Stamp Duty Land Tax Handbook

Other titles available from Law Society Publishing:

Housing Law Handbook, 2nd edition
General Editor: Stephen Cottle

Conveyancing Handbook, 26th edition
General Editor: Frances Silverman; Consultant Editors: Russell Hewitson and Anne Rodell

Conveyancing Protocol, 2019 edition
The Law Society

Conveyancing Quality Scheme Toolkit, 3rd edition
The Law Society (Russell Hewitson and Sarah Dwight)

Property Development, 3rd edition
Gavin Le Chat

Titles from Law Society Publishing can be ordered from all good bookshops or direct (telephone 0370 850 1422, or visit our online shop at **www.lawsociety.org.uk/bookshop**).

STAMP DUTY LAND TAX HANDBOOK

A Guide for Residential Conveyancers

Sean Randall

For Eve
***

All rights reserved. No part of this publication may be reproduced in any material form, whether by photocopying, scanning, downloading onto computer or otherwise without the written permission of the Law Society except in accordance with the provisions of the Copyright, Designs and Patents Act 1988. Applications should be addressed in the first instance, in writing, to Law Society Publishing. Any unauthorised or restricted act in relation to this publication may result in civil proceedings and/or criminal prosecution.

The author has asserted the right under the Copyright, Designs and Patents Act 1988 to be identified as author of this work.

Whilst all reasonable care has been taken in the preparation of this publication, neither the publisher nor the author can accept any responsibility for any loss occasioned to any person acting or refraining from action as a result of relying upon its contents.

The views expressed in this publication should be taken as those of the author only unless it is specifically indicated that the Law Society has given its endorsement.

© The Law Society 2020

Crown copyright material is reproduced with the permission of the Controller of Her Majesty's Stationery Office

ISBN-13: 978-1-78446-108-9

Published in 2020 by the Law Society
Reprinted with corrections in 2021
113 Chancery Lane, London WC2A 1PL

Typeset by Columns Design XML Ltd, Reading
Printed by Hobbs the Printers Ltd, Totton, Hants

The paper used for the text pages of this book is FSC® certified. FSC (the Forest Stewardship Council®) is an international network to promote responsible management of the world's forests.

Contents

About the author and consultant editors	x
Foreword	xi
Preface	xiii
Table of cases	xviii
Table of statutes	xix
Table of statutory instruments	xxiii
Abbreviations	xxiv

1   The scheme of the tax — 1

   1.1   Background — 1
   1.2   What is taxed? — 2
   1.3   Who is liable? — 4
   1.4   What tax is due? — 5
   1.5   Debt — 9
   1.6   Exempt transactions — 18
   1.7   When is the tax due? — 18
   1.8   The meaning of 'substantial performance' — 19
   1.9   How does the liable person comply? — 19
   1.10 When is the tax position final? — 21
   1.11 Anti-avoidance — 22

2   Excluded transactions — 25

   2.1   Background — 25
   2.2   Not a chargeable interest or an exempt interest — 25
   2.3   Exempt interests — 26
   2.4   Same person — 27
   2.5   Exempt transactions — 28

3   Freehold and leasehold transfers — 30

   3.1   Background — 30
   3.2   What tax rates and tax bands apply? — 30
   3.3   The residential higher rates — 41
   3.4   The residential super rate — 77
   3.5   The surcharge for overseas purchasers — 93

CONTENTS

4	**Common reliefs**		**95**
	4.1	Background	95
	4.2	First-time buyer relief	96
	4.3	Multiple dwellings relief	101
	4.4	Charities relief	108
	4.5	Relief for part-exchanges made by house-building companies	110
	4.6	Relief for property traders acquiring dwelling from customer of house-building company	110
	4.7	Relief for property traders acting as chain-breakers	111
	4.8	Relief for property traders acquiring dwelling from personal representatives	112
	4.9	Relief for property traders in case of relocation of employment	113
	4.10	Relief for employers	114
	4.11	Relief for grant-funded purchases by registered providers of social housing	115
5	**Leases**		**116**
	5.1	Background	116
	5.2	Grants of new leases	116
	5.3	Lease variations	126
	5.4	Lease assignments	128
	5.5	Assignment of agreement for lease	130
	5.6	Termination of leases	131
	5.7	Continuation of leases	134
	5.8	Special charging rules and reliefs	136
	5.9	Lease to nominee	137
	5.10	Sale and leaseback relief	138
6	**Collective enfranchisement**		**139**
	6.1	Background	139
	6.2	Landlord and Tenant Act 1987	142
	6.3	Leasehold Reform, Housing and Urban Development Act 1993	142
	6.4	Collective enfranchisement relief between 2003 and 2009	144
	6.5	Collective enfranchisement relief after 2009	145
	6.6	Identifying the purchaser	146
	6.7	Corporate purchasers	147
	6.8	Six or more flats	152
	6.9	Mixed-use buildings	154
	6.10	The residential higher rates	155
	6.11	Multiple dwellings relief	157
	6.12	Summary of potential alternative tax rates and reliefs	158

7	**Pre-completion transactions**	**161**
7.1	Background	161
7.2	Meaning of 'pre-completion transaction'	162
7.3	Effect of pre-completion transaction	162
7.4	'Assignments of rights' and 'free-standing transfers'	162
7.5	Relief	163
7.6	Registration	164

8	**Transfers between spouses and civil partners**	**166**
8.1	Background	166
8.2	Higher rates exemption	167
8.3	Transfers subject to existing debt	167
8.4	Divorce, dissolution of civil partnership, etc.	170
8.5	Assignments and sub-sales	171
8.6	Transfers to/from partnerships	171

9	**Gifts, assents, appropriations and appointments**	**173**
9.1	Background	173
9.2	Debt	174
9.3	Assents and appropriations by personal representatives	174
9.4	Variation of testamentary dispositions	175
9.5	Transfers between relatives	175
9.6	Transfers to a connected company	176
9.7	Distributions *in specie*	177
9.8	Contributions to partnerships	177
9.9	Distributions by, and withdrawals from, partnerships	178
9.10	The SDLT general anti-avoidance rule	179

10	**Right to buy transactions, shared ownership leases, etc.**	**182**
10.1	Background	182
10.2	Shared ownership leases	182
10.3	Shared ownership trusts and rent to shared ownership lease schemes	191
10.4	Right to buy transactions	198
10.5	Rent to mortgage transactions	199

11	**Alternative property finance**	**200**
11.1	Background	200
11.2	Land sold to financial institution and leased to individual	201
11.3	Land sold to financial institution and resold to individual	203
11.4	Alternative finance investment bonds	204

12 Transactions involving public bodies — 206

- 12.1 Background — 206
- 12.2 Compulsory purchase — 206
- 12.3 Compliance with planning obligations — 207
- 12.4 Public bodies relief — 208
- 12.5 Arrangements involving public or educational bodies — 208
- 12.6 Other reliefs involving public bodies — 209

13 Options and rights of pre-emption — 211

- 13.1 Background — 211
- 13.2 Options — 212
- 13.3 Rights of pre-emption — 216

14 Release of negative obligations — 218

- 14.1 Background — 218
- 14.2 Chargeable consideration — 219
- 14.3 Rates of tax — 220

15 Transfers to connected companies — 222

- 15.1 Background — 222
- 15.2 Connection — 223
- 15.3 Exceptions — 224

16 Partnerships — 226

- 16.1 Background — 226
- 16.2 General rules — 226
- 16.3 Introduction to special rules — 228
- 16.4 Transfer by partner (or connected person) to partnership — 228
- 16.5 Transfer by partnership to partner (or connected person) — 230
- 16.6 Capital withdrawals and loan repayments — 232
- 16.7 Transfer of interest in partnership — 234
- 16.8 Other special rules — 237
- 16.9 Other areas of difficulty — 237

17 Promote arrangements and development licences — 239

- 17.1 Background — 239
- 17.2 The scope of Finance Act 2003, s.44A — 240

18 Corporate reliefs — 243

- 18.1 Background — 243
- 18.2 Group relief — 244

	18.3 Reconstruction relief	251
	18.4 Acquisition relief	256
19	**Compliance and disputes**	**260**
	19.1 Background	260
	19.2 What transactions require an SDLT return?	260
	19.3 How to make an SDLT return	261
	19.4 Liability	265
	19.5 How to make payment	265
	19.6 When to make payment	266
	19.7 How to make a deferral application	266
	19.8 How to amend an SDLT return	268
	19.9 When to make an SDLT return	268
	19.10 How to reclaim overpaid tax	270
	19.11 HMRC intervention	272
	19.12 Penalties and interest	276
	19.13 Further time, reasonable excuse and special circumstances	278
	19.14 Information notices and inspections	278
	19.15 Record-keeping	279
	19.16 Enforcement	279
	19.17 Disputes	279
	19.18 Asking HMRC for help	281
	19.19 Accelerated payment notices	284
	19.20 Follower notices	284
	19.21 Disclosure of tax avoidance schemes	284
	19.22 Dishonest tax agents	286

APPENDICES

A	**Fee-earner checklist**	**289**
B	**Stamp duty land tax client questionnaire (human purchasers only)**	**293**
C	**Potential problem areas**	**296**
D	**Glossary**	**298**
Index		303

About the author and consultant editors

Author

Sean Randall is a partner at Blick Rothenberg Ltd. He has 20 years' experience advising on property transactions, including residential property transactions. He is the author and editor of *Sergeant and Sims on Stamp Taxes* (LexisNexis UK), a fellow of the Chartered Institute of Taxation, the chairman of the Stamp Taxes Practitioners Group and a former winner of 'Tax Writer of the Year'. He has contributed to the development of government policy, tax authority practice and statute on stamp taxes, including stamp duty land tax (SDLT), over many years. He lives in Kent with his wife and their three children.

Consultant editors

Helen Curtis-Goulding is a partner and head of the real estate department at Fladgate LLP. She specialises in high-value and complex property sales. She is described in the Legal 500 as 'speedy, efficient and commercially excellent' and is a former winner of eprivateclient's 'Top 35 Under 35 – the definitive annual list of young private client practitioners'. She lives in North London with her wife, daughter Mya and dog Basil.

Paul Clark qualified as a solicitor in 1970, and has specialised in commercial property since 1972, at Linklaters, DJ Freeman (where he was head of property for 10 years) and, since 2003, at what is now Cripps Pemberton Greenish in Tunbridge Wells, where he also lives. He has specialised in SDLT since 2003. He now trains lawyers and accountants throughout England. He is passionate about the use of plain legal language, and has created many standard forms, including the 'Leasebook' and the Royal Institution of Chartered Surveyors (RICS) Common Auction Conditions. For 10 years he was Practice and Precedents Editor of *The Conveyancer and Property Lawyer* (Sweet & Maxwell). He is a member of the Stamp Taxes Practitioners Group.

Foreword

Stamp duty land tax (SDLT) was almost an afterthought for residential property practitioners up until some 5–10 years ago. The rates of tax applicable were fairly clear-cut and you could, with a fair degree of certainty, advise a client on initial instruction what the amount of tax due on completion of a transaction would be.

Unfortunately, with the introduction of numerous amendments to the rates of SDLT in that time-frame and the differing and sometimes complex reliefs available, the current situation faced by residential property lawyers is extremely difficult. Navigating the correct rate of tax due has almost become a separate client instruction in itself. The differences in getting the advice right can run into thousands of pounds for clients and can often make or break a deal. The rate of tax payable more often than not these days, needs to come with a professional opinion as to why this rate applies.

It is not uncommon to have to run various different calculations applying different reliefs and exemptions so as to decide which one best suits your client. These are all with the benefit of a taxation department at our firm who specialise in providing such advice.

In the past, clients who were acquiring more complex assets, or who had their own complicated tax status, expected bespoke taxation advice. My experience now is that it is not uncommon for the seemingly most straightforward purchasers to need to seek advice.

There are no doubt hundreds of firms across England and Wales that specialise in residential conveyancing and who perhaps do not have the comfort of SDLT specialists to defer to for advice, but whose clients perhaps require or expect it. In many cases, a client does not want to pay for this advice, as they feel that their lawyer should be advising on this.

The result of the above has led to an influx of HM Revenue and Customs (HMRC) enquiries, and a spike in negligence claims being brought by clients for incorrect returns being submitted.

We hope this book goes some way to clarifying some of the grey areas which arise now more frequently on a daily basis.

I would like to thank Sean for asking me to become involved in this book as I feel it really will be of huge benefit to the wider profession and our clients – his wisdom has taught me a lot about this area.

Finally I would like to thank Fladgate LLP for their continued support in my work on this book.

Helen Curtis-Goulding
Partner & Head of Residential Property
Fladgate LLP
London

Preface

Stamp duty land tax (SDLT) has become a very complex area to advise on, even for practitioners that specialise in the tax. Driven by attempts to combat tax avoidance schemes and by changes in fiscal policy, the tax has been the subject of regular change since its introduction in 2003. As a result, so far as SDLT on residential property transactions is concerned, a gap has developed between the level of knowledge required to advise on the subject competently and the level of knowledge possessed by the largest body of persons that administer the tax, residential property lawyers.

Efforts have been made, and continue to be made, by HM Revenue and Customs (HMRC) to improve the level of awareness, ranging from multiple tiers of successively more detailed online guidance to 'webinars'. However, at the time of writing, the gap is still large. This has had consequences that include: the emergence of numerous 'boutiques' making unsolicited approaches to buyers of residential property offering to reclaim overpaid tax; underwriters charging increased premiums for professional indemnity insurance policies; HMRC receiving hundreds of queries every month from buyers and residential property lawyers; estate agents including perceived tax advantages inherent in property sales within sales particulars; and the making of professional negligence claims against residential property lawyers for failing to advise that partial relief was or might have been available or, conversely, for advising that partial relief was available when it was not. It is likely to be only a matter of time before HMRC tries to deter the public from using boutiques to make aggressive reclaims.

It has also driven me to write this book in conjunction with the Law Society. It does not attempt to answer every question and cover every area. Rather, its modest aim is to improve the awareness of residential property lawyers and to enable complex matters in respect of which specialist SDLT advice should be sought to be filtered from the standard matters in respect of which the residential property lawyer can advise confidently. In order to make the commentary as helpful as possible, particular areas sensitive to the most common conveyancing transactions are covered in detail and other areas, which are not, are covered at high level only.

The first part of the book (**Chapter 1**) covers the scheme of SDLT in overview. The second (**Chapters 2–18**) looks at the application of SDLT to specific types of residential property transactions in no particular order. The last (**Chapter 19**) gives practical help on matters including compliance. It is not written as an academic authority with a comprehensive list of statutory and case law references – though

PREFACE

statutory references and the main case law references are given. Instead, it tries to explain the rules as clearly and simply as possible using examples to illustrate points. The reader will be the judge of whether I have succeeded. I hope that it becomes the first point of reference for residential property lawyers. I have resisted including flow-charts. In my opinion, they (and the online tools on which they are based) tend to suffer from over-simplifying the rules. If they were adequate, the 300 pages or so that follow would not be necessary.

At various points text is shown in boxes. The information in those boxes comprises helpful tips, warnings, examples or references. References are made to HMRC's guidance manual, the Stamp Duty Land Tax Manual, as well as to statutes and case law. This is an acknowledgement that HMRC's guidance manual contains useful examples and confirms HMRC's interpretation of the legislation in key areas. It is wrong, however, to rely on HMRC's guidance manual as if it were the law. HMRC is known to resile from its guidance occasionally. Although in theory the remedy of judicial review may be available to prevent HMRC from doing so, the possibility of bringing claims in the High Court and First-tier Tribunal is unattractive and unrealistic for most.

Many of the principles apply to commercial transactions, but it would be wrong to use the work as a guide to commercial transactions. There are many complex areas in the SDLT code that touch on commercial transactions that are omitted from this work.

At the end of this book are three things that I hope are useful. The first is a 'fee-earner checklist'. It is designed to serve two purposes: a prompt for the fee-earner to consider certain things before advising the client on the correct amount of SDLT to pay and an evidential record that those things have in fact been considered in the event that there is a dispute. The second is a 'client questionnaire'. It does not pull every item of information required to advise on the tax, but it should pull most items and it does identify the occasions when extra information may be required. The third is a list of potential problem areas to help the residential property lawyer identify the occasions when specialist SDLT advice might add value.

This work does not cover the equivalent tax treatment of residential property transactions in Wales or Scotland. The devolved taxes – land transaction tax and land and buildings transaction tax – apply in Wales and Scotland, respectively, in place of SDLT.

To make the text as concise and readable as possible, references to the buyer as 'he' are to be read 'he' or 'she' as appropriate. No offence is intended to female readers.

Finally, I would like to thank the Law Society's commissioning editor, Christa Biervliet; the consultant editors, Helen Curtis-Goulding and Paul Clark (Paul, in particular, used his experience of training residential property lawyers on SDLT to clarify aspects and correct false assumptions, and made significant contributions, especially to the chapters on shared ownership leases and collective enfranchisement); LexisNexis UK, the publisher of my other work, *Sergeant and Sims on Stamp Taxes*; Blick Rothenberg Ltd for permitting me to write for the Law Society;

and finally, my wife, for her patience and encouragement throughout. All errors in this book are my responsibility alone.

The law is stated as at 25 November 2019.

Sean Randall
Partner, Blick Rothenberg Ltd
London

POSTSCRIPT

In light of the Stamp Duty Land Tax (Temporary Relief) Act 2020 (as amended), which was passed after this book was written, the author would like the reader to take into account the following tax rate changes.

Addendum[1]

On 8 July 2020, the government announced temporary increases to the SDLT nil rate bands for residential property transactions. The new rules, which were initially made by regulations and are the subject of the Stamp Duty Land Tax (Temporary Relief) Act 2020, as amended by Budget 2021 resolutions, increase the nil rate band from £125,000 to £500,000 in the three tables for residential property transactions (see below) where sale contracts are completed or substantially performed between 8 July 2020 and 30 June 2021 inclusive (the 'initial temporary rates'). The temporary rates do not apply where the contract was substantially performed or completed before 8 July 2020. A further set of temporary rates (the 'further temporary rates') set the nil rate band threshold at £250,000 where sale contracts are completed or substantially performed between 1 July 2021 and 30 September 2021 inclusive. First-time buyer relief is suspended while the initial temporary rates apply.

Initial temporary rates

Standard rates transactions

Relevant consideration	Tax rate
£0–£500,000	0%
£500,001–£925,000	5%
£925,001–£1,500,000	10%
The remainder (if any)	12%

---

[1] This addendum appeared in its original form with the first edition published in June 2020, and has been updated for this July 2021 reprint. See **www.gov.uk/stamp-duty-land-tax** for the latest information.

PREFACE

Higher rates transactions

Relevant consideration	Tax rate
£0–£500,000	3%
£500,001–£925,000	8%
£925,001–£1,500,000	13%
The remainder (if any)	15%

Grants of new rental leases of residential property

Rate bands	Tax rate
£0–£500,000	0%
£500,000+	1%

Further temporary rates

Standard rates transactions

Relevant consideration	Tax rate
£0–£250,000	0%
£250,001–£925,000	5%
£925,001–£1,500,000	10%
The remainder (if any)	12%

Higher rates transactions

Relevant consideration	Tax rate
£0–£250,000	3%
£250,001–£925,000	8%
£925,001–£1,500,000	13%
The remainder (if any)	15%

Grants of new rental leases of residential property

Rate bands	Tax rate
£0–£250,000	0%
£250,000+	1%

Finally, a two per cent non-resident surcharge applies to 'non-resident transactions' with an effective date on or after 1 April 2021. All these changes, and all other relevant changes, will be covered in detail in the second edition of this book (due 2022).

Table of cases

Elizabeth Court (Bournemouth) Ltd *v.* Revenue and Customs Comrs [2008] EWHC 2828 (Ch) 6.4
Farnborough Airport Properties Co *v.* Revenue and Customs Comrs [2019] EWCA Civ 118 .... 18.2.2.3
Hannover Leasing Wachstumswerte Europa Beteiligungsgesellschaft MBH *v.* Revenue and Customs Comrs [2019] UKFTT 262 (TC) 1.11, 9.10, 19.18.3
Hyman (David and Sally) *v.* Revenue and Customs Comrs [2019] UKFTT 469 (TC) 3.2.1
Mansion Estates Ltd *v.* Hayre & Co [2016] EWHC 96 (Ch) 7.1
Marshall (HM Inspector of Taxes) *v.* Kerr [1995] 1 AC 148; [1994] BTC 258 .... 6.7
Marzouk (Nadia Ibrahim) *v.* Revenue and Customs Comrs [2016] UKFTT 548 (TC) 19.13
PN Bewley Ltd *v.* Revenue and Customs Comrs [2019] UKFTT 65 (TC) 3.2.3
Project Blue Ltd *v.* Revenue and Customs Comrs [2018] UKSC 30 .... 9.10
R *v.* IRC, *ex parte* MFK Underwriting Agencies Ltd [1990] 1 WLR 1545; [1990] STC 873 .... 19.18.3
Ramsay (Elisabeth Moyne) *v.* Revenue and Customs Comrs [2013] UKUT 226 (TCC) 8.6
Smallman (Derek and Susan) *v.* Revenue and Customs Comrs [2018] UKFTT 0680 (TC) 1.7.1, 5.2.4
Stokes *v.* Cambridge [1961] 13 P&CR 77 .... 14.2
Street *v.* Mountford [1985] AC 809 .... 5.2.2
Swayne *v.* IRC [1899] 1 QB 335 .... 5.4.1
Uratemp Ventures Ltd *v.* Collins [2001] UKHL 43 .... 3.2.3

Table of statutes

Civil Partnership Act 2004
    Sched.5
        para.7(1)(b) 3.3.11
    Sched.7
        para.9 .... 3.3.11
    Sched.15
        para.7(a)(b) 3.3.11
    Sched.17
        para.9 .... 3.3.11
Commonhold and Leasehold
    Reform Act 2002 .... 10.3.2
Corporation Tax Act 2010
    s.448 .... 1.5.4.3
    s.450 .... 1.5.4.3, 6.7,
                      15.2, 16.4, 16.5
    s.451 .... 1.5.4.3, 15.2, 16.4, 16.5
    s.1122 ...... 1.5.4.3, 6.7, 15.2, 16.4,
                               16.5
    s.1123 .... 15.2
    s.1124 .... 18.2.2.3
Finance Act 2003
    Part 4 ....
    s.43 .... 2.4, 14.1
        (3) 1.3.1, 5.6.5
            (d) 5.3, 5.7.1
                (i) 5.2.10
        (4) 1.3.1, 9.1
        (5) 1.3.1
    s.44 .... 7.2
        (7)(c)(ii) 5.2.5
        (8) 1.7.1, 1.8
    s.44A 2.2, 17.1
    s.45 .... 7.1
    s.46 .... 2.2, 13.1
    s.47 .... 1.5.2, 1.5.3, 14.2
    s.48 .... 14.1
        (2) 1.2.4, 2.3
            (b) 5.2.2
            (c)(i) 5.2.2
        (3) 1.2.4, 2.3
    s.49 .... 1.6, 2.5

s.53 .... 6.7, 9.6, 9.7, 15.1
s.54 .... 9.6, 15.3
    (4) 9.7
s.55 ... 3.3.5.1, 5.2.3, 5.2.8, 14.3
s.56 .... 5.2.3
s.57A 5.10
s.57B 4.2
s.58A ... 3.3.1, 4.5, 4.6, 4.7, 4.8,
                          4.9, 4.10
s.58D 3.2.4, 3.2.5, 3.4.5, 4.3,
                             6.11
s.60 .... 12.2
s.61 .... 12.3
s.66 .... 12.4
s.67 .... 19.9
s.68 .... 4.4
s.69 .... 12.6.4
s.70 .... 10.1
s.71 .... 4.11
s.71A 11.1, 11.2
s.73 .... 11.1, 11.3
s.73C 11.4
s.74 .... 3.4.5, 6.4, 6.5
s.75A 1.11, 9.1, 9.10, 16.7,
                          16.9, 19.2
s.75B 1.11, 9.10
s.75C 1.11, 9.10
    (8)(a) 16.9
    (8A) 16.9
s.77 .... 1.6, 5.2.9, 5.6.5, 19.2
s.77A 5.2.9, 5.6.5, 19.2
    (1) 1.6
s.79 .... 19.2
s.80 .... 6.4
s.81ZA 3.4.2
s.81A 13.2.2
s.86 .... 19.6
s.90 .... 19.7
s.95 .... 19.12.1
s.97 .... 19.13
s.107 .... 12.6.4

TABLE OF STATUTES

Finance Act 2003 – *continued*
  Part 4 – *continued*
    s.108 .... 1.5.4.2, 5.2.7
    s.116 .... 3.2.1, 3.2.3
      (1) 14.3
      (7) 3.2.5, 3.3.5.1
    s.117 .... 13.1, 14.2, 17.2
    s.119 .... 1.7.1
    s.123 .... 11.4
    Sched.2A 5.5, 7.1
    Sched.3 .... 1.6, 2.5
      para.1 .... 9.1
      para.3 .... 8.4, 9.2, 9.3
      para.3A 8.4, 9.2
      para.4 .... 9.4
    Sched.4
      para.1 .... 14.2
      para.5 .... 1.5.2, 1.5.3, 14.2
      para.8 .... 8.3, 9.2
        (2) 1.5.2
      para.8A(1) 9.3
        (2) 9.4
      para.15 .... 12.5
    Sched.4ZA 3.3.1
      Part 1 .... 3.3.5.1
      Part 2
        para.5 .... 3.3.3, 6.10
        para.5CA 3.4.4.8
        para.6 .... 6.10
        para.7A 3.3.10.2, 6.10
      Part 3
        para.8 .... 19.10.2
        para.9 .... 3.3.6
        para.9A 3.3.9.5, 8.2
        para.9B 3.3.11
        para.10 .... 5.9
        para.11 .... 3.3.7, 5.9
        para.12 .... 3.3.8
        para.14 .... 3.3.9
        para.15 .... 11.2, 11.3
        para.16 .... 3.3.12
    Sched.4A 3.4.1
      paras.2, 3 .... 3.4.2
      para.4 .... 3.4.3
      para.5 .. 3.4.4.1, 3.4.4.2, 3.4.4.3,
                                3.4.4.4
      para.5A 3.4.4.5
      para.5B 3.4.4.6
      para.5C 3.4.4.7
      para.5D 3.4.4.10
      para.5EA 3.4.4.11
      para.5F 3.4.4.9

      para.5G 3.4.4.2, 3.4.4.3,
                                3.4.4.4
      para.5H 3.4.4.6
      para.5I 3.4.4.7
      para.5IA 3.4.4.8
      para.5J 3.4.4.10
      para.5JA 3.4.4.11
      para.5K 3.4.4.9
      para.6 .... 3.4.5
      paras.6A–6H 3.4.2, 3.4.5,
                              11.2, 11.3
    Sched.5 .... 5.2.1
      para.2 .... 5.2.3
    Sched.6ZA 4.2
      para.3 .... 11.2
    Sched.6A
      para.1 .... 4.5
      para.2 .... 4.6
      para.3 .... 4.8
      para.4 .... 4.7
      para.5 .... 4.10
      para.6 .... 4.9
    Sched.6B ... 3.2.4, 3.2.5, 3.4.5, 4.3,
                                  6.11
    Sched.7
      Part 1 .... 18.1, 18.2.1
      paras.1, 2, 2A, 2B .. 18.2.2.3
      para.3 .... 18.2.3
        (2) 1.5.2
      paras.4ZA, 4A, 4, 5, 6 ......
                                18.2.3
      Part 2 .... 18.1, 18.3.1, 18.4.1
      para.7 .... 18.3.2
      para.8 .... 18.4.2
      para.9 .... 18.3.3, 18.4.1
        (2) 1.5.2
      paras.10, 11, 12 ...... 18.3.3,
                                18.4.1
    Sched.8 .... 4.4
    Sched.9 .... 10.1
      para.1 .... 10.4
      paras.2, 3, 4A, 4B, 5 .... 10.2
      para.6 .... 10.5
      paras.7–14 .... 10.3.2
      para.15 .... 10.2
      para.15A 4.2, 10.2
      para.15B 4.2, 10.3.2
      para.16 .... 4.2, 4.4.4.1, 10.2,
                                10.3.2
    Sched.10
      Part 1
        paras.3–5 .... 19.12.1
        para.6 ... 5.2.4, 19.8, 19.10.2

TABLE OF STATUTES

Part 2 .... 19.15
Part 3 .... 19.11.2
   para.17 .... 19.11.2
Part 4 .... 19.11.3
   para.25(1) 19.11.3
Part 5 .... 19.11.4
   para.31 .... 19.11.5
Part 6
   para.34 .... 5.2.4, 19.10.2
   para.34E 19.17.4
Part 7
   paras.35, 36 .... 19.17.1
   para.36B 19.17.2
   para.36D 19.17.3
Sched.12 .... 19.16
Sched.15 .... 16.1
   Part 1 .... 16.2
      para.2 .... 16.9
   Part 2 .... 16.2
   Part 3 .... 1.5.2, 8.6, 16.9
      paras.10, 11, 12 .... 9.8, 16.4
      para.12A 16.4
      para.14 .... 2.2, 16.7, 16.9
      para.16 .... 16.8
      para.17 .... 16.7
      para.17A 9.9, 16.6
      paras.18, 19, 20, 21 ...... 9.9
      paras.18, 19, 20, 21, 22 ..... 16.5
      para.23 .... 16.8
      para.24 .... 16.5, 16.8
      para.27A 16.4
      para.28 .... 16.8
      paras.29, 30, 31, 32 .... 16.7
      para.35 .... 9.8
      para.36 .... 16.7
      para.37 .... 9.9
Sched.16
   para.3 .... 2.5, 3.3.7, 6.7
      (1) 6.6
      (3) 5.9
Sched.17A 5.2.1
   para.1A 5.2.5
   para.2 .... 5.2.6
   para.3 .... 5.2.10, 5.7.2, 5.7.3
   para.3A 5.2.10, 5.7.3
   para.4 .... 5.2.10
   para.5 .... 5.2.7, 5.7.3
   para.7(5) 5.2.5
   paras.7A, 8 .... 5.2.5
   para.9 .... 5.3, 5.7.1
   para.10 .... 5.2.8
   para.11 .... 5.2.10, 5.4.1

   para.12 .... 5.4.1, 10.2
   para.12A 5.2.10
   para.12B 5.5
   para.12B(3B) 1.7.1, 5.2.4
   para.15A 5.3
   para.16 .... 5.3, 5.6.3, 5.7.1
   para.17 .... 5.4.1
Sched.61 .... 11.4
Finance Act 2004
   Part 7 .... 6.7, 19.21
Finance Act 2007
   Sched.24 .... 19.12.1
Finance Act 2008
   Sched.36 .... 19.14
Finance Act 2009 .... 6.4
   Part 7
      ss.101–105 .... 19.12.2
      Scheds.53, 54 .... 19.12.2
Finance Act 2012
   Sched.38
      para.2 .... 19.22
Finance Act 2013
   Part 5 .... 1.11, 6.7
Finance Act 2014
   Part 4
      Ch.2 .... 1.11, 19.20
      Ch.3 .... 1.11, 19.19
   Part 5 .... 1.11
Financial Services and Markets
   Act 2000 .... 11.1
Housing Act 1985 .... 10.2, 10.3.2
   Part V 10.2, 10.4, 10.5
      s.126 .... 10.5
      s.171 .... 10.2
      s.171A 10.4
Housing Act 1988
   Part 3 .... 10.2, 10.3.2
Housing Act 1996
   s.18 .... 4.11
Housing and Regeneration Act
   2008
      s.19 .... 4.11, 10.2, 10.3.2
Housing Associations Act
   1985 .... 10.2, 10.3.2
Income Tax Act 2007
   s.1011 .... 8.2
Landlord and Tenant Act
   1987 .... 6.2
   Part I 3.4.2, 3.4.5, 4.3, 6.1
Law of Property (Miscellaneous
   Provisions) Act 1989
      s.2 .... 2.5, 8.4

Leasehold Reform, Housing and
 Urban Development Act
 1993 .... 3.3.10.2, 6.3, 6.4, 6.5,
       6.6, 6.7
  Part I
   Ch I 3.4.2, 3.4.5, 4.3, 6.1
   s.4A 6.4
Limited Liability Partnerships
 Act 2000 .... 16.2
Limited Liability Partnerships
 Act (Northern Ireland)
 2002 .... 16.2
Limited Partnerships Act
 1907 .... 16.2

Matrimonial and Family
 Proceedings Act 1984
  s.1(1)(a)(ii) 3.3.11
Matrimonial Causes Act 1973
  s.24(1)(b) 3.3.11
Mental Capacity Act 2005 ..... 3.3.7, 3.3.8
Mental Capacity Act (Northern
 Ireland) 2016 .... 3.3.7, 3.3.8
New Towns Act 1981 .... 10.2, 10.3.2
Partnership Act 1890 .... 3.3.9, 8.3,
       8.6, 16.2
Town and Country Planning Act
 1990
  s.55 .... 12.2
  s.106 .... 12.3

Table of statutory instruments

Housing (Northern Ireland) Order 1992
    Part 2 .... 10.2, 10.3.2
Matrimonial and Family Proceedings (Northern Ireland) Order 1989
    art.21(a)(ii) 3.3.11
Matrimonial Causes (Northern Ireland) Order 1978
    art.26(1)(b) 3.3.11
Planning (Northern Ireland) Order 1991
    art.40 .... 12.3
Stamp Duty Land Tax (Administration) Regulations 2002, SI 2003/2837
    Part 4 .... 19.7
Stamp Duty Land Tax Avoidance Schemes (Prescribed Descriptions of
    Arrangements) Regulations 2005, SI 2005/1868 .... 19.21
Stamp Duty Land Tax Avoidance Schemes (Prescribed Descriptions of
    Arrangements) (Amendment) Regulations 2010, SI 2005/1868 ..... 19.21
Stamp Duty Land Tax Avoidance Schemes (Prescribed Descriptions of
    Arrangements) (Amendment) Regulations 2012, SI 2010/407 ...... 19.21
Tax Avoidance Schemes (Information) Regulations 2012, SI 2012/836 .... 19.21
Tribunal Procedure (First-tier Tribunal) (Tax Chamber) Rules 2009, SI
    2009/273
        Ch 2 .... 19.17.6
        rules 10, 15, 18, 23, 39 .... 19.17.6

Abbreviations

ADR	alternative dispute resolution
APN	accelerated payment notice
CGT	capital gains tax
CIOT	Chartered Institute of Taxation
CPI	consumer price index
DOTAS	disclosure of tax avoidance schemes
EU	European Union
FA	Finance Act
GAAR	general anti-abuse rule
HMRC	HM Revenue and Customs
HRAD	higher rates for additional dwellings
LBTT	land and buildings transaction tax
LLP	limited liability partnership
LTT	land transaction tax
NHS	National Health Service
NI	National Insurance
NPV	net present value
PCRT	Professional Conduct in Relation to Taxation (Chartered Institute of Taxation)
PCT	primary care trust
PFI	private finance initiative
POTAS	promoters of tax avoidance schemes
PPP	public–private partnership
RPI	retail price index
RSL	registered social landlord
RTE	right to enfranchise
SDLT	stamp duty land tax
SRA	Solicitors Regulation Authority
UTR	Unique Taxpayer Reference
UTRN	Unique Transaction Reference Number
VAT	value added tax

CHAPTER 1
The scheme of the tax

1.1 BACKGROUND

Stamp duty land tax (SDLT) applied to land transactions in the United Kingdom (UK) from 1 December 2003 (subject to transitional provisions). It replaced stamp duty, which now only applies to transactions in stock and marketable securities and interests in partnerships that hold stock or marketable securities. Since 1 April 2018, SDLT applies to land transactions in England and Northern Ireland only. Transactions in land situated in Wales and Scotland are subject to land transaction tax (LTT) and land and buildings transaction tax (LBTT), respectively. LTT is administered by the Welsh Revenue Authority. LBTT is administered by Revenue Scotland.

In summary, the scheme of SDLT is to charge transactions where a land interest passes in return for value, regardless of why or how, or where the parties are resident or where the documents are executed. The temptation is to assume that only sales of freehold and leasehold estates are taxable and that the tax is based on what is given by way of consideration. In fact, various rules apply in certain circumstances to deem a person to have acquired something he has not and to deem the purchaser to have given consideration he has not. The main dangers to the residential property lawyer are making assumptions regarding how the tax *should* work, underestimating the complexity of the rules and not knowing of the existence of special rules.

Putting that warning to one side for the moment, in order to calculate the amount of tax chargeable on an SDLT transaction, answers are needed to the following questions:

- What is taxed?
- Who is liable?
- What tax is due?
- When is the tax due?
- What are exempt transactions?
- How does the liable person comply?
- When is the tax position final?
- What anti-avoidance rules apply?

Each of those questions is answered (or at least the answer to each question is introduced) in turn in this chapter. The questions are also explained in more detail in the chapters that follow in the context they relate to.[1]

1.2 WHAT IS TAXED?

1.2.1 The components of an SDLT transaction

An SDLT transaction means an 'acquisition' of a 'chargeable interest'. Those two terms are examined below. Where there is no 'acquisition' or no 'chargeable interest' is acquired the transaction is outside the scope of the tax: it is not an SDLT transaction.

> **WARNING**
>
> An exception applies if the transaction is in pursuance of a contract made before 19 July 2003, in which case it may be chargeable to stamp duty, not SDLT. This work does not cover the transitional rules for SDLT. Consequently, specialist advice should be sought if the contract was made before 19 July 2003.

1.2.2 The meaning of 'acquisition'

'Acquisition' takes a wide and circular meaning. It is the act or event by which the purchaser acquires a new or existing chargeable interest (e.g., a leasehold estate is granted or assigned) or a chargeable interest already held by the purchaser is benefited or enlarged in some way by something done to another chargeable interest (e.g., a lease is surrendered so as to benefit the reversionary interest). For the meaning of 'chargeable interest', see **1.2.3**.

The cause, method and purpose of the acquisition are irrelevant to the incidence of the tax, but may affect the tax calculation. The acquisition may occur by something done (or not done) by the parties; by court order; by operation of law; or by an SDLT rule. In other words, the acquisition may happen in the 'real world' or in the 'SDLT world'.

> **WARNING**
>
> One should not assume that the absence of a transfer or the creation of a land interest is outside the scope of the tax.

---

[1] For more information see *Sergeant and Sims on Stamp Taxes*, Division AA1: SDLT–general principles and rates (LexisNexis UK).

THE SCHEME OF THE TAX

Example 1.1

In certain circumstances, SDLT may apply to a person's acquisition or increase of a share in a partnership that owns land and to a person's entitlement to direct or request a landowner to dispose of the land to another person.

1.2.3 The meaning of 'chargeable interest'

'Chargeable interest' also takes a wide meaning. It is an estate, interest, right or power in or over land in England or Northern Ireland or the benefit of an obligation, restriction, or condition affecting the value of any such estate, etc., other than an exempt interest (as to which, see **1.2.4**).

It includes, therefore, freehold and leasehold estates, options, easements (e.g., rights of way and rights to light), the benefit of a covenant and rentcharges.

Legal and equitable interests are recognised as chargeable interests equally with one exception. The equitable interest acquired by a purchaser on an uncompleted sale contract is disregarded (see **1.7**).

Chattels purchased with a property are not chargeable. The distinction between a fixture and a chattel is the subject of case law. HM Revenue and Customs (HMRC) has historically accepted that the following are chattels:

- carpets (fitted or otherwise);
- curtains and blinds;
- free-standing furniture;
- kitchen white goods;
- electric and gas fires (provided that they can be removed by disconnection from the power supply without causing damage to the property); and
- light shades and fittings (unless recessed).

HMRC has historically accepted that the following are *not* chattels:

- fitted kitchen units, cupboards and sinks;
- AGAs and wall-mounted ovens;
- fitted bathroom sanitary ware;
- central heating systems; and
- intruder alarm systems.

The proportion of the price apportioned to chattels (if any) must be defensible. If the apportionment is not reasonable, the tax is calculated as if it had been apportioned reasonably.

A person is treated as having acquired a chargeable interest in the 'SDLT world' in certain circumstances, including:

- taking possession of the property to be purchased (see **1.8**);

- lease variations (see **5.3**);
- assignments of rights (see **7.4**);
- transfers of partnership interests (see **16.7**);
- withdrawals from partnerships and loan repayments by partnerships (see **16.6**); and
- development licence arrangements (see **Chapter 17**).

1.2.4 The meaning of 'exempt interest'

There are six types of exempt interest.[2] They are:

1. security interests (except rentcharges);
2. licences to use or occupy land;
3. tenancies at will;
4. advowsons (the right to choose a vicar);
5. franchises (a Crown franchise); and
6. manors (the Lordship of a Manor).

The acquisition of an exempt interest is *not* an SDLT transaction.
See **Chapter 2**.

WARNING

Be careful that what is described as a licence to use or occupy land is not in fact a lease, which *is* a chargeable interest. Other works should be consulted, if necessary, to understand the distinction (see **5.2.2**).

1.3 WHO IS LIABLE?

With one limited exception, the liability to pay the tax rests solely with the 'purchaser'. There is no provision within the SDLT legislation for HMRC to recover the tax from another person.

The exception relates to a failure by the purchaser to repay certain types of tax relief that, due to the occasion of a disqualifying event, are withdrawn.

1.3.1 The meaning of 'purchaser' and 'vendor'

The 'purchaser' is the person that makes the acquisition of the chargeable interest. The 'vendor' is the person that makes the disposal of the chargeable interest. In most cases, identifying the vendor and purchaser will be obvious. In others, less so. The SDLT legislation gives some help in a limited number of cases; none is controversial.

---

[2] Finance Act (FA) 2003, s.48(2), (3).

- Where a chargeable interest is created (e.g., the grant of a lease or an option), the purchaser is the person entitled to the interest and the vendor is the person whose existing interest is subject to the interest created.
- Where a chargeable interest is surrendered or released (e.g., the surrender of a lease or release of a right to light), the purchaser is the person whose interest is benefited by the surrender or release and the vendor is the person that ceases to be entitled to the interest surrendered or released.
- Where a chargeable interest other than a lease is varied, the purchaser is the person whose interest is benefited by the variation and the vendor is the person whose interest is subject to the variation.
- Where a lease is varied to reduce the rent, the purchaser is the tenant and the vendor is the landlord.
- Where a lease is varied to reduce the term, the purchaser is the landlord and the vendor is the tenant.
- Where a lease is varied in the first five years of the term of the lease to increase the rent, the purchaser is the tenant and the vendor is the landlord.
- Where a lease is varied in some other way and the tenant gives consideration (other than an increase in rent), the purchaser is the tenant and the vendor is the landlord.
- Where the variation of a lease takes effect as a surrender and regrant (e.g., the term or demise is increased), the landlord is the purchaser on the surrender and the vendor on the regrant, and the tenant is the vendor on the surrender and the purchaser on the regrant.

The legislation also requires a person to give consideration for, or be a party to, the transaction in order to be a purchaser.[3]

WARNING

The identity of the vendor, and their relationship with the purchaser, affects the operation of special rules and the availability of reliefs.

1.4 WHAT TAX IS DUE?

The tax is calculated using tax rates and tax bands. So much of the 'relevant consideration' for the transaction that falls within each tax band is taxed at the rate corresponding to that band. The result of the tax payable in each tax band is aggregated. With a limited number of exceptions there are no flat rates, i.e., rates that apply to all the relevant consideration.

---

[3] FA 2003, s.43(3)–(5).

If the appropriate set of tax rates and tax bands and the correct amount of the relevant consideration are found, the SDLT calculation is usually simple. Unfortunately, finding the appropriate set of tax rates and tax bands and the correct amount of the relevant consideration is sometimes difficult, as we shall see.

'Relevant consideration' means the chargeable consideration given for the subject-matter of the transaction and any 'linked' transactions (as to which, see **1.5.4**).

'Chargeable consideration' means any consideration in money or money's worth given by the purchaser or a connected person for the subject-matter of the transaction. 'Consideration' takes its contract law meaning. HMRC's starting point is that it refers to everything that must be given by the purchaser to compel the seller to perform the contract. In some cases, in determining the chargeable consideration the actual consideration is replaced by deemed consideration. In others, some or all of the actual consideration is disregarded as chargeable consideration (see **1.5.2**).

1.4.1 Tax rates and tax bands

There are six alternative sets of tax rates and tax bands that could apply to an SDLT transaction concerning residential property. Obviously, it is essential to select the appropriate set. The factors that determine which set is appropriate include:

- Whether the purchased interest is in or over 'residential property' (see **3.2.1**).
- Whether the purchased interest is in or over more than five dwellings (see **3.2.5**).
- Where multiple interests in or over more than five dwellings are purchased, whether the purchases are in pursuance of a single contract or single bargain (see **3.2.5**).
- Whether the purchased interest is in or over exclusively residential property (see **3.2.2**).
- Whether the SDLT transaction is linked to another the main subject-matter of which is, to any extent, in or over non-residential property (see **3.2.2**).
- Whether the interest purchased is a new lease for rent greater than a peppercorn (see **5.2**).
- Whether the purchaser (or all the purchasers if there is more than one) is a 'natural person' or a 'non-natural person' (see **3.4**).
- Where a company, partnership or collective investment scheme purchases a dwelling, the use to which the dwelling will be applied (see **3.4**).
- Where an individual purchases a dwelling, whether he, his spouse or civil partner, his minor children or minor stepchildren beneficially own another interest in a dwelling, and whether he is replacing his main residence (see **3.3**).
- Where an individual purchases a dwelling, whether he or his spouse or civil partner is a partner in a property-investment partnership (see **16.7**).
- Whether the purchaser (or all the purchasers if there is more than one) is a 'first-time buyer' (see **4.2**).

THE SCHEME OF THE TAX

The six sets of tax rates and tax bands are as follows:

The residential standard rates (first-time buyers only)

Relevant consideration	Tax rate
£0–£300,000	0%
£300,001–£500,000	5%
£500,000+	n/a

The residential standard rates

Relevant consideration	Tax rate
£0–£125,000	0%
£125,001–£250,000	2%
£250,001–£925,000	5%
£925,001–£1,500,000	10%
£1,500,000+	12%

The residential higher rates

Relevant consideration	Tax rate
£0–£125,000	3%
£125,001–£250,000	5%
£250,001–£925,000	8%
£925,001–£1,500,000	13%
£1,500,000+	15%

The residential super rate

Relevant consideration	Tax rate
£500,000+	15%

The non-residential (or mixed-use) rates

Relevant consideration	Tax rate
£0–£150,000	0%
£150,001–£250,000	2%
£250,000+	5%

The residential lease rates

Net present value of rent	Tax rate
£0–£125,000	0%
£125,000+	1%

Example 1.2

A and his wife, B, purchase the freehold estate of a house for £1.2 million. The purchase is a replacement of their main residence. SDLT of £63,750 is payable by A and B (an effective rate of 5.3%): (£125,000 @ 0%) + (£125,000 @ 2%) + (£675,000 @ 5%) + (£275,000 @ 10%).

1.4.2 Chargeable consideration (other than rent)

Chargeable consideration means money or money's worth in pounds sterling. It can take many forms. The most common are:

- the payment of cash;
- the creation of debt (a receivable);
- the assumption of debt owed by the vendor;
- the release or discharge of debt owed to the purchaser;
- the issue of a loan note;
- the issue of shares;
- the provision of works or services;
- the disposal of another chargeable interest; and
- the market value of the chargeable interest purchased.

Whether the amount or value of the consideration is used as the chargeable consideration in the SDLT calculation depends on the form of the chargeable consideration. In the case of:

- the payment of cash, it is the *amount* of the cash paid;
- the creation of debt (receivable), it is the *amount* of the cash owed;
- the assumption of debt owed by the vendor, it is the *amount* of the debt assumed;
- the release or discharge of debt owed to the purchaser, it is the *amount* of the debt released or discharged;
- the issue of a loan note, it is the *value* of the loan note issued;
- the issue of shares, it is the *value* of the shares issued;
- the provision of works or services, it is the *value* of the works or services provided (not necessarily its cost to the purchaser, but what it would cost the purchaser to get the works or services on the open market from a third party); and

- the disposal of another chargeable interest, it is the *value* of the chargeable interest given.

Special rules apply to debt and to contingent or uncertain consideration (see **1.5.1**). There is no discount given for postponed consideration.

Where consideration is given for a chargeable interest *and* something that is not a chargeable interest (e.g., chattels), it must be apportioned on a reasonable basis. If it is not apportioned on a reasonable basis, the tax is calculated as if it were.

1.5 DEBT

There are special rules that apply where all or part of the chargeable consideration for an SDLT transaction is the assumption of debt by the purchaser or the release or discharge of debt due to the purchaser or owed by the vendor. The meaning of 'debt' includes a contingent obligation to pay a sum of money at a future date.

First, where a chargeable interest is owned by more than one person (e.g., husband and wife) and debt is secured on the subject-matter of the transaction, if the interest is transferred to one person, tax is charged according to the proportion of the debt assumed that corresponds to the purchaser's undivided share in the interest transferred (even where the co-owners are, in fact, jointly and severally liable for the debt). If the co-owners are joint tenants rather than tenants in common, they are treated as owning a 50 per cent undivided share each. These rules work in reverse, i.e., where a property is transferred from sole ownership to joint ownership.

Example 1.3

A and B own a property equally as tenants in common. Debt is secured on the property. A and B are jointly and severally liable for the debt. A agrees to give his share in the property to B subject to the debt. The chargeable consideration for the transaction is taken to be 50% of the debt.

Example 1.4

A owns a property in his sole name. Debt is secured on the property. A agrees to give B a half share of the property subject to the debt. The chargeable consideration for the transaction is taken to be 50% of the debt.

Second, where the amount of debt assumed, released or discharged exceeds the market value of the subject-matter of the transaction, tax is charged on the market value of the subject-matter of the transaction. In other words, the market value is a cap on the chargeable consideration.

Third, where debt is secured on the subject-matter of the transaction immediately before and immediately after the effective date of the transaction *and* there is any change in the rights or liabilities of the parties in relation to the debt as a result of, or in connection with, the transaction there is *deemed* to be an assumption of debt by the purchaser. This is important. It means that debt may be taken to be assumed in the 'SDLT world' even though in the 'real world' it is not.

Example 1.5

A owns the freehold estate of a house. Debt is secured on the property. A had granted a legal charge (a third party charge) over the property as security for debt owed by B to a bank. A transfers the property to B for no consideration subject to the charge. A's obligations (as chargor or guarantor under the loan agreement) extinguish as a result of the transfer. B is treated as having assumed all the debt in the 'SDLT world' even though he was primarily liable for the debt before and after the transaction in the 'real world'.

Fourth, these rules apply only to the assumption of 'existing debt', defined as debt that exists either side of the transaction, not debt incurred in order to do the transaction. Many transfers of equity involve the discharge of the transferor's (A's) existing debt and the creation of new debt by the transferee (B). B never assumes the existing debt, but A needs funds to enable A to discharge the old debt. If B transfers those funds to A, that is the consideration (or part of the consideration) paid by B for the transaction.

If A transfers a house to A and B jointly in equal shares, one might ask why – since A has merely transferred a half interest – SDLT is due on the whole consideration. In the 'SDLT world', A and B jointly is considered to be a different person from A or B individually. Furthermore, when A registers a transfer of the house to A and B, A does not (as a matter of land registration law) retain a half interest in the property. Instead, the effect of the transfer is to divest the transferor of all interest and vest it in the transferee. If an entry on the register has priority, it will burden the interests of both A and B; it could not do that if A retained an interest throughout the transfer process. The only way vendor A can access the loan raised by purchaser A and B is if the latter pays it to A. And that is the chargeable consideration.

There is a legitimate way to avoid this result. The use of a transfer deed disguises the fact that two transactions are occurring.

First, A transfers a 50 per cent undivided share in the house to B. That is done by A making a declaration of trust in favour of A and B in consideration of B assuming half the existing mortgage debt. That is a land transaction, the transfer of a half beneficial interest from A to B which ought to be in explicit consideration of B's assumption of half the existing mortgage debt. SDLT is payable on that amount.

Second, there is no reason why A needs to appoint B as a second trustee. A could continue to hold the legal estate in trust for the two of them. In many cases, however, B will want to become a second trustee, or a lender will require it, so A transfers legal title to A and B, appointing B as a second trustee. That transfer document is for no chargeable consideration, so no land transaction return is required.

The transfer of the beneficial interest and the legal estate could be dealt with in one transfer. HM Land Registry Practice Guide 21 explains how to do it. However, it is still a transfer of the whole estate from A to A and B, not just a transfer of the beneficial interest from A to B. And it is understood that if HMRC sees one document, it will assume it is all one land transaction and tax it accordingly.

1.5.1 Contingent or uncertain consideration

Where all or some of the chargeable consideration is contingent, the contingency is initially ignored. The tax is payable on the assumption that the contingent consideration *will* be payable.

Where all or some of the chargeable consideration is uncertain or unascertained, the tax is initially payable on the basis of a reasonable estimate of the consideration.

In both cases, the purchaser must re-notify HMRC if it becomes apparent that more tax is due and may re-notify HMRC if it becomes apparent that less tax is due. Interest would be payable on the overpaid or underpaid tax at HMRC's standard rates unless, in the case of underpaid tax, a successful application was made to defer payment of the tax attributable to the contingent or uncertain consideration.

The right to make a deferral application does not extend to unascertained consideration (which HMRC interprets to mean consideration that does not depend on an uncertain future event), nor to contingent or uncertain consideration in the form of rent and is subject to meeting certain conditions. One of the conditions is making the application within 30 days of the effective date. Although the normal filing period has been reduced to 14 days, 30 days is still allowed for a deferral application.

> **WARNING**
>
> Consider making a deferral application if all or part of the consideration for a transaction will be contingent or uncertain. The deadline for making such applications can expire unexpectedly. It is prudent to prepare the application before completion.

Example 1.6

A purchases the freehold estate of a house on its disposal by B, a developer, for £5 million. The agreement includes an 'anti-embarrassment clause'. In the event that A sells the house within three years, he must pay B 30% of the sale proceeds in excess of £5 million. A successfully makes an SDLT deferral application. A sells the house within two years for £7.5 million and triggers the obligation to make a further payment to B of £750,000 (30% of £2.5 million). A must pay further SDLT on the £750,000 within 30 days of the sale. No interest is due on the further SDLT, provided that the tax is paid within 30 days, due to A having made the deferral application. If no deferral application had been made, interest would have been payable from the filing date (14 days after completion of A's purchase) until the date of payment, at HMRC's standard rate for unpaid tax.

1.5.2 Market value rules

There are eight market value rules in the SDLT legislation (below). They operate in different ways. Some operate as a cap (market value is the maximum) or collar (market value is the minimum) to the amount of the chargeable consideration. Others completely override the actual consideration regardless of its amount or value. In each case, the market value of the chargeable interest purchased that is used as the chargeable consideration for the transaction is the amount that the interest might reasonably sell for between willing parties on the open market.

The rules apply where:

- the purchaser is a company connected with the vendor (collar) (see **Chapter 15**);
- the consideration includes the issue or transfer of shares in a company with which the vendor is connected (collar) (see **Chapter 15**);
- the purchaser is a partnership and the vendor is a partner or a connected person (override) (see **16.4**);
- the vendor is a partnership and the purchaser is a partner or a connected person (override) (see **16.5**);
- the subject-matter of the transaction is an interest in a property-investment partnership (override) (see **16.7**);
- the amount of debt assumed, released or discharged by way of consideration is greater than the market value of the property (cap) (see **1.5**);
- part of the consideration given by the purchaser for a transaction is met by entering into another transaction as vendor (collar); and
- certain SDLT reliefs are withdrawn due to a disqualifying event occurring within the control period (override) (see **18.2.3**, **18.3.3** and **18.4.2.6**).[4]

> **WARNING**
>
> Familiarising oneself with the market value rules is vital. In many cases the rules are complex. Where it appears that a set of market value rules applies, consider taking specialist advice. In each case, particular conditions need to be met, and carve-outs or exceptions to the conditions are common.

---

[4] For more information, see FA 2003, ss.47, 53, Sched.15, Part 3, Sched.4, paras.5, 8(2), Sched.7, paras.3(2), 9(2). See also *HMRC internal manual – Stamp Duty Land Tax Manual* ('SDLT Manual') (HMRC, 19 March 2016, updated 16 January 2020, available at: **www.gov.uk/hmrc-internal-manuals/stamp-duty-land-tax-manual**): SDLTM04040, SDLTM04040A, SDLTM30220, SDLTM33300.

1.5.3 Exchanges

Where the whole or part of the consideration given for an SDLT transaction is met by the purchaser disposing of a chargeable interest (whether or not to the vendor), then the chargeable consideration given for each leg of the exchange of interests is based on the higher of what each party gives and gets, provided that the subject-matter of at least one of the legs is a major interest (freehold or leasehold estate).[5] It is impossible to treat this as a single sale, such that only one lot of SDLT is payable, as used to be the case under SDLT's predecessor, stamp duty.

Where the exchange does not involve a major interest, the market value rule does not apply and the tax is only chargeable to the extent that another type of consideration is given (e.g., cash).

Example 1.7

A sells the freehold estate of a house worth £1.5 million to B in return for B giving A the freehold estate of a house worth an equal amount. Both parties must pay SDLT based on £1.5 million.

Where the value of the interests exchanged is unequal and the party giving the lower-value interest also gives cash to equalise the bargain, HMRC accepts that SDLT is due on the lower-value interest received, not the higher value given. It accepts that part of the higher-value interest given is attributable to the receipt of cash. HMRC may struggle to accept that analysis where nothing else is given other than the exchanged interests unless it is obvious (e.g., due to the relationship between the parties) that the difference is a gift.

Example 1.8

A sells the freehold estate of a house worth £1.5 million to B in return for B giving A the freehold estate of a house worth £1.25 million and £250,000 of cash. A must pay SDLT based on £1.25 million. B must pay SDLT based on £1.5 million. Part of the £1.5 million house given by A as consideration for the house transferred by B is attributable to the receipt of cash: £250,000.

Example 1.9

A is B's grandmother. A wishes to downsize and make a gift to her granddaughter, B. A transfers the freehold estate of her house worth £1.5 million to B in return for B giving A the freehold estate of a house worth £1.25 million. A must pay SDLT based on £1.25 million. B

---

[5] FA 2003, s.47, Sched.4, para.5.

must pay SDLT based on £1.25 million. Part of the £1.5 million house given by A as consideration for the house transferred by B is a gift.

Where the transaction is a sale and leaseback, HMRC accepts that the interest sold should be valued subject to the leaseback. HMRC also indicates that the leaseback is not part of the consideration given for the sale, perhaps because the obligation to grant the leaseback is inherent in the interest acquired.[6]

Special rules apply to the following types of exchange:

- surrender and regrants (see **5.7.1**);
- part-exchanges involving house-builders (see **4.5**); and
- exchanges involving a partnership interest (see **16.8**).

1.5.4 'Linked' transactions

1.5.4.1 The impact of the rule

The concept of 'linked' transactions is primarily to stop avoidance of tax by dividing a single transaction into multiple transactions to benefit from lower tax rates. Where transactions are linked, the tax is calculated as if there were a single transaction for the total chargeable consideration given for the transactions (the 'relevant consideration') before it is pro-rated to the transactions.

Example 1.10

Without the 'linked' transactions rule, a freehold interest in a dwelling (worth £500,000) and its garden and grounds (worth £100,000) could be sold in two tranches to the same purchaser. The dwelling would attract £15,000 of SDLT if it was a standard-rates transaction (an effective rate of 2.5%): (£125,000 @ 0%) + (£125,000 @ 2%) + (£250,000 @ 5%); and the garden and grounds would not be chargeable as the chargeable consideration would fall within the nil rate band (£100,000 @ 0%).

With the rule, the two transactions would attract £20,000 of SDLT in total (an effective rate of 3.3%): (£125,000 @ 0%) + (£125,000 @ 2%) + (£350,000 @ 5%). Five-sixths of the £20,000 would be apportioned to the dwelling and one-sixth to the garden and grounds.

The concept of linked transactions also has three consequences.

1. If the subject-matter of the SDLT transaction is exclusively residential property (though not an interest in or over more than five dwellings) and the transaction is 'linked' to another that either occurred in the past or occurs at the same time, the tax rates and tax bands for non-residential transactions

---

[6] SDLT Manual: SDLTM04020.

would apply to the transaction if the subject-matter of that other transaction includes any non-residential property unless multiple dwellings relief is claimed.

Example 1.11

A agrees to sell to B a freehold estate in a dwelling for £1 million. A's son agrees to sell to B a freehold estate in land used for agricultural purposes for £200,000. The dwelling is a replacement of B's main residence. The two transactions are linked and are taxed in accordance with the non-residential rates as if there were one transaction. SDLT of £49,500 is chargeable (an effective rate of 4%): (£150,000 @ 0%) + (£100,000 @ 2%) + (£950,000 @ 5%). One-sixth of the £49,500 must be apportioned to the agricultural land and five-sixths to the dwelling.

---

2. The occurrence of a later linked transaction requires the purchaser in the earlier transaction to review the sufficiency of the tax paid on the earlier transaction, and, if necessary, re-notify HMRC and pay any additional tax in respect of the earlier transaction.

Example 1.12

The facts are as before but the two transactions complete at different times. The sale of the freehold estate in the dwelling completes first. SDLT of £43,750 is paid by B (an effective rate of 4.4%): (£125,000 @ 0%) + (£125,000 @ 2%) + (£675,000 @ 5%) + (£75,000 @ 10%). Three months later, the sale of the freehold in the agricultural land completes.

The two transactions are linked and are taxed in accordance with the non-residential rates as if there were one transaction. SDLT of £49,500 is chargeable (an effective rate of 4%): (£150,000 @ 0%) + (£100,000 @ 2%) + (£950,000 @ 5%). As £43,750 has already been paid, B pays an additional £5,750. One-sixth of the £49,500 is apportioned to the agricultural land and five-sixths to the dwelling. As the fraction of the tax payable on the dwelling is less than the tax already paid, B must amend the SDLT return made earlier to reduce the amount of tax chargeable.

---

3. Concurrent linked transactions may be notified in a single SDLT return. As a single return has been made, the transactions are treated as if they were a single transaction and the purchasers were acting jointly, but that has the effect of making each purchaser liable for the whole SDLT if the others do not pay, so the facility is rarely, if ever, used.

1.5.4.2 What are 'linked transactions'?

Transactions are 'linked' if they form part of a single scheme, arrangement or series of transactions between the same vendor and purchaser or, in either case, connected persons.[7]

'Single scheme', in the author's view, means one over-arching agreement or bargain.

'Arrangement', in the author's view, means a plan (whether or not legally enforceable) involving both parties to the transaction to reduce the amount of tax payable by the purchaser.

'Series of transactions', in the author's view, means consecutive transactions that are involved in connection with each other or are interdependent.

Whether transactions form part of a single scheme, arrangement or series, is a question of fact. A good indication that transactions are linked is if the price for one is influenced by the other: e.g., if a bulk purchase discount is offered. If consecutive transactions are entered into, the timing of the transactions is only relevant to whether it would be reasonable for HMRC (and ultimately a court or tribunal) to infer that the transactions form part of a single scheme, arrangement or series. In other words, transactions that span many years may be linked; and transactions that are entered into in close proximity to each other may not. Likewise, the number of sale contracts does not determine whether or not the transactions are linked.

An example of successive transactions entered into between the same parties that are not linked would be purchases made at an auction.[8]

Example 1.13

A purchases two adjoining dwellings from the same vendor on the same date at an auction. A had agreed with the seller that if the dwellings failed to reach their reserve then he would purchase the dwellings for a sum equal to the reserve. The properties failed to reach their reserve at a competitive auction.

The author would argue that the transactions are not linked. The transactions were independent of each other. It was outside the control of the parties whether or not a person other than A would purchase the properties, and the consideration for one transaction was not set by reference to A having bought the other. At the time of setting the reserve for each property, neither party could have known whether or not A would be successful in purchasing one or both of the properties.

1.5.4.3 What are 'connected persons'?

Persons can be connected for tax purposes via:

---

[7] FA 2003, s.108.
[8] SDLT Manual: SDLTM30100.

THE SCHEME OF THE TAX

- *Marriage, civil partnership or family relationship.* As an individual, you are connected with the following:
  - your spouse or civil partner, if you have one;
  - your 'relatives', meaning your parents and remoter ancestors, your children and remoter descendants, your brother and your sister; you are *not* connected with a relative of a relative (such as an uncle, aunt, nephew, niece or cousin);
  - the 'relatives' of your spouse or civil partner; and
  - the spouse or civil partner of all those 'relatives'.
- *A trust.* For instance, a trustee is connected with the settlor.
- *Their participation in a partnership (except in relation to transactions involving assets of the partnership pursuant to genuine commercial arrangements).* An individual partner is connected with each other partner, their spouses or civil partners, and their 'relatives'. Odd though it is, a person is connected with their partner's son, but not their brother's son.
- *Their control of a company as a shareholder.*
- *One company controlling another or the same person controlling two or more companies.*

A person is treated as having control of a company if he exercises, or is able to exercise, or is entitled to acquire direct or indirect control of the company's affairs by virtue of owning the majority of the shares in the company, or the majority of the voting power in the company, or an entitlement to receive the greater part of the profits and assets available for distribution to the shareholders of the company. In determining whether the control test is met, there may be attributed to a person the rights and powers of any company of which the person has, or the person and his 'associates' have control. The meaning of 'associates' includes relatives, partners and trustees of settlements.[9]

> **WARNING**
>
> The connection rules are complex. If you are concerned that the parties to a transaction are connected and the transaction is linked to another, consider seeking specialist advice to determine the impact of the linked transactions rule and possibly market value rules which might be engaged due to the connection.

Example 1.14

A, B and C are siblings. They own the shares in a company in equal proportions. Although none controls the company individually, the rights and powers of their siblings are attributed

---

[9] Corporation Tax Act 2010, ss.448, 450, 451, 1122.

such that each person is treated as controlling the company; hence, A, B and C are connected to each other by virtue of being relatives and each is also connected to the company.

1.6 EXEMPT TRANSACTIONS

There are five types of exempt transaction. An exempt transaction is not a chargeable or notifiable transaction. This means that no tax is payable, no relief needs to be claimed and no SDLT return needs to be made in respect of such a transaction.[10]

The five types of exempt transaction are:

1. transactions for no chargeable consideration (remember there may be chargeable consideration due to a market value rule even though there is no actual consideration) (see **Chapter 9**);
2. grants of certain leases by registered social landlords (RSLs) (only met by those who act for RSLs);
3. transactions in connection with divorce or the dissolution of a civil partnership (see **8.4**);
4. assents and appropriations by personal representatives (see **9.3**); and
5. variations of testamentary dispositions (see **9.4**).

See **Chapter 2**.

> **TIP**
>
> Exempt transactions are automatically exempt. HMRC does not need to be notified. The purchaser's agent may apply to amend the land register without a revenue certificate; but see **1.9.3**.

1.7 WHEN IS THE TAX DUE?

1.7.1 The meaning of 'effective date'

The 'effective date' is a key concept in the SDLT code. It defines the tax point. This is the point at which certain time periods begin running, most importantly the 14-day or 30-day period for paying tax and/or making an SDLT return. It is also the point at which the subject-matter of the transaction needs to be examined to determine its type – residential property, dwelling, non-residential property or mixed-use property.

In most cases, there will be a contract for an SDLT transaction which is to be completed by an instrument (usually a conveyance). In such cases, the effective date of the transaction is completion of the transaction provided that completion is

---

[10] FA 2003, ss.49, 77, 77A(1), 79, Sched.3; SDLT Manual: SDLTM00520.

between the same parties and in substantial conformity with the contract. An exception applies where the contract is substantially performed, in which case the effective date is the date of substantial performance. Where a substantially performed contract is subsequently completed, both the contract and the transaction effected on completion are notifiable but tax is only payable on the latter transaction to the extent that the amount of tax chargeable on it is greater than the amount of tax chargeable on the contract. Where the contract is not completed, the tax paid on substantial performance may be recovered by amending the return (for up to 12 months from the filing date) after which a claim may be made for the refund of overpaid tax. The recovery of the tax by amending the return is not in doubt. The recovery of the tax by making a claim is not certain, though a First-tier Tribunal decision is supportive.[11]

The treatment of agreements for lease is slightly different – see **5.2.4**.

1.8 THE MEANING OF 'SUBSTANTIAL PERFORMANCE'

A transaction is substantially performed when the purchaser or a connected person takes possession of the whole or substantially the whole of the subject-matter of the contract or a substantial amount of the consideration is given. The term 'possession' for this purpose includes receipt of rents or profits or the right to receive rents or profits, and it is immaterial whether possession is taken under the contract or under a licence or a lease.[12]

> **TIP**
>
> HMRC says that a 'substantial amount' means 90 per cent or more. It refuses to set a percentage to define 'substantially the whole'.

Where the transaction is the grant of a lease, an alternative trigger for substantial performance of the agreement for lease is the first payment of rent.

1.9 HOW DOES THE LIABLE PERSON COMPLY?

1.9.1 Self-assessment (or pay now and check later)

Like most taxes in the UK, SDLT is self-assessed. In other words, it works on a 'pay-now-and-check-later' basis. The sufficiency of the tax self-assessed is not accepted by HMRC immediately. Instead, it is accepted by HMRC:

- in response to a request for clearance;

---

[11] See *Derek Smallman and another* v. *Revenue and Customs Comrs* [2018] UKFTT 0680 (TC). See also FA 2003, ss.44(8), 119, Sched.17A, para.12A(3B); SDLT Manual: SDLTM07600.
[12] FA 2003, s.44(4) (contract and conveyance); SDLT Manual: SDLTM07950.

- on the closure of a check (enquiry) into the SDLT return;
- on a 'review';
- by entering into a contract settlement;
- on determination of an appeal;
- where no enquiry is opened and no determination or revenue assessment is made, by the passage of time.

The purchaser has a limited number of options to request HMRC to confirm its position or to accelerate the point at which HMRC is time-barred from making a challenge.

See **1.10**.

WARNING

The potential for HMRC to challenge the sufficiency of the tax self-assessed after a transaction has completed should be understood to prevent an unwelcome surprise, possibly years later.

1.9.2 Making a return and payment

The purchaser must make an SDLT return for all notifiable transactions. The purchaser must pay tax for all chargeable transactions unless a relief is claimed that relieves fully the amount of tax chargeable. All claims for relief must be made in an SDLT return or an amendment to an SDLT return. Generally, an SDLT return may only be amended within one year of the 'filing date', which is usually 14 days after the effective date of the transaction.

It is easier to describe the types of transactions that are notifiable by exception. Transactions that are *not* notifiable are:

- exempt transactions (see **1.6**);
- freehold purchases for chargeable consideration of less than £40,000 (unless the total amount of the chargeable consideration for any linked transactions is £40,000 or more);
- the purchase of a new lease for a premium of less than £40,000, provided that the annual rent is less than £1,000 and the original term of the lease is seven years or more;
- transfers or surrenders of an existing lease for chargeable consideration of less than £40,000, provided that the original term of the lease is seven years or more;
- the purchase of a new lease for a premium of less than £40,000 where the residential higher rates apply or £125,000 or less (where the residential standard rates apply) or £150,000 or less (where the non-residential rates apply), provided that the annual rent is less than £1,000 and the original term of the lease is less than seven years;

- transfers or surrenders of an existing lease for chargeable consideration of less than £40,000 (where the residential higher rates apply) or £125,000 or less (where the residential standard rates apply) or £150,000 or less (where the non-residential rates apply), provided that the original term of the lease is less than seven years;
- certain notional land transactions (see, e.g., **Chapter 7**);
- certain purchases funded by alternative property finance (see **Chapter 11**).

1.9.3 The link to registration

Where an SDLT transaction is notifiable, HM Land Registry is prevented from updating the land register for most types of SDLT transaction unless a certificate is enclosed (a 'revenue certificate' in form SDLT5) to confirm that the purchaser has made an SDLT return in respect of the transaction.

> **TIP**
>
> The certificate does *not* confirm that SDLT has been paid or that, in HMRC's view, the amount of SDLT self-assessed is sufficient. It is merely a receipt for the submission of an SDLT return.

Where an SDLT transaction is not notifiable, HM Land Registry should not reject an application to amend the land register due to the omission of a revenue certificate. However, in practice HM Land Registry may refer the matter to HMRC to check that the transaction is not notifiable or ask the purchaser's agent to explain why no revenue certificate is enclosed.

> **TIP**
>
> To facilitate registration, in certain cases consider including a covering letter to HM Land Registry explaining why the transaction is not notifiable and, therefore, why a revenue certificate is not enclosed.

Note that further returns may need to be made in respect of the SDLT transaction after the land register has been updated. Those returns do not relate to a fresh SDLT transaction and hence there is no link to registration. As a result, the obligation to make the returns may easily be missed (see **19.9**).

1.10 WHEN IS THE TAX POSITION FINAL?

Where an SDLT return is made, HMRC may check the sufficiency of the self-assessment by sending a notice confirming its intention to open an enquiry into the return. Such a notice must be sent within nine months of the 'filing date' (usually 14 days after the effective date). On closure of the enquiry, HMRC must either confirm that it is satisfied that the self-assessment in the return is correct or make amendments to the return giving effect to its conclusion that the self-assessment is incorrect. In certain circumstances, the exchange of correspondence may constitute an 'enquiry notice' or a 'closure notice'. If amendments are made to the SDLT return, the purchaser can choose to accept them or appeal the decision to make them. If the purchaser appeals the decision, he may request a review of the decision or notify the tribunal of the appeal.

Where no SDLT return is made, HMRC may make a determination of the amount of SDLT it thinks should have been self-assessed by the purchaser or, after four years beginning with the effective date of the transaction, make a revenue assessment to recover the loss of tax. There are strict time limits within which determinations and revenue assessments may be made. The latest period is 20 years beginning with the effective date of the transaction. The purchaser may generally appeal the decision to make a determination or revenue assessment. See **19.11.3** and **19.11.4**.

Penalties may be imposed for a number of reasons, including failure to make an SDLT return. Penalties cannot be imposed for failure to pay tax; instead, only interest may be imposed. See **19.12**.

Provision is made for the purchaser to amend the SDLT return and to reclaim overpaid tax. But in both cases particular conditions must be met. See **19.10**.

There is no concept of a 'self-certificate'. If the purchaser believes that the transaction is not notifiable, nothing needs to be presented to HMRC or HM Land Registry – though see **1.9.3**. The purchaser may, however, choose to send a 'nil return' without prejudice to his self-assessment that the transaction is not notifiable. This is to invite HMRC to open an enquiry into the return if it is dissatisfied with the purchaser's self-assessment and to prevent a penalty for failure to make an SDLT return. The purchaser may also choose to give additional information to HMRC within the enquiry period. There is no blank space in the SDLT return; hence, the provision of such information must be made by letter.

1.11 ANTI-AVOIDANCE

HMRC has at its disposal a range of weapons to deter and defend against attacks on the integrity of the SDLT code. They are (arguably in order of priority):

- market value rules and special charging rules;
- the requirement to read the legislation purposively and apply it so read to the facts viewed realistically;
- mini general anti-avoidance rules (so-called 'motive tests') that restrict the availability of specific reliefs where a main purpose of the relevant transaction is tax avoidance;
- the SDLT-specific general anti-avoidance rule, Finance Act 2003, s.75A (anti-avoidance), which requires tax to be paid on a notional transaction if the

THE SCHEME OF THE TAX

amount of tax payable on the notional SDLT transaction exceeds the amount of tax paid or payable on the actual SDLT transaction(s) – see below; and
- the ability to 'counteract' abusive arrangements under the general anti-abuse rule (GAAR) in Finance Act 2013, Part 5 (general anti-abuse rule).

Sitting alongside those defences are numerous things that act as warnings or sanctions at HMRC's disposal, including:

- the requirement to notify HMRC of proposals or the use of arrangements that have as a main benefit an SDLT advantage under the disclosure of tax avoidance schemes (DOTAS);
- the requirement to pay SDLT before an enquiry into an SDLT return is closed or an SDLT appeal is determined on receipt of an accelerated payment notice (APN);[13]
- the threat of a penalty equal to 50 per cent of the tax found to be payable on determination of an SDLT appeal where a follower notice is made;[14]
- graduated sanctions for certain promoters of tax avoidance schemes requiring, for example, such promoters to disclose details of their products and clients to HMRC and to tell clients that they are a monitored promoter under the promoters of tax avoidance schemes (POTAS) rules;[15]
- the Code of Practice on Taxation for Banks;
- the Solicitors Regulation Authority (SRA) warning notice issued on 21 September 2017 (updated 25 November 2019) headed 'Tax avoidance – your duties', which warns that solicitors involved in advising on and facilitating unsuccessful tax avoidance are in breach of the SRA Principles and Codes of Conduct as set out in the Standards and Regulations;
- government procurement rules that require potential suppliers to declare whether they have had an 'occasion of non-compliance' due to the use of a failed tax avoidance scheme; and
- the Chartered Institute of Taxation's (CIOT's) Professional Conduct in Relation to Taxation (PCRT).

Other works exist that examine these provisions, and the powers afforded to HMRC by them, in more detail. However, a brief mention should be made about FA 2003, s.75A. The provision is a controversial anti-avoidance rule for which there is no precedent. It was introduced in December 2006 in response to the disclosure of SDLT avoidance schemes. To determine whether it applies, the amount of tax paid (if any) on the real SDLT transaction is compared with the amount of tax that would be payable on a notional SDLT transaction. In making this comparison, any intermediate transactions that are SDLT transactions are disregarded and the tax that would be payable on the notional transaction is the largest amount given or received by way of consideration for the 'scheme transactions'.

---
[13] FA 2014, Part 4, Chapter 2.
[14] FA 2014, Part 4, Chapter 3.
[15] FA 2014, Part 5.

It follows that considerable stress is placed on the meaning of 'scheme transactions'. The concept determines whether the provision is engaged. The legislation describes 'scheme transactions' as anything that is 'involved in connection with' the real SDLT transaction. There is a debate (probably to be settled by case law) as to whether those four words 'involved in connection with' should be read literally to include things that are merely commercially interdependent or purposively to include only things that produce a tax loss that was not intended by parliament. Until 2019, HMRC's guidance indicated that it would interpret the provision purposively. In 2019, HMRC argued in an appeal, and the First-tier Tribunal found in that appeal, that HMRC's guidance was wrong. This illustrates the danger of relying on HMRC's guidance.[16]

See **9.10**.

WARNING

Whenever an SDLT transaction is factually connected to one or more other transactions (not necessarily SDLT transactions) for which consideration is given, pause to consider the potential application of FA 2003, s.75A. If necessary, take specialist advice and/or seek confirmation from HMRC of its interpretation of the legislation. Do not assume merely because the arrangements of which the SDLT transaction forms part are not driven by tax or are not driven by tax avoidance, that section 75A cannot apply.

---

[16] FA 2003, ss.75A–75C. See also *Hannover Leasing Wachstumswerte Europa Beteiligungsgesellschaft MBH and another* v. *Revenue and Customs Comrs* [2019] UKFTT 4 (TC). See also SDLT Manual: SDLTM09050.

CHAPTER 2

Excluded transactions

2.1 BACKGROUND

This chapter covers 'excluded' land transactions – i.e., land transactions that are excluded from being stamp duty land tax (SDLT) transactions or land transactions that are exempt from charge. Their exclusion or exemption is automatic: no relief or exemption needs to be claimed. None of the transactions is a notifiable transaction: no SDLT return needs to be made in order for the land register to be updated (assuming the transaction is registrable).

A transaction may be 'excluded' because:

- the interest acquired is not a chargeable interest (or an exempt interest);
- the interest acquired is an exempt interest;
- the parties to it are the same person; or
- it is an exempt transaction.[1]

2.2 NOT A CHARGEABLE INTEREST OR AN EXEMPT INTEREST

'Chargeable interest' takes a wide meaning. It is an estate, interest, right or power in or over land in England or Northern Ireland or the benefit of an obligation, restriction, or condition affecting the value of any such estate, etc., other than an exempt interest.

It includes, therefore, freehold and leasehold estates, options, easements (e.g., rights of way and rights to light) and rentcharges.

Legal and equitable interests are recognised as chargeable interests equally with one exception. The equitable interest acquired by a purchaser on an uncompleted sale contract is disregarded unless the contract is 'substantially performed' (see **1.7**).

Consequently, if the subject-matter of the transaction is not an estate, interest, right or power in or over land or the benefit of an obligation, restriction or condition affecting the value of any such estate, interest right or power in or over land, the

---

[1] For more information see *Sergeant and Sims on Stamp Taxes* (LexisNexis UK), Division AA1.8: Exceptions and exemptions.

STAMP DUTY LAND TAX HANDBOOK

transaction is not an SDLT transaction. Another way of putting this is that property rights (rights *in rem*) generally count and personal rights (rights *in personam*) generally do not.

In most cases it will be obvious that the subject-matter of the transaction is or is not a chargeable interest.

There are three exceptions where the SDLT legislation deems a person to acquire a chargeable interest (or have entered into a land transaction) even though the subject-matter of the transaction does not fall within the meaning of 'chargeable interest'. They are:

- acquisition of an interest in a 'property-investment partnership' (see **16.7**);
- development licence arrangements (see **Chapter 17**); and
- put options and rights of pre-emption (see **Chapter 13**).[2]

2.3 EXEMPT INTERESTS

There are six types of chargeable interests that are exempt. The exempt interests are:

1. security interests;
2. licences to use or occupy land;
3. tenancies at will;
4. advowsons;
5. franchises; and
6. manors.

The acquisition of an exempt interest is *not* an SDLT transaction.

Advowsons, franchises and manors are uncommon. 'Franchise' means for this purpose a grant from the Crown, such as the right to hold a market or take tolls.

The meaning of 'security interest' is wider than a conventional mortgage. It covers 'an interest or right (other than a rentcharge) held for the purpose of securing the payment of money or the performance of any other obligation'.[3]

A 'tenancy at will' is a lease that is exempt from charge. HM Revenue and Customs (HMRC) describes a tenancy at will in its guidance as 'an arrangement, whether documented or not, where a tenant occupies land as tenant (for example, not as servant or agent) with the consent of the owner, on the basis that the arrangement can be brought to an end by either party at any time. The arrangement will also automatically cease if either party dies or if the owner sells the land. A tenancy at will does not create an estate and thus cannot be assigned.' HMRC warns that a lease described as a tenancy at will may in fact constitute a periodic tenancy and, therefore, be chargeable.

HMRC used to publish a list of those terms which, it thought, indicated whether a person's right to occupy land constituted a licence or a lease. That list is missing

---

[2] Finance Act (FA) 2003, ss.44A, 46, Sched.15, para.14.
[3] FA 2003, s.48(3).

EXCLUDED TRANSACTIONS

from its latest guidance; though a copy of its old guidance, the Stamp Office Manual, is accessible in the National Archive. However, the list is still a good source of reference. It is set out below.

Terms which indicate that a lease or tenancy agreement has been granted are as follows:
- The right of the occupier to exclusive possession of the property.
- An authorisation to enter upon, use and enjoy the premises.
- A fixed term.
- An obligation on the occupier to repair the premises.
- An obligation not to 'waste' the property, a term of art meaning that the reversion is not to be damaged or prejudiced.
- An obligation on the occupier not to alter the premises.
- An obligation to allow the owner 'at all reasonable times to enter the premises to inspect them and for all other reasonable purposes'.
- An obligation on the occupier to 'deliver up' the premises at the end of the agreement period.
- An obligation on the occupier to insure the premises.
- A covenant on the part of the owner to afford the occupier 'quiet enjoyment' of the premises.
- The owner's right to re-enter and determine the agreement.
- A prohibition on sub-letting.
- An obligation on the occupier to pay for services, such as gas and electricity.

Terms which indicate that no more than a licence has been granted are as follows:
- Possession for part only of each day or for specific days each week.
- An obligation on the occupier not to impede the owner or his agents in the exercise of his rights of possession and control of the premises.
- A right for the owner to install additional occupiers.
- An obligation on the occupier to share with other occupiers installed by the owner.
- An obligation on the occupier not to cause nuisance to the other occupiers.
- A reference to the licence being personal to the licensee.
- An obligation on the occupier to pay a daily rate for the premises.
- A requirement that visitors are to leave by a certain time.
- No notice period required of the occupier.[4]

2.4 SAME PERSON

A requirement of an SDLT transaction is an *acquisition* of a chargeable interest. Subject to one exception, if the purchaser is the same person as the vendor, there is no acquisition. Logically, a person cannot acquire something he already owns. The paradigm example of this is where a bare trustee transfers property held on trust to the beneficiary. The act of the trustee is deemed to be an act of the beneficiary in the SDLT world. The beneficiary, therefore, is treated as making both the disposal *and*

---

[4] FA 2003, s.48(2), (3); *HMRC internal manual – Stamp Duty Land Tax Manual* ('SDLT Manual') (HMRC, 19 March 2016, updated 16 January 2020, available at: **www.gov.uk/hmrc-internal-manuals/stamp-duty-land-tax-manual**): SDLTM10050; *Stamp Taxes Manual* (last updated in 2001 and archived, available at: **https://webarchive.nationalarchives.gov.uk/20141203221719/http://www.hmrc.gov.uk/so/manual.htm**): paras.5.3–5.4.

the acquisition. Therefore, the beneficiary does not acquire the trust property for the purposes of SDLT, as he already owned it.

The exception is if the person making the disposal acts in a different capacity from the capacity in which he acts making the acquisition. For example, a person might grant a lease of trust property as bare trustee (at the direction of the beneficiary) to himself in his personal capacity. The same person would be regarded as making the disposal *and* acquisition (note the bare trustee would be treated as disposing of the entire interest in the lease under a deeming rule). Nevertheless, the person arguably has made an acquisition due to the different capacity in which he holds the trust property.[5]

2.5 EXEMPT TRANSACTIONS

There are five types of exempt transaction. An exempt transaction is not a chargeable or notifiable transaction. This means that no tax is payable, no relief needs to be claimed and no SDLT return needs to be made.

The five types are:

1. *Transactions for no chargeable consideration.* This includes the appointment of trust property by trustees to beneficiaries. (Note: There may be chargeable consideration even though there is no actual consideration due to a market value rule – see **1.5.2** and **Chapter 9**.)
2. *Grants of certain leases by registered social landlords (RSLs).* This refers to accommodation that the RSL holds on a lease for five years or less and lets as temporary rented accommodation to individuals nominated by a housing authority. Those leases are exempt from SDLT.
3. *Transactions in connection with divorce or the dissolution of a civil partnership.* The transfer of property between spouses or civil partners in pursuance of certain types of court order, an agreement in contemplation of, or in connection with, divorce or dissolution, judicial separation or a separation order is exempt regardless of whether the relevant spouse or civil partner assumes secured debt. Since an agreement relating to real property cannot exist unless it is in writing and complies with Law of Property (Miscellaneous Provisions) Act 1989, s.2, a formal contract between the parties is advisable, and they would normally need to be advised independently. See **8.4**.
4. *Assents and appropriations by personal representatives.* The transfer of property to one or more beneficiaries under a will or under the law of intestacy is exempt provided that no consideration is given for the transfer other than the assumption of secured debt or an obligation to pay inheritance tax. See **9.3**.
5. *Variations of testamentary dispositions.* A land transaction resulting from the variation of a disposition of property (regardless of whether the disposition

---

[5] FA 2003, s.43, Sched.16, para.3.

was in pursuance of a will or the law of intestacy) is exempt provided that it occurs within two years of the legatee's death and no consideration is given other than the variation of another disposition or the assumption of secured debt. See **9.4**.[6]

---

[6] FA 2003, s.49, Sched.3; SDLT Manual: SDLTM00520, SDLTM00530, SDLTM00540, SDLTM00550, SDLTM00560, SDLTM00570, SDLTM00570A.

CHAPTER 3

Freehold and leasehold transfers

3.1 BACKGROUND

This chapter covers the stamp duty land tax (SDLT) treatment of transfers of freehold and leasehold estates in or over residential property. It is the largest and most important topic for the residential property lawyer.[1]

It is divided into four parts. The first examines the meaning of 'residential property' and 'dwelling'. The second discusses the three per cent surcharge for purchases of 'additional' dwellings by individuals and purchases of dwellings by companies (the 'higher rates'). The third summarises the rules on the alternative surcharge for purchases of dwellings worth more than £500,000 by 'non-natural persons' (the 'super rate'). The final part discusses the surcharge for overseas purchasers.

References to 'higher-rates transaction', 'standard-rates transaction' and 'super-rate transaction' are to an SDLT transaction that is taxed in accordance with the higher rates, standard rates or super rate, respectively.

> **WARNING**
>
> A decision of the Financial Ombudsman in 2019 throws this subject into stark focus for firms providing financial services in connection with the sale process. It ordered a mortgage broker to compensate the purchaser for the interest payable on the amount borrowed to fund the additional amount of SDLT attributable to the higher rates because the broker had assured the purchaser in writing that the higher rates would not apply to the transaction.

3.2 WHAT TAX RATES AND TAX BANDS APPLY?

Five alternative sets of tax rates and tax bands apply to freehold and leasehold transfers in or over residential property – see **1.4.1**. These include a special set of tax

---

[1] For more information see *Sergeant and Sims on Stamp Taxes* (LexisNexis UK), AA2A: SDLT–super rate for certain residential property transactions, AA2B: SDLT–higher rates for additional dwellings acquired by individuals and dwellings acquired by companies.

FREEHOLD AND LEASEHOLD TRANSFERS

rates and tax bands that applies to first-time buyers purchasing for no more than £500,000 subject to meeting conditions (see **4.2**).

With the exception of the super rate and the first tax band for the higher rates, the rates apply to so much of the chargeable consideration given for the transaction and any linked transactions that falls within each tax band.

The switch to a progressive (or 'slice') system occurred in 2014. Prior to that, one tax rate applied to the *whole* of the chargeable consideration. This is referred to as the 'slab' system. Subject to transitional provisions, residential property transactions with an effective date on or after 4 December 2014 are taxed in accordance with the slice system. The move from a slab system to a slice system for commercial property transactions followed. The change took effect from 1 April 2016, again subject to transitional provisions.

Example 3.1

A buys the freehold estate in a London house for £1.5 million. The transaction is a standard-rates transaction. The amount of SDLT payable is £93,750 (an effective rate of 6.3%): (£125,000 @ 0%) + (£125,000 @ 2%) + (£675,000 @ 5%) + (£575,000 @ 10%). The amounts of tax charged within each tax band are aggregated to give the total amount of tax payable.

Example 3.2

As above, but the transaction is a higher-rates transaction. The amount of SDLT payable is £138,750 (an effective rate of 9.3%): (£125,000 @ 3%) + (£125,000 @ 5%) + (£675,000 @ 8%) + (£575,000 @ 13%). As before, the amounts of tax charged within each tax band are aggregated to give the total amount of tax payable.

With two exceptions, the five sets of tax bands and tax rates are alternatives. Only one set may apply to the transaction. The chargeable consideration given for the transaction is not apportioned such that part of the consideration is taxed in accordance with one set of tax rates and tax bands and another part is taxed in accordance with another set.

The first exception is the super rate. Where it applies, so much of the price that is attributable to a dwelling worth more than £500,000 is taxed at 15 per cent and the remainder of the price is taxed in accordance with the relevant set of rates applicable to the rest of the purchased property (e.g., non-residential rates where the purchased property is mixed-use). The second exception applies where multiple dwellings relief is claimed in mixed-use transactions. The proportion of the price attributable to the dwellings (the 'dwellings consideration') is calculated in accordance with the standard rates and added to a fraction of the tax that would be payable on the total price calculated in accordance with the non-residential rates. That fraction is the fraction that the price attributable to the non-dwellings (the 'non-dwellings consideration') bears as a proportion of the total consideration given for the transaction.

This hard-edged method has winners and losers. Engaging the non-residential (or mixed) rates on the whole of the price for a mixed transaction is often beneficial. Conversely, engaging the higher rates on the whole of the price for the replacement of a main residence and other residential property can be very costly.

Example 3.3

A buys a farmhouse for £2 million from a farmer. A owns another property abroad and the farmhouse is not a replacement of his main residence. He also buys fields that are the subject of a farm business tenancy for an additional £200,000. The total price (£2.2 million) is taxed in accordance with the non-residential (or mixed) rates. The amount of tax payable is £99,500 (an effective rate of 4.5%): (£150,000 @ 0%) + (£100,000 @ 2%) + (£1,950,000 @ 5%).

If the two interests had been purchased in two (unlinked) transactions, £115,250 more tax would have been payable, a total of £214,750 (an effective rate of 9.8%): on the house: (£125,000 @ 3%) + (£125,000 @ 5%) + (£675,000 @ 8%) + (£575,000 @ 13%) + (£500,000 @ 15%) and on the land: (£150,000 @ 0%) + (£50,000 @ 2%) = £1,000 total on the land.

Example 3.4

A buys two flats in a new residential development from a house-builder under a single contract for £1.5 million. A intends to use one (worth £1 million) as his new main residence and the other (worth £500,000) as a source of rent (buy-to-let). A sells his old main residence to fund the purchase. There is a single SDLT transaction. It is a higher-rates transaction. The whole of the £1.5 million paid is taxed in accordance with the higher rates even though part of the purchase is a replacement of a main residence. The amount of tax payable is £100,000 if a claim for multiple dwellings relief is made (an effective rate of 6.7%). This is the amount of tax due on the average price per dwelling ((£125,000 @ 3%) + (£125,000 @ 5%) + (£500,000 @ 8%) = £50,000) multiplied by the number of dwellings (two).

If, changing the facts, the two flats had been bought under two linked SDLT transactions, approximately half that amount of tax would have been payable (an effective rate of 3.2%). For an explanation of the method used to calculate the tax payable on a higher-rates transaction linked to a standard-rates transaction, see **3.3.5.4**. The calculation involves prorating the tax that would have been due if the standard rates had applied and prorating the tax that would have been due if the higher rates had applied before adding the two amounts together.

3.2.1 Meaning of 'residential property'

In order to determine which set of tax rates to apply, it is necessary to establish whether the 'main subject-matter of the transaction' (defined to mean the chargeable interest acquired) consists entirely of 'residential property'. If it does not, the non-residential (or mixed) rates apply to the whole of the chargeable consideration given for the transaction unless the super rate applies (see **3.4**).

The term 'residential property' is defined to mean:

- a building that:
    - is used as a dwelling; or
    - is suitable for use as a dwelling; or
    - is in the process of being constructed or adapted for use as a dwelling; and
- land that is or forms part of the garden or grounds of a building within such a building; or
- an interest in or right over land that subsists for the benefit of such a building.[2]

'Non-residential property' means any property that is not residential property.

So far as the first limb of the definition is concerned, whether a building is used as a dwelling, suitable for use as a dwelling or in the process of being constructed or adapted for use as a dwelling is fact sensitive. It is also nuanced. Determining whether a building is 'suitable' for use as a dwelling may depend on a blend of physical and legal factors. In 2019, the First-tier Tribunal held that a derelict dwelling was not suitable for use as a dwelling (see **3.2.3**).

Determining whether a building is 'in the process of' construction or adaptation for use as a dwelling ought to be easier. In the author's view, the test requires physical works to have started and for those works to *add* something to the land or building in question rather than take something away. So stripping out, demolition, land remediation and excavating foundations by themselves are unlikely to count. HM Revenue and Customs (HMRC) says that the start of the construction process is marked by building on the foundations:

> Relevant properties that are in the process of being constructed will be treated as dwellings at the point where building works on top of the foundations have begun. This will be more than a hole in the ground. Furthermore, preparatory works, including demolition of previous buildings, site preparation etc., are not considered sufficient to determine that construction of a dwelling has started. These may be considered 'construction works' but they do not involve the construction of the building for use as a dwelling, as the legislation specifies.[3]

---

[2] Finance Act (FA) 2003, s.116.
[3] *HMRC internal manual – Stamp Duty Land Tax Manual* ('SDLT Manual') (HMRC, 19 March 2016, updated 16 January 2020, available at: **www.gov.uk/hmrc-internal-manuals/stamp-duty-land-tax-manual**): SDLTM00400.

In most cases this will probably be the same test as 'golden brick' for value added tax (VAT) purposes. Once a building is 'in the process of' being constructed or adapted for use as dwellings, all the dwellings within the building are recognised for SDLT purposes.

> **TIP**
>
> A building that is in the process of construction or adaptation for use as one or more dwellings would generally be regarded as 'residential property'. This might engage the residential higher rates depending on the value of the dwellings in their partially completed state and the number of dwellings to be developed. It might also mean that multiple dwellings relief is available to provide a partial exemption from charge (see **4.3**) or if there are six or more dwellings under construction, they would be treated as non-residential (see **3.2.5**).

So far as the second limb of the definition is concerned, it is unclear at what point land that is purchased with a dwelling ceases to be part of the garden or grounds of the dwelling. Relevant factors include:

- planning permission;
- restrictions on use;
- the habitual use of the land;
- size, accessibility, distance and physical separation from the dwelling;
- the duration and nature of any non-residential use;
- whether that non-residential use was carried on with a view to profit;
- liability to pay business rates; and
- single payment scheme receipts.

No one factor is determinative.

Until 2019, HMRC's position on the meaning of garden and grounds for SDLT purposes was uncertain. Its guidance had stated that it would apply a test similar to the capital gains test. Land in excess of that which is required for the reasonable enjoyment of the dwelling would not be treated as part of the garden or grounds of the dwelling. However, it appeared to argue privately that land bought with a dwelling would be treated as part of the garden or grounds of the dwelling unless it was in active non-residential (e.g., agricultural) use on the effective date of the transaction.

The SDLT legislation (unlike the capital gains tax (CGT) legislation) does not specify a 'permitted area' or require the land to be occupied and enjoyed with the dwelling. Likewise there is no requirement for land that is not residential property to be actively used for non-residential purposes. Consequently, HMRC's original guidance and its practice were wrong.

In 2019, HMRC published nine pages of new guidance.[4] The guidance refers to the types of factors listed above, acknowledging (correctly, in the author's view) that no one factor is determinative. Accordingly, identifying the point at which land ceases to be part of the garden or grounds of a dwelling can be tricky.

In 2019, the First-tier Tribunal considered the meaning of garden or grounds in an SDLT appeal.[5] The appellants had bought a farmhouse with 3.5 acres of land comprising two gardens, a duck pond, a barn and a meadow. They paid SDLT in accordance with the standard rates and brought an appeal against HMRC's decision to refuse to repay tax on the basis that the tax should have been paid in accordance with the non-residential (or mixed) rates. The appellants argued that:

- the barn, meadow and bridleway did not subsist for the benefit of the farmhouse;
- the barn, meadow and bridleway were not part of the garden or grounds of the farmhouse;
- the barn, meadow and bridleway were separated from the farmhouse by hedges;
- the bridleway was used by the public and could not be used for private or recreational purposes;
- the barn was classified as a non-residential building; and
- the meadow and barn were not integral parts of the dwelling and could not be used for ornamental or recreational purposes.

The tribunal held that the term 'grounds' has, and is intended to have, a wide meaning. Its ordinary meaning is land attached to, or surrounding, a house which is occupied with the house or available to the owners of the house for them to use. The grounds do not need to be used for any particular purpose. It is not relevant that the grounds and garden are separated from each other by hedges or fences; the grounds do not need to be used for ornamental or recreational purposes; and it does not matter that there is a right of way over the grounds. Applying this to the meadow and bridleway, the tribunal held that they were part of the grounds of the farmhouse and that the barn was a building on that land. The appeal was dismissed.

> **TIP**
>
> Where land is purchased that is not obviously part of the garden or grounds of a dwelling, consider taking specialist advice to categorise the land properly for SDLT purposes, taking into account all the facts, HMRC guidance and case law.

Certain types of communal buildings used for institutional purposes are expressly treated as residential property or not. School dormitories, purpose-built

---

[4] SDLT Manual: SDLTM00395, SDLTM00440, SDLTM00445, SDLTM00450, SDLTM00455, SDLTM00460, SDLTM00465, SDLTM00470, SDLTM00475, SDLTM00480.
[5] See *David and Sally Hyman* v. *Revenue and Customs Comrs* [2019] UKFTT 469 (TC).

student accommodation arranged as cluster flats and barracks, for example, are treated as residential property. Care homes, hospices, prisons and hotels, for example, are treated as non-residential property. In some circumstances, establishing whether the purchased property falls within one of these classes of use is subjective. For example, it may not be obvious whether a building used as serviced apartments consists of dwellings (residential property) or is a 'hotel or inn or similar establishment' (non-residential property).

> **TIP**
>
> Where the purchased property is some type of communal accommodation and is to be used as a source of rents (e.g., serviced apartments), consider taking specialist advice to categorise the land properly for SDLT purposes, taking into account all the facts, HMRC guidance and case law.

Where the whole or part of a garden or grounds of a dwelling is purchased without the dwelling it serves, it is unclear whether the subject-matter of the transaction is residential or non-residential and, therefore, whether the transaction is taxed in accordance with the standard rates or non-residential (mixed) rates. The residential higher rates would never apply, as the main subject-matter of the transaction would not consist of a *dwelling*.

In the author's opinion, the transaction should be taxed in accordance with the non-residential rates even though the underlying land it benefits is used for residential purposes (see **14.3**). HMRC's view – which is shared by a significant proportion of advisers – is different, however. Its 'firm' view is that the land remains residential, even if it has been made inaccessible to the seller; but a subsequent sale by the purchaser may be non-residential if there is no dwelling on the sold land at the effective date of the subsequent sale. This was discussed in a meeting between HMRC and the Chartered Institute of Taxation (CIOT) in June 2018. The position has not been tested before the courts.

3.2.2 Mixed-use

A mixed-use transaction may be one of three types:

1. the purchase of a single chargeable interest that answers the description of both residential and non-residential property: e.g., the purchase of a country house with land in commercial use falls within this category;
2. the purchase of more than one chargeable interest in a single transaction where one or more of the interests consists exclusively of one or more dwellings and at least one other interest consists of, or includes, non-residential property; or
3. the purchase of one or more chargeable interests that consist of one or more

dwellings (the 'first purchase') that is 'linked' (either successively or concurrently) to the purchase of one or more chargeable interests that consist of, or include, non-residential property, provided that the first purchase is not a 'higher-rates transaction' and a claim for multiple dwellings relief is not made (see **3.3**).

In the second and third types, the relationship and proximity of the two types of property are irrelevant.

The SDLT treatment of each type is the same. Subject to the application of the super rate, the *whole* of the chargeable consideration is taxed in accordance with the non-residential (or mixed) rates unless, where more than one dwelling is purchased, a claim for multiple dwellings relief is made (see **4.3**).

3.2.3 The meaning of 'dwelling'

Subtly different definitions of 'dwelling' apply in different SDLT contexts. It generally means a self-contained residential property. According to case law, the term means a place where one lives and which one treats as home. It must have the facilities required for such use, including, as a minimum, facilities for personal hygiene, the preparation and consumption of meals, storage of personal belongings and a place to rest and sleep.

In 2019, the First-tier Tribunal considered whether the purchase of a derelict bungalow that was to be demolished and replaced with a new dwelling by a company should have been taxed in accordance with the residential standard rates or, as HMRC had argued, the residential higher rates.[6] After taking into account the dilapidated state of the building, including the absence of radiators and copper pipes and the presence of asbestos that would have needed to have been removed before repairs or alterations could have been carried out, the tribunal held that the building was not 'suitable' for use as a dwelling on the effective date of the transaction. Consequently, the tribunal found that the appellant had made an overpayment of tax and was entitled to a repayment. The tax should have been paid in accordance with non-residential (or mixed) rates.

In October 2019, HMRC published nine pages of guidance on the meaning of dwelling and single dwelling.[7] So far as material, HMRC says:

- The use of the dwelling at the effective date of the transaction is a very significant factor, but long-standing past use will also be considered. The intended use by the purchaser is irrelevant for the purpose of determining the building's use or suitability for use as a dwelling.
- Legal restrictions on dwelling use and whether the building is subject to council tax or business rates are factors in assessing suitability for use, but they are not necessarily determinative.

---

[6] See *PN Bewley Ltd v. Revenue and Customs Comrs* [2019] UKFTT 65 (TC).
[7] SDLT Manual: SDLTM00380 *et seq.*

- Dwellings that are essentially habitable, but in need of modernisation, renovation or repair, which can be addressed without materially changing the structural nature of the property will be considered suitable for use as a dwelling.
- Where a building is used partly as a dwelling and partly for other purposes, the degree of conversion and separation from residential areas will be key factors to determine whether the building is suitable for use as a dwelling or mixed-use.[8]

> **TIP**
>
> Where the purchased property is a derelict or dilapidated dwelling, consider taking specialist advice to categorise the land properly for SDLT purposes, taking into account all the facts, HMRC guidance and case law.

3.2.4 Purchase of more than one dwelling

The purchase of more than one dwelling is relevant to whether the higher rates apply to the transaction and the availability of partial relief, multiple dwellings relief (see **4.3**).

A building or part of a building may count as a dwelling even if it was not last used (and is not to be used) as a dwelling if it is 'suitable' for use as a single dwelling.

HMRC says:

> **Meaning of 'Single Dwelling'**
>
> Dwelling takes its everyday meaning (See SDLTM09750). It must be sufficiently self-contained to be considered a 'single dwelling.'
>
> The test of whether a property is 'suitable for use' as a single dwelling is a more stringent test than whether it forms a self-contained part of a larger dwelling. Furthermore, whether or not it is suitable for use as a single dwelling requires consideration of whether it is sufficiently independent to be considered a dwelling on its own. In the case where a building is considered to contain more than one dwelling, evidence will be needed to show that each 'dwelling' in question is sufficiently independent to count as a separate dwelling in its own right. In the absence of sufficient evidence, it may be decided that it is more appropriate to consider that there is one dwelling, not two or more.[9]

Accordingly, a house with a lower-ground floor flat, for example, should be regarded as two dwellings, provided that each part of the building:

- has separate external access or they share a single point of external access via common parts;
- enables its occupants to enjoy privacy from the occupants of the other;

---

[8] See *Uratemp Ventures Ltd* v. *Collins* [2001] UKHL 43.
[9] SDLT Manual: SDLTM00410. See also SDLTM00410, SDLTM00415, SDLTM00420, SDLTM00425, SDLTM00430, SDLTM09755.

- has adequate facilities for personal hygiene, the preparation and consumption of meals, the storage of personal belongings, and a place to rest and sleep; and
- is supplied with gas, electricity and water, and their supply is able to be adjusted and switched off independently – as is their source of heating.

The absence of any or all of the following factors in respect of each part of the property is unlikely to be conclusive, but may be relevant, in determining whether or not there are separate dwellings:

- separate recognition for council tax purposes;
- classification for non-domestic use;
- separate utility meters;
- the difficulty or impossibility of selling each part of the building without the other;
- the use of the building historically.

The intended use of the purchased property is irrelevant. Occupying the whole of the purchased building (or the whole of the purchased land) as one dwelling after completion does not prevent there being more than one dwelling at the effective date of the transaction for the purposes of SDLT. However, note that making alterations to the purchased building or land that reduce the number of dwellings (because one or more cease to be suitable for use as a single dwelling) within the three-year period beginning with completion would trigger a withdrawal of multiple dwellings relief.[10]

TIP

Where part of the purchased property is suitable for use as a single dwelling (e.g., it contains an annex or lower-ground floor flat), consider taking specialist advice to determine whether the characteristics of the relevant part could reasonably support a claim for multiple dwellings relief.

WARNING

1. Where the buyer claims multiple dwellings relief, either initially or within one year of completion, the possibility of the relief being withdrawn should be brought to their attention.
2. Overpaid tax due to a failure to claim multiple dwellings relief cannot be reclaimed more than one year after completion – see **19.10.2**.

---

[10] FA 2003, s.58D, Sched.6B.

STAMP DUTY LAND TAX HANDBOOK

Example 3.5

A buys the freehold estate in a London townhouse for £4 million. It is a replacement of his main residence. The house is arranged over five floors, including a lower-ground floor. The lower-ground floor includes a separate kitchenette/utility room, toilet and shower. It can be accessed both externally and internally by lockable doors. A (reasonably) is under the impression that he has bought one dwelling and pays tax in accordance with the standard rates – a sum of £393,750 (an effective rate of 9.8%): (£125,000 @ 0%) + (£125,000 @ 2%) + (£675,000 @ 5%) + (£575,000 @ 10%) + (£2,500,000 @ 12%).

More than one year after completion he realises that he could have claimed multiple dwellings relief to save £86,250 of tax, paying £307,500 (an effective rate of 7.7%): ((£125,000 @ 0%) + (£125,000 @ 2%) + (£675,000 @ 5%) + (£575,000 @ 10%) + (£500,000 @ 12%)) = £153,750 x 2. Sadly, he is too late to apply to reclaim the overpaid tax.

For an explanation of the method used to calculate the tax payable where multiple dwellings relief is available, see **4.3**.

3.2.5 Purchases of more than five dwellings

The purchase of more than five dwellings in a 'single transaction' engages the non-residential (or mixed) rates notwithstanding the absence of any non-residential property in the transaction.[11] The dwellings are treated as if they were non-residential property except for the purposes of multiple dwellings relief and the super rate. This means that where the super rate does not apply, purchasers of more than five dwellings can choose to pay SDLT in accordance with the non-residential (or mixed) rates of tax (the base case) or pay SDLT in accordance with the standard rates or higher rates of tax in conjunction with a claim for multiple dwellings relief.[12] The minimum rate of one per cent would apply where none of the purchased dwellings is worth more than £40,000 (note that the average price per dwelling is irrelevant). Where one or more of the purchased dwellings is worth more than £40,000, the higher rates would apply unless all but one of the dwellings are 'subsidiary dwellings' (see **3.3.3**). Two calculations should be made to determine whether the purchaser should claim the relief or treat the purchase of more than five dwellings as non-residential.

Example 3.6

A buys the freehold estate in a building consisting of six studio apartments for £2.5 million. If A claims multiple dwellings relief, £240,000 of tax would be payable (an effective rate of 9.6%): (£125,000 @ 3%) + (£125,000 @ 5%) + (£166,666 @ 8%) x 6.

---

[11] FA 2003, s.116(7).
[12] FA 2003, s.58D, Sched.6B.

FREEHOLD AND LEASEHOLD TRANSFERS

If he does not claim the relief, £125,500 less tax would be payable (an effective rate of 4.6%): (£150,000 @ 0%) + (£100,000 @ 2%) + (£2,250,000 @ 5%).

For an explanation of the method used to calculate the tax payable in this type of transaction, see **4.3**.

Example 3.7

A buys the freehold estate in a building composed of six studio apartments for £1.5 million. If A claims multiple dwellings relief, £60,000 of tax would be payable (an effective rate of 4%): (£125,000 @ 3%) + (£125,000 @ 5%) x 4.

If he does not claim the relief, £4,500 more tax would be payable (an effective rate of 4.3%): (£150,000 @ 0%) + (£100,000 @ 2%) + (£1,250,000 @ 5%).

In some cases it may not be clear whether more than five dwellings have been purchased in a single transaction, linked transactions or separate (unlinked) transactions. Reasonable views differ on the meaning of 'single transaction'. HMRC appears to accept that it can be read to include a single bargain.

3.3 THE RESIDENTIAL HIGHER RATES

3.3.1 Background

The higher rates regime (referred to by HMRC as 'HRAD' or higher rates for additional dwellings) is an especially complex part of the SDLT legislation. The legislation runs to almost 100 subparagraphs.[13] So the potential for making errors is high. The regime is also likely to be the part of the SDLT code most relevant to a residential property lawyer's practice. The regime is often referred to as the 'surcharge' and the 'three per cent surcharge'. In this work, the term 'higher rates' is used. The reference to 'additional dwellings' is omitted deliberately. While the ownership of an additional dwelling is needed for an individual to be liable to the higher rates, it is not needed for a company to be so liable. Consequently, the higher rates are the default for purchases by companies (subject to the super rate – see **3.4**). There is no exemption from the higher rates for companies. The government chose not to include one. Instead, it pointed to the 'flexibilities' within the SDLT rules for investors: namely, the rule that deems the purchase of six or more dwellings in a single transaction to be treated as if non-residential property had been purchased (see **3.2.5**) and multiple dwellings relief (see **4.3**).

The higher rates regime applies to transactions with an effective date on or after 1 April 2016 subject to transitional provisions. It has been changed twice since it was introduced. More changes are possible. Its stated purpose is to dampen demand

---

[13] FA 2003, s.58A, Sched.4ZA; SDLT Manual: SDLTM09730.

for additional dwellings like buy-to-lets and second homes to help families buy a home. It can sometimes be a challenge explaining to a purchaser why their liability to pay the higher rates achieves that objective. The rules are prescriptive and occasionally arbitrary in nature. Where they apply, the higher rates add three per cent to every tax band in the set of rates for residential transactions and reintroduce a slab rate for the first tax band. Where the chargeable consideration given for the purchased property is £40,000 or more, so much of it as does not exceed £125,000 is taxed at three per cent. There is no zero per cent rate band for the first £40,000 of the chargeable consideration. The tax rates for non-residential (or mixed) transactions and the super rate are untouched.

Example 3.8

The amount of SDLT payable on the purchase of a dwelling for £400,000 would be £20,000 if the higher rates apply (an effective rate of 5%): (£125,000 @ 3%) + (£125,000 @ 5%) + (£150,000 @ 8%).

Example 3.9

The amount of SDLT payable on the purchase of a dwelling for £400,000 would be £10,000 if the standard rates apply (an effective rate of 2.5%): (£125,000 @ 0%) + (£125,000 @ 2%) + (£150,000 @ 5%).

There are multiple tiers of HMRC guidance available online. Each tier explains the rules progressively in more detail. It is impossible to explain complex legislation in a concise way that covers all fact patterns. Consequently, the basic and intermediate tiers of guidance, in particular, as helpful as they are, should be used with care.

Where a transaction is a higher-rates transaction, code 04 should be entered at question 1 ('type of property') of the SDLT return.

WARNING

1 The information needed to determine whether the higher rates apply to a transaction can be voluminous, personal in nature and obscure. The client questionnaire should be reviewed to establish whether it is adequate in pulling the right information to alert the residential property lawyer that the transaction is or might be a higher-rates transaction. A suggested client questionnaire can be found at the back of this work.
2 To protect against professional negligence claims, there should be an audit trail confirming what information or advice was given to the purchaser and the reasoning for the advice. The audit trail might include an attestation from the client that he does not own (and is not beneficially entitled to) an additional dwelling in the UK or overseas or is separated from his spouse or civil partner (where his spouse or civil partner owns, or is beneficially entitled to, an additional dwelling in the UK or overseas).

> 3   Note that a higher-rates transaction may become a standard-rates transaction after completion. This means that the purchaser is entitled to reclaim the SDLT attributable to the difference in the rates. The purchaser should be alerted of this possibility, the conditions that must be met and the time limit for making the reclaim.

In the rest of this part:

- references to 'main residence' are to a person's only or main residence; and
- references to 'additional dwelling' are to a freehold or leasehold estate (or an undivided share of such an estate, or the relevant foreign equivalent of such an estate) in a dwelling, other than the purchased dwelling, worth £40,000 or more situated anywhere in the world that is not subject to a lease with more than 21 years to run.

3.3.2 The conditions

The conditions that need to be met for a transaction to be a higher-rates transaction vary according to factors, including:

- whether the purchaser is a legal or natural person;
- the number of purchasers;
- the marital status of the purchaser;
- the state of the purchaser's marriage or civil partnership;
- whether the purchaser has children or stepchildren;
- the age of the purchaser's children or stepchildren; and
- the number of dwellings purchased.

At the cost of repetition, the various scenarios, and the corresponding conditions for each, are listed in turn below.

In some cases, the condition that the purchaser owns an 'additional' dwelling (referred to below merely as 'Condition C') is met if a dwelling is owned by certain persons other than the purchaser. The list of persons is specified in full immediately below and abbreviated to '(etc.)' in the main text subsequently. The list of persons is as follows:

- the purchaser's spouse or civil partner (unless separated) (see **3.3.6**);
- the purchaser's children (unless aged 18 or over) (see **3.3.8**);
- the purchaser's stepchildren (unless aged 18 or over, or the purchaser and the child's parent are separated) (see **3.3.8**);
- the trustees of a bare trust under which the purchaser, his spouse or civil partner (unless separated), or children or stepchildren (unless aged 18 or over, or, in the case of stepchildren, the purchaser and the child's parent are separated), are beneficiaries (see **3.3.7**);
- the trustees of a settlement under which the purchaser, his spouse or civil partner (unless separated), or children or stepchildren (unless aged 18 or over,

or, in the case of stepchildren, the purchaser and the child's parent are separated), are entitled to occupy the dwelling for their lifetime or to the income earned in respect of the dwelling, but not necessarily for their lifetime (see **3.3.7**); and
- any property-investment partnership in which the purchaser, or the purchaser's spouse or civil partner (unless separated), is a partner (see **3.3.9**).

3.3.2.1 Individuals purchasing one dwelling

Where the only purchaser is an individual and is purchasing one dwelling (for the meaning of 'dwelling' and 'single dwelling', see **3.2.3** and **3.2.4**, respectively), the following conditions must be met for the transaction to be a higher-rates transaction:

- The amount of the chargeable consideration given must be £40,000 or more.
- The purchased interest must be a freehold or leasehold estate (or an undivided share of such an estate) in or over a dwelling, except a lease of seven years or less.
- The purchased interest must not be subject to (i.e., reversionary on) a lease that has more than 21 years to run on the effective date.
- At the end of the effective date, the purchaser (etc.) must own an additional dwelling: this is referred to in the legislation, HMRC guidance and this work as 'Condition C'.
- The purchased dwelling must not be a replacement of the purchaser's main residence (see **3.3.10.1**).
- The purchaser must not already own the freehold (or another leasehold) estate in the purchased dwelling – although there are extra conditions that apply (see **3.3.10.2**).
- The vendor must not be the purchaser's spouse or civil partner (see **3.3.10.3**).
- The non-residential (or mixed) rates must not apply (see **3.3.5.1**).
- The super rate must not apply (see **3.4**).

Example 3.10

A inherited a 50% share of a dwelling worth more than £200,000, now held as an investment (buy-to-let). He rents his current home and has done so for more than three years. He buys a house to live in as his new home from a third party. It is his first purchase. A's share in the buy-to-let dwelling was inherited more than three years ago. A's purchase is a higher-rates transaction. It does not matter that he only owns half of the other dwelling, nor does it matter in this example that he did not purchase the other dwelling and merely inherited it (but see **3.3.12**), nor does it matter that he intends to live in the purchased dwelling as his main residence. All the relevant conditions for the higher rates are met.

FREEHOLD AND LEASEHOLD TRANSFERS

Example 3.11

A is selling her Spanish holiday villa before buying her first home in the UK for £650,000. Completion is set for Tuesday. On Tuesday, the purchase completes in the morning, but at lunchtime the Spanish lawyers report that the sale has been delayed until Wednesday. At the end of Tuesday, A still owns the Spanish villa, a dwelling additional to her purchased dwelling. So she must pay SDLT in accordance with the higher rates – £42,000 rather than £22,500 – and there is no mechanism for reclaiming the extra £19,500 following the sale of the villa (as her purchase was not a replacement of her main residence).

3.3.2.2 Individuals jointly purchasing one dwelling

Where there is more than one person purchasing one dwelling (for the meaning of 'dwelling' and 'single dwelling', see **3.2.3** and **3.2.4**, respectively), the following conditions must be met in respect of each purchaser for the transaction to be a higher-rates transaction:

- The amount of the chargeable consideration given must be £40,000 or more. (This means the consideration given for the whole transaction, not just the part that the joint purchaser is paying.)
- The purchased interest must be a freehold or leasehold estate (or an undivided share of such an estate) in or over a dwelling (except a lease of seven years or less).
- The purchased interest must not be subject to (i.e., reversionary on) a lease that has more than 21 years to run on the effective date.
- At the end of the effective date, at least one of the purchasers (etc.) must own an additional dwelling: this is referred to in the legislation, HMRC guidance and this work as 'Condition C'.
- The purchased dwelling must not be a replacement of the relevant purchasers' main residence (see **3.3.10.1**).
- The purchasers must not already own the freehold (or another leasehold) estate in the purchased dwelling – although there are extra conditions that apply (see **3.3.10.2**).
- The non-residential (or mixed) rates must not apply (see **3.3.5.1**).
- The super rate must not apply (see **3.4**).

Example 3.12

A and B are married. They wish to buy their first home together. A buys the property in his sole name. B owns a small flat that is let out. A is a first-time buyer. The transaction is a higher-rates transaction because B owns a dwelling on the completion date of his purchase. The sale of B's flat after A's purchase would entitle him to make a reclaim only if he had lived

STAMP DUTY LAND TAX HANDBOOK

in B's flat as his main residence at some point within three years of the completion date for his purchase (see **3.3.10.1**).

3.3.2.3 Individuals purchasing more than one dwelling

Where more than one dwelling is purchased in a single transaction (for the meaning of 'dwelling' and 'single dwelling', see **3.2.3** and **3.2.4**, respectively), the following conditions must be met for the transaction to be a higher-rates transaction:

- In relation to two or more of the purchased dwellings, the amount of the chargeable consideration given for the dwelling must be £40,000 or more.
- In relation to two or more of the purchased dwellings, the purchased interest must be a freehold or leasehold estate (or an undivided share of such an estate) in a dwelling (except a lease of seven years or less).
- In relation to two or more of the purchased dwellings, the purchased interest must not be subject to (i.e., reversionary on) a lease that has more than 21 years to run on the completion date.
- In relation to two or more of the purchased dwellings, the purchased dwelling must not be 'subsidiary' to another of the purchased dwellings (see **3.3.3**).
- The vendor must not be the purchaser's spouse or civil partner (see **3.3.10.3**).
- The non-residential (or mixed) rates must not apply (see **3.3.5.1**).
- The super rate must not apply (see **3.4**).

Example 3.13

A does not own any dwellings. He buys two in a single transaction from a third party. They are both worth more than £40,000 each and neither is 'subsidiary' to the other. The transaction is a higher-rates transaction.

Where any of the first four conditions listed above for the purchase of multiple dwellings are met in relation to *only one* of the purchased dwellings (the 'relevant' purchased dwelling), the following additional conditions must be met for the transaction to be a higher-rates transaction:

- At the end of the day of completion, the purchaser (etc.) must own an additional dwelling – this is referred to in the legislation, HMRC guidance and this work as 'Condition C'.
- The relevant purchased dwelling must not be a replacement of the purchaser's main residence (see **3.3.10.1**).
- The purchaser must not already own the freehold (or another leasehold) estate in the relevant purchased dwelling (see **3.3.10.2**).

FREEHOLD AND LEASEHOLD TRANSFERS

Example 3.14

A buys two dwellings in a single transaction from a third party. They are both worth more than £40,000 each. One is 'subsidiary' to the other (see **3.3.3**) and that other dwelling is not A's replacement main residence. A owns another dwelling overseas worth more than £40,000, which he uses as a holiday home. The transaction is a higher-rates transaction.

3.3.2.4 Company purchasing one or more dwellings

Where the purchaser is a company (or any of the purchasers include a company), the following conditions must be met for a transaction to be a higher-rates transaction:

- The amount of the chargeable consideration given must be more than £40,000.
- The purchased interest must be a freehold or leasehold estate (or an undivided share of such an estate) in or over a dwelling (except a lease of seven years or less).
- The purchased interest must not be subject to (i.e., reversionary on) a lease that has more than 21 years to run on the effective date.
- The non-residential (or mixed) rates must not apply (see **3.3.5.1**).
- The super rate must not apply (see **3.4**).

Example 3.15

A sets up a new company, A Ltd, to purchase a house as an investment (buy-to-let). The super rate does not apply, because the dwelling is purchased exclusively to exploit as a source of rents in the course of a property-rental business. The transaction is a higher-rates transaction. It does not matter that A does not own a dwelling, nor that this is A Ltd's first acquisition, nor that A Ltd will let out the property for investment income.

Where a company buys a freehold or leasehold estate in more than one dwelling, but fewer than six dwellings, the higher rates would apply if £40,000 or more is attributable to at least one of the dwellings and the purchased interest in that dwelling is not subject to (i.e., reversionary on) a lease that has more than 21 years to run on the effective date.

Where a company buys a freehold or leasehold estate in more than five dwellings, the non-residential rates would apply unless a claim for multiple dwellings relief were made, in which case the higher rates would apply if £40,000 or more is attributable to at least one of the dwellings and the purchased interest in that dwelling is not subject to (i.e., reversionary on) a lease that has more than 21 years to run on the effective date (see **3.3.5.2**).

3.3.3 Granny annexes

Where an individual buys more than one dwelling in a single transaction, the transaction would not be a higher-rates transaction merely due to the fact that more than one dwelling is purchased provided that two-thirds of the chargeable consideration given is reasonably attributable to one of the dwellings (the 'main dwelling') and the other dwelling (the 'subsidiary dwelling') is located in the same building as, or on the grounds of, the main dwelling.[14]

There may be more than one subsidiary dwelling. However, in order for more than one dwelling to be a subsidiary dwelling, all those dwellings must be in the same building as, or on the grounds of, the main dwelling and not more than one-third of the chargeable consideration given may be attributable to the subsidiary dwellings.

The rule is aimed to prevent the purchase of a family home that has a 'granny annex' automatically being taxed in accordance with the higher rates.

Where the transaction consists of one dwelling and the other dwelling (or each of the other dwellings) purchased is a subsidiary dwelling, it would be a higher-rates transaction if the following conditions for a single-dwelling transaction are met:

- At the end of the day of completion, any of the purchasers (etc.) must own an additional dwelling: this is referred to in the legislation, HMRC guidance and this work as 'Condition C'.
- The purchased main dwelling must not be a replacement of the purchasers' main residence (see **3.3.10.1**).
- The purchasers must not already own the freehold (or another leasehold) estate in the purchased main dwelling (see **3.3.10.2**).
- The non-residential (or mixed) rates must not apply (see **3.3.5.1**).
- The residential super rate must not apply (see **3.4**).

Example 3.16

A and B purchase a large townhouse to live in as their main residence. They do not own any other dwellings. They are not replacing their main residence. The house is arranged over five floors with a lower-ground floor comprising a self-contained flat. The purchase price is £4 million. The proportion of the £4 million reasonably attributable to the lower-ground floor flat is £750,000. Consequently, the lower-ground floor flat is 'subsidiary' to the rest of the property; hence, the transaction is not a higher-rates transaction.

Example 3.17

A and B purchase a farmhouse to live in as their main residence. They do not own any other dwellings. They are not replacing their main residence. There are three small dwellings on the grounds of the farmhouse that are used as holiday lets. The purchase price is £2.1

---

[14] FA 2003, Sched.4ZA, para.5; SDLT Manual: SDLTM09766, SDLTM09755.

million. The proportion of the £2.1 million reasonably attributable to the farmhouse is £1.3 million. Consequently, none of the three holiday lets is a 'subsidiary dwelling'; hence, the transaction *is* a higher-rates transaction.

WARNING

1 Although a 'subsidiary dwelling' may be disregarded as a separate dwelling for the purposes of the higher rates, it is nevertheless respected as a separate dwelling for the purposes of multiple dwellings relief (see **3.3.5.2**). This is an important distinction and a frequent cause of individuals overpaying SDLT.
2 If a subsidiary dwelling cannot be purchased in the same transaction as the main dwelling, perhaps because an annex is owned by a parent of the owners of the main dwelling, so the transactions are 'linked', the main dwelling will be taxed at that fraction of the standard rates for the total consideration for both dwellings that its consideration bears to the total consideration, and the subsidiary dwelling will be taxed at its fraction of the higher rates on the total consideration.

3.3.4 Overseas dwellings

As indicated above at **3.3.2**, the incidence of the higher rates requires the purchaser or their spouse or civil partner (etc.) to own an additional dwelling (Condition C); the condition is met if the relevant person owns a dwelling situated outside England or Northern Ireland provided that the type of interest in the dwelling owned is equivalent to a freehold or leasehold estate or an undivided share and the interest held is worth £40,000 or more. In some cases, legal advice local to the country in which the dwelling is located will be required to determine the equivalence of the interest. Interest held by the purchaser that must be valued, not the dwelling, to determine whether Condition C is met, at least that is how HMRC interprets the legislation. See **3.3.7**.

Example 3.18

A purchases the freehold estate of a house to live in as his main residence. He is not replacing his main residence. He has a temporary usufruct (the right of use and enjoyment of a property for a set period) in respect of a €400,000 dwelling in France. The temporary usufruct is valued at 23% of the value of the full ownership of the dwelling; thus it is worth approximately €90,000. The transaction would be a higher-rates transaction if the usufruct is equivalent to a leasehold interest or beneficial ownership of a leasehold interest.

3.3.5 Interaction with other SDLT provisions

3.3.5.1 Mixed-use transactions

The higher rates only apply to residential transactions. A transaction is not a residential transaction for this purpose (unless multiple dwellings relief is claimed – see **4.3**) if:

- the purchased interest consists of, or includes, land or buildings that are not 'residential property' (see below);
- one or more freehold or leasehold estates are purchased in or over more than five dwellings in a single transaction (see **3.2.5**).

Where the purchased interest consists of one or more dwellings (the 'first purchase') and the purchase is 'linked' (either successively or concurrently) to the purchase of an interest that consists of, or includes, non-residential property, the first purchase, if it is a higher-rates transaction, would retain its status as a higher-rates transaction notwithstanding its linkage to the non-residential (or mixed) transaction, but that would only matter if a claim for multiple dwellings relief is made (see **4.3**). Absent such a claim, in the author's opinion, both purchases would be taxed at the non-residential (or mixed) rates.

Where the transaction is mixed-use, the amount of the chargeable consideration is not apportioned between the two types of property unless a claim for multiple dwellings relief is made or the super rate applies (see **3.3.5.2** and **3.4**, respectively). Only one set of rates applies, the non-residential (or mixed) rates.[15]

Example 3.19

A buys the freehold estate of a building. The ground floor of the building was last used to run a marketing agency. A total of 12 staff worked in the space. The building had a number of features consistent with that use. The rest of the building was last used as a dwelling and separated internally from the part used to run the marketing agency with lockable doors. The vendor had paid business rates. Consequently, not all of the building is suitable for use as a dwelling. The transaction is not a residential property transaction, it is a mixed-use transaction. It is irrelevant, therefore, whether A owns an additional dwelling. The transaction would not be a higher-rates transaction under any circumstances.

Example 3.20

A Ltd buys a portfolio of seven properties in a single transaction as an investment. Five of the properties are freehold estates in dwellings let out on assured shorthold tenancies. Two of the properties are leasehold estates over buildings used as offices. The transaction is not a residential property transaction, it is a mixed-use transaction. It is irrelevant, therefore, that the purchaser is a company. The transaction is not a higher-rates transaction. A Ltd should

---

[15] FA 2003, ss.55.

FREEHOLD AND LEASEHOLD TRANSFERS

calculate the tax that would be due if multiple dwellings relief was claimed and compare that to the amount of tax payable in accordance with the non-residential (or mixed) rates to determine whether or not to claim the relief. For multiple dwellings relief, see **3.3.5.2**.

Example 3.21

A Ltd buys the freehold estate of a building composed of six studio flats. The transaction is not a residential property transaction. The flats are treated as non-residential property. It is irrelevant, therefore, that the purchaser is a company. The transaction is not a higher-rates transaction. A Ltd should calculate the tax that would be due if multiple dwellings relief was claimed and compare that to the amount of tax payable in accordance with the non-residential (or mixed) rates to determine whether or not to claim the relief.

3.3.5.2 Multiple dwellings relief

Where multiple dwellings relief is claimed, the transaction is taxed in accordance with the residential standard rates or higher rates as follows:

- Where the subject-matter includes non-residential property (not dwellings that are deemed to be non-residential property because six or more are purchased in a single transaction – see **3.2.5**), the standard rates apply; though see below.
- Where more than five dwellings are purchased in a single transaction, the higher rates apply if the conditions for a higher-rates transaction are met – see, in particular, **3.3.3**.
- Where more than one dwelling, but fewer than six dwellings, are purchased, the higher rates apply if the conditions for a higher-rates transaction are met – see, in particular, **3.3.3**.

A condition of the higher rates is that the chargeable interest 'consists of' one or more dwellings. In the author's opinion, this means that the chargeable interest should consist *exclusively* of one or more dwellings before the higher rates are engaged. Accordingly, where multiple dwellings relief is claimed on a mixed-use transaction, the residential standard rates should be used, not the higher rates. This might make quite a difference. It is not known whether HMRC would agree to this interpretation.

Example 3.22

A Ltd buys the freehold estate in a building consisting of 10 flats for £1 million. It first calculates the tax that would be due if multiple dwellings relief was claimed. The transaction is a higher-rates transaction. The amount of SDLT due would be £30,000 (an effective rate of 3%). This is the amount of tax due on the average price per dwelling of £100,000 (£100,000 @ 3%) multiplied by the number of dwellings (10). It then calculates the tax that would be due in accordance with the non-residential (or mixed) rates. The amount of SDLT due would be £39,500 (an effective rate of 4%): (£150,000 @ 0%) + (£100,000 @ 2%) + (£750,000 @ 5%). Accordingly, A Ltd claims the relief.

Example 3.23

As above, except that the purchase price is £3 million. A Ltd first calculates the tax that would be due if multiple dwellings relief was claimed. The transaction is a higher-rates transaction. The amount of SDLT due would be £140,000 (an effective rate of 4.7%). This is the amount of tax due on the average price per dwelling of £300,000 ((£125,000 @ 3%) + (£125,000 @ 5%) + (£50,000 @ 8%)) multiplied by the number of dwellings (10). It then calculates the tax that would be due in accordance with the non-residential (or mixed) rates. The amount of SDLT due would be £139,500 (an effective rate of 4.7%): (£150,000 @ 0%) + (£100,000 @ 2%) + (£2,750,000 @ 5%). Accordingly, A Ltd does *not* claim the relief.

Example 3.24

As above, except that the building is mixed-use: the ground floor consists of retail premises (worth £100,000). A Ltd first calculates the tax that would be due if multiple dwellings relief was claimed. The transaction is not a higher-rates transaction. The amount of SDLT due would be £49,650 (an effective rate of 1.7%). This is the amount of tax due on the average price per dwelling of £290,000 ((£125,000 @ 0%) + (£125,000 @ 2%) + (£40,000 @ 5%)) multiplied by the number of dwellings (10) plus the fraction of the tax that would be due under the non-residential (or mixed) rates that its consideration bears to the total consideration (£100,000/£3 million). It then calculates the tax that would be due in accordance with the non-residential (or mixed) rates. The amount of SDLT due would be £139,500 (an effective rate of 4.7%): (£150,000 @ 0%) + (£100,000 @ 2%) + (£2,750,000 @ 5%). Accordingly, A Ltd claims the relief.

Example 3.25

As above, except that a lease of the ground floor retail premises (again, worth £100,000) and separate leasehold estates of the dwellings are purchased in two linked transactions because the vendors are connected persons rather than the same person: the subject-matter of one transaction is the ground floor lease, and the subject-matter of the other (the dwellings transaction) is the 10 leases of the dwellings. A Ltd first calculates the tax that would be due if multiple dwellings relief was claimed on the dwellings transaction. The dwellings transaction *is* a higher-rates transaction. The amount of SDLT due would be £146,500 (an effective rate of 4.8%). This is the amount of tax due on the average price per dwelling of £290,000 ((£125,000 @ 3%) + (£125,000 @ 5%) + (£40,000 @ 8%)) multiplied by the number of dwellings (10) plus the fraction of the tax that would be due under the non-residential (or mixed) rates that its consideration bears to the total consideration (£100,000/£3 million). It then calculates the tax that would be due in accordance with the non-residential (or mixed) rates. The amount of SDLT due would be £139,500 (an effective rate of 4.7%): (£150,000 @ 0%) + (£100,000 @ 2%) + (£2,750,000 @ 5%). Accordingly, A Ltd does *not* claim the relief.

3.3.5.3 First-time buyer relief

Where the purchaser is an individual, he meets the conditions for a 'first-time buyer' and the amount of the chargeable consideration given for the transaction is not more than £500,000, the relief that would be available, first-time buyer relief (see **4.2**) is not available if the purchase is a higher-rates transaction. In other words, the first-time buyer relief is incompatible with higher-rates transactions. This might be a surprise to the purchaser. He may reasonably be under the impression that the relief is available because he has not previously purchased a dwelling in England or Northern Ireland. His purchase might be a higher-rates transaction notwithstanding that he is a 'first-time buyer' (using the term in the loose sense) for reasons including:

- he owns a greater than 50 per cent share of a dwelling that he had inherited within the last three years;
- he owns a 50 per cent or lower share of a dwelling that he had inherited more than three years ago;
- his wife or civil partner owns a dwelling;
- any of his children or stepchildren aged under 18 beneficially own a dwelling;
- he owns a dwelling overseas.

Of course, he might suffer twice in these circumstances. First, he loses the benefit of the relief, which might be a full or partial relief depending on whether the amount of the consideration given for the transaction exceeds £300,000. Second, he has to pay tax in accordance with the higher rates, not the standard rates.

Example 3.26

A and B are married. They live in a flat that is owned by B. A does not own a dwelling and has never done so. A and B wish to move into a larger property together. They find a house worth £300,000. A is able to fund the purchase alone. B had recently remortgaged her property and chose a five-year fixed rate mortgage. She reluctantly decides to retain her flat and let it out because selling it would trigger a large redemption penalty. A is under the impression that because he is a first-time buyer and he is buying in his sole name, no SDLT would be due. In fact, the transaction is a higher-rates transaction and SDLT of £14,000 would be due (an effective rate of 4.7%): (£125,000 @ 3%) + (£125,000 @ 5%) + (£50,000 @ 8%). In determining whether Condition C is met, B's flat counts against A; hence the condition is met.

3.3.5.4 'Linked' transactions

The SDLT legislation does not specify how the tax should be calculated where a higher-rates transaction is 'linked' to a standard-rates transaction. For the meaning of 'linked', see **1.5.4**. It is worth repeating that a higher-rates transaction can never

STAMP DUTY LAND TAX HANDBOOK

be linked to a non-residential or mixed transaction unless multiple dwellings relief is claimed (see **3.3.5.1**). The recommended method of calculating the tax is as follows:

1. Calculate the tax that would be due on the total amount of the chargeable consideration given in accordance with the standard rates.
2. Calculate the tax that would be due on the total amount of the chargeable consideration given in accordance with the higher rates.
3. Multiply the tax due under the standard rates by the fraction produced by dividing the consideration given for the standard-rates transaction by the total consideration.
4. Multiply the tax due under the higher rates by the fraction produced by dividing the consideration given for the higher-rates transaction by the total consideration.

One context in which this may arise in practice is the purchase of more than one dwelling from the same seller where one is the replacement of the purchaser's main residence and the other is not (see **3.3.10.1**). It is vital in such circumstances that there are two land transactions, which will almost certainly be linked. Either use two contracts or have one contract providing for two transfers.

Example 3.27

A buys two flats in a new development from a house-builder under a single contract for £1.5 million. A intends to use one (worth £1 million) as his new main residence and the other (worth £500,000) as a source of rent (buy-to-let). A sells his main residence to fund the purchase. There is a single SDLT transaction. It is a higher-rates transaction. The whole of the £1.5 million paid is taxed in accordance with the higher rates even though part of the purchase is a replacement of a main residence. The amount of tax payable is £100,000 if a claim for multiple dwellings relief is made (an effective rate of 6.7%): (£125,000 @ 3%) + (125,000 @ 5%) + (£500,000 @ 8%) x 2 (see **4.3**).

If the two flats had been bought under two linked SDLT transactions, just over two-thirds of that amount would have been payable. This is found by calculating the amount of tax that would be payable if the transaction were a standard-rates transaction, then calculating the amount of tax that would be payable if the transaction were a higher-rates transaction before prorating the two tax amounts. The amount of tax payable applying the standard rates would be £55,000 (an effective rate of 3.7%): (£125,000 @ 0%) + (125,000 @ 2%) + (£500,000 @ 5%) x 2. The £100,000 is pro-rated to give £33,333: £100,000 x (£0.5 million / £1.5 million). The £55,000 is pro-rated to give £36,667: £55,000 x (£1 million / £1.5 million). The £33,333 and £36,667 are aggregated to give a total tax charge of £70,000.

3.3.6 Spouse or civil partner buying alone

Where the purchaser is an individual, married or in a civil partnership and makes the purchase alone, the transaction is a higher-rates transaction if it would have been had he bought it jointly with his spouse or civil partner.[16]

In other words, in determining whether the purchaser owns the freehold or leasehold estate (or an undivided share of such an estate, or the relevant foreign equivalent of such an estate) in another dwelling worth £40,000 or more situated anywhere in the world, at the end of the day of completion, such an estate, undivided share or foreign equivalent held by his spouse or civil partner counts against him unless he is 'separated' from his spouse or civil partner on the effective date.

'Separated' means separated by a court order or deed of separation, or separation that is likely to be permanent.

The ownership of one or more dwellings by the purchaser's cohabitant does not count against him, even where they live together as if they were married or in a civil partnership.

Example 3.28

A lives with B in a house that B owns. They are unmarried and not in a civil partnership. A is not beneficially entitled to a share of B's house. A buys a house for A and B to live in as their main residence. B's house is to be let out. B is not beneficially entitled to a share of A's house. The transaction is not a higher-rates transaction. In determining whether Condition C is met, the dwelling owned by B does not count against A; hence, the condition is not met.

3.3.7 Trusts

Where the purchaser is an individual, in determining whether he owns the freehold or leasehold estate (or an undivided share of such an estate, or the relevant foreign equivalent of such an estate) in another dwelling worth £40,000 or more situated anywhere in the world, at the end of the effective date, such an estate, undivided share or foreign equivalent held by the following persons counts against him:

- The trustees of a bare trust under which he, his spouse or civil partner, children or stepchildren (unless aged 18 or over, or, in the case of stepchildren, the purchaser and the child's parent are separated), are beneficiaries.
- The trustees of an interest in possession trust under which he, his spouse or civil partner, or children or stepchildren (unless aged 18 or over, or, in the case of stepchildren, the purchaser and the child's parent are separated), are entitled to occupy the dwelling for their lifetime or to the income earned in respect of the dwelling (not necessarily for their lifetime).[17]

---

[16] FA 2003, Sched.4ZA, para.9; SDLT Manual: SDLTM09820.
[17] FA 2003, Sched.4ZA, para.11, Sched.16, para.3; SDLT Manual: SDLTM09815; Inheritance Tax Manual: IHTM27054.

A person is a beneficiary under a bare trust if he is 'absolutely entitled' to the trust property as against the trustee: i.e., where the beneficiary may call for a transfer of the trust property to him and end the trust at any time. The purpose of the bare trust is irrelevant. Subject to one exception, it does not matter that the beneficiary is not capable of owning a property legally due to their age or mental capacity. The exception applies to transactions completing on or after 21 November 2017 by trustees acting on behalf of a child in pursuance of their powers under the Mental Capacity Act 2005 or the Mental Capacity Act (Northern Ireland) 2016.

Example 3.29

A is married. His wife (B) is the beneficiary under a bare trust. The trust property includes a dwelling worth £150,000. A does not own a dwelling. He buys the freehold estate of a house to live in as his (and B's) main residence. The purchase is a higher-rates transaction. Although A does not own another dwelling (legally or beneficially) and B does not own the other dwelling legally, her beneficial interest in the other property counts against A when determining whether Condition C is met; hence, the condition is met.

Example 3.30

A is in a civil partnership. His civil partner (B) has a child (C) aged 16 who is the life tenant under an interest in possession trust settled by B's father. A does not own a dwelling. He buys the freehold estate of a house to live in as his (and B's, but not C's) main residence. The purchase is a higher-rates transaction. Although neither A nor B own another dwelling (legally or beneficially) and C does not own the other dwelling legally, C's beneficial interest in the other property counts against A when determining whether Condition C is met; hence, the condition is met.

This means that where the purchaser is an individual, in determining whether he owns the freehold or leasehold estate (or an undivided share of such an estate, or the relevant foreign equivalent of such an estate) in another dwelling worth £40,000 or more situated anywhere in the world, at the end of the day of completion, such an estate, undivided share or foreign equivalent held by the following persons does *not* count against him:

- the trustees of a discretionary trust; or
- the trustees of an interest in possession trust under which neither he, his spouse or civil partner, nor children or stepchildren, are entitled to occupy the dwelling for their lifetime or to the income earned in respect of the dwelling. This might be because they are 'remaindermen' rather than 'life tenants'.

Example 3.31

A is a trustee of a discretionary trust. He has discretion to give the whole or some of the income earned from the trust property (which includes residential properties) to a class of beneficiaries that includes B. B does not own any properties personally. B buys a house as an investment (buy-to-let). The purchase is not a higher-rates transaction. A's ownership of the trust property does not count against B when determining whether Condition C is met; hence, the condition is not met.

Conversely, such an estate, undivided share or foreign equivalent held by a trustee *does* count against him where:

- he is a trustee of a discretionary trust; or
- he is a trustee of an interest in possession trust under which no one is currently entitled to occupy the dwelling for their lifetime or to the income earned in respect of the dwelling,

regardless of whether he acts in his personal capacity rather than his fiduciary capacity (or, put another way, regardless of whether or not the purchased dwelling is trust property).

However, HMRC accepts that the trustee's interest in the trust property must be valued, not the dwelling that is held as trust property. So unless the trustee's interest in the dwelling held as trust property is worth £40,000 or more, HMRC would say that Condition C is not met where the trustee buys a dwelling in his personal capacity. Although obviously beneficial to the taxpayer, HMRC's view does seem to rub against the scheme of the legislation, which is to treat the trustee of a settlement as owning the whole of the trust property.

Example 3.32

A is a trustee of an interest-in-possession trust. The trust owns residential property for two life tenants and their children (remaindermen). A buys a house to live in as his home. In making the purchase, A acts in his personal capacity, not as trustee. The trust property (to the extent that it consists of, or includes, dwellings) counts against A when determining whether Condition C is met. The value of A's interest in each dwelling held as trust property is less than £40,000. Consequently, HMRC should accept that the condition is not met on the facts and, therefore, the transaction is not a higher-rates transaction.

Note that the purchase of a dwelling by a trustee in his fiduciary capacity in either of the two circumstances listed above is always a higher-rates transaction. It is treated in the same way as if the trustee were a company. Condition C does not apply.

Example 3.33

A is a trustee of a discretionary trust. The trust property does not include residential property. A buys a house as an investment (buy-to-let). A's intention is to accumulate income within the trust before it is appointed to the beneficiaries (at his discretion). The purchase is a higher-rates transaction. Condition C does not apply.

Where an individual is a trustee and he buys a dwelling, in determining whether he owns the freehold or leasehold estate (or an undivided share of such an estate, or the relevant foreign equivalent of such an estate) in another dwelling worth £40,000 or more situated anywhere in the world, at the end of the day of completion, such an estate, undivided share or foreign equivalent held by him does *not* count against him where:

- he is a trustee of a bare trust under which one or more other persons are the beneficiaries; or
- he is a trustee of an interest-in-possession trust under which one or more other persons are entitled to occupy the dwelling for their lifetime or to the income earned in respect of the dwelling.

Example 3.34

A is the trustee of a bare trust. The trust property, which includes dwellings, is held for B as beneficiary. A does not own any dwellings personally. A buys a house to live in as his home. The transaction is not a higher-rates transaction. In determining whether Condition C is met, the dwellings held as trust property do not count against him, but count against the beneficiary; hence, the condition is not met.

Note that these rules only apply where the purchaser is a trustee or a beneficiary and are only relevant for the purpose of determining whether the purchaser meets Condition C. In other words, they only affect whether the transaction is a higher-rates transaction or a standard-rates transaction. They do not affect who is liable to the tax under the general rules. The liable person continues to be:

- the beneficiaries where the trust is a bare trust; or
- the trustees where the trust is not a bare trust (see **2.4**).

Example 3.35

A is a bare trustee for B. A buys the freehold estate in a house for B. A owns other dwellings both in his personal capacity and as trustee for other beneficiaries. B does not own another dwelling. The purchase is not a higher-rates transaction. In determining whether Condition C is met, the dwellings owned by A do not count against B; hence, the condition is not met. B is liable to the tax, not A.

Example 3.36

A is a trustee in respect of a discretionary trust for a class of beneficiaries that includes B. A buys the freehold estate in a house as trust property. A does not own another dwelling, either personally or in his fiduciary capacity. The purchase is a higher-rates transaction. The type of trust (a settlement) means that Condition C does not need to be met in order for the transaction to be a higher-rates transaction. A is liable to the tax, not B (but the cost will normally be met from trust assets).

Example 3.37

A is a trustee in respect of an interest-in-possession trust. B is the life tenant. A buys the freehold estate in a house as trust property. The trust property includes another dwelling. In determining whether Condition C is met, the other dwelling held as trust property counts against A; hence, the condition is not met. A is liable to the tax, not B (but the cost will normally be met from trust assets).

The converse of the rules applies. Where a person is treated as owning a dwelling held by:

- the trustees of a bare trust under which he, his spouse or civil partner, children or stepchildren (unless aged 18 or over), are beneficiaries; or
- the trustees of an interest in possession trust under which he, his spouse or civil partner, or children or stepchildren (unless aged 18 or over), are entitled to occupy the dwelling for their lifetime or to the income earned in respect of the dwelling,

and the trustees dispose of the dwelling, then he is treated as having made the disposal.

Where the buyer has an interest in an overseas dwelling it is necessary to examine whether the nature of that interest is equivalent to legal or beneficial ownership of a freehold or leasehold estate. In the case of usufructs the position is not clear. A usufruct is a civil law concept found in many overseas jurisdictions. It gives a person the right to use or enjoy another person's property. There is no direct equivalent under the laws of England and Wales. In particular, it is unclear whether the right of the property owner should be treated as if it were subject to a lease, whether the arrangement should be treated as if it were an interest-in-possession trust and whether the value of the property-owner's interest is depressed by the arrangement. See **3.3.4**.

3.3.8 Children

Where the purchaser is an individual, in determining whether he owns the freehold or leasehold estate (or an undivided share of such an estate, or the relevant foreign equivalent of such an estate) in another dwelling worth £40,000 or more situated anywhere in the world, at the end of the day of completion, such an estate, undivided share or foreign equivalent beneficially held by any of his children or stepchildren (unless aged 18 years or over, or, in the case of stepchildren, the purchaser and the child's parent are separated) count against him.[18] In other words, he is treated as owning the freehold or leasehold estate (etc.) that, in fact, beneficially belongs to his children or stepchildren.

The purchase of a dwelling on behalf of a child is usually a higher-rates transaction if the child's parents or, if they are unmarried, their spouses or civil partners own the freehold or leasehold estate (etc.) in another dwelling. However, for purchases with a completion day date on or after 21 November 2017, this is not the case when a trustee makes the purchase on behalf of the child in pursuance of his powers under the Mental Capacity Act 2005 or the Mental Capacity Act (Northern Ireland) 2016.

The trustee's ownership of the dwelling on trust for the child does not count against him when determining whether Condition C is met on his purchase of a dwelling.

Example 3.38

A buys the freehold estate of a dwelling on trust for his son aged 16. A owns other residential properties, but his son does not. The transaction is a higher-rates transaction. The purchase is treated as made by A, not his son, and A's ownership of the other properties meets Condition C.

Example 3.39

A buys the freehold estate of a dwelling for himself to live in as his main residence. The purchase is not the replacement of his main residence. A does not own another residential property other than one that he holds on trust for his son aged 16. The transaction is a higher-rates transaction. In determining whether Condition C is met, the dwelling beneficially owned by A's son counts against A; hence, the condition is met.

Example 3.40

Infant child A is mentally incapacitated. The Court of Protection appointed B as trustee for A. In pursuance of B's powers, B buys the freehold estate in a dwelling for A to live in as his main residence. A does not own the freehold or leasehold estate (etc.) in another dwelling. The

---

[18] FA 2003, Sched.4ZA, para.12; SDLT Manual: SDLTM09815.

transaction is not a higher-rates transaction regardless of whether A's parents own another dwelling. Condition C is not met. It is also not met by virtue of B's ownership of a dwelling.

3.3.9 Partnerships

Where the purchaser is an individual, in determining whether he owns the freehold or leasehold estate (or an undivided share of such an estate, or the relevant foreign equivalent of such an estate) in another dwelling worth £40,000 or more situated anywhere in the world, at the end of the day of completion, such an estate, undivided share or foreign equivalent held by a partnership in which the purchaser is a partner is treated as held by the purchaser unless it is used by the partnership for the purposes of a trade carried on by the partnership (e.g., a bed-and-breakfast). A property-letting business is not a trade. Consequently, dwellings held by a partnership that is carrying on a property-letting business are treated as held by the partners. The type of partnership and the jurisdiction in which it is established are irrelevant.[19]

Example 3.41

A rents his home and does not own any properties personally. He is a partner in a property-letting partnership carried on by him and two others. That partnership owns 10 dwellings in England and overseas. A buys a dwelling to live in as his main residence. His purchase is a higher-rates transaction, as he is treated as owning the 10 dwellings held by the partnership for the purposes of its business.

Example 3.42

A rents his home and does not own any properties personally. He is a partner in a partnership that carries on the trade of a care home. That partnership owns a dwelling. A buys a dwelling to live in as his main residence. His purchase is not a higher-rates transaction, as he is not treated as owning the dwelling held by the partnership for the purposes of its trade.

The purchase of a dwelling by a partnership is treated as if it were by all the partners. Consequently, if any of the partners is a company or, where they are all individuals, any of the partners owns a freehold or leasehold estate (etc.) in another dwelling, the purchase of a dwelling by the partnership will be a higher-rates transaction. The amount of SDLT payable is not pro-rated according to the percentage partnership share held by the contaminating partner. The application of the higher rates is all or nothing.

---

[19] FA 2003, Sched.4ZA, para.14; SDLT Manual: SDLTM09790.

Example 3.43

An English limited partnership buys a dwelling as an investment (buy-to-let). The partnership is composed of A and B as limited partners each owning a 49.5% partnership share and C Ltd as a general partner owning 1%. A and B are married. Neither A nor B own another dwelling. The purchase is a higher-rates transaction, as one of the purchasers (C Ltd) is a company. It is irrelevant that between them A and B are entitled to 99% of the income profits of the partnership and the company is entitled to only 1% of the income profits. The whole of the purchase price is taxed in accordance with the higher rates.

A dwelling held by a partnership is not disregarded when another dwelling is purchased by the partnership.

Example 3.44

A partnership established under the Partnership Act 1890 owns a dwelling as an investment (buy-to-let). It is composed of two individuals, neither of whom own a dwelling personally. That initial purchase is a standard-rates transaction. The partnership buys another dwelling as an investment. The purchase is a higher-rates transaction.

3.3.9.1 Companies

Where the purchaser is an individual, in determining whether he owns the freehold or leasehold estate (or an undivided share of such an estate, or the relevant foreign equivalent of such an estate) in another dwelling worth £40,000 or more situated anywhere in the world, at the end of the day of completion, such an estate, undivided share or foreign equivalent held by a company in which the purchaser is a shareholder is disregarded. The corporate veil is not broken. The type of company and the country in which it is incorporated are irrelevant.

Example 3.45

A owns the entire issued share capital of a company, B Ltd, that holds a dwelling. A does not own a dwelling personally. A buys a house to live in as his home. The transaction is not a higher-rates transaction. In determining whether Condition C is met, the dwelling owned by B Ltd does not count against him; hence, the condition is not met.

3.3.10 The exceptions

There are three exceptions to the higher rates:

- replacement of main residence;

- lease extensions (etc.); and
- transfers between spouses and civil partners.

The exceptions are subject to meeting various conditions. They do not provide an exemption from charge generally – hence, a transaction that would be a higher-rates transaction but for an exception is chargeable at the residential standard rates. None of the exceptions needs to be claimed and none may be withdrawn due to a change of circumstances. The most important to the reader is the first, the replacement of main residence exception.

3.3.10.1 Replacement of main residence

The first exception is the replacement of main residence exception.[20] The purchased dwelling may be taken to be a replacement of a main residence either initially or subsequently, depending on whether the main residence that has been replaced is sold (or otherwise disposed of) before or after the effective date of the purchase. In the first case, the purchase is a standard-rates transaction. In the second case, the purchase is a higher-rates transaction, but a refund of the tax attributable to the difference in rates (three per cent) may be claimed when the former main residence is disposed of.

The two possibilities are taken in turn in that order.

The transaction would be a replacement of the purchaser's main residence so long as all the following five requirements are met. If any are not, the purchase will not be a replacement of the purchaser's main residence:

1. On the effective date, the purchaser intends to live in the purchased dwelling as his only or main residence.
2. Within three years before the effective date, the purchaser (or his spouse or civil partner unless they are 'separated', see below, at the effective date) disposed of the freehold or leasehold estate (or an undivided share of such an estate, or an equivalent foreign interest) in another dwelling (the 'sold dwelling'). That interest could have a value of less than £40,000. (Note: The three-year limit does not apply where the effective date was on or before 26 November 2018.)
3. Immediately after the disposal of the sold dwelling, neither the purchaser, nor his spouse or civil partner, owned any freehold or leasehold estate (or an undivided share of such an estate, or an equivalent foreign interest) in the sold dwelling. (Note: This condition does not apply where the effective date of the purchase was before 22 November 2017.)
4. The purchaser had lived in the sold dwelling as his only or main residence at some point within three years before the effective date. (Note: This requirement does not apply where the effective date was on or before 26 November 2018.)

---
[20] FA 2003, Sched.4ZA, para.3(6), (7); SDLT Manual: SDLTM09800.

5. Between the effective date of disposal of the sold dwelling and the effective date of purchase of the purchased dwelling, neither the purchaser, nor his spouse or civil partner, acquired the freehold or leasehold estate (or an undivided share of such an estate, or equivalent foreign interest) in another dwelling with the intention of it being the purchaser's only or main residence. (Note: Renting is disregarded unless he acquires a lease of a main residence for a term of more than seven years.)

'Separated' means separated by a court order or deed of separation, or separation that is likely to be permanent. Other than making the disposal to the purchaser's spouse or civil partner, which does not qualify, the purchaser may dispose of the sold dwelling to a relative or a connected company (though the disposal may be taxable for that person in the usual way).

Example 3.46

A and B are married. Each spouse owns a house. They live in A's house as their home. B's house is let out. A and B buy a new house together to live in as their new home. To fund the purchase, A sells his house on the open market. The purchase is not a higher-rates transaction because A disposed of a dwelling that had been used by him and his spouse as their main residence within three years before the completion date, neither spouse retained an interest in the sold house nor acquired another dwelling between the date of the sale and the date of the purchase. As a result, A and B pay SDLT in accordance with the residential standard rates even though B retains her house.

Note that the requirement to have disposed of, and lived in, the sold dwelling within three years before the effective date of the purchase of the purchased dwelling does not apply where the effective date was on or before 26 November 2018. This is an important transitional rule. Many purchasers have paid tax in accordance with the higher rates wrongly believing that the disposal of their last main residence did not count, either because it took place more than three years before their purchase or because they had not lived in the property at some point within the previous three years. They have four years from the effective date of their purchase to apply to reclaim the overpaid tax. Note that this period is longer than the one-year period given for reclaiming SDLT where the disposal of the sold dwelling occurs after the purchase of the replacement main residence: see below.

Example 3.47

On 31 October 2018, A and B purchased the freehold estate of a house in London for £4 million. They intended to live in the house as their main residence. They sold their previous main residence in 2010 when they went to the United States to work, and they lived in rented accommodation while there. A and B paid £513,750 of SDLT wrongly believing that their purchase was a higher-rates transaction (an effective rate of 12.8%): (£125,000 @ 3%) + (£125,000 @ 5%) + (£675,000 + 8%) + (£575,000 @ 13%) + (£2,500,000 @ 15%). The conditions for the replacement of main residence exception were met. As the completion date for their purchase occurred before 27 November 2018, there was no requirement to have sold the previous dwelling or lived in the sold dwelling within the previous three years. They overpaid SDLT in the amount of £120,000: (£125,000 @ 0%) + (£125,000 @ 2%) + (£675,000 + 5%) + (£575,000 @ 10%) + (£2,500,000 @ 12%).

Note: Although a disposal of the sold dwelling does not need to be by the purchaser – a disposal by the purchaser's spouse or civil partner is enough – the fact that the spouse or civil partner has lived in the dwelling is not enough – it is the purchaser who must have lived in the sold dwelling at some point during the three-year period.

Example 3.48

A and B are married but live apart due to work. They both own their own homes. Their work commitments change and they choose to buy a new house to live in together as their home. Their purchase is funded by the sale of A's former home. B retains her former home. Although the purchase is a replacement of A's main residence, it is not a replacement of B's main residence. She did not live in the sold dwelling as her main residence at some point within three years before the sale. It would not matter if A had bought their new home in his sole name. The transaction would continue to be a higher-rates transaction due to his marriage to B (see **3.3.6**).

Note: Moving out of the dwelling that was the purchaser's main residence and into rented accommodation so that the old main residence could be let out and used as a source of rents does not count as a disposal of that former residence, because the purchaser retains an interest in it.

Example 3.49

A and B own their home and another dwelling overseas used as a second home. Prior to purchasing their new home, A and B move out of their home and let it to a third party for rental profits. A and B's purchase is not regarded as a replacement of a main residence. A and B have not made a qualifying disposal of their old home; hence, their purchase is a higher-rates transaction.

Note: The disposal of the purchaser's main residence by the spouse or civil partner qualifies even if the purchaser and his spouse or civil partner were not married at the relevant time provided they are married (and 'living together') at the effective date of the purchase.

Example 3.50

A and B live together in a house owed by B. They are unmarried. A owns his former home, since let to a third party. A and B marry and subsequently purchase a house as their new home. B sells her house to fund the transaction. A and B's purchase is a replacement of their main residence, even though A and B were not married during the period they lived together in B's house.

Finally, note that the conditions are potentially sensitive to the sequence in which transactions are undertaken.

Example 3.51

A and B own their home. They do not own another dwelling. They sell their home and move into rented accommodation. They later buy a dwelling for investment (buy-to-let). The purchase of the buy-to-let dwelling is not a higher-rates transaction, as Condition C is not met. They later buy a property to use as their new home. Completion of their purchase falls within the period of three years of the sale of the old home. The purchase of their new home is *not* a higher-rates transaction, as it is a replacement of their main residence.

Example 3.52

Suppose the facts are the same, but A and B buy their new home before they buy the dwelling for investment. The purchase of their new home would not be a higher-rates transaction, as Condition C would not be met. But the purchase of the buy-to-let dwelling would be a higher-rates transaction, as it is *not* a replacement of their main residence.

If the new dwelling is purchased before the old one is disposed of and tax at the higher rates is paid, the transaction would become a replacement of the purchaser's main residence and a refund of the tax attributable to the difference in rates (three per cent) may be claimed where all four of the following requirements are met:

1. On the effective date, the purchaser intended to live in the purchased dwelling as his only or main residence.
2. Within three years after the effective date, the purchaser (or his spouse or civil partner) completes the disposal of the freehold or leasehold estate (or an undivided share of such an estate, or equivalent foreign interest) in another dwelling (the 'sold dwelling').
3. Immediately after the disposal of the sold dwelling, neither the purchaser, nor his spouse or civil partner, owned the freehold or leasehold estate (or an undivided share of such an estate, or equivalent foreign interest) in the sold

dwelling. (Note: This condition does not apply where the effective date of the purchase was before 22 November 2017, nor does it apply where the couple are separated – see below.)
4. The purchaser had lived in the sold dwelling as his only or main residence at some point within three years before the effective date of his purchase of the new dwelling.

'Separated' means separated by a court order or deed of separation, or separation that is likely to be permanent.

This would entitle the purchaser to reclaim the difference in tax between the standard rates and higher rates with interest provided that the purchaser acts within one year of the disposal of the sold dwelling. For disposals made before 29 October 2018, the one-year deadline was three months. The day after that one-year deadline, the purchaser would be time-barred from making a reclaim. There is no provision for HMRC or the First-tier Tribunal to exercise discretion to allow a late application.

Making a reclaim can be done online at HMRC's website. Alternatively, the online form can be completed, printed off and sent to HMRC by post. The information set out below must be input. When a form is completed online the form automatically calculates the amount of tax to be refunded. The purchaser must indicate whether he agrees or disagrees with the calculation. The usual requirement to give HMRC a copy of the sale contract and land transfer form or lease with the reclaim application does not apply. The required information is as follows:

- the Unique Transaction Reference Number (UTRN) of the SDLT return made in respect of the purchased dwelling. This can be found on the Revenue certificate (form SDLT5) and the submitted version of the SDLT return (form SDLT1);
- the effective date of the purchase (usually the completion date);
- the purchaser's contact details;
- the effective date of the sale (usually the completion date);
- the name of the purchaser of the sold dwelling;
- the address of the sold property;
- the amount of SDLT paid on the purchase under the higher rates;
- the amount of SDLT payable on the purchase under the standard rates;
- the amount of SDLT refundable;
- the bank details of the purchaser; and
- a declaration by the purchaser that the contents of the form are correct.

Example 3.53

A and B relocate. They struggled to sell their old home and, as they wished to be in their new home for the start of the new school year, they completed on their purchase before finding a buyer for their old home. They pay £1 million for their new home. They pay £73,750 of SDLT (an effective rate of 7.4%): (£125,000 @ 3%) + (£125,000 @ 5%) + (£675,000 @ 8%) + (£75,000 @ 13%). Six months later, they complete their sale of their old home. They are entitled to reclaim SDLT, provided they apply on a timely basis, as the sale took place within three years after the purchase, and they had lived in their former dwelling in the three years prior to their purchase. The amount they can reclaim is £30,000. That is the difference between the £43,750 of SDLT due under the standard rates (an effective rate of 4.4%) – (£125,000 @ 0%) + (£125,000 @ 2%) + (£675,000 @ 5%) + (£75,000 @ 10%) – and the £73,750 of SDLT paid.

It is not necessary for the sold dwelling to be (or have been) sold in order for the disposal to qualify. Any disposal would qualify provided that the purchaser ceases to beneficially own any part of the sold dwelling. Nor is it necessary for the sold dwelling to be (or have been) disposed of to a third party. The disposal would qualify if made to a relative of the purchaser provided that it is not made to the purchaser's spouse or civil partner or to trustees for an infant child of either.

Example 3.54

A owns his main residence. He also owns several buy-to-let properties. He wishes to buy a new dwelling as his new main residence. To save the difference in SDLT between the residential standard rates and higher rates, before the completion date of his purchase he declares a bare trust in favour of his brother, effectively giving the beneficial interest in his old main residence to his brother out of love and natural affection. The declaration of trust qualifies as a disposal of his main residence. It is irrelevant that a person who made the acquisition (A's brother) is related to the person who made the disposal (A). It is also irrelevant that A continues to own the dwelling legally, as for the purposes of the higher rates, the beneficiary, rather than the trustee, is treated as the purchaser.

Where a person stays in more than one dwelling, which property is their 'main residence' is a question of fact. The purchaser cannot make an election, though making a CGT principal private residence election would be relevant. The main residence will not necessarily be the property in which the person spends most of his or her time. HMRC (and ultimately a court or tribunal) will have regard to things including: where the person's family spend its time; where the children go to school; where the person is registered to vote; where the person is registered with a dentist and doctor; where the person works; how each residence is furnished; and which address is used for correspondence.

Example 3.55

A owns a flat in London and a house in Newcastle. A typically works in London between Monday and Thursday, staying in the London flat from Monday evening until Thursday morning. He typically works from his Newcastle house every Friday, staying there from Thursday evening until Monday morning. A's wife and child live in the Newcastle house. A is registered to vote in Newcastle and he is registered with a medical practice in Newcastle. A

FREEHOLD AND LEASEHOLD TRANSFERS

spends roughly an equal amount of time in the London flat, but his main residence is almost certainly the Newcastle house.

The purchaser must *intend* to live in the purchased dwelling as his only or main residence. It is not necessary for the purchaser to begin to live in the purchased dwelling immediately. There may be a good reason to delay moving in. However, obviously if the period of delay is long, the reason for the delay is unclear, or the purchaser never moves in because his plans change or are frustrated in some way, the purchaser will be on the back foot in satisfying HMRC that on the completion date his intention was to live in the purchased dwelling.

Example 3.56

A and B own a house in Hertfordshire. They live in it as their home. They buy a flat in central London to live in as their new home. The transaction is a higher-rates transaction. They do not move in straightaway. Instead, they let it out on an assured shorthold tenancy. The reason for their decision is that their son cannot start his new school (a boarding school) until he reaches a certain age. Near the end of the academic year, almost one year later, they give notice to their tenants. One month later they move into their central London flat and put their Hertfordshire house on their market. On completion of the sale of their Hertfordshire house, A and B apply to reclaim the tax attributable to the higher rates. On the day of completion of their purchase of the central London flat, they had intended to live in the property as their home. The delay in moving in was driven by the restriction on their son starting his new school. It was not driven by a change of mind.

Where a disposal converts what was a higher-rates transaction into a standard-rates transaction, it cannot also be used to make a later purchase the replacement of a main residence.

Example 3.57

A and B are married and own a house together, but are separated. A and B also own a buy-to-let property. A buys a house as his main residence. His purchase is a higher-rates transaction, as he continues to own a share of the former matrimonial home. B continues to occupy the former matrimonial home for a period of time before it is sold. On its sale, A's purchase ceases to be a higher-rates transaction and A duly reclaims the corresponding amount of SDLT. B later buys a house as her new main residence. Her purchase is a higher-rates transaction, as she continues to own a share in the buy-to-let. The sale of the former matrimonial home does not make her purchase a replacement of a main residence.

(There is, incidentally, a good reason for this apparently unfair rule. If it did not exist, A could buy home 2 before selling home 1, paying the higher rates. When A sells home 1, he could reclaim the tax attributable to the higher rates. A couple of years later, he could buy home 3 and rely on the sale of home 1 to avoid paying tax at the higher rates – without needing to dispose of home 2.)

Note: A disposal of a dwelling by the purchaser's spouse or civil partner is not enough. The sold dwelling must have been used by the purchaser as his only or main residence 'at some point' within the three years before his purchase of the new one.

Example 3.58

A and B are married but live apart due to work. They both own their own homes. Their work commitments change and they choose to buy a new house to live in together as their home. They both retain their former homes. Later A sells his former home. Although the purchase would become a replacement of A's main residence, it is not a replacement of B's main residence. She did not live in the sold dwelling as her main residence at some point within three years before the purchase of their new home. It would not matter if A had bought their new home in his sole name. The transaction would continue to be a higher-rates transaction for him due to his marriage to B (see **3.3.6**).

The exception puts those who already own their home at an advantage over those that do not.

Example 3.59

A owns his home and a portfolio of 10 buy-to-let properties. A buys a house as his new home. The sale of his former home within three years of the purchase would make the purchase a replacement of a main residence; hence, the transaction would be a standard-rates transaction. In contrast, B owns a buy-to-let property but rents his home. B buys a house as his new home. The purchase would not be a replacement of a main residence; hence, the transaction would be a higher-rates transaction.

As discussed near the start of this chapter, either a transaction is a higher-rates transaction or it is not. The transaction is not split into two with the relevant proportion of the chargeable consideration given being taxed in accordance with one set of rates and the remaining proportion being taxed in accordance with the other set of rates. This can hurt a person purchasing two or more dwellings in a single transaction where one will be a replacement of his main residence. HMRC is sympathetic to this hard-edged effect of the legislation and is prepared to treat the two types of purchase as linked transactions. However, in order to secure this treatment, the dwellings must be the subject of separate contracts or a single contract that is to be completed by two transfers.

Example 3.60

A buys two flats in a new residential development from a house-builder under a single contract and transfer for £1.5 million. A intends to use one (worth £1 million) as his new main residence and the other (worth £500,000) as an investment (buy-to-let). A sells his old main residence to fund the purchase. There is a single SDLT transaction. It is a higher-rates transaction. The whole of the £1.5 million paid is taxed in accordance with the higher rates, even though part of the purchase is a replacement of a main residence. The amount of tax payable is £100,000 if a claim for multiple dwellings relief is made (an effective rate of 6.7%). This is the amount of tax due on the average price per dwelling (((£125,000 @ 3%) + (£125,000 @ 5%) + (£500,000 @ 8%)) multiplied by the number of dwellings (two).

If, changing the facts, the two flats had been bought under two linked SDLT transactions, approximately half that amount of tax would have been payable (an effective rate of 3.2%). For an explanation of the method used to calculate the tax payable on a higher-rates transaction linked to a standard-rates transaction, see **3.3.5.4**. The calculation involves prorating the tax that would have been due if the standard rates had applied and prorating the tax that would have been due if the higher rates had applied, and adding the two amounts together: ((£125,000 @ 0%) + (£125,000 @ 2%) + (£500,000 @ 5%)) x 2 = £27,500 x (£1 million / £1.5 million) + ((£125,000 @ 3%) + (£125,000 @ 5%) + (£500,000 @ 8%)) x 2 = £100,000 x (£500,000 / £1.5 million).

WARNING

1 Where a purchased dwelling will be a replacement of the purchaser's main residence and another purchased dwelling will not, consider using two sale contracts or two transfers and seeking specialist advice or HMRC's approval of paying tax as if there were two linked transactions. Although the strategy of splitting one transaction into two to access the replacement of main residence exception on part of the purchase would be reasonable in the author's opinion, it may be prudent to stress-test this against the facts, or get 'clearance' from HMRC in advance.
2 Where a higher-rates transaction is linked to a standard-rates transaction, the tax calculation is complicated – see **3.3.5.4**.

3.3.10.2 *Lease extensions (etc.)*

The second exception applies to the purchase of a freehold or leasehold estate (or an undivided share in a dwelling) by an individual who already holds a freehold or leasehold estate or undivided share in the same dwelling immediately before completion. It only applies to purchases with an effective date on or after 22 November 2017. It is aimed at preventing transactions including staircasing, and lease extensions and collective enfranchisement transactions from being higher-rates transactions.[21]

---

[21] FA 2003, Sched.4ZA, para.7A; SDLT Manual: SDLTM09814.

Where the conditions are met, it is not necessary to determine whether the purchaser (etc.) owns another dwelling (Condition C). The transaction is excluded from being a higher-rates transaction and, therefore, would be chargeable in accordance with the standard rates.

The conditions that need to be met as at the effective date are as follows:

- The purchaser holds the whole or at least a 25 per cent share (as joint tenant or tenant in common) of the freehold or leasehold estate in the purchased dwelling.
- The purchased dwelling has been the purchaser's main residence throughout the previous three years.
- Where the estate is a leasehold estate, the lease must have 21 years or more to run.

This would relieve the purchase of additional equity in a dwelling purchased using a shared ownership lease where no market value election is made on the initial acquisition of the lease. Where the purchase results in the purchaser's share in the dwelling exceeding 80 per cent, SDLT would be chargeable in accordance with the standard rates regardless of the ownership of other dwellings by the purchaser provided the conditions listed above are met. See **Chapter 10**.

Similarly, the purchase of an extended lease (e.g., in pursuance of the Leasehold Reform, Housing and Urban Development Act 1993) would not be a higher-rates transaction provided that the unexpired term of the pre-existing lease over the dwelling is 21 years or more.

For the SDLT treatment of collective enfranchisement transactions, see **Chapter 6**.

Example 3.61

A owns a 60-year lease of a flat which he lives in as his main residence. He bought the flat and began using it as his main residence many years ago. He also owns a number of properties as an investment (buy-to-let) in the UK and overseas. He exercises his statutory right to acquire an extended lease of the flat. The transaction is a standard-rates transaction. His ownership of the buy-to-let properties is irrelevant.

Example 3.62

A has just acquired a 60-year lease of a flat as his replacement main residence together with an assignment of the previous owner's statutory right to acquire a 90-year lease extension from the landlord. He also owns a number of properties as an investment (buy-to-let) in the UK and overseas. The purchase of the 60-year lease is a replacement of his main residence and, therefore, a standard-rates transaction. However, the purchase of the new 150-year lease from the landlord is a higher-rates transaction. The exception does not apply, because

FREEHOLD AND LEASEHOLD TRANSFERS

the purchased dwelling has not been the purchaser's main residence throughout the last three years. Consequently, his ownership of the buy-to-let properties *is* relevant.

Example 3.63

A and B are siblings who have jointly owned their freehold home for 10 years. B is moving abroad and A agrees to buy her half interest for £300,000. A's purchase will be a standard-rates transaction. His interest is more than 25 per cent of the freehold and he has lived in the house as his main residence throughout the previous three years.

3.3.10.3 *Transfers between spouses and civil partners*

The third exception applies to the purchase of the freehold or leasehold estate in a dwelling (or an undivided share in a dwelling) on its disposal by the purchaser's spouse or civil partner. It only applies to purchases with a completion date on or after 22 November 2017. The exception applies where the spouses or civil partners are the only parties to the transaction and they not separated. 'Separated' means separated by a court order or deed of separation, or separation that is likely to be permanent. It is irrelevant whether or not the dwelling is used by the purchaser or to be used by the purchaser as his main residence.[22]

If A and B are spouses or civil partners and they are the only parties to the transaction, the exception applies to transactions between:

- A and B;
- B and A;
- A and AB;
- B and AB;
- AB and A; and
- AB and B.

The exception is especially helpful where there are transfers of equity.

Example 3.64

A and B are married and own a buy-to-let dwelling worth £750,000 equally as tenants in common. B owns another buy-to-let dwelling worth £500,000. A transfers his 50% undivided share in the £750,000 dwelling to B. The outstanding mortgage on the property is £500,000. B becomes solely liable to repay the mortgage and pays A £125,000 (50% of the equity). B's purchase is not a higher-rates transaction, even though B owns another dwelling worth more than £40,000 and the purchased dwelling will not be used by B as her main residence. The chargeable consideration for the transaction is £375,000 (£250,000 +

---

[22] FA 2003, Sched.4ZA, para.9A; SDLT Manual: SDLTM09820.

£125,000). The amount of tax payable is £8,750 (an effective rate of 2.3%): (£125,000 @ 0%) + (£125,000 @ 2%) + (£125,000 @ 5%).

Example 3.65

A and B are married. A owns a buy-to-let dwelling worth £1 million. B owns another buy-to-let dwelling worth £500,000. A transfers the £1 million dwelling to himself and B equally as tenants in common. The outstanding mortgage on the property is £750,000. B becomes jointly and several liable to repay the mortgage and pays A £125,000 (50% of the equity). B's purchase is not a higher-rates transaction even though B owns another dwelling worth more than £40,000 and the purchased dwelling will not be used by B as her main residence. The chargeable consideration for the transaction is £500,000 (£375,000 + £125,000). The amount of tax payable is £15,000 (an effective rate of 3%): (£125,000 @ 0%) + (£125,000 @ 2%) + (£250,000 @ 5%).

Example 3.66

A and B are married and own a house worth £1 million equally as tenants in common. They separate. B owns a buy-to-let dwelling worth £250,000. A transfers his 50% undivided share in the £1 million house to B and C, B's new partner. The outstanding mortgage on the property is £750,000. B and C become jointly and severally liable to repay the mortgage and pay A £125,000 (50% of the equity). B and C's purchase *is* a higher-rates transaction as B owns another dwelling worth more than £40,000 and someone other than A and B acquires the dwelling (namely, C), though, in any case, even if the parties to the transfer had been only A and B, and C had acquired his share in the dwelling sometime later, the exception would still not have applied because A and B were separated on the completion date. The chargeable consideration for the transaction is £375,000 (£250,000 + £125,000). The amount of tax payable is £20,000 (an effective rate of 5.3%): (£125,000 @ 3%) + (£125,000 @ 5%) + (£125,000 @ 8%).

3.3.11 Property adjustment orders

Where the purchaser is an individual, in determining whether he owns another dwelling at the end of the day of completion, the freehold or leasehold estate in a dwelling (etc.) held by him is disregarded where:

- the dwelling is not the individual's main residence;
- the dwelling is another person's main residence; and
- a 'property adjustment order' has been made in respect of the dwelling in favour of the other person.

The aim of the rule – which only applies to purchases with a completion day date on or after 22 November 2017 – is to prevent the retention of the former matrimonial home counting against the purchaser if he was ordered to retain an interest in it. Such orders tend to be made where the only significant asset is the home and if it were sold there would not be enough money to provide a home for children, so one party is ordered to stay in the home (and look after the children) and the other party is ordered to leave it – but retain a financial interest in it.

'Property adjustment orders' are those made under:

- Matrimonial Causes Act 1973, s.24(1)(b);
- Matrimonial and Family Proceedings Act 1984, s.17(1)(a)(ii) (property adjustment orders after overseas divorce);
- Matrimonial Causes (Northern Ireland) Order 1978, art.26(1)(b) (property adjustment orders in connection with divorce proceedings, etc.);
- Matrimonial and Family Proceedings (Northern Ireland) Order 1989, art.21(a)(ii) (property adjustment orders after overseas divorce);
- Civil Partnership Act 2004, Sched.5, para.7(1)(b) or Sched.15, para.7(1)(b) (property adjustment orders in connection with dissolution, etc. of civil partnership); or
- Civil Partnership Act 2004, Sched.7, para.9 or Sched.17, para.9 (property adjustment orders in connection with overseas dissolution, etc. of civil partnership).

Note: Many of these orders can be consent orders, agreed to by the parties.[23]

Example 3.67

A and B were married. As part of the divorce proceedings, a property adjustment order was made to delay the sale of their former matrimonial home, which is held by A and B jointly. A buys a new dwelling to live in as his new main residence. The purchase is not a higher-rates transaction. In determining whether Condition C is met, his ownership of an undivided share in the former matrimonial home is disregarded, as a property adjustment order has been made; hence, the condition is not met.

Example 3.68

A and B were married. A agrees with B to delay the sale of their former matrimonial home, which is held by A and B jointly, but that agreement is not the subject of a property adjustment order. A buys a new dwelling to live in as his new main residence. The purchase is a higher-rates transaction. In determining whether Condition C is met, his ownership of an undivided share in the former matrimonial home counts against him, as no property adjustment order had been made; hence, the condition is met.

3.3.12 Inherited dwellings

Where the purchaser is an individual, in determining whether he owns another dwelling, at the end of the effective date, the freehold or leasehold estate in a dwelling (etc.) held by him is disregarded where:

---

[23] FA 2003, Sched.4ZA, para.9B; SDLT Manual: SDLTM09797.

- he inherited it jointly with one or more others within the last three years; and
- his share of it (together with any share of it owned by his spouse or civil partner) has not exceeded 50 per cent within the last three years.[24]

The freehold or leasehold estate (or an undivided share of such an estate, or the relevant foreign equivalent of such an estate) in another dwelling inherited more than three years ago counts.

The date on which the purchaser became beneficially entitled to the property is the relevant date. This date may vary where the inheritance is governed by foreign law. An interest in an un-administered estate is not a relevant interest. The interest must be transferred to, or be appropriated by, the purchaser before he is taken to own it for this purpose (but do not forget that if the administration of the estate is complete, such an appropriation may be implied).

Example 3.69

A and B are brothers. Their father died. He had owned a number of buy-to-let properties in the UK and overseas. Two of those properties were transferred to A and B equally in pursuance of a bequest made in their father's will. Within the period of three years of the transfer of the properties, A buys a house to live in as his main residence. He owns no properties other than the properties he inherited. There are no changes to the ownership of the two properties. A's purchase is not a higher-rates transaction. In determining whether Condition C is met, his 50% undivided share of the two properties previously owned by his late father does not count against him; hence, the condition is *not* met.

Example 3.70

A and B are brothers. Their father died. He had owned a number of buy-to-let properties in the UK and overseas. Two of those properties were transferred to A and B equally in pursuance of a bequest made in their father's will. Three years and one day after the transfer of the properties, A buys a house to live in as his main residence. He owns no properties other than the properties he inherited. A's purchase is a higher-rates transaction. In determining whether Condition C is met, his 50% undivided share of the two properties previously owned by his late father counts against him; hence, the condition is met.

Example 3.71

A and B are brothers. Their father died. He had owned a number of buy-to-let properties in the UK and overseas. Two of those properties were transferred to A and B in the ratio 51:49 in pursuance of a bequest made in their father's will. Within three years of the transfer of the properties, A buys a house to live in as his main residence. He owns no properties other than the properties he inherited. A's purchase is a higher-rates transaction. In determining whether Condition C is met, his 51% undivided share of the two properties previously owned

---

[24] FA 2003, Sched.4ZA, para.16; SDLT Manual: SDLTM09795.

by his late father count against him; hence, the condition is met. It would not have mattered if A had transferred 1% of the two properties to B before the completion day. He would have owned more than 50% of the two properties within the three-year period.

Example 3.72

A and B are brothers. Their father died. He had owned a number of buy-to-let properties in the UK and overseas. Two of those properties were transferred to A and B equally in pursuance of a bequest made in their father's will. B sells his 50% undivided share in the properties to A's wife. Within three years of the transfer of the properties, A buys a house to live in as his main residence. He owns no properties other than the properties he inherited. A's purchase is a higher-rates transaction. In determining whether Condition C is met, his 50% undivided share of the two properties previously owned by his late father is aggregated with his wife's. As the combined percentage share of the inherited properties owned by A and his wife exceeds 50%, A is treated as owning the properties; hence, the condition is met.

3.4 THE RESIDENTIAL SUPER RATE

3.4.1 Background

In 2012, the government introduced a punitive rate of SDLT to deter individuals from the practice of 'enveloping' (the use of a special purpose company by an individual to acquire and hold a dwelling) and to prevent a loss of tax arising on sales of the dwelling. The rate – a flat 15 per cent on purchases for more than £500,000 (reduced from £2 million in March 2014) – was (and continues to be) fraught with contradictions. For example,

- There was no loss of tax when a company made the purchase – the same amount of tax was paid by the company as the amount that would have been payable if the individual had made the purchase. The loss of tax only arose when the company (then owning the dwelling) was sold. Consequently, the rate punishes an individual in case he chooses to sell the company. If the company sells the dwelling directly, as was (and continues to be) common, full SDLT was paid by the purchaser, meaning that there has been no loss of tax at any point in the process.
- Originally, and for many years, the coverage of reliefs from the super rate was inadequate, meaning that businesses were forced to pay the punitive rate despite using a company for genuine commercial reasons.
- In most cases, the decision to use a company was driven by inheritance tax planning, not saving SDLT. The inheritance tax advantage was not stopped until six years later.
- The rate acted like a season ticket or toll charge – the rate was more than twice the top rate of tax at the time of its introduction (seven per cent) and three times the previous top rate of tax (five per cent). That effect has been eroded

significantly for 'super prime' residential property – the catalyst for the measure – due to the multiple rate increases for residential property transactions since 2012. The difference between the super rate and the alternative marginal rate for a higher-rates transaction may now only be a fraction of a percent for a dwelling costing £20 million, but it is in relation to transactions between £500,000 and £1 million that the super rate operates most unfairly. A company purchasing a house for £550,000 would pay £34,000 of SDLT if the higher rates applied (an effective rate of 6.2 per cent) and £82,000 of SDLT if the super rate (15 per cent) applied.

In a sense, then, the super rate is somewhat an anachronism. Nevertheless, it is incumbent on the residential property lawyer to understand when it applies and when it does not. Another tax, annual tax on enveloped dwellings, applies to every day that a company charged to the super rate owns the property. The super rate takes priority over the higher rates. It also applies to mixed-use transactions.

The super rate applies to transactions completing on or after 21 March 2012 subject to transitional provisions.[25]

3.4.2 The conditions

In order for a transaction to be a super-rate transaction, the following conditions need to be met:

- The chargeable interest must consist of, or include, at least one dwelling.
- The proportion of the consideration attributable to the interest in the dwelling and appurtenant rights must be more than £500,000.
- The purchaser (or at least one of the purchasers) must be a company or partners in a partnership including, to any extent, a company, or the purchase must be made for the purposes of a collective investment scheme. (Note: The super rate applies if a company (etc.) is one of the purchasers of a dwelling costing more than £500,000 even if the company's contribution to that price is minimal.)
- The purchase must not be made by a trustee of a settlement for the purpose of the settlement. A settlement is any type of trust that is not a bare trust.
- If the purchase is made by a trustee of a bare trust, one or more of the beneficiaries must be a company (etc.).
- None of the 'reliefs' must apply (see **3.4.4**).
- The transaction must not be a collective enfranchisement transaction made under Landlord and Tenant Act 1987, Part 1 (right of first refusal) or Leasehold Reform, Housing and Urban Development Act 1993, Part 1, Chapter 1 (right to collective enfranchisement); or if it is, the average amount of the consideration given for the transaction must exceed £500,000 and one or more of the participating flat-owners must be a company (etc.) (see **Chapter 6**).

---

[25] FA 2003, Sched.4A; SDLT Manual: SDLTM09500.

Example 3.73

A sets up a company, B Ltd, to purchase the freehold estate in a London dwelling worth £1 million. The purpose of the purchase is to make the dwelling available for occupation by A's children while they study at university. B Ltd must pay £150,000 of SDLT: £1 million @ 15%. If A had made the purchase personally (and assuming he owns another dwelling) he would have paid £73,750 of SDLT (an effective rate of 7.4%): (£125,000 @ 3%) + (£125,000 @ 5%) + (£675,000 @ 8%) + (£75,000 @ 13%).

Example 3.74

Assume the same facts, but A settles £1 million of cash on trust for his children. The trust is an interest in possession trust. A's children – all of whom are over 18 and none of whom own another dwelling – are the life-tenants. B Ltd is the trustee. B Ltd must pay £43,750 of SDLT (an effective rate of 4.4%): (£125,000 @ 0%) + (£125,000 @ 2%) + (£675,000 @ 5%) + (£75,000 @ 10%).

The three types of qualifying purchaser – company, partnership and collective investment scheme – are sometimes referred to collectively as 'non-natural persons', though this term is not used in the legislation. The three categories are referred to collectively below as 'company (etc.)' in the rest of this chapter for simplicity.

The meaning of 'dwelling' is substantially similar to the meaning used for the purposes of multiple dwellings relief. As one would expect, communal or institutional residential accommodation is excluded as 'residential property'.

In certain circumstances, the ('off-plan') purchase of a dwelling to be built under the sale contract is taxed as if the dwelling was in existence.

Where the subject-matter of the transaction consists of one or more dwellings worth more than £500,000 and interests in non-residential property and/or dwellings worth less than £500,000, the consideration given for the transaction must be apportioned between the dwelling(s) worth more than £500,000 and everything else. The super rate must then be applied to the proportion of the consideration attributable to the dwelling(s) worth more than £500,000 and either the non-residential (mixed) rates or higher rates must be applied to the remainder of the consideration. The purchaser is treated as having entered into two transactions and separate SDLT returns must be made for each. Dwellings that are subject to the super rate are taken into account when determining whether or not more than five dwellings are purchased but are not taken into account when determining whether or not multiple dwellings relief is available. See **3.4.5**.

The rules governing the super rate are modified for cases that involve alternative property finance arrangements, including Islamic mortgages. The scheme is to impose the super rate where the person receiving the finance is a company (etc.)

subject to the availability of relief. Provision is made for the relief to be withdrawn in certain circumstances.[26]

3.4.3 Composite transactions

Where the buyer or a connected person buys more than one chargeable interest in the same dwelling from the same seller or a connected person, whether or not at the same time provided they are 'linked' transactions, the total consideration given is used to determine whether the super rate applies to each transaction. In other words, if the total amount of the consideration given is more than £500,000, the super rate applies to each transaction notwithstanding that the amount of the consideration given for that transaction in isolation does not exceed £500,000. This is an anti-avoidance rule designed to stop parties artificially splitting a transaction in lots worth £500,000 or less to avoid the super rate.[27]

Example 3.75

A Ltd buys a 50% undivided share of the freehold estate in a dwelling for £500,000. The purpose of A Ltd's purchase is to make the dwelling available for occupation by A Ltd's member, B. The super rate does not apply because the amount of the consideration given does not exceed £500,000. A Ltd pays SDLT of £30,000 in accordance with the higher rates (an effective rate of 6%): (£125,000 @ 3%) + (£125,000 @ 5%) + (£250,000 @ 8%). One month later, B acquires the remaining 50% undivided share of the freehold estate from the same seller. Both transactions are super-rate transactions. The tax chargeable on the two 'linked' transactions is £150,000 (£1 million @ 15%). This is pro-rated equally between the two transactions. A Ltd must make a further return and pay SDLT of £45,000 (£75,000 – £30,000) within 30 days of completion of B's purchase. B must make an initial return and pay SDLT of £75,000 within 14 days of completion of his purchase.

3.4.4 The 'reliefs'

There are various exclusions from the super rate. They all apply automatically where the relevant conditions are met; hence, their operation is not dependent on making a claim for relief in an SDLT return or an amendment to an SDLT return. Notwithstanding this, HMRC encourages them to be claimed in an SDLT return and this is recommended. Failure to do so is likely to increase the likelihood that an enquiry is opened into the SDLT return. Consequently, the exclusions are referred to in this work as 'reliefs'. Each relief is claimed by entering code 35 at question 9 ('are you claiming relief?') of the SDLT return.

The reliefs do not provide a complete exemption from charge – rather they merely exclude the tax from being calculated in accordance with the super rate. Instead, the tax is calculated in accordance with the non-residential (mixed) rates or

---

[26] FA 2003, s.81ZA, Sched.4A, paras.2, 3, 6A, 6B, 6C, 6D, 6E, 6F, 6G, 6H.
[27] FA 2003, Sched.4A, para.4; SDLT Manual: SDLTM09540.

FREEHOLD AND LEASEHOLD TRANSFERS

the residential higher rates. (The residential standard rates would not apply to the purchase of a dwelling made by companies unless the amount of the consideration given for a dwelling does not exceed £40,000.) The non-residential (or mixed) rates would apply where more than five dwellings are purchased in a single transaction or part of the purchased property is not 'residential property'. In all other cases, the residential higher rates would apply.

Each of the reliefs may be withdrawn if the requirements for the relief cease to be met within a three-year control period unless frustrated by events outside the purchaser's control. A disposal of the property does not trigger such a withdrawal. In the case of certain reliefs, the relief is also withdrawn if a 'non-qualifying individual' is permitted to occupy the property. Where there is a withdrawal, it means that the difference between the amount of tax that would have been payable had the super rate applied initially and the amount of tax paid must be paid, and an SDLT return must be made, within 30 days of the relevant disqualifying event.

The reliefs apply to the purchase of dwellings:

- by landlords (see **3.4.4.1**);
- by developers (see **3.4.4.2**);
- by property traders (see **3.4.4.3**);
- for use in trades (see **3.4.4.4**);
- open to the public (see **3.4.4.6**);
- by banks, etc. (see **3.4.4.7**);
- under a home reversion plan (also known as an 'equity release scheme') (see **3.4.4.8**);
- for use as a farmhouse (see **3.4.4.9**);
- for occupation by employees, etc. (see **3.4.4.10**); and
- for use as a caretaker flat (see **3.4.4.11**).

Each relief is taken in turn below.

WARNING

1   Significant changes were made in 2013 and 2016 to extend the coverage of reliefs. The changes did not have retrospective effect. It should not be assumed that the summary of the reliefs that follows applies to transactions that completed before 1 April 2016.
2   Although the incidence of the super rate and annual tax on enveloped dwellings is intended to be aligned – hence, if relief from one applies it is tempting to assume that relief from the other should too – that is generally the case, but not always.

3.4.4.1   Purchases by landlords

The super rate does not apply where:

- the chargeable interest is acquired exclusively …

- to exploit as a source of rents ...
- in the course of a property-rental business run from the UK or overseas ...
- on a commercial basis with a view to profit ...
- or to use (or to develop for use) as business premises for the purposes of such a business ...
- unless a 'non-qualifying individual' (see **3.4.4.5**) will be permitted to occupy the dwelling.[28]

Example 3.76

A Ltd buys a newly developed block of flats with vacant possession. At least one of the flats is worth more than £500,000. The super rate does not apply to the extent that the purchased flats are worth more than £500,000 because the only purpose for acquiring the property was to let the flats to third parties for a market rent. That purpose is evidenced in the board minutes of the company, the covenants given when drawing down debt to fund the company's purchase and the commencement of letting within a reasonable time.

The relief is withdrawn if, within three years of completion of the purchase, the purchased dwelling (or a derived interest) is not held exclusively for letting, trading or developing or for use in the purchaser's trade unless starting or carrying on that activity has been frustrated due to unforeseen circumstances outside the purchaser's control and reasonable steps are taken to start or resume the activity.[29] Alternatively, the relief is withdrawn if a 'non-qualifying individual' is permitted to occupy the dwelling. For the meaning of 'non-qualifying individual', see **3.4.4.5**.

Example 3.77

A Ltd buys a dwelling to exploit as a source of rents in the course of its property-rental business. The company is owned by an individual (B). Within a short time, A Ltd instructs a letting agent to market the property for rental. Noting that the rental market is slow and without having found a third party tenant, three months later A Ltd permits B and his family to occupy the property for six months. After six months, A Ltd re-instructs the letting agent to market the property for rental and this time a third party tenant is found and the property is let to him on a periodic tenancy. Relief from the super rate is available initially. However, when the dwelling is made available for occupation by B and his family, the difference between the amount of tax that would have been payable in accordance with the super rate and the amount of tax paid would become payable. It is not a defence that the decision to make the property available for occupation by B and his family was due to unforeseen circumstances outside A Ltd's control (the state of the rental market), nor that the property was let to a third party when the rental market recovered.

---

[28] FA 2003, Sched.4A, para.5; SDLT Manual: SDLTM09555, SDLTM09655, SDLTM09660.
[29] FA 2003, Sched.4A, para.5G.

FREEHOLD AND LEASEHOLD TRANSFERS

> **WARNING**
>
> Switching between letting, trading or developing or using the dwelling for the purposes of a trade does not trigger a withdrawal of the relief, but switching from one of those purposes to another relievable activity does. There is no obvious reason for this. So where the purchaser intends to let the dwelling at completion but, due to unforeseen circumstances outside the purchaser's control or merely due to a change of mind, the property is sold or used in the purchaser's trade, the relief is available and is not withdrawn.

Example 3.78

A Ltd buys the freehold estate of a house to exploit as a source of rents. After failing to find a tenant willing to pay the desired rent, A Ltd decides to sell the property. The transaction was not, and has not become, a super-rate transaction.

3.4.4.2 Purchases by developers

The super rate does not apply where:

- the chargeable interest is acquired exclusively ...
- for the purpose of development or redevelopment and resale ...
- in the course of a 'property-development trade' ...
- unless a 'non-qualifying individual' (see **3.4.4.5**) will be permitted to occupy the dwelling.[30]

A 'property-development trade' means a business that consists of, or includes, buying and developing or redeveloping for resale, land and buildings (not necessarily dwellings). So buying a dwelling to convert into commercial premises for resale would qualify.

The extent to which the dwelling must be developed or redeveloped before it is resold is not specified. HMRC (correctly) accepts that a range of activity qualifies, from renovation to demolition and construction. This is implicit in the use of separate terms: 'development' and 'redevelopment'. The point at which something ceases to be a development and becomes a redevelopment is not clear, but this has no practical significance.

Alternatively, the super rate does not apply where the chargeable interest is acquired by a property developer as part of a 'qualifying exchange'.

A 'qualifying exchange' means satisfying part of the purchase price for a new dwelling by transferring to the seller (the property developer) an existing dwelling in part exchange. The new dwelling must not have been previously occupied since it was constructed or adapted for use as a single dwelling. Note that there is a separate

---

[30] FA 2003, Sched.4A, para.5; SDLT Manual: SDLTM09560, SDLTM0956, SDLTM09655, SDLTM09660.

relief, which operates to provide a complete exemption from charge, for part-exchanges made by house-building companies: see **4.5**. Accordingly, the relief from the super rate is only relevant where the conditions for that other relief are not met.

Example 3.79

A Ltd adapts an existing dwelling into multiple flats for resale. One of the flats is sold to an individual in part exchange for a dwelling owned by the individual. The individual had not lived in that other dwelling; hence, the conditions for full part-exchange relief are not met. However, the super rate does not apply to A Ltd's purchase.

The relief is withdrawn if, within three years of completion of the purchase, the purchased dwelling is not held exclusively for letting, trading, developing or for use in the purchaser's trade unless starting or carrying on that activity has been frustrated due to unforeseen circumstances outside the purchaser's control and reasonable steps are taken to start or resume the activity.[31] Alternatively, the relief is withdrawn if a 'non-qualifying individual' is permitted to occupy the dwelling. Note that switching from letting, trading, developing or use in the purchaser's trade is permitted, but switching from one of those four purposes to another relievable activity is not. For the meaning of 'non-qualifying individual', see **3.4.4.5**.

Example 3.80

A Ltd buys the freehold estate of a house to redevelop and resell on the open market. After redeveloping the property, the board of directors of A Ltd considers that the residential property market has declined and rather than sell the property for less than expected and/or put the property on the market for longer than expected, it decides to let the property to a relative of the company's shareholder. The transaction was not a super-rate transaction.

However, when the dwelling is made available for occupation by the shareholder's relative, the difference between the amount of tax that would have been payable in accordance with the super rate and the amount of tax paid would become payable. It is not a defence that the decision to make the property available for occupation by the shareholder's relative was due to unforeseen circumstances outside A Ltd's control (the state of the market), nor that the property is sold when the market recovers, nor that the relative pays a market rent.

WARNING

Switching between letting, trading or developing or using the dwelling for the purposes of a trade does not trigger a withdrawal of the relief, but switching from one of those purposes to another relievable activity does. There is no obvious reason for this. So

---

[31] FA 2003, Sched.4A, para.5G.

> where the purchaser intends to develop or redevelop and resell the dwelling at completion but, due to unforeseen circumstances outside the purchaser's control or merely due to a change of mind, the property is sold undeveloped or let out after it has been developed, the relief is available and is not withdrawn.

Example 3.81

A Ltd buys the freehold estate of a house to redevelop and resell on the open market. After redeveloping the property, A Ltd considers that the residential property market has declined and rather than sell the property for less than expected and/or put the property on the market for longer than expected, it decides to let the property to a third party for rental profits. The transaction was not, and has not become, a super-rate transaction.

3.4.4.3 Purchases by property traders

The super rate does not apply where:

- the chargeable interest is acquired exclusively ...
- for resale ...
- in the course of a 'property-trading business' ...
- run on a commercial basis with a view to profit ...
- unless a 'non-qualifying individual' (see **3.4.4.5**) will be permitted to occupy the dwelling.[32]

A 'property-trading business' means a business that consists of, or includes, the buying and selling of dwellings in the nature of a trade. The meaning of 'trade' is established by case law, rather than statute. The issue of whether or not the activity is in the nature of a trade is fact sensitive. HMRC is likely to test this, especially where the activity appears to be isolated or speculative.

Example 3.82

A Ltd buys the freehold estate of a house to resell on the open market in the course of its property-trading business. The transaction was not a super-rate transaction. The fact that the dwelling is not sold immediately or even in close proximity to the purchase does not cause the transaction to be a super-rate transaction. The test is of intention. A Ltd's board of directors had intended, and continues to intend, to sell the property.

The relief is withdrawn if, within three years of completion of the purchase, the purchased dwelling is not held exclusively for letting, trading, developing or for use in the purchaser's trade unless starting or carrying on that activity has been

---

[32] FA 2003, Sched.4A, para.5; SDLT Manual: SDLTM09570, SDLTM09655, SDLTM09660.

frustrated due to unforeseen circumstances outside the purchaser's control and reasonable steps are taken to start or resume the activity.[33] Alternatively, the relief is withdrawn if a 'non-qualifying individual' is permitted to occupy the dwelling. Note that switching from letting, trading, developing or use in the purchaser's trade is permitted, but switching from one of those four purposes to another relievable activity is not. For the meaning of 'non-qualifying individual', see **3.4.4.5**.

Example 3.83

As above, except that after failing to find a buyer within a reasonable period of time, the board of directors of A Ltd decides to let the property to a relative of the company's shareholder temporarily while the search for a buyer continues. The transaction was not a super-rate transaction. The test is of intention. A Ltd's board of directors had intended, and continues to intend, to sell the property. However, when the dwelling is made available for occupation by the shareholder's relative, the difference between the amount of tax that would have been payable in accordance with the super rate and the amount of tax paid would become payable. It is not a defence that the decision to make the property available for occupation by the shareholder's relative was due to unforeseen circumstances outside A Ltd's control (the state of the market), nor that the property is sold when the market recovers, nor that the relative pays a market rent.

WARNING

Switching between letting, trading or developing or using the dwelling for the purposes of a trade does not trigger a withdrawal of the relief, but switching from one of those purposes to another relievable activity does. There is no obvious reason for this. So where the purchaser intends to resell the dwelling at completion but, due to unforeseen circumstances outside the purchaser's control or merely due to a change of mind, the property is exploited as a source of rents, the relief is available and is not withdrawn.

Example 3.84

A Ltd buys the freehold estate of a house to resell on the open market. After failing to find a person willing to buy the property for the desired price, the board of directors of A Ltd considers that the residential property market has declined and rather than sell the property for less than expected and/or put the property on the market for longer than expected, it decides to let the property to a third party for rental profits. The transaction was not, and has not become, a super-rate transaction.

---

[33] FA 2003, Sched.4A, para.5G.

3.4.4.4 Purchases for use in trades

The super rate does not apply where:

- the chargeable interest is acquired exclusively ...
- for use (or for development for use) for the purposes of a trade ...
- run on a commercial basis with a view to profit ...
- unless a 'non-qualifying individual' (see **3.4.4.5**) will be permitted to occupy the dwelling.[34]

Example 3.85

A Ltd runs a care-home business. It buys the freehold estate of a house to use for the purposes of its trade. Specifically, the house is to be made available for occupation to employees of the business on a short-term basis and to use as a training centre. The super rate does not apply. All the conditions for the relief are met.

The relief is withdrawn if, within three years of completion of the purchase, the purchased dwelling is not held exclusively for letting, trading, developing or for use in the purchaser's trade unless starting or carrying on that activity has been frustrated due to unforeseen circumstances outside the purchaser's control and reasonable steps are taken to start or resume the activity.[35] Alternatively, the relief is withdrawn if a 'non-qualifying individual' is permitted to occupy the dwelling. Note that switching from letting, trading, developing or use in the purchaser's trade is permitted, but switching from one of those four purposes to another relievable activity is not. For the meaning of 'non-qualifying individual', see **3.4.4.5**.

3.4.4.5 Non-qualifying individuals

None of the reliefs for landlords, developers and traders, and for use in trades, applies where there is an intention at completion for a 'non-qualifying individual' to be permitted to occupy the dwelling at any time, not just during the first three years. Furthermore, the start of such occupation during the first three years would trigger a withdrawal of the relief, meaning that the purchaser must make a further SDLT return and pay the difference between the amount of tax that would have been payable had the super rate applied initially and the amount of tax paid within 30 days.

A 'non-qualifying individual' includes any of:

- a purchaser (e.g., where the individual purchased the property jointly with a company) unless acting as a partner in a partnership;

---

[34] FA 2003, Sched.4A, para.5.
[35] FA 2003, Sched.4A, para.5G.

- a purchaser acting as a partner in a partnership holding a 50 per cent or greater partnership share; or
- an individual connected with the purchaser (or any of the purchasers) or the spouse or civil partner of such an individual.[36]

3.4.4.6 Purchases for dwellings open to the public

The super rate does not apply where:

- the chargeable interest is acquired with the intention ...
- that it will be used in a trade ...
- run on a commercial basis with a view to profit ...
- that involves offering the public the opportunity to make use of, or enjoy, the dwelling (or a significant part of its interior) as customers of the trade on 28 days or more per year.[37]

In determining whether the public is offered the opportunity to make use of, or enjoy, a significant part of the interior of the dwelling, the size (relative to the size of the whole dwelling), nature and function of the relevant area are taken into account.

Example 3.86

A Ltd buys the freehold estate of a large country house for use in its trade. The trade consists of providing a venue and associated services for weddings and other private events. A significant part of the interior of the property and all of its gardens and grounds will be made available for this purpose. There is no period of the year during which the property is not available, other than times required for periodic repairs and renovation. The super rate does *not* apply. All the conditions for the relief are met.

The relief is withdrawn if, within three years of completion of the purchase, the purchased dwelling is not used as a source of income in a trade that involves offering the public the opportunity to make use of, or enjoy, the dwelling as customers of the trade unless starting or carrying on that activity has been frustrated due to unforeseen circumstances outside the purchaser's control and reasonable steps are taken to start or resume the activity.[38]

Example 3.87

As above, but within three years of the transaction A Ltd ceases to trade. The property is instead held by the company for redevelopment and resale. The difference between the

---

[36] FA 2003, Sched.4A, para.5A; SDLT Manual: SDLT09575, SDLT09580.
[37] FA 2003, Sched.4A, para.5B; SDLT Manual: SDLTM09590, SDLTM09595, SDLTM09600, SDLTM09605, SDLTM09610.
[38] FA 2003, Sched.4A, para.5H.

amount of tax that would have been payable in accordance with the super rate and the amount of tax paid would become payable. It is not a defence that the decision to cease to trade was due to unforeseen circumstances outside A Ltd's control, nor that the property is held for an alternative relievable purpose.

3.4.4.7 Purchases by banks, etc.

The super rate does not apply where:

- the purchaser is a bank or another type of financial institution ...
- the purchaser runs a business that involves the lending of money ...
- and the chargeable interest is acquired in the course of that business for the purpose of resale.[39]

The relief is withdrawn if, within three years of completion of the purchase, the purchaser ceases to be a financial institution or ceases to run a business that involves the lending of money, or the purchased dwelling ceases to be held for the purpose of resale in the course of its money-lending business unless starting or carrying on that activity has been frustrated due to unforeseen circumstances outside the purchaser's control and reasonable steps are taken to start or resume the activity.[40]

3.4.4.8 Home reversion plans

The super rate does not apply where:

- the purchaser is authorised to provide 'home reversion plans' ...
- and the chargeable interest is acquired under such a plan.[41]

Broadly, a 'home reversion plan' (also known as an 'equity release scheme') is an arrangement under which the plan provider buys a dwelling from an individual in return for an annuity or lump sum and a lifetime tenancy. The seller of the reversion or a related person must be entitled to occupy at least 40 per cent of the dwelling under the lifetime tenancy. On the death of the seller, the arrangement terminates and the dwelling is sold.

The relief is withdrawn if, within three years of completion of the purchase, the dwelling ceases to be held for the purpose of the home reversion plan unless, after the dwelling ceases to be held for the purpose of the home reversion plan, the dwelling is sold (ignoring any reasonable and unavoidable delay) provided that a 'non-qualifying individual' is not permitted to occupy the dwelling.[42] For the meaning of 'non-qualifying individual', see **3.4.4.5**.

---

[39] FA 2003, Sched.4A, para.5C; SDLT Manual: SDLTM09670, SDLTM09690, SDLTM09700.
[40] FA 2003, Sched.4A, para.5I.
[41] FA 2003, Sched.4ZA, para.5CA.
[42] FA 2003, Sched.4A, para.5IA.

3.4.4.9 Purchases for use as a farmhouse

The super rate does not apply where:

- the chargeable interest is, or is to be, a farmhouse …
- occupied by a farm worker that has a substantial involvement in the day-to-day work or management of the trade …
- for the purpose of a farming trade …
- run on a commercial basis with a view to profit.[43]

The relief is withdrawn if, within three years of completion of the purchase, the dwelling ceases to be occupied for the purposes of a farming trade by a qualifying farm unless starting or carrying on that activity has been frustrated due to unforeseen circumstances outside the purchaser's control and reasonable steps are taken to start or resume the activity.[44]

3.4.4.10 Purchases for occupation by employees, etc.

The super rate does not apply where:

- the chargeable interest is acquired for the purpose of making the dwelling available to employees or partners for use as living accommodation …
- for the purposes a trade or property-rental business …
- run on a commercial basis with a view to profit.[45]

'Qualifying employees or partners' means employees or partners of the purchaser unless they hold a 10 per cent or greater share in the income profits of the trade or partnership, in the purchaser or the purchased dwelling, or they provide domestic services to an individual that is connected to the purchaser. Complicated rules apply to determine whether, and to what extent, an individual holds a share in a company. In certain circumstances, the rights of another person in respect of the company may be attributed to the individual.

For the meaning of 'trade', see **3.4.4.3**.

Example 3.88

A Ltd is a bank. It buys the freehold estate in a house to make the house available for occupation to its overseas directors when visiting the UK branch. The transaction is not a super-rate transaction. All the directors that occupy the house 'qualify'. None hold a 10% or greater share in the company (etc.).

---

[43] FA 2003, Sched.4A, para.5F; SDLT Manual: SDLTM09640, SDLTM09645, SDLTM09650, SDLTM09680.
[44] FA 2003, Sched.4A, para.5K.
[45] FA 2003, Sched.4A, para.5D; SDLT Manual: SDLTM09620, SDLTM09625, SDLTM09630, SDLTM09635, SDLTM09665, SDLTM09675.

The relief is withdrawn if, within three years of completion of the purchase, the dwelling ceases to be made available for the purposes of a qualifying trade or property-rental business as living accommodation by qualifying employees or partners unless starting or carrying on that activity has been frustrated due to unforeseen circumstances outside the purchaser's control and reasonable steps are taken to start or resume the activity.[46]

3.4.4.11 Purchases by management company of flat for occupation by caretaker

The super rate does not apply where:

- the chargeable interest of a flat in a building that contains at least two more flats ...
- is acquired by a tenants' management company ...
- for the purpose of making the flat available for use as caretaker accommodation.[47]

The relief is withdrawn if, within three years of completion of the purchase, the dwelling ceases to be made available for the purposes of caretaker accommodation.[48]

3.4.5 Interaction with other SDLT provisions

A dwelling worth more than £500,000 purchased by a company (etc.) counts when determining whether the number of dwellings purchased in a single transaction exceeds five so as to engage the non-residential rates (see **3.2.5**). However, the non-residential rates only apply to the dwelling worth £500,000 or more if a relief from the super rate is available.

A dwelling worth more than £500,000 purchased by a company (etc.) does not count when determining whether more than one dwelling is purchased for the purposes of multiple dwellings relief unless a relief from the super rate is available (see **4.3**).[49]

Where the parties to the transaction consist of, or include, a partnership and a partner or a connected person, the chargeable consideration given for the transaction is calculated in accordance with special rules. The super rate applies only if the amount of the chargeable consideration found by using those rules is more than £500,000. The super rate also applies to the transfer of an interest in a property-investment partnership where one or more of the partners is a company (etc.) and the

---

[46] FA 2003, Sched.4A, para.5J.
[47] FA 2003, Sched.4A, para.5EA.
[48] FA 2003, Sched.4A, para.5JA.
[49] FA 2003, s.58D, Sched.6B; SDLT Manual: SDLTM09710.

partnership property includes a dwelling; and to withdrawals from, or repayments of loans by, partnerships in certain circumstances: see **16.7** and **16.6**, respectively.[50]

Collective enfranchisement transactions made under Landlord and Tenant Act 1987, Part 1 (right of first refusal) or Leasehold Reform, Housing and Urban Development Act 1993, Part 1, Chapter 1 (right to collective enfranchisement) are subject to the super rate if the average amount of the consideration given for the transaction by the participating flat-owners exceeds £500,000 and one or more of the participating flat-owners is a company (etc.) (see **Chapter 6**).[51]

Where a dwelling worth more than £500,000 is purchased using alternative property finance arrangements entered into between a financial institution and a person, the financial institution's acquisition of the dwelling is exempt from the super rate provided that relief from the rate applies to the person's acquisition of the lease. The relief from the super rate may be withdrawn if the qualifying conditions cease to be met within a three-year period (see **Chapter 11**).[52]

Example 3.89

A Ltd purchases six dwellings in a single transaction for £5 million. Two of the dwellings are to be made available for occupation by individuals connected with the company. The rest are to be let to third parties. The proportion of the price reasonably attributable to the two dwellings to be occupied by the connected individuals is £3 million, apportioned equally between the two dwellings. In calculating the amount of tax payable (and notifying HMRC) in respect of the transaction, A Ltd must divide the transaction into two parts: a super-rate transaction (the acquisition of the two dwellings by the connected individuals) and a non-residential property transaction (the acquisition of the four dwellings to be let to third parties). The four dwellings to be let to third parties are treated as non-residential property, as more than five dwellings are purchased in a single transaction. The total amount of SDLT payable is £539,500 (an effective rate of 10.8%). The amount of SDLT payable on the super-rate transaction is £450,000: £3 million @ 15%. The amount of SDLT payable on the non-residential transaction is £89,500: (£150,000 @ 0%) + (£100,000 @ 2%) + (£1,750,000 @ 5%). (NB In this example, claiming multiple dwellings relief on the purchase of the four dwellings to be let to third parties would have produced a greater tax charge.)

Example 3.90

A building is composed of 10 flats. All 10 of the qualifying tenants choose to purchase the freehold estate of the building collectively in exercise of their rights under the Leasehold Reform, Housing and Urban Development Act 1993. The participating tenants set up a company and hold shares in the company in specified proportions. The company acts as nominee for the participating tenants, one of whom is a company. The nominee company buys the freehold estate in the building in return for paying £5.1 million. The average price per qualifying flat is £510,000 or £5.1 million divided by 10. As one of the qualifying

---

[50] FA 2003, Sched.4A, para.6; SDLT Manual: SDLTM09705.
[51] FA 2003, s.74.
[52] FA 2003, Sched.4A, paras. 6A, 6B, 6C, 6D, 6E, 6F, 6G, 6H.

tenants is a company and the average price per qualifying flat exceeds £500,000, collective enfranchisement relief is not available (see **Chapter 6**). The proportion of the £5.1 million attributable to two of the flats exceeds £500,000 each. The total share of the purchase price attributable to those two flats is £1.2 million. As the proportion of the price attributable to at least one flat is more than £500,000, the tax is calculated in accordance with the super rate. The amount of tax chargeable in accordance with the super rate is £180,000 (£1.2 million @ 15%). The amount of tax chargeable in accordance with the non-residential rates is £184,500 (£150,000 @ 0%) + (£100,000 @ 2%) + (3.65 million @ 5%). The total amount of tax due on the transaction is £364,500 (£180,000 + £184,500), an effective tax rate of 7.1%. The 10 participating tenants are jointly and severally liable for the tax.

Example 3.91

A Ltd buys the freehold estate of a building composed of five flats for £2 million. The purpose of the acquisition does not meet the conditions for a relief from the super rate. One of the flats is worth more than £600,000; the rest are worth less than £500,000 each. In calculating the amount of tax payable (and notifying HMRC) in respect of the transaction, A Ltd must divide the transaction into two parts: a super-rate transaction (the acquisition of the £600,000 flat) and a higher-rates transaction (the acquisition of the four flats worth less than £500,000 each). A claim for multiple dwellings relief may be made for the higher-rates transaction. The amount of SDLT payable is £162,000 (an effective rate of 8.1%). The amount of tax payable on the super-rate transaction is £90,000: £600,000 @ 15%. The amount of tax payable on the higher-rates transaction is £72,000. This is the amount of tax payable on the average price per dwelling (£18,000: (£125,000 @ 3%) + (£125,000 @ 5%) + (£100,000 @ 8%)) multiplied by the number of purchased dwellings that are not subject to the super rate (four). (Note: In this example, fewer than six dwellings are purchased in total, thus the purchase of the four dwellings worth less than £500,000 each is a higher-rates transaction rather than a non-residential transaction.)

Example 3.92

A Ltd is a 51% partner in a property-letting partnership. A dwelling worth £1 million is sold by the partnership to A Ltd. The board of directors of A Ltd intends to make the dwelling available for occupation to its shareholder. The transaction is not a super-rate transaction. The operation of the special rules for transactions involving partnerships (see **Chapter 16**) sets the chargeable consideration at an amount below the super-rate threshold (£500,000).

3.5 THE SURCHARGE FOR OVERSEAS PURCHASERS

In February 2019, the government published a consultation on introducing a surcharge (the third type of surcharge) for purchases of residential property situated in England and Northern Ireland by non-resident persons (legal and natural persons).[53] It had previously been announced at the 2018 budget three months earlier.

---

[53] *Stamp Duty Land Tax: non-UK resident surcharge consultation* (HM Treasury and HMRC, 11 February 2019).

The surcharge would be at the rate of one per cent on top of the existing rates (residential higher rates, standard rates, super rate and lease duty rate). Therefore, the marginal rate of tax payable by non-resident individuals purchasing an 'additional' dwelling would be four per cent higher than the rate payable by resident individuals purchasing their first home. Purchases of mixed-use buildings, mixed purchases and purchases of more than five dwellings in a single transaction would continue to be treated as non-residential and thus fall outside the surcharge. Multiple dwellings relief would also continue to be available, though the tax due on the average price per dwelling would be calculated in accordance with the surcharge. The aim is to dampen demand from non-residents so as to help residents purchase their first home.

Particular rules would determine whether a person is a resident depending on the type of person: individual, company or trustee. This would be the first time that the purchaser's place of residence matters for SDLT and would bring further complexity to the regime. The residency test proposed for individuals is specific to SDLT. An individual would be treated as resident if they have been in the UK (at midnight) on 183 days or more in the year preceding completion of their purchase. Therefore, an individual could be treated as resident for income tax but non-resident for SDLT. Non-residents would not avoid the surcharge by using a UK-resident company to make the purchase. Closely held UK companies would be treated as non-resident if controlled by a non-resident.

The government has yet to publish its response to the feedback received during the consultation. However, it has confirmed that the surcharge would *not* be introduced in the Finance Bill 2019–20.

CHAPTER 4

Common reliefs

4.1 BACKGROUND

Seven stamp duty land tax (SDLT) reliefs are common to residential property transactions. They are, in no particular order:

1. first-time buyer relief;
2. multiple dwellings relief;
3. charities relief;
4. relief for part-exchanges made by house-building companies;
5. reliefs for property traders:
   – acquiring dwelling from customer of house-building company;
   – acquiring dwelling from personal representative;
   – acting as chain-breakers;
   – acquiring dwelling from personal representatives;
   – in case of relocation of employment;
6. relief for employers; and
7. relief for grant-funded purchases by registered providers of social housing.

This chapter discusses each in turn. Having an awareness of them is important. Some are 'true' reliefs in the sense that they must be claimed in an SDLT return or an amendment to an SDLT return. Some are not and apply automatically. That distinction matters. Where an SDLT return is made, the purchaser forfeits the right to reclaim the tax attributable to his failure to claim a relief more than one year after the filing date (14 days after the effective date) – see **19.10.2**. Some provide a full exemption, others provide a partial exemption. Some, but not all, may be withdrawn on the happening of a disqualifying event.

This chapter does not cover the reliefs set out below. Instead, they are covered in the context in which they appear in this work. With the exception of relief for overpaid tax and relief for pre-completion transactions, none of the reliefs listed below needs to be claimed in an SDLT return or an amendment to a return: they all operate automatically. Nevertheless, this does not mean that such transactions are not notifiable – they are. In the majority of cases, HM Revenue and Customs

(HMRC) provides relief codes and the author would encourage their use in the SDLT return to avoid confusion. The reliefs not covered in this chapter are:

- collective enfranchisement relief (see **Chapter 6**);
- exceptions from the residential super rate (see **3.4.4**);
- exceptions from the residential higher rates (see **3.3.10**);
- sale and leaseback relief (see **5.10**);
- relief for surrender and regrant (see **5.7.1**);
- overlap relief (see **5.7.1**);
- relief for incorporation of limited liability partnership (see **16.8**);
- relief for overpaid tax (see **19.10.2**);
- compulsory purchase relief (see **12.2**);
- alternative property finance relief (see **Chapter 11**);
- relief for pre-completion transactions (see **Chapter 7**);
- compliance with planning obligations (see **12.3**); and
- group relief, acquisition relief and reconstruction relief (see **Chapter 18**).

The following reliefs also are not covered in this work, as they are considered too specialist relative to the context – other works should be consulted to understand them:

- relief for 'seeding' a property authorised investment fund or co-ownership authorised contractual scheme; and
- transfers in consequence of reorganisation of parliamentary constituencies.[1]

4.2 FIRST-TIME BUYER RELIEF

Relief for first-time buyers was reintroduced permanently in 2017 for transactions completing on or after 22 November 2017. It had previously been introduced in 2010 for a limited period of two years. It is a full relief for qualifying purchases up to £300,000 and a partial relief for qualifying purchases up to and including £500,000. Purchases over £500,000 do not qualify. The relief takes effect by increasing the threshold of the nil rate band in the set of tax rates and tax bands for standard-rates transactions from £125,000 to £300,000 and taxing the rest of the consideration at five per cent (see **1.4.1**).[2]

4.2.1 Conditions for the relief

Qualifying purchases are those that meet the following conditions:

---

[1] For more information see *Sergeant and Sims on Stamp Taxes* (LexisNexis UK), AA6: SDLT–general exceptions and exemptions; AA7: SDLT–relief for corporations; AA8: SDLT–relief for public and national purposes; AA9: SDLT–relief for social purposes.

[2] Finance Act (FA) 2003, s.57B, Sched.6ZA, Sched.9, paras.15A, 15B, 16; *HMRC internal manual – Stamp Duty Land Tax Manual* ('SDLT Manual') (HMRC, 19 March 2016, updated 16 January 2020, available at: **www.gov.uk/hmrc-internal-manuals/stamp-duty-land-tax-manual**): SDLTM29800.

COMMON RELIEFS

- A freehold or leasehold estate in a *single* dwelling is purchased (except a lease that has an unexpired term of less than 21 years at the beginning of the day after it was acquired). That also means a purchaser whose only interest in a dwelling has been one or more leases of less than 21 years remains a first-time buyer.

> **WARNING**
>
> The purchase of more than one dwelling does not count. The presence of a 'granny annex' on the grounds of the purchased dwelling or a basement flat in the same building as the purchased dwelling could cause the purchaser to lose the relief but gain multiple dwellings relief (see **4.3**). Splitting a transaction into two linked transactions would not work. Subject to a limited exception, linked transactions are also excluded.

Example 4.1

A is a first-time buyer. He has only ever lived in rented accommodation, taking 6- or 12-month tenancies. The tenancies do not change his status as a first-time buyer. He buys a 15-year lease of a flat in London for £300,000. First-time buyer relief is not available, as the lease had less than 21 years to run at the beginning of the day after he bought it. A year later he buys a house in the suburbs for £450,000. A is still a first-time buyer (but if he still owns his London flat he will not be eligible for relief as his house purchase will be a higher-rates transaction – see below).

> **WARNING**
>
> Where a person acquires a new lease of a dwelling (for a term of more than 21 years) as bare trustee, or he acquires the freehold or leasehold estate of a dwelling as trustee of a settlement, for SDLT purposes he is regarded as the purchaser of that interest, even though he is not beneficially entitled to the property. This means that he does not qualify for first-time buyer relief on the purchase of his first home.

- The amount or value of the consideration given (other than rent) is not more than £500,000. Rent is totally ignored.

> **WARNING**
>
> The relief is not tapered for purchases for more than £500,000. The rule is hard-edged. No relief would be available if the purchase price were, for example, £500,001.

- The purchaser (or each purchaser if there is more than one) is an individual.

> **WARNING**
>
> Where a spouse or civil partner buys in his sole name, the relief is not lost merely because his spouse or civil partner is not a first-time buyer. However, if his spouse or civil partner holds another dwelling, the relief would be denied if their ownership of another dwelling converts the purchase into a higher-rates transaction – see below.

- The purchaser (or each purchaser if there is more than one) intends to occupy the purchased dwelling as their only or main residence.
- The purchaser (or each purchaser if there is more than one) has not previously *acquired* (not necessarily bought) a freehold or leasehold estate (or equivalent interest) in a dwelling anywhere in the world (ignoring a lease with a term of less than 21 years at the point it was acquired).

> **WARNING**
>
> An acquisition by way of inheritance or gift would count. The term 'purchaser' is used in the SDLT sense to refer to the person making the acquisition rather than the method of acquisition.

- The transaction is not 'linked' to another transaction unless that linked transaction relates to the purchase of the garden or grounds of the purchased dwelling (or land that subsists for the benefit of the dwelling or its garden or grounds).
- The transaction is not a 'higher-rates transaction' (as to which, see **3.3**).

> **WARNING**
>
> A first-time buyer may not be eligible for the relief because his purchase is a higher-rates transaction due to the ownership of a dwelling by his spouse or civil partner, his minor children, his minor stepchildren, and in some cases the trustees of a trust under which the purchaser or any of the foregoing persons are beneficiaries, or a property-investment partnership of which the purchaser or his spouse or civil partner is a partner.

4.2.2 Meaning of 'dwelling'

A 'dwelling' for these purposes means:
- a building (or part of a building) used as a single dwelling;
- a building (or part of a building) suitable for use as a single dwelling;
- a building (or part of a building) that is in the process of being converted or adapted for use as a single dwelling;
- land that is, or is to be, the garden or grounds of the dwelling and land that subsists, or is to subsist, for the dwelling; or

- a building (or part of a building) that is to be constructed or adapted for use as a dwelling under a contract that is 'substantially performed' before the construction or adaptation has begun. For the meaning of 'substantial performance', see **1.8**.

It does not include certain types of institutional or communal accommodation, e.g., residential accommodation for students.

It is not clear whether the acquisition of an undivided share of a dwelling counts against the purchaser for the purposes of the relief. There used to be a similar uncertainty in relation to the higher rates, but when the legislation for the higher rates was amended in 2018 to make this explicit the legislation for first-time buyer relief was not. However, this was almost certainly an oversight, as HMRC guidance assumes that undivided shares do count. The burden of satisfying a court or tribunal that parliament had intended to exclude an undivided share of a freehold or leasehold estate would be heavy.

Unlike for higher-rates purposes, however, there is no minimum threshold of £40,000. Any interest counts against the buyer, whatever its value.

Example 4.2

When A was a student in the North East, he and three other students were able to buy a run-down dwelling for £100,000, which they occupied for three years and then sold at a modest profit. Even though A's interest was never worth more than £30,000, he is not a first-time buyer.

The relief must be claimed in an SDLT return, or an amendment to an SDLT return, by entering code 32 at question 9 ('are you claiming relief?') of the SDLT return.

Example 4.3

A is a first-time buyer. He is married to B, who is not. They purchase a house together for less than £500,000. A cannot claim first-time buyer relief. This is because he purchases jointly with B. Every purchaser must be a first-time buyer in order for the relief to apply.

Example 4.4

A is a first-time buyer. He is married to B, who is not. She owned a dwelling (since sold) before her marriage to A. A purchases a house alone for less than £500,000 in his sole name. B does not own another dwelling. A can claim first-time buyer relief. The transaction is not a higher-rates transaction, which would have disqualified it from the relief.

Example 4.5

A is a first-time buyer. He is married to B, whose six-year-old daughter (C) from a previous relationship was one of six grandchildren to whom her deceased grandfather's cottage was left in bare trust. C's interest is worth £50,000. A purchases a house alone for less than £500,000. A cannot claim first-time buyer relief, as the transaction is a higher-rates transaction – for A is treated as the owner of his stepdaughter's £50,000 interest.

4.2.3 Shared ownership leases

The relief is available on purchases of shared ownership leases. How it applies to such transactions varies depending on whether the purchaser makes a market value election on the grant of the lease or instead pays SDLT in stages. The relief was not originally available for the latter type, i.e., where a market value election was *not* made. The legislation was amended retrospectively – i.e., to cover all first-time buyers purchasing shared ownership properties on or after 22 November 2017 – to benefit purchasers that chose to pay SDLT in stages. See **10.2**.

4.2.3.1 Market value election

Where a market value election is made, the relief applies if the market value of the property at completion does not exceed £500,000. No SDLT would be payable on subsequent shares purchased or on the rent payable under the lease.

Example 4.6

A is a first-time buyer. He pays £275,000 for a 50% share in a shared ownership property worth £550,000. A makes a market value election. A cannot claim the relief, as the market value of the property is more than £500,000. He must pay £17,500 of SDLT (an effective rate of 3.2%): (£125,000 @ 0%) + (£125,000 @ 2%) + (£300,000 @ 5%). As a result of A making the market value election, no additional amount of SDLT will be payable on any further shares in the property purchased and no SDLT is payable on the rent payable under the lease.

Example 4.7

A is a first-time buyer. He pays £140,000 for a 50% share in a shared ownership property worth £280,000. A makes a market value election. A claims the relief, as the market value of the property is not more than £500,000. He pays no SDLT (£280,000 @ 0%). As a result of A making the market value election, no additional amount of SDLT will be payable on any further shares in the property purchased and no SDLT is payable on the rent payable under the lease.

Example 4.8

A is a first-time buyer. He pays £175,000 for a 50% share in a shared ownership property worth £350,000. A makes a market value election. A claims the relief, as the market value of the property is not more than £500,000. He pays £2,500 of SDLT (an effective rate of 0.71%): (£300,000 @ 0%) + (£50,000 @ 5%). As a result of A making the market value election, no additional amount of SDLT will be payable on any further shares in the property purchased, and no SDLT is payable on the rent payable under the lease.

4.2.3.2 Payment in stages

Where a market value election is not made, the relief applies to the amount paid for the initial share of the property purchased if the market value of the property on completion does not exceed £500,000 (it is irrelevant that the amount paid for the initial share does not exceed £500,000 if the market value of the property exceeds £500,000). Where the relief is claimed, no SDLT is payable on the rent payable under the lease. The relief only applies to the initial share purchased.

The relief is not withdrawn if the total amount paid for the initial share together with any further shares in the property subsequently purchased ('staircasing') is more than £500,000. No additional amount of SDLT is payable unless and until the purchaser increases his share in the property to more than 80 per cent. The ordinary rules apply for calculating the amount of SDLT payable on the transaction that makes the purchaser's total share in the property tip over 80 per cent and on any subsequent staircasing transactions (see **10.2**).

Example 4.9

A is a first-time buyer. He pays £150,000 for a 40% share in a shared ownership property worth £375,000. A does not make a market value election. A claims the relief, as the market value of the property is not more than £500,000. He pays no SDLT (£150,000 @ 0%), regardless of the net present value (NPV) of the rent payable over the term of the lease. No additional amount of SDLT will be payable on any further shares in the property purchased unless and until A's total share in the property is more than 80%.

Substantially similar rules apply to shared ownership trust transactions (see **10.3**).

4.3 MULTIPLE DWELLINGS RELIEF

A partial relief is available where one or more chargeable interests in more than one dwelling are purchased in a single transaction or 'linked' transactions (including in connection with the purchase of non-residential property) unless:

- the transaction is made under Landlord and Tenant Act 1987, Part 1 (right of first refusal) or Leasehold Reform, Housing and Urban Development Act 1993, Part 1, Chapter 1 (right to collective enfranchisement) (see **Chapter 6**);
- certain types of alternative SDLT relief are, or would be, available or have been withdrawn (specifically: group relief; acquisition relief; reconstruction relief; seeding relief for property authorised investment funds and co-ownership authorised contractual schemes; and charities relief) (see **Chapter 18**);
- the purchased interest in the dwelling is subject to a lease that was granted for an initial term of more than 21 years, in which case that interest is disregarded in determining whether more than one dwelling is purchased (subject to a limited exception for lease and leaseback transactions involving housing associations and certain other qualifying bodies).[3]

WARNING

This is a potential trap. It is not enough to check how long the term of the lease has to run. One must check how long the initial term of the lease was.

Example 4.10

A buys a house for £1 million divided into four independent flats, each let on six-month assured shorthold tenancies. A can claim multiple dwellings relief, so pays SDLT of £40,000, an effective rate of 4% (£10,000 being the SDLT at the higher rates payable on the average price of £250,000 per flat multiplied by the number of flats).

Example 4.11

B buys a house for £1 million divided into four independent flats, each originally leased on 50-year leases, where there is only six months left to run. B cannot claim multiple dwellings relief. He must pay £73,750 of SDLT (an effective rate of 7.4%): (£125,000 @ 3%) + (£125,000 @ 5%) + (£675,000 @ 8%) + (£75,000 @ 13%).

The relief, where it is claimed, modifies the 'linked' transactions rule – see **1.5.4**. But for claiming the relief, the amount of SDLT chargeable on the purchase of more than one dwelling would be calculated in accordance with the relevant rates (i.e., the residential standard rates or higher rates or the non-residential rates, as to which see **1.4.1**) on the *total* amount or value of the consideration given for the transaction. A claim for the relief 'switches off' the SDLT linked transactions rule (but only for the dwellings that qualify for the relief) meaning that the amount of tax payable on the

---

[3] FA 2003, s.58D, Sched.6B; SDLT Manual: SDLTM29900, SDLTM00380, SDLTM00385, SDLTM00390, SDLTM00395.

dwellings is calculated on the average price per dwelling before it is multiplied by the number of dwellings purchased. However, any property bought in the linked transactions that does not qualify for multiple dwellings relief attracts tax at the rate applicable to the total price as if the relief had not been claimed, but only on its fraction of the total price.

Example 4.12

A purchases for £1 million a shop with two adjoining terraced cottages. A purchases the cottages from B and the shop from B's company, B Ltd. The transactions are 'linked' and, if multiple dwellings relief were not claimed, would normally be taxed at the non-residential (or mixed) rates on £1 million. If the shop costs £500,000 and the cottages £250,000 each, the shop is not eligible for multiple dwellings relief so still attracts tax at the rates applicable to £1 million (but on just half of that total tax, as its price is half the total price). However, if the relief were claimed, the cottages would attract tax just on their average price as dwellings, £250,000 each. Whether the cottages bear SDLT at normal or higher rates is discussed at **3.3.5.1**.

The relief is similar in design to the partial SDLT relief for collective enfranchisement transactions (see **Chapter 6**). It means that the amount of tax payable by the purchaser is more in line with the amount of tax that he would have suffered if he had purchased the dwellings individually. Aside from needing to claim the relief, there are three ways in which multiple dwellings relief differs from collective enfranchisement relief:

- Multiple dwellings relief has a one per cent collar. The amount of tax payable cannot be lower than one per cent of the total consideration given for the dwellings. There is no such collar for collective enfranchisement relief. As the residential higher rates are usually engaged for purchases of more than one dwelling, the collar rarely bites.
- Multiple dwellings relief has no cap. In contrast, collective enfranchisement relief is not available where the purchaser (or, if there is more than one purchaser, a purchaser) is a company and the average price per qualifying flat is more £500,000. However, dwellings that are within the residential super rate (see **3.4**) are disregarded as dwellings for the purposes of multiple dwellings relief unless relief from the super rate is available.
- There is provision for the withdrawal of multiple dwellings relief if a disqualifying event happens within three years (see below). There is no provision for the withdrawal of collective enfranchisement relief.

As the purchase of more than five dwellings in a single transaction is taxed as if the dwellings were non-residential property (see **3.2.5**), where more than five dwellings are purchased, the purchaser must make a choice:

- claim multiple dwellings relief in accordance with the residential standard rates or (more usually) the higher rates; or
- do not claim multiple dwellings relief and instead pay tax in accordance with the non-residential rates.

In practice, two sets of calculations should be made to determine which choice to make. As a rule of thumb, where the average price per qualifying dwelling is under £275,000 it is better to claim the relief; where it is over £333,333 it is better not to; and where it is between £275,000 and £333,333 it depends on the number of dwellings purchased.

4.3.1 Method to calculate tax

Where the relief is claimed, the method used to calculate the tax payable is as follows:

1. Split the consideration between the part apportionable to the qualifying dwellings (the 'dwellings consideration') and the part (if any) apportionable to non-residential property and any non-qualifying dwellings, such as those subject to leases initially granted for more than 21 years (the 'non-dwellings consideration').
2. Divide the dwellings consideration by the number of qualifying dwellings purchased to produce an average price per qualifying dwelling.
3. Find the tax that would be payable on the average price per qualifying dwelling using the residential standard rates or higher rates (as appropriate – see later).
4. Multiply the tax due on the average price per qualifying dwelling by the number purchased.
5. Compare the tax found in the preceding step with one per cent of the dwellings consideration and use whichever is higher – this is the tax due on the dwellings consideration.
6. If there is non-dwellings consideration, find the tax that would be payable on the total consideration given for the transaction in accordance with the non-residential rates.
7. Prorate the tax found in the preceding step according to the fraction that the non-dwellings consideration bears as a proportion of the total consideration given for the transaction – this is the tax due on the non-dwellings consideration.
8. Add the tax due on the dwellings consideration and the tax due on the non-dwellings consideration to give the total amount of tax chargeable.

Example 4.13

A buys the freehold estate in a building containing five studio flats for £1.5 million for investment purposes (buy-to-let). The freehold estate is not subject to a lease granted for an

COMMON RELIEFS

initial term of more than 21 years. The studio flats are occupied by tenants under assured shorthold tenancies. A claims multiple dwellings relief. The average price per qualifying dwelling is £300,000 (£1.5 million / 5). The tax that would be chargeable on a notional flat worth £300,000 in accordance with the higher rates is £14,000 (an effective rate of 4.7%): (£125,000 @ 3%) + (£125,000 @ 5%) + (£50,000 @ 8%). The amount of tax chargeable on the transaction is £70,000 (£14,000 x 5), an effective tax rate of 4.7%, as this is more than £15,000 (1% of £1.5 million).

Example 4.14

A buys the freehold estate in a building that is the process of being adapted for use as six flats for £2.4 million for investment purposes (buy-to-let). The freehold estate is not subject to a lease granted for an initial term of more than 21 years. A considers claiming multiple dwellings relief. The average price per dwelling is £400,000 (£2.4 million / 6). The tax that would be chargeable on a notional flat worth £400,000 in accordance with the higher rates is £22,000 (an effective rate of 5.5%): (£125,000 @ 3%) + (£125,000 @ 5%) + (£150,000 @ 8%). If the relief were claimed, the amount of tax chargeable on the transaction would be £132,000 (£22,000 x 6), an effective tax rate of 5.5%, as this is more than £24,000 (1% of £2.4 million). If the relief were not claimed, the amount of tax chargeable in accordance with the non-residential rates would be £109,500 (an effective rate of 4.6%): (£150,000 @ 0%) + (£100,000 @ 2%) + (£2,150,000 @ 5%). A decides not to claim the relief, as £22,500 more tax would be payable if he did so.

4.3.2 Meaning of 'dwelling'

A 'dwelling' for these purposes means:

- a building (or part of a building) used as a single dwelling;
- a building (or part of a building) suitable for use as a single dwelling;
- a building (or part of a building) that is in the process of being converted or adapted for use as a single dwelling;
- land that is, or is to be, the garden or grounds of the dwelling and land that subsists, or is to subsist, for the dwelling (note: no guidance has yet been issued as to what is meant by the phrases 'is to be' or 'is to subsist' or how one can claim multiple dwellings relief on land that is not already the garden or grounds of a dwelling); or
- a building (or part of a building) that is to be constructed or adapted for use as a dwelling under a contract that is 'substantially performed' before the construction or adaptation has begun.

It does not include certain types of institutional or communal accommodation (e.g., a hotel, inn or similar establishment), but it does include purpose-built residential accommodation for students.

It also does not include dwellings worth more than £500,000 purchased by a company, collective investment scheme or partnership with one or more corporate partners unless 'relief' from the residential super rate applies (see **3.4**).

Where a transaction is a non-residential transaction because more than five dwellings are purchased or the transaction is mixed, claiming the relief does not make the transaction a higher-rates transaction provided that, where more than five dwellings are purchased, not more than £40,000 of the consideration is attributable to each dwelling. In those cases, the tax chargeable under multiple dwellings relief is calculated in accordance with the standard rates. However, where more than five dwellings are purchased and £40,000 or more is attributable to any of the purchased dwellings, the tax chargeable under multiple dwellings relief is calculated in accordance with the higher rates if the purchaser is a company or an individual who already owns a dwelling worth £40,000 or more, or two or more of the dwellings are worth £40,000 or more.

Where more than one dwelling is purchased in the same transaction (not linked transactions) and one of them (the 'main dwelling') would be taxed at the residential standard rates, the other dwelling(s) must be 'subsidiary' to the main dwelling, otherwise their existence would make the whole transaction a higher-rates transaction (see **3.3.3**).

'Single dwelling' takes its ordinary meaning. However, determining when a building consists of a single dwelling or multiple dwellings may be difficult and will always be fact sensitive. A number of factors should be taken into account, including (but not limited to):

- the physical suitability of the building or part of the building for use as a single dwelling;
- whether there are adequate facilities for independent living; and
- whether there is separate external access or whether shared external access would interfere with the privacy of the occupants of the other dwelling(s).

HMRC agrees. It says that in determining whether or not a property includes one or more dwellings, a wide range of factors should be taken into consideration and, where the factors conflict, it is necessary to weigh up all the factors to come to a balanced judgement. The factors which HMRC considers are relevant include:

- the facilities of the dwelling (e.g., for cooking and personal hygiene);
- independent access to the dwelling;
- privacy from other dwellings;
- control of electricity, gas, water and heating from within the dwelling;
- legal constraints (e.g., planning conditions, restrictive covenants);
- separate recognition for council tax;
- marketing material; and
- individual letter boxes.

The first three factors (described collectively as 'physical configuration') are described by HMRC as 'very important' in determining how many dwellings there are. It is reasonable to infer from this that HMRC regards those factors as having more significance than the others – but that does not mean they are determinative.

Example 4.15

A purchases the freehold estate in a London townhouse for £4 million. The transaction is not a higher-rates transaction. The house has six floors: the ground floor, four floors above the ground floor and a lower-ground floor. The lower-ground floor has its own external access, kitchenette, bathroom and living/sleeping accommodation and can be shut off from the rest of the house. A intends to permit his au pair to live in the lower-ground floor space. A single property is recognised for council tax purposes. The lower-ground floor and the rest of the property share an electricity and heating supply. The lower-ground floor does not have its own hot-water boiler. The value of the lower-ground floor is £500,000. A claims multiple dwellings relief on the basis that the purchased property consists of two dwellings: the lower-ground floor and the rest of the property. Claiming the relief reduces A's SDLT liability by £86,250, from £393,750 to £307,500. The amount of tax chargeable in accordance with the standard rates for a single dwelling worth £4 million is £393,750 (an effective rate of 9.8%): (£125,000 @ 0%) + (£125,000 @ 2%) + (£675,000 @ 5%) + (£575,000 @ 10%) + (£2.5 million @ 12%). The amount of tax chargeable in accordance with the standard rates for a single dwelling worth £2 million is £153,750 (an effective rate of 7.7%): (£125,000 @ 0%) + (£125,000 @ 2%) + (£675,000 @ 5%) + (£575,000 @ 10%) + (£500,000 @ 12%); £153,750 multiplied by two (the number of dwellings purchased) is £307,500, giving an effective rate of 7.7%.

The relief must be claimed in an SDLT return, or an amendment to an SDLT return, by entering code 33 at question 9 ('are you claiming relief?') of the SDLT return.

4.3.3 Withdrawal of relief

Some or all of the relief is withdrawn if, to any extent, something happens within three years of the effective date of the transaction and, had it happened immediately before the effective date, more tax would have been payable. Such disqualifying events include the reduction in the number of dwellings (e.g., due to fewer dwellings being constructed or adapted, or existing dwellings being amalgamated) or the conversion of the building from residential use to non-residential use. HMRC appears to accept that the grant of a lease of the dwelling is not a disqualifying event, even if the term of the lease is more than 21 years, regardless of the amount of rent payable, as it constitutes a part disposal of the dwelling.

Note that the three-year period is a maximum period. If a dwelling is disposed of to an unconnected person, what happens to that dwelling later does not affect the original purchaser.

Where a disqualifying event occurs, the tax must be recalculated as if the event had occurred immediately before the effective date of the transaction and if the amount of tax payable is greater than had been originally self-assessed, the excess must be paid (and a further SDLT return must be made) within 30 days of the event.

Example 4.16

Repeating the previous example, A claims multiple dwellings relief on the basis that the purchased property consists of two dwellings. Two years later, A makes changes to the lower-ground floor to reconfigure the space into a gym. The lower-ground floor ceases to be suitable for use as a single dwelling and A must pay additional tax. The amount of tax payable in this case is the tax that would have been payable but for claiming the relief less the tax paid: £393,750 – £307,500 = £86,250.

Example 4.17

Repeating the first example from **4.3.1**, A buys the freehold estate in a building containing five studio flats for £1.5 million for investment purposes (buy-to-let) and claims multiple dwellings relief based on five dwellings. Two years after his purchase of the property, A begins to adapt the building for use as a 'bed-and-breakfast'. A recalculates the amount of tax that would have been chargeable if the adaptation had started immediately before completion. The £1.5 million would have been chargeable in accordance with the non-residential rates: (£150,000 @ 0%) + (£100,000 @ 2%) + (£1.25 million @ 5%), giving a total tax charge of £64,500 (an effective rate of 4.3%). As £64,500 is not more than £70,000, no further tax needs to be paid and no further return needs to be made.

4.4 CHARITIES RELIEF

The purchase or co-joint purchase of a property by a charity may be fully or partly relieved where:

- the charity intends to hold all or the greater part of the property for use in furtherance of its charitable purposes (or those of another charity) or as an investment from which the profits are applied to its charitable purposes; and
- the transaction is not entered into for the purpose of avoiding SDLT.[4]

HMRC says that the 'greater part of the property' should be determined by reference to value rather than the internal area of the purchased property. While this interpretation of the phrase is reasonable, it is not explicit in the SDLT legislation.

Example 4.18

A charity buys a residential building composed of five flats and intends to dispose of three of the flats at completion. More than half the purchase price is attributable to the two flats to be

---

[4] FA 2003, s.68, Sched.8; SDLT Manual: SDLTM26000.

retained. HMRC should accept that the charity may claim full relief as it intended to hold the 'greater part of the land', even though in terms of internal area it would have disposed of more than half.

4.4.1 Withdrawal of relief

The relief is withdrawn where:

- either:
  - the purchaser ceases to be established for charitable purposes only; or
  - the purchased property (or a derived interest) is used by the purchaser for non-charitable purposes;

  and:

- at the relevant time, the purchaser continues to hold the relieved property (or a derived interest),

provided that the relevant event or act happens within three years of the purchase or in pursuance of arrangements made within three years of the purchase.

The relief is retained to the extent that the purchaser no longer holds all of the relieved property at the relevant time or continues to use the relieved property for charitable purposes.

Where the purchaser did not intend to hold all of the property for qualifying charitable purposes, there is an additional trigger for a withdrawal of the relief. The relief is withdrawn where the purchased property is sold, either by way of transfer or by the grant of a lease for rent of less than £1,000 per year, unless the sale is in furtherance of the purchaser's charitable purposes.

Provision is made for the relief to be claimed by a charity where it purchases a property jointly with a non-charity.

Example 4.19

Continuing the example above, the charity sells the three flats. It must pay SDLT on the proportion of the price attributable to the sold flats. Let us suppose the purchase price for all five was £1.5 million and the proportion of the price attributable to the sold flats was £675,000 (45% of £1.5 million), then £44,000 of SDLT is payable (£125,000 @3%) + (£125,000 @ 5%) + (£425,000 @ 8%). The charity cannot claim multiple dwellings relief. The availability of multiple dwellings relief is restricted where certain reliefs (including charities relief) are available or have been withdrawn.

The relief must be claimed in an SDLT return, or an amendment to an SDLT return, by entering code 20 at question 9 ('are you claiming relief?') of the SDLT return.

STAMP DUTY LAND TAX HANDBOOK

4.5 RELIEF FOR PART-EXCHANGES MADE BY HOUSE-BUILDING COMPANIES

A transaction is exempt where an individual (alone or jointly) disposes of his former main residence (the 'sold dwelling') to a house-building company where:

- the individual acquires a new dwelling from the house-building company;
- the individual intends to occupy the new dwelling as his only or main residence;
- the individual occupied the sold dwelling as his only or main residence at some point within the two years ending with the acquisition by the company;
- the acquisition of the sold dwelling and acquisition of the new dwelling are in consideration of each other; and
- the sold dwelling's garden or grounds are not more than 0.5 of a hectare unless they are required for the reasonable enjoyment of the dwelling having regard to its size and character. (Note: Where the garden or grounds are more than this area and are not required for the reasonable enjoyment of the dwelling, the exemption is pro-rated.)[5]

A 'house-building company' means a company that carries on the business of constructing or adapting buildings (or parts of buildings) for use as dwellings and includes a company connected with it.

A 'new dwelling' means a dwelling that has not previously been occupied since its construction or adaptation as a dwelling.

A claim for relief does not need to be made in an SDLT return or an amendment to an SDLT return. The exemption is automatic. Nevertheless, this does not mean that such transactions are not notifiable – they are. HMRC provides a relief code (code 08) and the author would encourage its use when answering question 9 ('are you claiming relief?') of the SDLT return to avoid confusion. There is no provision for the withdrawal of the relief; hence, there is no negative impact if the individual ceases to use the new dwelling as his main residence.

4.6 RELIEF FOR PROPERTY TRADERS ACQUIRING DWELLING FROM CUSTOMER OF HOUSE-BUILDING COMPANY

A transaction is exempt where an individual (alone or jointly) disposes of his former main residence (the 'sold dwelling') to a property trader where:

- the individual acquires a new dwelling from a house-building company;
- the individual intends to occupy the new dwelling as his only or main residence;
- the individual occupied the sold dwelling as his only or main residence at some point within the two years ending with the acquisition by the trader;
- the transaction is made in the course of the property trader's business, a business that consists of, or includes, acquiring dwellings from individuals who acquire new dwellings from house-building companies;

---

[5] FA 2003, s.58A, Sched.6A, para.1; SDLT Manual: SDLTM21020.

- the sold dwelling's garden or grounds are not more than 0.5 of a hectare unless they are required for the reasonable enjoyment of the dwelling having regard to its size and character (note: where the garden or grounds are more than this area and are not required for the reasonable enjoyment of the dwelling, the exemption is pro-rated);
- the property trader does not intend to spend more than £10,000 or five per cent of the consideration given for the dwelling (subject to a cap of £20,000), whichever is the greater, on the refurbishment of the dwelling;
- the property trader does not intend to grant a lease or a licence of the dwelling except to the individual for a period of no more than six months; and
- the property trader does not intend to permit any of its principals or employees (or, in either case, connected persons) to occupy the dwelling.[6]

A 'property trader' means a company, a limited liability partnership or a partnership that is composed entirely of companies or limited liability partnerships that carries on the business of buying and selling dwellings.

A 'house-building company' means a company that carries on the business of constructing or adapting buildings (or parts of buildings) for use as dwellings and includes a company connected with it.

A claim for relief does not need to be made in an SDLT return or an amendment to an SDLT return. The exemption is automatic. Nevertheless, this does not mean that such transactions are not notifiable – they are. HMRC provides a relief code (code 28) and the author would encourage its use when answering question 9 ('are you claiming relief?') of the SDLT return to avoid confusion.

The relief is withdrawn fully if, to any extent, the property trader spends more than the permitted amount on the refurbishment of the dwelling, grants a lease or a licence of the dwelling other than to the individual for a period of no more than six months or permits any of its principals or employees (or, in either case, connected persons) to occupy the dwelling. There is no negative impact if the individual ceases to use the new dwelling as his main residence.

4.7 RELIEF FOR PROPERTY TRADERS ACTING AS CHAIN-BREAKERS

A transaction is exempt where an individual (alone or jointly) disposes of his former main residence (the 'sold dwelling') to a property trader where:

- the individual occupied the sold dwelling as his only or main residence at some point within two years of the property trader's acquisition;
- the individual made arrangements to sell the sold dwelling and buy another dwelling as his only or main residence, those arrangements failed and the acquisition of the sold dwelling is to enable the purchase of the other dwelling to proceed;

---

[6] FA 2003, s.58A, Sched.6A, para.2; SDLT Manual: SDLTM21030.

- the transaction is made in the course of the property trader's business, a business that consists of, or includes, buying dwellings in these circumstances;
- the sold dwelling's garden or grounds are not more than 0.5 of a hectare unless they are required for the reasonable enjoyment of the dwelling having regard to its size and character (note: where the garden or grounds are more than this area and are not required for the reasonable enjoyment of the dwelling, the exemption is pro-rated);
- the property trader does not intend to spend more than £10,000 or five per cent of the consideration given for the dwelling (subject to a cap of £20,000), whichever is the greater, on the refurbishment of the dwelling;
- the property trader does not intend to grant a lease or a licence of the dwelling except to the individual for a period of no more than six months; and
- the property trader does not intend to permit any of its principals or employees (or, in either case, connected persons) to occupy the dwelling.[7]

A 'property trader' means a company, a limited liability partnership or a partnership that is composed entirely of companies or limited liability partnerships that carries on the business of buying and selling dwellings.

A claim for relief does not need to be made in an SDLT return or an amendment to an SDLT return. The exemption is automatic. Nevertheless, this does not mean that such transactions are not notifiable – they are. HMRC provides a relief code (code 28) and the author would encourage its use when answering question 9 ('are you claiming relief?') of the SDLT return to avoid confusion.

The relief is withdrawn fully if, to any extent, the property trader spends more than the permitted amount on the refurbishment of the dwelling, grants a lease or a licence of the dwelling other than to the individual for a period of no more than six months or permits any of its principals or employees (or, in either case, connected persons) to occupy the dwelling.

The meaning of 'failed' is not defined.

4.8 RELIEF FOR PROPERTY TRADERS ACQUIRING DWELLING FROM PERSONAL REPRESENTATIVES

A transaction is exempt where the personal representatives of a deceased individual dispose of his former main residence (the 'sold dwelling') to a property trader where:

- the deceased individual occupied the sold dwelling as his only or main residence at some point within two years of his death;
- the transaction is made in the course of the property trader's business, a business that consists of, or includes, acquiring dwellings from personal representatives of deceased individuals;

---

[7] FA 2003, s.58A, Sched.6A, para.4; SDLT Manual: SDLTM21050.

COMMON RELIEFS

- the sold dwelling's garden or grounds are not more than 0.5 of a hectare unless they are required for the reasonable enjoyment of the dwelling having regard to its size and character (note: where the garden or grounds are more than this area and are not required for the reasonable enjoyment of the dwelling, the exemption is pro-rated);
- the property trader does not intend to spend more than £10,000 or five per cent of the consideration given for the dwelling (subject to a cap of £20,000), whichever is the greater, on the refurbishment of the dwelling;
- the property trader does not intend to grant a lease or a licence of the dwelling; and
- the property trader does not intend to permit any of its principals or employees (or, in either case, connected persons) to occupy the dwelling.[8]

A 'property trader' means a company, a limited liability partnership or a partnership that is composed entirely of companies or limited liability partnerships that carries on the business of buying and selling dwellings.

A claim for relief does not need to be made in an SDLT return or an amendment to an SDLT return. The exemption is automatic. Nevertheless, this does not mean that such transactions are not notifiable – they are. HMRC provides a relief code (code 28) and the author would encourage its use when answering question 9 ('are you claiming relief?') of the SDLT return to avoid confusion.

The relief is withdrawn fully if, to any extent, the property trader spends more than the permitted amount on the refurbishment of the dwelling, grants a lease or a licence of the dwelling or permits any of its principals or employees (or, in either case, connected persons) to occupy the dwelling.

4.9 RELIEF FOR PROPERTY TRADERS IN CASE OF RELOCATION OF EMPLOYMENT

A transaction is exempt where an individual disposes of his only or main residence (the 'sold dwelling') to a property trader where:

- the individual occupied the sold dwelling as his only or main residence at some point within the last two years;
- the transaction is driven by the individual's relocation of employment (from a place that is not within reasonable daily travelling distance of his new place of employment to one that is);
- the transaction is made in the course of the property trader's business, a business that consists of, or includes, acquiring dwellings from individuals in connection with a change of residence resulting from relocation of employment;
- the consideration given for the sold dwelling does not exceed the market value of the dwelling;

---
[8] FA 2003 s.58A, Sched.6A, para.3; SDLT Manual: SDLTM21040.

- the sold dwelling's garden or grounds are not more than 0.5 of a hectare unless they are required for the reasonable enjoyment of the dwelling having regard to its size and character (note: where the garden or grounds are more than this area and are not required for the reasonable enjoyment of the dwelling, the exemption is pro-rated);
- the property trader does not intend to spend more than £10,000 or five per cent of the consideration given for the dwelling (subject to a cap of £20,000), whichever is the greater, on the refurbishment of the dwelling;
- the property trader does not intend to grant a lease or a licence of the dwelling except to the individual for a period of no more than six months; and
- the property trader does not intend to permit any of its principals or employees (or, in either case, connected persons) to occupy the dwelling.[9]

A 'property trader' means a company, a limited liability partnership or a partnership that is composed entirely of companies or limited liability partnerships that carries on the business of buying and selling dwellings.

A claim for relief does not need to be made in an SDLT return or an amendment to an SDLT return. The exemption is automatic. Nevertheless, this does not mean that such transactions are not notifiable – they are. HMRC provides a relief code (code 28) and the author would encourage its use when answering question 9 ('are you claiming relief?') of the SDLT return to avoid confusion.

The relief is withdrawn fully if, to any extent, the property trader spends more than the permitted amount on the refurbishment of the dwelling, grants a lease or a licence of the dwelling other than to the individual for a period of no more than six months or permits any of its principals or employees (or, in either case, connected persons) to occupy the dwelling.

4.10 RELIEF FOR EMPLOYERS

A transaction is exempt where an individual disposes of his only or main residence (the 'sold dwelling') to his existing or new employer where:

- the individual occupied the sold dwelling as his only or main residence at some point within the last two years;
- the transaction is driven by the individual's relocation of employment (from a place that is not within reasonable daily travelling distance of his new place of employment to one that is);
- the consideration given for the sold dwelling does not exceed the market value of the dwelling; and
- the sold dwelling's garden or grounds are not more than 0.5 of a hectare unless they are required for the reasonable enjoyment of the dwelling having regard to

---

[9] FA 2003, s.58A, Sched.6A, para.6; SDLT Manual: SDLTM21070.

its size and character (note: where the garden or grounds are more than this area and are not required for the reasonable enjoyment of the dwelling, the exemption is pro-rated).[10]

A claim for relief does not need to be made in an SDLT return or an amendment to an SDLT return. The exemption is automatic. Nevertheless, this does not mean that such transactions are not notifiable – they are. HMRC provides a relief code (code 09) and the author would encourage its use when answering question 9 ('are you claiming relief?') of the SDLT return to avoid confusion. There is no provision for the withdrawal of the relief.

4.11 RELIEF FOR GRANT-FUNDED PURCHASES BY REGISTERED PROVIDERS OF SOCIAL HOUSING

A transaction is exempt where the purchaser is a registered provider of social housing (regardless of whether it is profit-making) if the transaction is funded 'with the assistance of' a public subsidy or, in the case of non-profit-making registered providers only, the purchaser is controlled by its tenants or the vendor is a qualifying body.[11]

'Public subsidy' means any grant of other financial assistance made or given by the Greater London Authority or under certain specific Acts: e.g., Housing Act 1996, s.18 (social housing grants) and Housing and Regeneration Act 2008, s.19 (financial assistance by Homes England).

The extent to which the transaction must be funded by a public subsidy is not defined, either in the statute or in HMRC guidance. The condition merely requires that the purchase is made 'with the assistance of' the public subsidy. HMRC appears to accept that 'recycled grant' held in a Recycled Capital Grant Fund qualifies as public subsidy.

A claim for relief does not need to be made in an SDLT return or an amendment to an SDLT return. The exemption is automatic. Nevertheless, this does not mean that such transactions are not notifiable – they are. HMRC provides a relief code (code 23) and the author would encourage its use when answering question 9 ('are you claiming relief?') of the SDLT return to avoid confusion. There is no provision for the withdrawal of the relief.

---

[10] FA 2003, s.58A, Sched.6A, para.5; SDLT Manual: SDLTM21060.
[11] FA 2003, s.71; SDLT Manual: SDLTM27500.

CHAPTER 5
Leases

5.1 BACKGROUND

This chapter covers the stamp duty land tax (SDLT) consequences of transactions in residential leases.[1] It begins with the creation (grant) of a lease; it continues with variations and assignments; and it ends with the termination of a lease (e.g., surrender). There are traps for the unwary, including the obligation to make further returns in respect of the grant of a lease many years after the grant of the lease (which is assumed by an assignee on an assignment of a lease) and transactions that are taxed as if they were grants of leases. For short-term residential leases, the obligations to notify and pay tax are not enforced by restrictions on registration. Consequently, they are easy to miss and, in the author's experience, frequently are.

For simplicity, the term 'lease' rather than 'tenancy' is used here to describe a term of years absolute even of residential premises, though, of course, there is no difference between the two terms.

5.2 GRANTS OF NEW LEASES

5.2.1 Background

The grant of a lease of residential property is potentially taxed in a different way from transfers of freehold and leasehold estates in residential property. The main difference arises if part of the consideration for the grant of the lease is rent. The reason is that where the consideration given for the transaction includes rent, an additional tax calculation is required using a specific set of tax rates and tax bands to determine the amount of tax chargeable on the rent.

The tax rates and tax bands for freehold transfers and leasehold assignments apply to any premium given (or deemed to be given) by the tenant or a connected person for the grant of the lease depending on factors including whether the demised premises are exclusively residential property and, if so, the number of dwellings the lease is over.

---

[1] For more information see *Sergeant and Sims on Stamp Taxes* (LexisNexis UK), AA5: SDLT–leases.

For more information on tax rates and tax bands, see **1.4.1**.[2]

5.2.2 Licences and tenancies at will

Licences and tenancies at will are exempt interests. Their acquisition does not give rise to a chargeable SDLT transaction. In the author's view, this is for the avoidance of doubt because neither type of interest is a property right enforceable against the world (*in rem*). They are personal rights enforceable against specific persons (*in personam*) only. HM Revenue and Customs (HMRC) uses the criteria established in case law to determine whether the nature of the right or interest granted is a licence or a lease regardless of how the parties refer to it. It places emphasis on the need to give exclusive possession in order for the interest to be a lease. However, the giving of exclusive possession is not always determinative of the issue. See **2.3**.[3]

5.2.3 The charge on rent

The SDLT charge on rent is calculated using tax rates that are applied to 'slices' of the net present value (NPV) of the rent.[4] (It is unlikely that the NPV of the rent under a lease of mixed-use premises or more than five dwellings would engage the top tax rate. It would need to exceed £5 million to do so.) A formula is provided in the legislation to calculate the NPV. It uses a temporal discount rate of 3.5 per cent.

In order to calculate the NPV of the rent it is necessary to know:

- the effective date of the transaction (see **5.2.4**);
- the amount of the rent payable in the first five years of the term of the lease (see **5.2.5**);
- the start date and end date of the lease (see **5.2.6**); and
- whether the grant is linked to another lease, irrespective of whether that other lease is over the same or different premises and whether it was granted at the same time or in the past (see **5.2.7**).

Each of those concepts is discussed in turn below.

An NPV calculator is available at HMRC's website. It is accurate for most types of lease transaction, but does not cover, for example, overlap relief calculations on surrender and regrants, which must be done manually.

The tax rates and tax bands that apply to rent are as follows:

---

[2] Finance Act (FA) 2003 Scheds.5, 17A; *HMRC internal manual – Stamp Duty Land Tax Manual* ('SDLT Manual') (HMRC, 19 March 2016, updated 16 January 2020, available at: **www.gov.uk/hmrc-internal-manuals/stamp-duty-land-tax-manual**): SDLTM10000.
[3] FA 2003, s.48(2)(b), (c)(i); SDLT Manual: SDLTM00320; *Street v. Mountford* [1985] AC 809.
[4] FA 2003, ss.55, 56, Sched.5, para.2; SDLT Manual: SDLTM11005.

Residential rates

Net present value	Tax rate
£0–£125,000	0%
£125,000+	1%

Non-residential (or mixed) rates

Net present value	Tax rate
£0–£150,000	0%
£150,001–£5,000,000	1%
£5,000,000+	2%

Example 5.1

A is granted a three-year lease of a large country house for rent of £10,000 per month. The NPV of the rent is £336,196 and the amount of SDLT payable is £2,111 (£125,000 @ 0%) + (£211,196 @ 1%). A must make an SDLT return and pay the tax within 14 days of the grant of the lease.

5.2.4 The effective date

Where an agreement for lease is entered into, no tax is payable until it is completed or, if earlier, it is substantially performed. The relevant event – completion or substantial performance – is the effective date of the transaction.

Where an agreement for lease is substantially performed, the agreement is taxed as if it were the grant of a lease in the 'SDLT world'. Where the agreement for lease is subsequently completed, the grant of the actual lease is disregarded except that the tax must be recalculated as if there were a notional lease granted on the date of substantial performance for a term that begins on the date of substantial performance and ends at the end of the actual lease and in consideration of the rent payable over that term and any other consideration given for the actual or notional lease. This is slightly different from the treatment of other contracts for a land transaction to be completed by a conveyance under which both the substantial performance of the contract and completion are notifiable transactions.

Where tax is paid on substantial performance and the agreement for lease is not completed for any reason (e.g., due to its rescission) the tax shall be repaid by HMRC, usually by the tenant amending the SDLT return. An SDLT return generally cannot be amended after 12 months of the filing date (14 days after substantial performance). It is uncertain whether tax can be recovered if there is a failure to complete the contract after that point. This is likely to be answered by case law. A tribunal decision in 2018 indicated that the tax can be recovered by making a claim for relief for overpaid tax.[5] However, the author is pessimistic that HMRC would accept that that decision is of general application.

To understand what acts constitute 'substantial performance', see **1.8**.

Example 5.2

A enters into an agreement for lease of a new-build flat. Before completion of the agreement, the seller permits A's contractor to take possession of the flat under licence to carry out the fit-out. A is required to make an initial return and pay SDLT within 14 days of his contractor taking possession. The completion of the agreement for lease does not, in this example, require A to make a further return.

Example 5.3

Take the same facts as in the previous example, but six months after the start of the fit-out works A discovers a material defect in the construction of the flat. As a result, the contract is rescinded. A amends the SDLT return made to reclaim the SDLT paid on substantial performance.

Example 5.4

Take the same facts as in the previous example, but 18 months after the start of the fit-out works A discovers a material defect in the construction of the flat. As a result, the contract is rescinded. It is not clear whether A can amend the SDLT return made to reclaim the SDLT paid on substantial performance even though he is not at fault in failing to amend the return within the one-year period.

5.2.5 The amount of rent payable

'Rent' is not defined in the SDLT legislation. The term takes its ordinary meaning: a periodic payment for the use of land or property. A separate payment to the landlord for insurance or service charge reserved as rent is disregarded as rent for SDLT purposes. However, a single sum payable as rent (whether or not it is expressed to be inclusive of services, insurance or other matters) is all subject to SDLT; it cannot be apportioned by the tenant, but only by the landlord – although the landlord's apportionment is not conclusive and may need to be adjusted if it is not just and reasonable. Sums paid pursuant to an obligation to pay utility bills are not rent. Where a market value applies, the market value of the lease is taxed as if it were a premium. The rent payable under the lease (if any) is *not* increased to a market rate.

---

[5] *Derek and Susan Smallman* v. *Revenue and Customs Comrs* [2018] UKFTT 0680 (TC); FA 2003, Sched.17A, para.12A, Sched.10, paras.6, 34; SDLT Manual: SDLTM17005.

Example 5.5

A is granted a two-year lease of a flat for rent of £6,000 per month 'inclusive of all services and insurance'. The entire £6,000 per month is treated as rent in the NPV calculation.

Example 5.6

A is granted a two-year lease of a flat for rent of £6,000 per month 'of which £800 is a contribution to the cost of services and insurance'. So long as that is a just and reasonable apportionment by the landlord (in other words, the service costs have not been overstated), A may calculate the NPV based on rent of £5,200 per month.

Where the term of the lease exceeds five years, only the rent payable in the first five years is used to calculate the NPV of the rent. The rent taxable from the beginning of year six onwards is treated as the highest amount of rent paid in the first five years of the term.

> **TIP**
>
> If the term of the lease is greater than five years and a rent-free period is given, it would be better to 'spread' the incentive over the first five years of the term of the lease rather than take it immediately. The rent profile of the lease would be 'smoothed' such that the rent that is taken into account for any period after the first five years of the term would be reduced.

Where the amount of rent payable in respect of the first five years of the term of the lease (if applicable) is variable or uncertain, a reasonable estimate of the amount of rent should be used in the NPV calculation. It is not open to apply to defer tax on contingent or uncertain rent. As soon as the amount of rent is known or, if later, at the expiry of the fifth year (the 'relevant date'), the tenant must recalculate the NPV using the actual rent paid in the first five years of the term of the lease. If the recalculation results in the grant becoming notifiable for the first time, an SDLT return (an 'initial return') and, if applicable, payment of SDLT must be made within 14 days of the relevant date. If the recalculation results in additional tax being payable, a new SDLT return (a 'further return') and payment of SDLT must be made within 30 days of the relevant date. If the recalculation results in less tax being payable, the tenant may make a claim for repayment of the amount overpaid. In both cases interest would be payable at HMRC's standard rates for overpaid and underpaid tax.

Where the amount of rent payable in the first five years of the term of the lease becomes certain due to the exercise of a break clause, it is unclear whether the reduced term is taken into account by the tenant when he makes the adjustment. If it is, as the author would argue, this would be an exception to the rule that break clauses are disregarded when determining the term of the lease (see **5.2.6**). It would also be an exception to the rule that no credit is given for the tax paid on the grant of a lease other than in the case of surrender and regrants where the lease terminates early. It is clear that if a break occurs during the first five years of the term, say after three years, the tenant cannot reclaim any rent where the amount of rent payable was fixed, not variable. All things being equal, it is better to acquire a lease for a shorter term with options to renew to avoid tax being wasted if the lease terminates early and to benefit from cashflow.

Rent increases linked to the retail price index (RPI) are disregarded unless the increase is determined by reference to a formula (e.g., RPI plus or minus X per cent) other than a simple cap or collar. However, where the NPV calculation has been made on an estimate of the rent payable in the first five years, any RPI rent increases made in the first five years *are* taken into account when making the adjustment. Where some other index is used (such as the consumer price index (CPI)), the NPV calculation must be done based on an estimate that is corrected when the final index figure is published.

Where the first or only rent review date falls in the final three months of the fifth year of the term of the lease and it is expressed to fall five years after a specific date that falls within the three-month period ending with the term commencement date, the rent review can be ignored.[6]

Example 5.7

On 1 January 2020, A is granted a three-year lease of a London flat. The amount of rent payable in year 1 is £96,000. The amount of rent payable in years 2 and 3 is found by using the RPI figure for the previous December and adding 1% (subject to a cap of 5% and a collar of 3%). A estimates that RPI will be 3% each year; hence, he estimates that the amount of rent payable in year 2 is £99,840 (£96,000 plus 4%) and the amount of rent payable in year 3 is £103,834 (£99,840 plus 4%). This produces an NPV of £279,201 and a tax charge on rent of £1,542. A must make a further return and pay the tax by 15 January 2020. The RPI figures for December 2020 (3.75%) and December 2021 (4%) are published each year on 15 December. Consequently, the amount of rent payable for year 3 becomes known on 15 December 2021. The amount of rent paid in year 2 was £100,560 (£96,000 plus 4.75%) and the amount of rent payable in year 3 is £105,588 (£100,560 plus 5%). This produces an NPV of £281,861 and a tax charge on rent of £1,568. A must make a further return and pay £26 of additional tax by 14 January 2022.

Any payment made for a period before the start of the lease is taxed as a premium. This is contradicted by the rule that treats the first payment of rent as substantial

---

[6] FA 2003, Sched.17A, paras.7(5), 7A, 8; SDLT Manual: SDLTM13155, SDLTM13190.

performance of the agreement for lease. However, that does not displace the instruction to tax such a payment as a premium.[7]

5.2.6 The start date and end date

A fixed-term lease has a term commencement date and a contractual expiry date. However, as case law shows, until a lease is granted no legal estate exists. The incidence of SDLT on a lease is complicated by the fact that the first year of the term when calculating the NPV of the rent cannot be earlier than the date of the lease. However, that date may not be the date from which the term of the lease is calculated.

Question 17 of the SDLT return requires one to enter 'the start date as specified in the lease' – and HMRC's guidance says that if this is earlier than 1 January 1500, we enter the date 1 January 1500. Clearly, this is not the date from which SDLT is calculated. It is merely a date from which a calculation of the length of the term is made. Often a landlord will want all leases to end together, so will grant all leases for a term of, say, 125 years starting on 1 January 2010. Sometimes leases are granted for a term that does not start until a future date. Such 'reversionary' leases are valid so long as the future date is no more than 21 years into the future. One would answer question 17 by inserting that future date.

However, when entering into the HMRC calculator the rents for each of the first five years of the term, then with two exceptions, the first year of the term cannot start earlier than the date of the lease. The exceptions are:

- If a lease is granted today for a term of 10 years starting on the date of the lease, then the term starts today for question 17 purposes, as does the first year of the term for NPV purposes.
- If a lease is granted today for a term of 10 years starting in five years' time, then the legal estate starts today and today is the effective date of the transaction. However, the term starts on the fifth anniversary of today, for both question 17 and NPV purposes.

However, if a lease is granted today for a term of 10 years starting on a term commencement date exactly one year ago, then for question 17 purposes one should put in last year's start date, but the first year of the term for NPV purposes starts today. That necessarily means that the term of the lease for SDLT purposes is just nine years. It also means that if there is a rent review after five years from the 'term commencement date' that review will happen during the first five years of the term (at the start of the fifth year) for SDLT purposes, meaning that any increase on review must be taken into account, not just for the fifth year, but for all succeeding years.

In many cases, of course, where the term commencement date is in the past, the tenant will not take possession or pay rent until the date of the lease. Effectively, the

---

[7] FA 2003, s.44(7)(c)(ii), Sched.17A, para.1A; SDLT Manual: SDLTM13155.

tenant only has a nine-year lease. However, what if the tenant actually went into possession a year ago? One then has to ask on what basis the tenant was allowed in, and whether rent has been paid. If there was an agreement for lease, for example, then it would have been substantially performed (see **5.2.4**).

The tenant may have been given a tenancy at will, or a licence, pending completion. Those are exempt interests, and any 'rent' payable under them will not be subject to SDLT.

In rare cases a tenant may be allowed in on licence paying no rent and having to pay the back rent as a lump sum on completion. Rent, for SDLT purposes, does not include any chargeable consideration for the grant of a lease that is payable in respect of a period *before* the grant of the lease. This lump sum will not, therefore, be taxed as rent and must be taxed as a premium.

Incidentally, when using the HMRC calculator the actual rents payable in respect of each of the first five years need to be entered. If the rent is £100,000 a year, but there is a three-month rent-free period in the first year, then one must enter £75,000. If the term is only two-and-a-half years long, then one must enter £100,000 for the first two years and £50,000 for the third. If the term is five-and-a-half years long, then one must enter £100,000 as the highest rent payable in any consecutive 12-month period in the first five years of the term; since the term is only five-and-a-half years, the calculator will work out that the rent payable in the sixth year of the term is only £50,000.

When determining the term of the lease, only the start date and end date are taken into account. Any break options and options to renew are disregarded. The exercise of an option to renew may have SDLT implications (see **5.7.2**). The exercise of a break option would not unless consideration is given by the landlord or, possibly, the rent was uncertain (see **5.6.2** and **5.2.5**, respectively).[8]

Example 5.8

A is granted a two-year lease of a London flat subject to an option to renew exercisable by the tenant only at the end of the term and a break clause exercisable by either party on giving the other six months' notice in writing. The term of the lease is two years for SDLT purposes. Both types of option are ignored when determining the term of the lease.

5.2.7 'Linked' leases

Where leases of different premises granted concurrently are 'linked', the NPV of each lease is calculated and added together to give a total NPV on which SDLT is calculated. That SDLT charge is then spread between the leases proportionate to their individual NPV. The general meaning of 'linked' transactions is used: see **1.5.4**.

---

[8] FA 2003, Sched.17A, para.2; SDLT Manual: SDLTM14080.

Linked leases may also be granted consecutively over the same premises, when they are called 'successive linked leases'. The context which mostly frequently produces successive linked leases is lease renewals (see **5.7.2**). Here, however, the definition of linkage is altered. Linkage normally needs, as well as a single scheme, etc., the same or connected vendors in each transaction and the same or connected purchasers. Where leases are concerned, however, a tenant who assigns a lease transfers his linkage status to his successor. In other words, successive lease transactions may be linked even though the tenant has changed.

The mischief at which the rule is aimed is artificially reducing the area demised or term of a lease into multiple concurrent or successive leases to benefit from the nil rate band. Accordingly, the effect of the rule is to ensure that the benefit of the nil rate band (£1,500) is enjoyed only once and spread between the 'linked' leases.[9]

Example 5.9

A is granted three leases of separate flats in one block by a developer for, respectively, two years, three years and four years. A is an employer and will make the flats available to its employees. The amount of rent payable under each lease is discounted to reflect the single bargain. The annual rent payable by A under the two-year lease is £48,000; the annual rent payable by A under the three-year lease is £60,000; and the annual rent payable by A under the four-year lease is £72,000. The NPV of each lease is £91,185, £168,098 and £264,461, respectively. The total NPV is £523,744. The amount of SDLT payable on that total is £3,987: (£125,000 @ 0%) + (£398,744 @ 1%). This SDLT is apportioned £694 to the two-year lease (£3,987 x £91,185/£523,744); £1,280 to the three-year lease (£3,987 x £168,098/£523,744); and £2,013 to the four-year lease (£3,987 x £264,461/£523,744).

5.2.8 The charge on premium

'Premium' means any consideration given for the grant of the lease other than rent. Where a market value rule applies (such as on the grant of a lease to a company by a connected person), the market value of the lease is taken to be the premium, if higher than the actual premium given (if any). The amount of rent payable under the lease (if any) is respected. There is no rule that increases the amount of rent to a market rate, if applicable. Obviously, such a rule is not necessary: if the lease is under-rented, it will be valuable.

The tax due on the premium given (if any) for the grant of the lease is calculated in the same way as if the transaction were the transfer of a freehold or leasehold estate, subject to the following exceptions (though they are mostly given for the avoidance of doubt only):

---

[9] FA 2003, s.108, Sched.17A, para.5; SDLT Manual: SDLTM17032.

- The following are disregarded as chargeable consideration (even if they are reserved as rent) and a payment made to release the tenant from any of the following obligations is not regarded as consideration on a surrender of a lease (see **5.6.3**):
  - any undertaking by the tenant to repair, maintain or insure the premises;
  - any undertaking by the tenant to pay any amount for services, repairs, maintenance or insurance or the landlord's management costs;
  - any other obligation undertaken by the tenant that would not affect the amount of rent that a tenant would be prepared to pay in the open market;
  - any guarantee given by the tenant of the payment of rent or the performance of any other obligation of the tenant under the lease;
  - any penal rent payable by the tenant in respect of the breach of any obligation of the tenant under the lease;
  - payment by the tenant of the landlord's costs on a collective enfranchisement transaction (see **Chapter 6**);
  - payment by the tenant of the landlord's reasonable costs on the grant (or the extension) of a lease; and
  - for agricultural tenants only, any obligation to surrender an entitlement to single farm payment to the landlord on termination of the lease.
- Payment of a deposit or the making of a loan is treated as a premium if the repayment of the deposit or loan is contingent on an act or omission by the tenant or on the tenant's death.
- A payment made by the landlord to the tenant is disregarded as consideration – it is a reverse premium.
- Consideration for the grant of the lease that is payable in respect of a period before the date of the lease is taxed as if it were a premium (see **5.2.5**).[10]

5.2.9 Grants requiring an SDLT return

The tenant must make an SDLT return on his acquisition of a new lease for a term of seven years or more where either the premium paid (or market value of the lease, if applicable) is £40,000 or more, or the relevant rent is £1,000 or more.

The tenant must make an SDLT return on his acquisition of a new lease for a term of less than seven years only if tax is payable on the premium and/or rent (or is only not payable because a relief is claimed).[11]

5.2.10 Grants of leases in the 'SDLT world'

The following types of transaction are taxed as if a lease had been granted:

- substantial performance of agreement for lease (see **5.2.4**);
- assignments of relieved leases (see **5.4.2**);

---

[10] FA 2003, s.55, Sched.17A, para.10; SDLT Manual: SDLTM11060.
[11] FA 2003, ss.77, 77A; SDLT Manual: SDLTM12005.

- lease extensions and other variations that take effect as a matter of law as a surrender and regrant (see **5.3** and **5.7.1**).[12]

5.3 LEASE VARIATIONS

Five types of lease variations are treated as SDLT transactions:

- a variation to increase the rent in the first five years of the term – an acquisition by the tenant;
- a variation to reduce the rent – an acquisition by the tenant;
- a variation to increase the term or area demised (or any other variation that takes effect as a matter of law as a surrender and regrant) – an acquisition by both parties;
- a variation to reduce the term – an acquisition by the landlord; and
- a variation to any other term of the lease where the tenant gives consideration (other than an increase in rent) – an acquisition by the tenant.[13]

In each case, the tax is charged on the amount or value of the consideration given, subject to the following exceptions:

- Where a lease is varied to increase the rent payable in the first five years of the term of the lease, the tenant is treated as if he had acquired a new lease in consideration of the additional rent. Rent increases after the fifth year are always ignored irrespective of the extent of the increase. Where the lease makes provision for rent increases in the first five years of the term, they must be estimated in calculating the NPV.
- Where a market value applies (e.g., the purchaser is a connected company), the chargeable consideration is the market value of the variation (e.g., the difference between the open market value of the lease before and after the variation).
- Where the variation is to increase the term or area demised (or any other variation that takes effect as a matter of law as a surrender and regrant), the deemed surrender of the pre-varied lease and the regrant of the post-varied lease are disregarded as chargeable consideration for each other.
- Where the variation is to increase the term or area demised (or any other variation that takes effect as a matter of law as a surrender and regrant), in calculating the NPV of the rent under the post-varied lease, any rent that was 'taken into account' in determining the NPV of the rent under the pre-varied lease is disregarded provided that the premises demised by the post-varied lease are the same or substantially the same as the premises demised by the pre-varied lease. In other words, in calculating the NPV of the lease that is deemed to be granted, a credit is given for the rent that was taxed under the lease

---

[12] FA 2003, s.43(3)(d)(i), Sched.17A, paras.3, 3A, 4, 11, 12A; SDLT Manual: SDLTM17005, SDLTM17085, SDLTM19025.
[13] FA 2003, s.43(3)(d), Sched.17A, paras.9, 15A, 16; SDLT Manual: SDLTM15000, SDLTM15020, SDLTM16005.

that is deemed to be surrendered. However, where the taxed rent is greater than the new rent, the credit cannot produce a negative figure. The rent under the new lease is taken to be nil. Express surrenders and regrants (where the premises are substantially the same) are taxed in the same way. This is referred to as 'overlap relief' and does not need to be claimed in an SDLT return. The return should state the NPV of the lease net of 'overlap relief'. (This is a very brief outline of overlap relief. In some cases, for instance, one cannot use the HMRC calculator; a manual NPV calculation is needed. Seek further advice.)

- Where a lease is varied to reduce the rent in return for the release of a tenant-only break clause or the tenant agreeing not to exercise a break clause, HMRC accepts that no chargeable consideration is given and the lease variation is exempt from charge.

Example 5.10

A is granted a three-year lease of a flat on 1 January 2020 ('the old lease'). Annual rent of £84,000 is payable under the old lease. The NPV of the rent payable under the old lease is calculated and tax is paid. On 1 January 2022, the old lease is surrendered and a new lease is granted for three years. Annual rent of £82,000 is payable under the new lease. The overlap period is from 1 January 2022 until 31 December 2022 (one year). The NPV calculation for the new lease should use rent of £0 for the first year (as the rent under the old lease is more than the rent under the new lease) and rent of £82,000 for the remaining four years of the term of the lease.

Example 5.11

On 1 January 2020, A is granted a five-year lease of a house. Annual rent of £96,000 is payable under the lease. On 1 July 2021, with three-and-a-half years of the lease left to run, A's landlord agrees to reduce the annual rent to a peppercorn in return for A making a payment of £250,000. The variation of the lease is a chargeable SDLT transaction; but it is not linked to the grant of the lease. A must pay tax on the £250,000 and make a return within 14 days.

5.3.1 Variations requiring an SDLT return

Unless the variation takes effect as the grant of a new lease, the relevant party that is treated as the purchaser does not need to make an SDLT return unless tax is payable or would be payable but for a relief.

Where the variation takes effect as the grant of a new lease for a term of seven years or more, the tenant must make an SDLT return where either the premium paid (or market value of the lease, if applicable) is £40,000 or more, or the relevant rent is £1,000 or more. For the market value rules, see **1.5.2**.

Where the variation takes effect as the grant of a new lease for a term of less than seven years, the tenant must make an SDLT return only if tax is payable on the premium and/or rent or would be payable but for a relief.

The landlord must make an SDLT return on the deemed surrender where the pre-varied lease was originally granted for a term of seven years or more and the chargeable consideration for the surrender is £40,000 or more.

The landlord must make an SDLT return on the deemed surrender where the pre-varied lease was originally granted for a term of less than seven years and tax is payable or would be payable but for a relief.

5.4 LEASE ASSIGNMENTS

5.4.1 General

The tax chargeable on the assignment of a leasehold estate is calculated in the same way as the transfer of a freehold estate (as to which, see **Chapter 3**), subject to two exceptions:

- As on the grant of a lease, the payment of a deposit or the making of a loan is treated as a premium if the repayment of the deposit or loan is contingent on an act or omission by the tenant or on the tenant's death.
- In certain circumstances, an assignment of a lease is taxed as if it were the grant of a lease in the 'SDLT world' (see **5.4.2**).[14]

5.4.2 Assignments of relieved leases

Where the assignment is the *first* assignment of a lease that does not qualify for certain SDLT reliefs and the grant of the lease was relieved by any of the same reliefs, the assignment is taxed as if it were the grant of a lease for a term equal to the unexpired term of the actual lease and on the same terms (including rent) as the actual lease. No time limit is set by the legislation or HMRC guidance. The first assignment of the lease may happen at any time after the grant of the lease. The special charging rule does not expire.

So far as material to residential conveyancing transactions, the SDLT reliefs in questions are:

- sale and leaseback relief;
- group relief, reconstruction or acquisition relief;
- transfers involving public bodies; and
- charities relief.

---

[14] FA 2003, Sched.17A, paras.11, 12, 17; SDLT Manual: SDLTM17085, SDLTM12050; *Swayne* v. *IRC* [1899] 1 QB 335.

The consequence of the assignment being taxed as if it were the grant of a lease is that the assignee is taxed on the NPV of the rent payable over the unexpired term of the assigned lease. In most residential cases the assigned lease will be for a peppercorn (or a nominal ground rent), so the re-characterisation of the assignment as the grant of a lease in the 'SDLT world' will have no (or no material) effect.

5.4.3 Assumption of assignor's obligations

As well as incurring an obligation to make an SDLT return and pay the tax on his acquisition of the assigned lease, the assignee would assume the assignor's obligation (if any) to make a further return in respect of the original grant of the lease. He would also take on whatever self-assessment the assignor had made. Consequently, provision should be made in the sale contract requiring the assignor to confirm what self-assessment has been made and, if applicable, to indemnify the assignee for any tax in respect of the grant that might become payable.

This might apply where:

- the premium for the grant was contingent or uncertain (see **1.5.1**);
- another lease is granted that is linked to the assigned lease (see **5.2.7**);
- the lease continues after the end date (see **5.7**);
- the amount of rent payable was uncertain (see **5.2.5**).

The assumption by the assignee of any tenant obligations under the lease, including the obligation to pay rent, is not treated as chargeable consideration. This principle is well established under case law and has been enshrined in the SDLT code for the avoidance of any doubt.

Example 5.12

A is granted a three-year lease of a London flat for no premium and uncertain rent. A pays SDLT based on an estimate of the rent. After one year, A assigns the lease to B for no premium. As soon as the total amount of rent becomes ascertainable, B must recalculate the NPV of the lease and pay tax if the amount paid by A is less than the amount due.

TIP

On an assignment of a lease, the possibility of the assignee being liable to pay additional tax in respect of the grant of the lease should be checked as part of the legal due diligence and, if necessary, provision should be made in the sale contract to cover the risk.

5.5 ASSIGNMENT OF AGREEMENT FOR LEASE

The assignment of an agreement for lease is treated like a novation: the assignee steps into the assignor's shoes. It is not a separate transaction. However, when the agreement is completed, the consideration given by the assignee for the lease is taken to include any consideration given by him for the assignment of the agreement. The treatment is far simpler than the equivalent regime for assignments of other types of contract for a land transaction: see **Chapter 7**. No relief needs to be claimed by the assignor. If you like, relief is embedded in the SDLT treatment. Neither the act of entering into the agreement for lease nor the act of assigning it is an SDLT transaction for the assignor. The assignor would only be liable to SDLT if he substantially performs the agreement (see **1.8**). There could be different results if rather than assigning (or novating) the agreement for lease, instead the tenant assigns it immediately or directs the landlord to grant it to another person.

Perhaps the most common 'sub-sale' that a residential conveyancer undertakes is the sub-sale of a new flat, which is usually done by assigning the original purchase contract. Flats are invariably leasehold, so an agreement to buy a new flat is an agreement for lease and its assignment is not a sub-sale for SDLT purposes. The regime for 'pre-completion transactions' in Finance Act 2003, Sched.2A explicitly states that it does not apply to the assignment of agreements for lease.[15]

Example 5.13

A buys a flat off-plan for £1 million. He pays a reservation fee and, on entering into an agreement for lease, the remainder of a 10% deposit. A does not substantially perform the agreement. Before completion, A assigns the benefit of the agreement to B for £200,000. On completion, B pays the seller the outstanding £900,000 and is granted the lease. B must pay SDLT on the total of the £900,000 paid to the seller for the grant and the £200,000 paid to A for the assignment. No SDLT is payable by A. A does not need to claim a relief or make an SDLT return to secure this treatment.

WARNING

If a tenant is to 'sub-sell' a lease on completion rather than merely assign his rights under an uncompleted agreement for lease, taking specialist advice may be appropriate to confirm the absence of any SDLT liability (and filing obligations) for the original tenant.

---

[15] FA 2003, Sched.17A, para.12B.

LEASES

5.6 TERMINATION OF LEASES

A lease may terminate by effluxion of time, operation of law, or an act of one or both of the parties. More specifically, a lease may end by:

- forfeiture;
- notice to quit;
- surrender (including a variation that takes effect as a matter of law as a surrender and regrant);
- assignment to the landlord (assuming a declaration of non-merger is not given by the landlord); or
- expiry.

Each is examined in turn below.

5.6.1 Forfeiture

The termination of the lease by forfeiture would not usually be a chargeable or notifiable transaction, as no chargeable consideration would be given for the acquisition.

Example 5.14

A granted a lease of a house to B, a third party. B has failed to pay rent for two consecutive months. A exercises his right to forfeit and re-enters the property after following the relevant statutory procedure. The termination of the lease is not chargeable to SDLT (or notifiable) as no chargeable consideration is given by A.

5.6.2 Notice to quit

A notice to quit may be given, usually, by landlord or tenant. Although it is a land transaction (the landlord's interest is no longer subject to the lease) the landlord does not need to make an SDLT return unless tax is payable or would be payable but for a relief. It would be rare indeed for there to be actual chargeable consideration on a notice to quit. There would be deemed chargeable consideration if a market value applies (such as where the landlord is a company connected to the tenant) – see **1.5.2**.

Example 5.15

A is in occupation of a house under an assured shorthold tenancy. A term of the tenancy gives A the right (but not the obligation) to 'break' the lease by giving the landlord one month's notice. The break clause cannot be exercised in the first six months of the term of the lease. A exercises the break clause. A's landlord makes an acquisition of a chargeable interest but he has not given any consideration for the transaction. Consequently, the transaction is an exempt transaction and is not notifiable.

5.6.3 Surrender

A surrender is an act of both parties to end a lease. It is an SDLT transaction. The chargeable consideration is anything given in money or money's worth by the landlord (not the tenant) as consideration for the surrender of the lease unless a market value applies, in which case the chargeable consideration is the value of the tenant's interest in the lease. Where a lease is granted in return for the surrender of an existing lease between the same parties, the grant is disregarded as chargeable consideration for the surrender (and the surrender is disregarded as chargeable consideration for the new lease) and there is no exchange of land transactions.[16] A payment made to release the tenant from certain obligations is not chargeable consideration (see **5.2.8**).

A surrender of a lease may be express or implied due to a variation of the lease taking effect as the grant of a new lease. The SDLT treatment of both is the same. For the special rules that apply to surrender and regrant transactions, see **5.3**.

The landlord must make an SDLT return on the tenant's surrender of the lease where the lease was originally granted for seven or more years and the chargeable consideration is £40,000 or more.

The landlord must make an SDLT return on the tenant's surrender of a lease where the lease was originally granted for less than seven years where the chargeable consideration is taxed at more than zero per cent.

Where there is a surrender and regrant of the same or substantially the same premises, including where the lease is terminated in pursuance of a court order, rent that was taken into account when calculating the NPV of the old lease is discounted (but not below nil) from the rent taken into account when calculating the NPV of the new lease during the period that the terms of the leases overlap. This is referred to as 'overlap relief' and does not need to be claimed in an SDLT return (see **5.3**).

Example 5.16

A is in occupation of a flat under a three-year lease. A's landlord wishes to re-occupy the property. He makes a payment to A in return for A surrendering the lease. The surrender is an SDLT transaction, as A's landlord has made an acquisition of a chargeable interest. As the initial term of the lease was less than seven years, tax would only be due if the amount paid by A's landlord exceeded the nil rate threshold (£125,000). (The higher rates are not relevant as a lease for seven years or less is not a major interest for the purposes of the higher rates.)

---

[16] FA 2003, Sched.17A, para.16.

5.6.4 Merger

The assignment of a lease to the landlord would be chargeable in the same way as any transfer of a freehold or leasehold estate. For lease assignments generally, see **5.4**. The charge would apply to the value or amount of the consideration given (if any) by the landlord or, if a market value rule applies, to the market value of the assigned lease. The termination of the lease by operation of law consequential on the assignment (assuming a declaration of non-merger is not given by the landlord) would not be a chargeable or notifiable transaction as no chargeable consideration would be given for the acquisition. For the market value rules, see **1.5.2**.

The landlord must make an SDLT return on the tenant's assignment of the lease where the lease was originally granted for seven years or more and the chargeable consideration is £40,000 or more.

The landlord must make an SDLT return on the tenant's assignment of the lease where the lease was originally granted for less than seven years where the chargeable consideration is taxed at more than zero per cent.

Example 5.17

On 1 January 2020, A granted a two-year lease of a flat to B. On 31 December 2020, with one year of the term left to run, B agrees to assign the lease to A in return for cash. A does not make a declaration of non-merger, hence the lease is extinguished on the assignment of the lease. A's acquisition of the lease is potentially a chargeable and notifiable SDLT transaction to the extent that the amount paid, or, if a market value rule applies, the market value of the lease if greater, is more than £125,000 (the threshold for paying tax).

5.6.5 Expiry

It is uncertain whether or not the expiry of a lease is an SDLT transaction – it is no defence that the transaction occurs by operation of law rather than intervention by the parties – but as the landlord would not give any consideration for the acquisition and, if a market value rule applies, the lease would not be valuable (it would not exist), the transaction would be exempt from charge and not notifiable. Consequently, the issue has no practical importance. The landlord would not need to make an SDLT return or claim any relief to secure this treatment.[17]

Example 5.18

On 1 January 2020, A granted a two-year lease of a flat to B, a third party. On 1 January 2022, the end of the term is reached and the lease expires. A's reversionary interest in the property is benefited by ceasing to be subject to the lease, so A has made an acquisition of a chargeable interest for the purposes of SDLT. But A's acquisition is exempt and not notifiable

---

[17] FA 2003, ss.43(3), 77, 77A; SDLT Manual: SDLTM11070.

(hence no tax is payable and no return needs to be made) because A has not given any consideration for the transaction.

5.7 CONTINUATION OF LEASES

A lease may continue by:

- extension;
- renewal;
- holding over; or
- grant of a reversionary lease.

The SDLT treatment of each varies and is described in turn below.

5.7.1 Lease extensions

The SDLT treatment of a variation of the lease to extend the term of the lease follows its legal treatment as a surrender and regrant (see **5.3**).[18]

Example 5.19

A occupies a house under a two-year lease. Within three months left to run, A agrees with the landlord to vary the lease to extend the term by a further two years. The original lease is treated as surrendered with effect from the date of the lease variation and a new lease for a two-year term is taken to have been granted with effect from the date of the lease variation. The rent that falls in the three-month overlap period that was taken into account when calculating the NPV of the old lease is deducted from the rent that is taken into account when calculating the NPV of the new lease.

5.7.2 Lease renewals

If the renewal of the lease is pursuant to a term of the lease (e.g., an option to renew), HMRC would argue that the new lease and old lease are part of a single scheme and, if the landlord remains the same (or a connected person), they are successive linked leases (see **5.2.7**). In contrast, if the lease contains no option to renew and the renewal is pursuant to fresh negotiations, HMRC should be satisfied that the leases are not successive linked leases. The author doubts that HMRC's view is correct. The purpose of the 'linked' transaction rule is to counter arrangements to avoid SDLT by artificially entering into a series of successive short leases rather than a single lease for a term equal to the aggregate of the terms of the short leases. That mischief is patently absent where, for example, the tenant (reasonably) does not wish to commit to a longer term and values flexibility.

---

[18] FA 2003, s.43(3)(d), Sched.17A, paras.9, 16; SDLT Manual: SDLTM14080.

Where the renewal is 'linked' to an earlier lease the tax is calculated as if the series of leases were one lease granted at the time the first lease in the series was granted, for a term equal to the total of the terms of all the leases in the series, and in consideration of the rent payable under all the leases in the series. In other words, where, for example, there is an assured shorthold tenancy for a one-year term that contains an option to renew for a further year, if the option is exercised the NPV is recalculated as if the term of the original lease was two years (and so on). It is easy to miss this obligation, especially because the lease is not registrable.

Where the renewal causes the grant of the lease to be notifiable, an initial return is due within 14 days of the end of the original term. Where the renewal causes additional tax to be payable in respect of the grant of the lease, a further return is due within 30 days of the end of the original term. This modifies the treatment of successive linked leases.[19]

Example 5.20

On 1 January 2020, A is granted a one-year lease of a flat for an annual rent of £60,000. It contains an option to renew. The grant of the lease is a chargeable but not a notifiable SDLT transaction. The NPV of the rent under the lease (£60,000) is under the nil rate threshold (£125,000). A renews the lease twice. He fails to realise that the renewals required him to recalculate the NPV of the rent under the lease. Fortunately, there were no consequences of the first renewal. The NPV of the rent under the lease (now for a term of two years) was still under the nil rate threshold (£113,981). However, the second renewal does have an SDLT consequence. The NPV of the rent under the lease (now for a term of three years) is more than the nil rate threshold (£168,098); hence, an SDLT return is due and payment of £430 is required (£125,000 @ 0%) + (£43,000 @ 1%). Interest and penalties would be imposed for late payment and late filing respectively if the tax payment and return are not made within 30 days of the end of the first extension.

5.7.3 Holding over

Where a tenant remains in occupation of a residential property after the term of the lease has expired and he continues to pay rent, he may be treated as occupying under a statutory periodic tenancy. This means that for SDLT purposes, the term of the original lease is taken to have 'grown' by one year (unless it was granted before 1 December 2003) irrespective of anything that might mean that the lease may be extended or determined sooner. This follows the same tax treatment for lease renewals (see **5.7.2**). Where a new lease is granted within one year of the expiry of the original lease (or of any one-year extension), the new lease is treated as if it had been granted on the day after the expiry of the original lease (or of the previous one-year's extension). In other cases, making an SDLT return and paying the tax or

---

[19] FA 2003, Sched.17A, para.3; SDLT Manual: SDLTM17035.

additional tax (calculated in accordance with the rates in force at the date of the original grant) must be made within 14 days after the *end* of the period of extension.[20]

5.7.4 Reversionary leases

A 'reversionary lease' is a lease that begins to run after the date of grant, usually at the expiry of an existing lease. The effective date of the transaction is the date of grant, not the term commencement date. The grant is taxed as a new (unlinked) lease using the tax rates and tax bands applicable at the date of grant. However, the NPV is calculated from the future term commencement date.

Example 5.21

A is in occupation of a residential property under a lease that ends on 30 June 2020. On 1 January 2020, he is granted a reversionary lease the term of which begins on 1 July 2020. The effective date of the grant is 1 January 2020. A must make an SDLT return and pay tax (if necessary) by 15 January 2020 (within 14 days of the effective date). The NPV calculation uses the rent payable from 1 July 2020.

In the author's view, where an agreement for a reversionary lease is entered into but its completion is deferred, the tenant's occupation of the demised premises under the existing lease does not mean that the tenant substantially performs the agreement. This is because the tenant has not 'taken possession' under the agreement. A First-tier Tribunal decision casts doubt on that opinion.[21] However, without any reasoning given in the decision for the finding that the purchaser had substantially performed the agreement, it is reasonable to infer that the decision is incorrect.

Example 5.22

As in the previous example, A is in occupation of a residential property under a lease that ends on 30 June 2020. On 1 January 2020, he enters into an agreement for a reversionary lease the term of which begins on 1 July 2020. Completion of the agreement is deferred until 1 July 2020. A must make an SDLT return and pay tax (if necessary) by 15 July 2020 (within 14 days of the effective date). The NPV calculation uses the rent payable from 1 July 2020.

5.8 SPECIAL CHARGING RULES AND RELIEFS

Certain other reliefs and special charging provisions may apply to transactions involving residential leases:

---

[20] FA 2003, Sched.17A, paras.3, 3A, 5; SDLT Manual: SDLTM17035, SDLTM14060.
[21] *Derek and Susan Smallman v. Revenue and Customs Comrs* [2018] UKFTT 0680 (TC).

- first-time buyer relief (see **4.2**);
- multiple dwellings relief (see **4.3**);
- sale and leaseback (see **5.10**);
- collective enfranchisement (see **Chapter 6**);
- shared ownership transactions (see **10.2** and **10.3**);
- alternative property finance (see **Chapter 11**); and
- transfers between partners and partnerships (see **16.4** and **16.5**).

With the exception of first-time buyer relief, multiple dwellings relief and shared ownership transactions where a claim or an election must be made in an SDLT return or an amendment to an SDLT return, the special charging rules and exemptions listed above are automatic and do not need to be claimed by the tenant. Nevertheless, this does not mean that such transactions are not notifiable – they are. In the majority of cases, HMRC provides relief codes and the author would encourage their use in the SDLT return to avoid confusion.

5.9 LEASE TO NOMINEE

Where a nominee or bare trustee enters into an SDLT transaction, the person for whom they act (i.e., the principal or beneficiary) is usually treated as the vendor or purchaser. The tax 'looks through' the nominee arrangement or trust. An exception applies where the transaction is the grant of a lease by or to a nominee or bare trustee. The nominee or bare trustee is treated as the person making the acquisition or disposal of the *whole* interest (legal and beneficial). For grants of leases *to* a nominee or bare trustee, this affects the liable person. It may also affect the availability of relief (e.g., sale and leaseback relief) if the relief is sensitive to which person makes the acquisition or disposal. HMRC appears to be sympathetic to the potentially disruptive effect the exception, read literally, can cause to ordinary transactions. However, the reader should not assume that this is the case. Requesting pre-transaction clearance is recommended if this applies to the facts.[22]

Example 5.23

A uses an offshore nominee company to purchase a new lease of a residential property. The decision is driven by his desire not to be shown on the land register as the owner of the property. The company, rather than A, is treated as the purchaser so far as SDLT is concerned and has the obligation to make an SDLT return and pay the tax. This is even though A is absolutely entitled to the property as against the company. However, the rule does not apply for the purposes of the higher rates, which are determined by reference to A's status as they would if the company were acting as nominee in the purchase of a freehold or existing lease.

---

[22] FA 2003, Sched.16, para.3(3), Sched.4ZA, paras.10, 11.

5.10 SALE AND LEASEBACK RELIEF

The leaseback on a lease and leaseback or sale and leaseback transaction is exempt from SDLT provided that:

- the two legs of the transaction are between the same parties;
- nothing else is given by the purchaser of the interest sold other than cash or debt;
- the sale is not a 'pre-completion transaction' (see **Chapter 7**); and
- the parties are not members of the same SDLT group (see **18.2**).

The relief does not need to be claimed in an SDLT return, but it is recommended that 'other' relief is claimed by the tenant by entering code 28 at question 9 ('are you claiming relief?') of the SDLT return.[23]

---

[23] FA 2003, s.57A; SDLT Manual: SDLTM16040.

CHAPTER 6
Collective enfranchisement

6.1 BACKGROUND

Collective enfranchisement is the name given to the statutory process under which tenants act together to exercise a statutory right to purchase the freehold estate of the building in which their premises are situated. It is a complex area legally. Practitioners specialise in the subject. It is regrettable, then, that the degree of complexity is made worse by stamp duty land tax (SDLT). The subject throws up many of the concepts that make SDLT on residential property transactions a difficult area. The practical impact on the sector is, the author suspects cynically, lessened by wide-scale inadvertent non-compliance. Of course, this is not satisfactory and the author has invited HM Revenue and Customs (HMRC) and HM Treasury to review the SDLT rules on collective enfranchisement transactions.

A partial SDLT 'relief' ('collective enfranchisement relief') is given for collective enfranchisement purchases made under Landlord and Tenant Act 1987, Part 1 (right of first refusal) or Leasehold Reform, Housing and Urban Development Act 1993, Part 1, Chapter 1 (right to collective enfranchisement) on or after 22 April 2009. It 'switches off' the SDLT 'linked' transaction rule (see **1.5.4**) meaning that the tax payable on the transaction is calculated on the average price attributable to the flats owned by the participating tenants before it is multiplied by the number of flats owned by the participating tenants. It is similar in design to the partial SDLT relief for purchases of multiple dwellings (see **4.3**). It means that the amount of the tax suffered by the participating tenants is more in line with the amount of tax that they would have suffered if they had purchased their share of the freehold estate individually. Collective enfranchisement relief is not a true relief in the sense that it must be claimed. Nevertheless, this does not mean that collective enfranchisement transactions are not notifiable – they are. HMRC provides relief code 25 (collective enfranchisement by leaseholders) and the author would encourage its use in the SDLT return to avoid confusion.

There is one condition. Where one of the participating tenants is a company, corporate partnership or collective investment scheme, the average price per qualifying flat cannot exceed £500,000. If it does, a flat 15 per cent rate (the 'super rate': see **3.4**) of SDLT would apply to the whole of the price unless 'relief' from the super rate is available.

Although the purchased freehold estate would be in more than one dwelling, multiple dwellings relief would generally not be available to collective enfranchisement transactions. This is because multiple dwellings relief is disapplied to the extent that the purchased interest is subject to a lease granted for an *initial* term of more than 21 years. In practice, as collective enfranchisement relief and multiple dwellings relief are substantially similar, the restriction on the availability of multiple dwellings relief (a restriction that will almost always apply to a collective enfranchisement transaction, but will not necessarily apply to a purchase following the exercise of a right of first refusal) is likely only to hurt purchases made outside the 1987 Act or 1993 Act.

With one exception (below), the rules to determine the amount of tax payable on a collective enfranchisement transaction work in a hard-edged way. The transaction as a whole is taxed in accordance with the non-residential rates, the residential standard rates or, exceptionally, the residential higher rates. There is no provision for the price to be apportioned. This is because the transaction is the joint purchase of an interest in land. It means, for example, that if the higher rates are engaged due to the participation of a corporate tenant and the remaining length of a flat-lease, the *whole* transaction is taxed in accordance with the higher rates, not the proportion of the price attributable to the corporate tenant. This may put pressure on the corporate tenant to exclude itself from the process to prevent its participation 'infecting' the transaction for the other participating tenants. In many cases that may not be possible.

The exception is the residential super rate. For transactions under the Act (see below) where the average price per qualifying dwelling is £500,000 or less and for transactions outside the Act, the super rate applies *to the extent that* the proportion of the purchase price attributable to any of the flats within the building (viewed individually) is worth more than £500,000.

It is worth stating upfront that the harshness and complexity of the rules apply to collective enfranchisement transactions especially where:

- a participating tenant is a company; or
- a flat-lease owned by any tenant (not necessarily a participating or qualifying tenant) has 21 years or less to run.

If either of those two features is present, particular caution should be taken.

The questions that a residential property lawyer must answer to calculate the correct amount of SDLT payable on a collective enfranchisement transaction and to establish who bears the obligation to make the SDLT return and pay the tax include:

- Is the purchase made under the Act or outside the Act?
- Who is the purchaser – the appointee or participating tenants?
- Is the purchaser, or are any of the purchasers, a company, partnership with one or more corporate partners or collective investment scheme?
- Is the average price per qualifying flat more than £500,000?
- What proportion of the purchase price is attributable to each flat?

- Do any of the purchasing/participating tenants (or a tenant's 'living together' spouse or civil partner, or the child of either unless aged 18 or over, or a property investment partnership of which a tenant, or a tenant's spouse or civil partner, is a member) own a 'major interest' in another dwelling anywhere in the world worth £40,000 or more?
- What is the unexpired term of the leases held by the purchasing/participating tenants?
- What was the initial term of the leases held by the purchasing tenants?
- Is the purchased freehold estate in six or more dwellings?
- Is the purchased freehold estate mixed-use?

This chapter explains the relevance of all those questions. It begins, however, with a brief summary of the 1987 Act and 1993 Act so far as relevant to the context.

References to 'under the Act' are to the purchase of the freehold estate made collectively in exercise of rights under the 1987 Act or the 1993 Act.

References to 'outside the Act' are to the purchase of the freehold estate made collectively otherwise than in exercise of rights under the 1987 Act or the 1993 Act.

References to 'participating tenants' are to the qualifying tenants that collectively participate in the purchase under the Act.

References to 'qualifying flats' are to the flats held by the participating tenants.

References to 'purchasing tenants' are to the tenants that collectively purchase the freehold estate outside the Act.

References to 'company (etc.)' are to company, partnership with one or more corporate partners or collective investment scheme.

References to 'freehold estate' are to the reversionary interest held by the landlord of the tenants, either the freehold estate in the building or the superior leasehold estate in the building.

For purchases made under the Act, it is assumed that the company making the purchase will acquire and hold the freehold estate on bare trust for the participating tenants.

A summary of the four potential alternative sets of tax rates and tax bands, and the two alternative reliefs can be found at the end of this chapter (see **6.12**). It is probably tempting for the reader to begin at that section. The author's recommendation is not to. The purpose of the summary is to draw together the various concepts discussed in the main body of this chapter. Its value, therefore, derives from the reader already being familiar with those concepts before reaching it.

For more information on tax rates and tax bands, see **1.4.1**.[1]

---

[1] For more information see *Sergeant and Sims on Stamp Taxes* (LexisNexis UK), SDLT AA9.3: Collective enfranchisement by leaseholders (relief from aggregation).

6.2 LANDLORD AND TENANT ACT 1987

The Landlord and Tenant Act 1987 gives tenants of certain premises the right of first refusal where the landlord intends to dispose of his interest in the premises. The Act applies to premises consisting of the whole or part of a building which contains two or more flats held by 'qualifying tenants' provided that more than half of the flats in the building are held by qualifying tenants. The offer to purchase made by the landlord to the qualifying tenants in accordance with their right must be accepted by a majority of the qualifying tenants. If the landlord's offer is accepted, the landlord cannot dispose of the interest to anyone other than the tenants' nominee (usually a company) during a specified period.

A new landlord who acquires a reversionary interest in flats from a vendor who is in breach of the provisions of the 1987 Act can be required to supply details of the transaction to the qualifying tenants' nominee. The qualifying tenants can then require him to dispose of his interest to their nominee on the same terms as he acquired the interest. Tenants are 'qualifying tenants' unless their tenancy is excluded for reasons including it is a protected shorthold tenancy or an assured tenancy, or the tenant owns two other flats in the same building.

6.3 LEASEHOLD REFORM, HOUSING AND URBAN DEVELOPMENT ACT 1993

The Leasehold Reform, Housing and Urban Development Act 1993 gives rights to tenants of a block of flats collectively to buy the freehold estate of the block (collective enfranchisement) and/or gives rights to the tenants individually to buy an extended lease of their flat (purchase of extended lease).

6.3.1 Collective enfranchisement

The qualifying tenants who exercise their right (participating tenants) must use a nominee company to purchase the freehold estate. The nominee company would hold the freehold estate on bare trust for the participating tenants so far as it is in the flats and hold the estate absolutely so far as it is in the common parts of the building. One-half or more of the qualifying tenants must participate in order for the landlord to be compelled to sell the freehold estate. To qualify, a tenant must be a tenant of a lease granted for an initial term of more than 21 years. Tenants who own three or more flats are excluded. Joint tenants are treated as one tenant.

The price payable to the landlord is the total of:

- the market value of the freehold estate;
- where the unexpired term of the leases held by participating tenants is 80 years or less, one-half of the 'marriage value' (i.e., the increase in the total value of the freehold and leasehold estates following collective enfranchisement);
- compensation for any loss suffered as a result of enfranchisement; and
- the landlord's reasonable costs.

COLLECTIVE ENFRANCHISEMENT

Participating tenants may fund part of the purchase price with the assistance of a third party, a 'white knight investor'. In return, the white knight investor usually receives a 999-year lease of the premises owned by the non-participating tenants. The white knight investor – which might be an individual or a company and is usually a company – would recover its investment by paying an amount that is usually less than the market value of the 999-year lease(s) it acquires (leaving the participating tenants to make up the balance), receiving the ground rents from the non-participating tenants and receiving a premium from the non-participating tenants if/when the tenants exercise their statutory right to extend their leases (see **6.3.2**). The white knight investor would also generally receive shares in the nominee company that owns the freehold estate, but the value for the investor is in the 999-year lease(s) it acquires. In practice, a white knight investor is often used where the unexpired term of the leases held by the qualifying tenants is short, meaning that the tenants cannot afford to participate in the acquisition.

Frequently, after the participating tenants have exercised their right to enfranchise they would individually exercise their right to acquire an extended lease (e.g., a 999-year lease) possibly in return for paying a premium to the nominee company. Where a premium is paid, the amount of the premium would usually depend (as explained at **6.3.2**) on factors including the unexpired term of the tenant's existing lease. The shorter the expired term, the greater the premium to extend the lease. A bear-trap exists where no premium is paid and one of the participating tenants or the white knight investor is a company: see **6.7**. As a consequence of extending the lease, the value of the freehold estate would be reduced proportionately.

6.3.2 Purchase of extended lease

Qualifying tenants also have the right to be granted a new lease to expire 90 years after expiry of the existing lease. This is not a collective right, but one exercisable by tenants individually. The consideration given for the new lease, which is to take effect immediately in substitution for the existing lease, must be a premium but no rent. The right does not prevent the tenant from later exercising their right to collective enfranchisement (or vice versa). A qualifying tenant is a tenant of a lease granted for an initial term of more than 21 years and who has held the lease for at least the previous two years. Tenants who own three or more flats in the building the subject-matter of the transaction are excluded.

The premium payable to the landlord is the total of:

- the diminution in the value of the landlord's interest;
- where the unexpired term of the tenant's existing lease does not exceed 80 years, 50 per cent of the marriage value (i.e., the increase in the total value of the landlord's interest and leasehold interest following collective enfranchisement); and
- compensation.

This chapter does not cover the right of a tenant to purchase an extended lease in more detail. The grant of the new lease might take effect as a surrender and regrant (see **5.6.3**); or, where it does not, the existing lease is usually terminated by operation of law when the new lease is granted.

However, if a tenant does exercise the right, do consider whether the premium paid for the extension (if it amounts to £40,000 or more) is subject to the residential higher rates.

If at the end of the day that the tenant purchases the extended lease (replacing the previous lease) the tenant (etc.) (see 'purchasers (etc.)' in **3.3.2**) has no major interest worth £40,000 in any other dwelling anywhere in the world, then the transaction will not be a higher-rates transaction and will be taxed at the residential standard rates.

If the tenant (etc.) does own a major interest in another dwelling, but:

- the tenant is extending the lease of the tenant's only or main residence (where the tenant has lived throughout the previous three years);
- the lease has more than 21 years left to run;
- the tenant is either the sole owner or owns at least a 25 per cent interest in the lease as a joint tenant or a tenant in common; and
- the purchase completes on or after 22 November 2017,

then the purchase will be a standard-rates transaction (see **3.3.10.2**).

Where the tenant purchases a replacement main residence together with an assignment of the previous tenant's right to extend the lease, the previous paragraph cannot apply as the tenant has not lived in the dwelling throughout the previous three years.

If the landlord can be persuaded to grant the extended lease subject to, and with the benefit of, the existing lease (in other words not to use the statutory scheme, which involves the surrender of the existing lease, but to grant an overriding lease that makes the tenant his own landlord in relation to the existing lease), then the tenant will have acquired a lease reversionary on a lease with an unexpired term of more than 21 years (in almost all cases) which means the acquisition fails one of the conditions for the residential higher rates to apply (see the third bullet point under **3.3.2.1**). The tenant can then merge the existing lease in the new extended lease.

6.4 COLLECTIVE ENFRANCHISEMENT RELIEF BETWEEN 2003 AND 2009

The provision that affords the SDLT relief for collective enfranchisement transactions, Finance Act 2003, s.74, originally only applied to purchases made by right to enfranchise (RTE) companies (as defined in Leasehold Reform, Housing and Urban Development Act 1993, s.4A). As the provisions relating to RTE companies were not brought into force, the relief could not be enjoyed. Section 74 was amended by the Finance Act 2009 to resolve the problem. The reference to RTE companies was removed, meaning that the relief can now be enjoyed by any nominee purchaser.[2]

6.5 COLLECTIVE ENFRANCHISEMENT RELIEF AFTER 2009

Collective enfranchisement relief only applies to collective enfranchisement purchases made under the Act. There is only one condition that must be met in order for the participating tenants to access the relief and it only applies if one or more of the participating tenants is a company (etc.): the average price per qualifying flat must not be more than £500,000.

The relief works by modifying the method of calculating the tax. Rather than being calculated on the purchase price, instead the tax is calculated by reference to the average price per qualifying flat. This is achieved by taking the purchase price and dividing it by the number of qualifying flats, then calculating the tax on that average price before multiplying the result by the number of qualifying flats. Where some of the qualifying tenants do not participate or reach a separate agreement with the nominee outside the Act, their flats are disregarded for the purpose of calculating the amount of SDLT chargeable for those that do participate. There is no minimum amount of tax payable where the relief applies. Note that the relief is not a true relief in the sense that it does not need to be claimed in an SDLT return or an amendment to an SDLT return and there is no provision for its withdrawal. Nevertheless, this does not mean that such transactions are not notifiable – they are. HMRC provides relief code 25 (collective enfranchisement by leaseholders) and the author would encourage its use in the SDLT return to avoid confusion. Importantly, the relief does not modify the other SDLT rules that determine which set of tax rates or tax bands apply to the transaction. This is apt to confuse, as we shall see.[3]

Example 6.1

A building is composed of 50 flats. Forty of the qualifying tenants choose to purchase the freehold estate of the building collectively in exercise of their rights under the 1993 Act. The participating tenants set up a company and hold shares in the company in specified proportions. The company acts as nominee for the participating tenants, all of whom are individuals. The company purchases the freehold estate in the building in return for paying £10 million. The average price per qualifying flat is £250,000 (£10 million / 40). The amount of tax that would be payable on a notional flat worth £250,000 in accordance with the *standard rates* is £2,500 (an effective rate of 1%): (£125,000 @ 0%) + (£125,000 @ 2%). The amount of tax that would be payable on a notional flat worth £250,000 in accordance with the *higher rates* is £10,000 (an effective rate of 4%): (£125,000 @ 3%) +

---

[2] Finance Act (FA) 2003, ss.74, 80; *Elizabeth Court (Bournemouth) Ltd* v. *Revenue and Customs Comrs* [2008] EWHC 2828 (Ch).
[3] FA 2003, s.55, Sched.74; *HMRC internal manual – Stamp Duty Land Tax Manual* ('SDLT Manual') (HMRC, 19 March 2016, updated 16 January 2020, available at: **www.gov.uk/hmrc-internal-manuals/stamp-duty-land-tax-manual**): SDLTM28500, SDLTM28505, SDLTM28510.

(£125,000 @ 5%). The amount of tax that would be payable on a notional flat worth £250,000 in accordance with the *non-residential rates* would be £2,000 (an effective rate of 0.8%): (£150,000 @ 0%) + (£100,000 @ 2%). The relevant amount of tax due on the notional flat is multiplied by the number of flats owned by the participating tenants (40) to give a total tax charge.

Depending on which set of tax rates and tax bands is used, the total amount of tax payable on the transaction ranges from £80,000 (an effective tax rate of 0.8%) to £400,000 (an effective rate of 4%). The 40 participating tenants are jointly and severally liable for the tax. For the reasons set out at **6.8**, in this example the author would argue that the non-residential rates apply; hence, £80,000 of tax would be payable.

6.6 IDENTIFYING THE PURCHASER

The identity of the purchaser for the purposes of SDLT is usually driven by whether or not the purchase is made under the Act.

If the purchase is made outside the Act, the purchaser does not need to be a nominee for the purchasing tenants. Accordingly, if the purchaser is a company owned by the purchasing tenants and does not act as a nominee for them, the company is the purchaser. Where there are more than four tenants in a building, a company is typically used to make the purchase. This is because no more than four persons can hold the legal title to a property.

If the purchase is made under the Act, then the purchaser *must* be a nominee for the participating tenants. The SDLT rules 'look through' the nominee and deem the participating tenants to be the purchasers, not the company.[4] Of course, one or more of the participating tenants may itself be a company: see **6.8**.

Which person is treated as making the purchase matters for SDLT purposes for three reasons:

- it defines the liable person – i.e., the person liable to make the SDLT return and pay the tax;
- it affects whether or not collective enfranchisement relief is available; and
- it may determine which tax rates and tax bands apply to the transaction.

Example 6.2

All 10 tenants in a building exercise their right under the 1993 Act to purchase the freehold estate of the building. They use a nominee company to make the purchase. The participating tenants are the purchasers, not the company.

---

[4] FA 2003, Sched.16, para.3(1); SDLT Manual: SDLTM31710.

Example 6.3

All four tenants in a building agree with the owner of the freehold estate of the building to purchase the owner's interest. The purchase is made outside the Leasehold Reform, Housing and Urban Development Act 1993. They use a company to make the purchase. The company does not act as a nominee for the purchasing tenants. The company is the purchaser, not the purchasing tenants.

6.7 CORPORATE PURCHASERS

So far as purchases made under the Act are concerned, the status of the purchaser (or any of the purchasers) – individual or company (etc.) – is relevant to determining whether or not collective enfranchisement relief applies and, for collective enfranchisement transactions involving buildings containing fewer than six flats, whether the tax should be calculated in accordance with the residential standard rates or higher rates: see **3.3**.

If collective enfranchisement relief is not available because one or more of the participating tenants is a company (etc.) and the average price per qualifying flat is more than £500,000, the tax might be calculated in accordance with the residential super rate (see **3.4**). Put another way, where the relief applies due to the average price per qualifying flat being £500,000 or less, the transaction is protected from the super rate.

Example 6.4

A building contains four flats, including a penthouse flat twice as big as each of the others. The cost of enfranchisement is £1.5 million: £300,000 per normal flat and £600,000 for the penthouse. All the flat-leases have an unexpired term of more than 21 years. If the tenants use a company to make the acquisition outside the Act, that company will be acquiring a major interest in a single dwelling (the penthouse) for more than £500,000, and if the company is not exempt from the residential super rate, the transaction will be split in two and two SDLT returns will be due: the residential super rate will apply to £600,000 and the residential standard rates will apply to £900,000. If the acquisition were made under the Act, then – even if the penthouse were owned by a company – the residential super rate would not apply since the average price per dwelling (£375,000) does not exceed £500,000.

For purchases made under the Act where the average price per qualifying flat is more than £500,000 and for purchases made outside the Act, it is always necessary to examine whether the super rate applies to the transaction. The super rate takes precedence over all other rules. It should, therefore, be considered at the start of the SDLT analysis.

For purchases made under the Act, the super rate applies, regardless of the number of flats in the building, where a purchasing tenant is a company (etc.), the average price per qualifying flat is more than £500,000 and 'relief' from the super rate does not apply: see below. Where it applies, a flat 15 per cent rate should be applied to the whole of the price paid for the freehold estate.

For purchases made outside the Act, the super rate applies, regardless of the number of flats in the building, where a purchasing tenant is a company (etc.) or the purchasing tenants use a company other than a nominee company to make the purchase, and the proportion of the purchase price attributable to *any* of the flats in the building is more than £500,000. To the extent that the freehold estate attributable to a flat is worth more than £500,000, that interest is referred to as a 'higher threshold interest'. The proportion of the purchase price paid by the purchasing tenants attributable to the higher threshold interest (or all the higher threshold interests if there is more than one) should be found and a flat 15 per cent rate should be applied to the total unless 'relief' from the super rate applies: see below. The balance of the purchase price should be taxed in accordance with the standard rates (unless the unexpired term of a flat-lease is 21 years or less, in which case it would be taxed at the higher rates due to the participation of the company as a co-purchaser) provided that there are fewer than six flats in the building, or in accordance with the non-residential rates if there are six or more flats in the building (see **6.8**).

'Relief' from the super rate would apply if the company (etc.) that owns the flat acquires the freehold estate 'exclusively' for one or more of permitted purposes, e.g.:

- exploitation as a source of rents in the course of a property-rental business;
- development or redevelopment and resale in the course of a property-development trade; or
- resale in the course of a property-trading business.

It is worth reiterating that the purpose of acquiring the freehold estate collectively with the other qualifying tenants, and not the purpose of holding the qualifying flat/flat, is relevant to determine whether the 'relief' from the super rate applies. The term 'relief' is used in the loose sense. Where the conditions for 'relief' are met, the super rate does not apply. The 'relief' does not need to be claimed. Nevertheless, this does not mean that such transactions are not notifiable – they are. HMRC provides relief code 35 (relief from 15 per cent rate of SDLT) and the author would encourage its use in the SDLT return to avoid confusion.

'Relief' from the super rate would not be available where the occupier is connected with the flat-owning company (e.g., by controlling the company).

Example 6.5

A building is composed of 10 flats. All 10 of the qualifying tenants choose to purchase the freehold estate of the building collectively in exercise of their rights under the 1993 Act. All the flat-leases have an unexpired term of more than 21 years. The participating tenants set up a company and hold shares in the company in specified proportions. The company acts as nominee for the participating tenants, one of whom is a company. That company is controlled by the occupier of the flat, a 'non-qualifying individual'. The nominee company purchases the freehold estate in the building in return for paying £5.1 million. The average price per qualifying flat is £510,000 (£5.1 million / 10). As one of the qualifying tenants is a company, the average price per qualifying flat exceeds £500,000 and relief from the super rate is not available (due to the 'non-qualifying occupation'), collective enfranchisement relief is not available. The proportion of the £5.1 million attributable to two of the flats (the 'higher threshold interests') exceeds £500,000 each. The total share of the purchase price attributable to the two higher threshold interests is £1.2 million. Nevertheless, the tax is calculated at the super rate of 15% on the *entire* £5.1 million: £5.1 million @ 15% = £765,000. The £5.1 million is *not* apportioned between the share of the price attributable to the higher threshold interests and the rest. The 10 participating tenants are jointly and severally liable for the tax.

If the company were replaced by an individual, the amount of tax chargeable would be £615,000 less. This is because collective enfranchisement relief *would* be available and the tax would be calculated solely in accordance with the non-residential rates. The amount of tax chargeable on a dwelling worth £510,000 in accordance with the non-residential rates (see **6.8**) is £15,000: (£150,000 @ 0%) + (£100,000 @ 2%) + (£260,000 @ 5%). The £15,000 is multiplied by the number of qualifying flats owned by the participating tenants (10) to give a total of £150,000 (an effective tax rate of 2.9%).

Example 6.6

A building is composed of 10 flats. All 10 of the qualifying tenants choose to purchase the freehold estate of the building collectively in exercise of their rights under the 1993 Act. The participating tenants set up a company and hold shares in the company in specified proportions. The company acts as nominee for the participating tenants, one of whom is a company. The nominee company purchases the freehold estate in the building in return for paying £3 million. The average flat price is £300,000 (£3 million / 10). As the average price per qualifying flat does not exceed £500,000, collective enfranchisement relief *is* available. This means that it is not necessary to determine whether there are any 'higher threshold interests': the transaction is protected from the super rate by virtue of collective enfranchisement relief. The amount of tax chargeable is £45,000 (an effective rate of 1.5%): £3 million / 10 = £300,000, and the amount of tax chargeable on a dwelling worth £300,000 in accordance with the non-residential rates (see **6.8**) is £4,500: (£150,000 @ 0%) + (£100,000 @ 2%) + (£50,000 @ 5%). The £4,500 is multiplied by the number of qualifying flats owned by the participating tenants (10) to give £45,000. The 10 participating tenants are jointly and severally liable for the tax.

So far as purchases made outside the Act are concerned, similar issues apply, albeit collective enfranchisement relief is not available. Whether or not the purchaser is a company or, where a nominee company used, any of the purchasing tenants is a company is relevant to determine whether the super rate applies or the higher rates apply, unless, in the case of the higher rates only, there are more than five qualifying flats or the freehold estate of the purchased building is mixed-use or the freehold estate is subject to (i.e., reversionary on) leases with an expired term of more than 21 years (see **6.8** and **6.9**). In this case, however, the super rate only applies *to the extent that* the price paid for the freehold estate is attributable to the 'higher threshold interest(s)'.

Example 6.7

A building is composed of 10 flats. All 10 of the tenants choose to purchase the freehold estate of the building collectively outside the Act. The tenants set up a company and hold shares in the company in specified proportions. The company acts as nominee for the tenants, one of whom is a company. That company is controlled by the occupier of the flat. The nominee company purchases the freehold estate in the building in return for paying £5.1 million. The proportion of the £5.1 million attributable to two of the flats (the 'higher threshold interests') exceeds £500,000 each. The total share of the purchase price attributable to the two higher threshold interests is £1.2 million. As the purchase is made outside the Act, a tenant is a company, relief from the 15% rate does not apply and the proportion of the price attributable to at least one flat is more than £500,000, the tax is calculated in accordance with the super rate (15% flat rate). The amount of tax chargeable in accordance with the super rate is £180,000 (£1.2 million @ 15%). The amount of tax chargeable in accordance with the non-residential rates (see **6.8**) is £184,500: (£150,000 @ 0%) + (£100,000 @ 2%) + (£3.65 million @ 5%). The total amount of tax due on the transaction is £364,500 (an effective rate of 7.1%): £180,000 + £184,500. The 10 participating tenants are jointly and severally liable for the tax.

If the company were replaced by an individual, the amount of tax chargeable would be £120,000 less. This is because the tax would be calculated solely in accordance with the non-residential rates. The total amount of tax chargeable on £5.1 million in accordance with the non-residential rates is £244,500 (an effective tax rate of 4.8%): (£150,000 @ 0%) + (£100,000 @ 2%) + (£4,850,000 @ 5%).

A bear-trap exists where a participating tenant is a company and after the collective purchase of the freehold estate the participating tenants acquire extended leases for no premium. It arises due to three anti-avoidance rules that, at least on literal reading of them, work in conjunction with each other.

The first rule deems the nominee company (not the participating tenants for whom it holds the freehold estate) to be the vendor on the lease grant (see **2.4**).[5]

The second rule deems the amount of the chargeable consideration to be not less than the market value of the extended lease where the corporate tenant is connected with the nominee company (see **Chapter 15**).[6]

The third rule provides that the corporate tenant is connected with the nominee company where it controls the company or acts together with others to do so.[7] The corporate tenant may not control the nominee company by itself, but it would usually control the nominee company together with the other participating tenants.

---

[5] FA 2003, Sched.16, para.3.
[6] FA 2003, s.53.
[7] Corporation Tax Act 2010, ss.450, 1122.

Where the participating tenants enter into a shareholders' agreement to regulate their relationship, their acting in concert would be evident from that agreement. Alternatively, it may be evident from other facts, including the participation agreement. A solution may be for an individual to acquire and hold the extended lease as bare trustee for the company. This is because the individual would be treated as purchaser of the whole of the lease, not merely purchaser of the bare legal title; hence, the market value rule would not apply. Before reverting to this tactic, though, the residential property lawyer should take advice to confirm that this is necessary, the arrangement is not disclosable under the disclosure of tax avoidance schemes (DOTAS) rules[8] and does not fall foul of the general anti-abuse rule (GAAR).[9]

It is arguable that, absent using an individual as bare trustee, the imposition of a market value charge in these circumstances is absurd and unjust. The participating tenants would have paid SDLT in full on purchasing the freehold estate. The purpose of purchasing the freehold estate is to enable them to acquire, for example, 999-year leases for no premium. In other words, in the 'real world' the parties to the lease grant are essentially the same. The purpose of the rule that deems the nominee company to be the vendor is to attack a specific SDLT-avoidance scheme. It is not to impose a full market value charge on the lease grant. HMRC might be prepared to accept that it can be read down applying a principle established in case law.[10] It has been prepared to read it down in other contexts where the consequence of not doing so would be absurdity or injustice. However, this is unpublished practice and HMRC's reaction to this fact pattern is uncertain. Consequently, one should not assume that HMRC would interpret the legislation in this way without seeking advance clearance on a formal basis.

Example 6.8

A building is composed of nine flats. Six of the nine qualifying tenants exercise their right to purchase the freehold estate for £12 million under the Leasehold Reform, Housing and Urban Development Act 1993. One of the six participating tenants is a company. That company is controlled by the occupier of the flat, a 'non-qualifying individual'. The nominee company purchases the freehold estate in the building. The average price per qualifying flat is £1,333,333 (£12 million / 9). As one of the qualifying tenants is a company, the average price per qualifying flat exceeds £500,000 and relief from the super rate is not available (due to the 'non-qualifying occupation'), collective enfranchisement relief is not available. Hence, SDLT is payable at the flat rate of 15%: £1.8 million (£12 million @ 15%). After the freehold estate is purchased, the nominee company grants 999-year leases to the participating tenants (its shareholders) for no premium. The pre-existing leases held by the participating tenants terminate by operation of law on the grant of the 999-year leases. The market value of the 999-year lease granted to the corporate participating tenant is £2 million. On a literal reading of the legislation, the corporate participating tenant would be liable to pay SDLT at the rate of 15% on £2 million on its acquisition of the 999-year lease (£300,000)

---

[8] FA 2004, Part 7.
[9] FA 2013, Part 5.
[10] *Marshall (HM Inspector of Taxes)* v. *Kerr* [1994] BTC 258.

STAMP DUTY LAND TAX HANDBOOK

despite: (a) the corporate participating tenant having borne its share of the SDLT cost incurred by the nominee company on the purchase of the freehold estate; (b) nothing being given by the corporate participating tenant for the 999-year lease; and (c) arguably there being only a 'technical' connection between the parties to the 999-year lease grant.

Where there is actual (or deemed) chargeable consideration for the grant of an extended lease, the transaction would be a standard-rates transaction:

1. where the grant of the extended lease is reversionary on the flat-lease and the flat-lease has 21 years or more to run; or
2. where:
   (a) the purchaser is an individual; and
   (b) the purchaser (etc.) (see 'purchasers (etc.)' in **3.3.2**) does not own the freehold or leasehold estate (or foreign equivalent) in another dwelling worth £40,000 or more (unless it is subject to a long lease); or
3. where:
   (a) the grant of the extended lease is not reversionary on the flat-lease and the flat-lease has 21 years or more to run; and
   (b) the flat-lease is held by the purchaser and no more than three other joint tenants or the purchaser is beneficially entitled as a tenant in common to 25 per cent or more of the flat-lease.

See **3.3.10.2**.

6.8 SIX OR MORE FLATS

The use of the tax rates and tax bands for non-residential transactions seems incongruous with collective enfranchisement transactions. Nevertheless, in the author's opinion, those tax rates and tax bands are compatible with collective enfranchisement transactions unless, in the case of purchases made outside the Act, multiple dwellings relief is available and claimed – when the residential rates must apply.

If the purchased freehold estate is in more than five flats and the super rate does not apply, the transaction is taxed in accordance with the non-residential rates. This is due to an SDLT provision that states (so far as material):

> ... where six or more separate dwellings are the subject of a single transaction involving the transfer of a [freehold estate] in ... them, then, for the purposes of [the SDLT code] as it applies in relation to that transaction, those dwellings are treated as not being residential property.[11]

---

[11] FA 2003, s.116(7).

This is referred to as the 'six-or-more rule' (see **3.2.5**).

The test is not whether the total number of qualifying flats owned by the participating tenants is more than five. The total number of qualifying flats owned by the participating tenants may be fewer than six. The test is whether the purchased interest (the freehold estate) is 'in' more than five dwellings.

In the author's view, on a plain reading of the legislation collective enfranchisement relief would continue to apply for purchases made under the Act even though the flats are treated as not being residential property. This is because collective enfranchisement relief, where it applies, merely modifies the amount of the chargeable consideration used in the tax calculation. That change is not sensitive to whether the freehold estate is treated as being in non-residential property. The transaction would, in the 'real world', be a collective enfranchisement transaction made under the Act. Deeming the subject-matter of the transaction to be non-residential property in the 'SDLT world' should not prevent the participating tenants from accessing the relief. The issue is different with multiple dwellings relief, which is only accessed if the transaction is a 'multiple dwelling transaction'. A transaction is a 'multiple dwelling transaction' only if its subject-matter consists of an interest in at least two dwellings. This is why, the author infers, the parliamentary draftsmen deemed it necessary to add an express provision in the multiple dwellings relief legislation confirming that the six-or-more rule is to be disregarded in determining whether a transaction qualifies for the relief.

If this is correct, the non-residential rates would apply to the average price per qualifying flat and the result would be multiplied by the number of qualifying flats owned by the participating tenants.

For purchases made outside the Act, a choice may need to be made: either (a) pay tax in accordance with the non-residential rates on the purchase price or (b) in the rare case where the conditions are met, claim multiple dwellings relief and pay tax in accordance with the standard rates or higher rates depending on whether one or more of the flat-leases has an unexpired term of 21 years or less; whether any of the purchasing tenants is a company (etc.); whether the flats are 'subsidiary' to a main dwelling; and whether any of the tenants (etc.) owns a major interest in another dwelling.

For more information on the tax rates and tax bands, see **1.4.1**.

Example 6.9

A building contains five flats. All five tenants exercise their right under the Act to purchase the freehold estate of the building for £2.75 million. Two of the five flat-leases have an unexpired term of 21 years or less. The tenants use a nominee company as required by the Act. None of the participating tenants is a company; hence, it is irrelevant that the average price per qualifying flat is more than £500,000. Although none of the participating tenants owns a 'major interest' in another dwelling, the flats within the building are not 'subsidiary' to a main dwelling. This means that the transaction is a higher-rates transaction (see **3.3**). The tax payable in accordance with the higher rates is as follows: £2.75 million divided by five equals £550,000; the tax due on a notional flat worth £550,000 in accordance with the higher rates is £34,000: (£125,000 @ 3%) + (£125,000 @ 5%) + (£300,000 @ 8%). The £34,000 is multiplied by the number of qualifying flats owned by the participating tenants (five) to give £170,000 (an effective tax rate of 6.2%). The five participating tenants are jointly and severally liable for the tax.

Example 6.10

A building contains six flats. Five tenants exercise their right under the Act to purchase the freehold estate of the building for £2.1 million. They use a nominee company as required by the Act. None of the participating tenants is a company. That the purchased freehold estate is in more than five dwellings means that the non-residential rates apply. It does not matter that there are only five qualifying flats. The amount of tax payable in accordance with the non-residential rates is as follows: £2.1 million divided by five equals £420,000. The tax due on a notional flat worth £420,000 calculated in accordance with the non-residential rates is £11,000: (£125,000 @ 0%) + (£125,000 @ 2%) + (£170,000 @ 5%). The £11,000 is multiplied by the number of qualifying flats owned by the participating tenants (five) to give £55,000 (an effective tax rate of 2.6%). The five participating tenants are jointly and severally liable for the tax.

6.9 MIXED-USE BUILDINGS

For all collective enfranchisement transactions – i.e., for purchases made under the Act and outside the Act – if, to any extent, the purchased freehold estate relates to non-residential property, subject to two exceptions, the *whole* of the chargeable consideration given for the transaction is taxed in accordance with non-residential rates. The chargeable consideration is not apportioned between the two types of use before the relevant set of rates is applied to each proportion. It is all or nothing. This is referred to as the 'mixed-use rule' (see **3.2.2**).

The first exception is where the residential super rate applies to the transaction (see **3.4**). To recap, the super rate would apply where:

- the purchaser, or a participating/purchasing tenant, is a company;
- the average price per qualifying dwelling is more than £500,000; or
- the proportion of the freehold attributable to *any* flat in the building is more than £500,000;

and:

- none of the reliefs from the rate applies.

For purchases made under the Act, where the conditions are met all of the purchase price is taxed at the super rate. For purchases made outside the Act, only the proportion of the purchase price attributable to the 'higher threshold interest(s)' is taxed at the super rate. The balance of the chargeable consideration is taxed in accordance with the non-residential rates.

The second exception, which applies to purchases made outside the Act, is where multiple dwellings relief is claimed. This will not be possible in relation to flats whose leases were initially for a term exceeding 21 years. Where multiple dwellings relief is claimed, the purchase price must be apportioned between the two types of use before the tax is calculated on each proportion (see **4.3**).

Of course, the mixed-use rule has no practical effect if the freehold estate is in more than five dwellings. The transaction would already be taxed in accordance with the non-residential rates, subject to the super rate being engaged or a claim for multiple dwellings relief being made, due to the six-or-more rule.

6.10 THE RESIDENTIAL HIGHER RATES

Unless the purchased freehold estate is in more than five flats or subject to a non-residential lease, the incidence of the residential higher rates depends on how many years the flat-leases have left to run. The rest of this part is only relevant to collective enfranchisement transactions involving buildings consisting of fewer than six flats and buildings that do not have non-residential use. It should also be read subject to the discussion on the residential super rate. A transaction that is subject to the residential higher rates is referred to as a 'higher-rates transaction'.

Where the purchase is made under the Act or, where it is made outside the Act, the purchasing tenants jointly make the purchase personally rather than using a company, it is necessary to determine whether the higher rates apply.

The higher rates would apply if any of the participating/purchasing tenants is a company where:

- the proportion of the freehold estate attributable to any of the flats (not necessarily qualifying flats) is £40,000 or more (the 'relevant flats');
- the unexpired term of the lease held by any tenant of the relevant flats (regardless of whether or not they are a participating/purchasing tenant) is 21 years or less; and
- the freehold is in fewer than six flats and is not in any non-residential property.

Example 6.11

A building contains four flats. All four tenants agree to purchase the freehold estate of the building for £1.5 million. One of the flat-leases has an unexpired term of 21 years or less. The transaction is made outside the Act. The tenants use a company to make the purchase. The price attributable to each flat does not exceed £500,000, so the super rate is not applicable. The transaction is a higher-rates transaction.

The higher rates would apply if all the participating/purchasing tenants are individuals and:

- the proportion of the freehold estate attributable to two or more of the flats (not necessarily qualifying flats) is £40,000 or more each (the 'relevant flats');
- in the case of two or more of the relevant flats, the unexpired term of the lease of the flat is 21 years or less;
- in the case of two or more of the relevant flats, the flats are not 'subsidiary' to another flat (the 'main dwelling') (note: in order to be 'subsidiary', the proportion of the price paid for the freehold estate which is attributable to the main dwelling must be two-thirds or more; hence, it is going to be very rare for the relevant flats to be 'subsidiary'); and
- the freehold is in fewer than six flats and is not in any non-residential property.

In the (very) unlikely event that all but one of the relevant flats is 'subsidiary', the following two conditions must be met before the transaction is a higher-rates transaction:

- a participating/purchasing tenant (etc.) (see 'purchasers (etc.)' in **3.3.2**) owns a 'major interest' in another dwelling anywhere in the world worth £40,000 or more; and
- the unexpired term of the relevant tenant's lease is less than 21 years (see **3.3.10.2**).

Example 6.12

A landlord notifies his tenants of his intention to sell the freehold estate in their building for £2.2 million. There are five flats in the building. Two of the flat-leases have an unexpired term of 21 years or less. In pursuance of the tenants' right of first refusal, the landlord offers to sell the freehold estate to the tenants for the same amount. All five tenants are qualifying tenants. All five leases were granted for an initial term of more than 21 years. None of the flats is 'subsidiary'; hence, the transaction is a higher-rates transaction even if none of the tenants owns another dwelling. The tax payable in accordance with the higher rates is as follows: £2.2 million / 5 = £440,000; the tax due on a notional flat worth £440,000 in accordance with the higher rates is £25,200: (£125,000 @ 3%) + (£125,000 @ 5%) + (£190,000 @ 8%). The £25,200 is multiplied by the number of qualifying flats owned by the participating tenants (5) to give £126,000 (an effective tax rate of 5.7%). The five participating tenants are jointly and severally liable for the tax.

Put another way, where the freehold is in fewer than six flats and is not in any non-residential property the residential standard rates, not the higher rates, would apply where:

- the proportion of the freehold estate attributable to each of the flats (not necessarily qualifying flats) is less than £40,000; or
- every flat-lease held by the tenants (not necessarily the participating/purchasing tenants) is more than 21 years.[12]

---

[12] FA 2003, Sched.4ZA, paras.5, 6, 7A; SDLT Manual: SDLTM09730.

6.11 MULTIPLE DWELLINGS RELIEF

Multiple dwellings relief is only relevant to purchases made outside the Act, and even then will only apply to those dwellings whose leases were originally granted for less than 21 years ('qualifying dwellings'), so it will rarely apply.

The relief works in a substantially similar way to collective enfranchisement relief. The consideration given for the transaction is divided by the number of dwellings (flats) to produce an average price per dwelling, and the tax is calculated on that average price before it is multiplied by the number of dwellings. However, there are some notable areas in which the operation of the two reliefs differs.

- Under multiple dwellings relief, the number of dwellings used to calculate the average price per dwelling is the total number of flats in the building to which the purchased freehold estate relates regardless of the number of tenants that participate in the purchase (provided they are 'qualifying dwellings' – see **4.3.1**). Under collective enfranchisement relief, only the qualifying flats owned by the participating tenants are taken into account.
- Multiple dwellings relief is subject to a collar: the amount of tax payable under the relief cannot be less than one per cent of the total dwellings consideration, though in practice this only affects low-value standard-rates transactions. There is no collar for collective enfranchisement relief.
- Multiple dwellings relief must be claimed in an SDLT return or in an amendment to an SDLT return. Collective enfranchisement relief does not need to be claimed. Nevertheless, this does not mean that collective enfranchisement transactions are not notifiable – they are. HMRC provides relief code 25 (collective enfranchisement by leaseholders) and the author would encourage its use in the SDLT return to avoid confusion.
- Multiple dwellings relief is subject to withdrawal if an event happens within three years of the transaction that would, if it had happened immediately before completion of the transaction, have resulted in less tax payable (e.g., the number of dwellings reduces). Collective enfranchisement relief cannot be withdrawn.

For more information on multiple dwellings relief, see **4.3**.[13]

Example 6.13

A building contains four flats. All four tenants agree to purchase the freehold estate of the building for £1.5 million. The transaction is made outside the Act. Three of the leases held by the tenants were granted for a term of less than 21 years. The proportion of the £1.5 million price attributable to those three leases is £1.3 million. The other lease was granted for a term of more than 21 years. None of the tenants is a company and none owns a 'major interest' in another dwelling. The transaction is a 'relevant transaction' for the purposes of multiple dwellings relief because the purchased freehold is in more than one dwelling and three of the

---

[13] FA 2003, s.58D, Sched.6B; SDLT Manual: SDLTM29900.

STAMP DUTY LAND TAX HANDBOOK

dwellings are 'qualifying dwellings' because the leases over them were not granted for a term of more than 21 years. The total dwellings consideration is £1.3 million. The average price per dwelling is £433,333 (£1.3 million / 3). The tax chargeable on a notional dwelling worth £433,333 applying the residential higher rates is £24,667: (£125,000 @ 3%) + (£125,000 @ 5%) + (£183,333 @ 8%). The total amount of tax chargeable on the dwellings consideration is £74,001 (£24,667 x 3). The total amount of tax chargeable on the transaction, but for the relief, is £112,750. The proportion of the £112,750 attributable to the non-qualifying dwelling is £15,033 or £200,000 / £1.5 million x £112,750. The total amount of tax payable on the transaction is £89,034 (£74,001 + £15,033), an effective tax rate of 5.9%.

6.12 SUMMARY OF POTENTIAL ALTERNATIVE TAX RATES AND RELIEFS

The result of the foregoing is that one or two of four alternative sets of tax rates and tax bands would apply to the transaction (assuming multiple dwellings relief is not available or not claimed):

1. The *residential higher rates* would apply where:

    (a) the purchasers are the participating/purchasing tenants;
    and either:
    (b) where:

       (i) the purchasing/participating tenants include a company; and
       (ii) the proportion of the purchase price attributable to any flat (not necessarily the qualifying flats) is £40,000 or more, and the unexpired term of the corresponding flat-lease is 21 years or less;

    or:
    (c) where the purchasing/participating tenants do not include a company;

       and either:

         (i) where:

           (A) the proportion of the purchase price attributable to two or more flats (not necessarily the qualifying flats) is £40,000 or more each, and the unexpired term of the corresponding flat-leases is 21 years or less; and
           (B) none of the flats is worth two-thirds or more of the total purchase price;

         or

         (ii) where:

           (A) the proportion of the purchase price attributable to only one of the flats (not necessarily the qualifying flats) is £40,000 or more, and the unexpired term of the corresponding flat-lease is 21 years or less; and

(B) a participating/purchasing tenant (etc.) owns the freehold or leasehold estate (or foreign equivalent) in another dwelling worth £40,000 or more (unless it is subject to a long lease) and the unexpired term of their flat-lease is 21 years or less;
(d) and in addition to the above, where:
(i) the freehold estate of the purchased building is subject to fewer than six flats; and
(ii) the freehold estate of the purchased building is not subject to a non-residential lease.

2. The *residential super rate* would apply where:

(a) the purchaser is a company (unless it is a nominee company) or, if not, one or more of the participating/purchasing tenants is a company and, for purchases made under the Act only, the average price per qualifying flat is more than £500,000; or
(b) for purchases outside the Act only, the share of the freehold attributable to *any* flat in the building is more than £500,000; and
(c) no 'relief' from the super rate applies.

3. The *non-residential rates* would apply where:

(a) for all transactions, the freehold estate of the purchased building is subject to more than five flats; or
(b) for all transactions, the freehold estate of the purchased building is subject to a non-residential lease; and
(c) for purchases made under the Act only, one or more of the participating tenants is a company and the average price per qualifying flat is £500,000 or less (or the average is more than £500,000 and 'relief' from the super rate applies);
(d) for purchases made outside the Act, the purchaser or one or more of the purchasing tenants is a company and the share of the freehold attributable to *any* flat in the building (not necessarily the flat owned by the company) is £500,000 or less (or the share attributable to a flat is more than £500,000 and 'relief' from the super rate applies); and
(e) for all transactions, none of the participating/purchasing tenants is a company.

4. The *residential standard rates* would apply where none of the other rates applies.

Additionally, one of two reliefs may apply to the transaction.

1. *Collective enfranchisement relief* would apply where:

(a) the purchase is made under the Act; and

(b)   none of the participating tenants is a company, or, if any is a company, the average price per qualifying flat is £500,000 or less (or the average is more than £500,000 and 'relief' from the super rate applies).

2. *Multiple dwellings relief* would be available where:
   (a)   the purchase is made outside the Act;
   (b)   none of the purchasing tenants is a company, or, if any is a company, the share of the freehold attributable to *any* flat in the building is £500,000 or less;

   but only in relation to the flat-leases granted for an initial term of no more than 21 years.

CHAPTER 7

Pre-completion transactions

7.1 BACKGROUND

This chapter covers transactions entered into before completion of a sale contract that result in a person other than the original purchaser in the sale contract being entitled to call for a transfer of the property to them. Such transactions – which are referred to in the stamp duty land tax (SDLT) legislation, HM Revenue and Customs (HMRC) guidance and this work as 'pre-completion transactions' – include sub-sales, assignments of contracts and novations. A separate regime exists for sub-sales (etc.) of development licences (see **Chapter 17**) and assignments of agreements for leases (see **5.5**).[1]

The pre-completion transaction regime is complex. It covers more than 10 pages of legislation. Where a transaction falls within it (see **7.2**), the reader should consider taking specialist SDLT advice to ensure that the outcome for the original purchaser or end purchaser is as anticipated. By way of warning, in 2016 a solicitor was found to be negligent in relation to a conveyancing transaction in failing to structure a sub-sale so as to take advantage of SDLT sub-sale relief.

The summary in this chapter is necessarily 'light' and should not be relied on as an exhaustive guide to the rules. It does not cover things including:

- successive pre-completion transactions (e.g., where there is more than one assignment of rights or sub-sale, or a combination of assignment of rights and sub-sale, before completion);
- sub-sales between connected parties;
- the combination of sub-sales and exchanges; or
- sub-sales to partnerships.

The regime was radically altered in 2013 to prevent its use in SDLT avoidance schemes. Only the 2013 regime is discussed in this work.

---

[1] For more information see *Sergeant and Sims on Stamp Taxes* (LexisNexis UK), AA2.5: Transactions entered into before completion of contract; *Mansion Estates Ltd v. Hayre & Co.* [2016] EWHC 96 (Ch); Finance Act (FA) 2003, s.45, Sched.2A; *HMRC internal manual – Stamp Duty Land Tax Manual* ('SDLT Manual') (HMRC, 19 March 2016, updated 16 January 2020, available at: **www.gov.uk/hmrc-internal-manuals/stamp-duty-land-tax-manual**): SDLTM21500.

References in this work to 'A', 'B' and 'C' refer to the vendor under the original sale contract, the purchaser under the original sale contract and the purchaser under the pre-completion transaction (or end purchaser), respectively.

7.2 MEANING OF 'PRE-COMPLETION TRANSACTION'

A transaction is a 'pre-completion transaction' if the following conditions are met:

- A and B enter into a contract for the acquisition of a chargeable interest;
- that contract is to be completed by an instrument (typically, a transfer of the chargeable interest);
- before completion or substantial performance (see **1.8**) B enters into a transaction with another person (C) resulting in C becoming entitled to call for a transfer of some or all of the chargeable interest;
- that other transaction is not the grant or assignment of an option.

The requirement for C to be entitled to call for a transfer means that if, at completion, B directs A to transfer the property to C and, before completion, C had no remedy available to it if B failed to do so, there has not been a pre-completion transaction.

7.3 EFFECT OF PRE-COMPLETION TRANSACTION

The pre-completion transaction has no immediate effect. C is not regarded as entering into an SDLT transaction. This mimics the effect of B entering into the original sale contract. The effect is only apparent on substantial performance or completion.

7.4 'ASSIGNMENTS OF RIGHTS' AND 'FREE-STANDING TRANSFERS'

A distinction is drawn between two types of pre-completion transaction: (a) an assignment of rights under the original sale contract and (b) everything else including sub-sales (referred to in the legislation as 'assignments of rights' and 'free-standing transfers', respectively). An assignment of rights is any pre-completion transaction that gives C an entitlement to exercise rights under the original contract.

On an assignment of rights, C is taxed on the consideration he gives A under the original contract and the consideration he gives B for the assignment of the original contract. The vendor is generally taken to be A, but in certain circumstances is taken to be B. This is relevant to the application of those SDLT rules sensitive to the identity of the vendor: e.g., the deemed market value rule for transfers to connected companies and special charging rules for transfers between partners (and connected persons) and partnerships. At completion, B is treated in the 'SDLT world' as making a separate acquisition even though in the 'real world' he does not.

On a free-standing transfer, B and C are also treated as making separate acquisitions regardless of whether, in the case of a sub-sale, there is a direct transfer of the property by A to C or two successive transfers of the property, A to B and B to C. A sub-sale effected by two transfers is popular where B does not wish A to know that he has on-sold the property or for how much. Obviously, the choice between using an assignment of rights or a sub-sale will be affected by what is permitted under the original sale contract, including what standard conditions are included. C is taxed on the consideration he gives B. The vendor is generally taken to be A, but in certain circumstances is taken to be B.

7.5 RELIEF

In both cases, B may claim a full or partial SDLT relief provided that, in the case of an assignment of rights, the original contract had not been substantially performed when the pre-completion transaction was entered into and, in the case of free-standing transfers that are sub-sales, the substantial performance or completion of the sub-sale takes place 'at the same time as, and in connection with' the corresponding substantial performance or completion of the original sale contract.

It is practically impossible to design completion mechanics permitting two transfers to occur exactly simultaneously. In recognition of this, HMRC appears to accept that the words 'at the same time' are met when the transfers occur on the same day as near to each other as possible. In case HMRC opens an enquiry, evidence should be retained to demonstrate the proximity between the two transfers.

The relief must be claimed in an SDLT return, or an amendment to an SDLT return, by entering code 34 at question 9 ('are you claiming relief?') of the SDLT return.

The relief is denied where it is reasonable to conclude that B had a main purpose of securing an SDLT advantage for any person. The legislation does not explicitly carve-out the relief available for pre-completion transactions – the meaning of 'tax advantage' includes relief from tax – but this must be implicit otherwise the relief would never be available.

Partial relief is available where C acquires only part of the subject-matter of the original contract.

No relief needs to be claimed where the free-standing transfer is a novation. B is not regarded as making an acquisition in those circumstances. So the effect of the novation is to clear B of any SDLT liability automatically.

Where B and C are connected for tax purposes or do not act at arm's length, the chargeable consideration for C's acquisition may be increased under a 'minimum consideration rule'. The rule compares the amount of the chargeable consideration given for the transaction with two amounts:

- the purchase price for the property under the original sale contract (unless only part of the property is on-sold in which case a proportion of the purchase price attributable to the part on-sold is used); and
- the net amounts of the consideration given by the parties (where the net amount of the consideration given by any party is the amount of consideration given by the party less the amount of consideration given to the party).

See **8.5**.

7.6 REGISTRATION

Where B wishes to amend the land register to note his acquisition of the property, he must produce a revenue certificate (SDLT5) in the usual way. The revenue certificate is generated by B making an SDLT return.

Where B does not wish to amend the land register, and there are two transfers (A-to-B and B-to-C), HMRC says that C must produce a revenue certificate *and* written confirmation that B acquired the property on its disposal by A and transferred it to C. Such written confirmation is unnecessary where there is only one transfer (A-to-C).

Example 7.1

A agrees to sell the freehold estate in a house to B (an unconnected party) for £1 million. B pays a 10% deposit (£100,000) on exchange of contracts. Before completion, B assigns his rights under his contract with A to C for £150,000. The £150,000 represents the £100,000 deposit paid by B and £50,000 of profit. C completes the contract and pays A the outstanding £900,000. On completion, B acquires the property in the 'SDLT world'. B must make an SDLT return within 14 days of the A-to-C transfer. The chargeable consideration for his acquisition is £1 million; the vendor is A. B should claim relief in that return to obtain a complete exemption from charge. At completion, C acquires the property in the 'real world'. C must make an SDLT return within 14 days of the A-to-C transfer. The chargeable consideration for his acquisition is £1,050,000 (£900,000 plus £150,000); the vendor is also A. C must pay tax on £1,050,000.

Example 7.2

A agrees to sell the freehold estate in a house to B (an unconnected party) for £1 million. B pays a 10% deposit (£100,000) on exchange of contracts. Before completion B agrees to sell the property to C for £1,050,000. C pays a 10% deposit (£105,000) on exchange of contracts. On completion, B pays A the outstanding £900,000 and A transfers the property to B. On the same day, C pays B the outstanding £945,000 and B transfers the property to C. Both B and C acquire the property in the 'real world'. Both must make separate SDLT returns within 14 days of the A-to-B and B-to-C transfers. The chargeable consideration for B's acquisition is £1 million; the vendor is A. B should claim relief in that return to obtain a complete exemption from charge. The chargeable consideration for C's acquisition is £1,050,000; the vendor is also A. C must pay tax on £1,050,000.

Example 7.3

A agrees to sell the freehold estate in a house to B (an unconnected party) for £1 million. B pays a 10% deposit (£100,000) on exchange of contracts. B finds an unconnected person that wishes to purchase the property, C. A, B and C enter into a deed of novation under which B is released from his rights and obligations under the sale contract and C 'steps into B's shoes'. C pays B £150,000 in return for B giving up his rights under the contract. At completion, C pays A the outstanding £900,000 and A transfers the property to C. Although the novation is a pre-completion transaction, B is not treated as having made an acquisition. B does not need to make an SDLT return or claim relief. C must make an SDLT return within 14 days of the A-to-C transfer. The chargeable consideration for his acquisition is £1,050,000 (£900,000 plus £150,000); the vendor is A. C must pay tax on £1,050,000.

Example 7.4

A agrees to sell the freehold estate in two houses to B (an unconnected party) for £2 million. B pays a 10% deposit (£200,000) on exchange of contracts. Before completion B agrees to sell one property to C for £1,200,000. C pays a 10% deposit (£120,000) on exchange of contracts. At completion, B pays A the outstanding £1.8 million and A transfers both properties to B. On the same day, C pays B the outstanding £1,080,000 and B transfers the relevant property to C. Both B and C acquire the property in the 'real world'. Both must make separate SDLT returns within 14 days of the A-to-B and B-to-C transfers. The chargeable consideration for B's acquisition is £2 million; the vendor is A. B should claim relief in that return to provide a partial exemption from charge. The effect of the claim for the relief is to reduce the chargeable consideration for B's acquisition to £800,000 (£2 million less £1.2 million). B must pay tax on £800,000. The chargeable consideration for C's acquisition is £1.2 million; the vendor is also A. C must pay tax on £1.2 million.

CHAPTER 8

Transfers between spouses and civil partners

8.1 BACKGROUND

This chapter covers the stamp duty land tax (SDLT) treatment of transfers of property between spouses and civil partners. Five sets of rules are relevant.[1]

However, it is equally relevant to set out here what rules do *not* apply. Subject to what is said below, no reliefs, exemptions, special charging provisions or market value rules apply to transfers between spouses or civil partners. Accordingly, the tax is generally calculated in accordance with the ordinary rules – i.e., on the amount or value of the consideration given in the 'real world'. If chargeable consideration is given and its amount or value is more than the relevant nil rate band (£125,000 for standard-rates transactions and £150,000 for non-residential or mixed transactions), the purchaser would be liable to pay tax. If no chargeable consideration is given or its amount or value is not more than the nil rate band, the purchaser would not be liable to pay tax. Note that the nil rate band for higher-rates transactions (£40,000) does not apply where certain conditions are met due to a specific exemption from the higher rates.

The five sets of rules that deserve attention are:

- an exemption from the higher rates;
- transfers subject to debt;
- transfers on divorce or dissolution of a civil partnership;
- assignments and sub-sales; and
- transfers to/from partnerships.

Each set of rules is discussed in turn below.

---

[1] For more information see *Sergeant and Sims on Stamp Taxes* (LexisNexis UK), AA2: SDLT–land transactions, AA2B [AA39AI] Married couples and civil partners, AA3.2 Transfer of land to a partnership, AA3.7 Transfer of land from a partnership.

8.2 HIGHER RATES EXEMPTION

For property transfers between spouses or civil partners made on or after 22 November 2017, an exemption from the higher rates applies. The transfer will always be a standard-rates transaction; hence, it is irrelevant whether or not the purchaser (or the spouse or civil partner of the purchaser) owns another dwelling at the end of the day that is the completion date. The exemption is not a complete exemption, merely an exemption from the higher rates.

In order for the exemption to apply, two conditions must be met:

- the only parties to the transfer must be the spouses or civil partners; and
- the couple must be 'living together'.

Married couples and civil partners are treated as 'living together' unless they are legally separated (by court order or deed of separation) or are, in fact, separated in circumstances in which the separation is likely to be permanent.[2]

Example 8.1

A is married to B. A and B own a residential property in England in equal shares as tenants in common. It is not their only or main residence. A transfers his 50% undivided share in the property to B so that, after the transfer, B owns the property entirely. The property is mortgaged. The amount of debt outstanding is £100,000. B owns a number of buy-to-let properties in her own name. But for the exemption from the higher rates, SDLT would apply at 3% on 50% of the £100,000 debt. As the only parties to the transfer are A and B, A and B are married and A and B are not separated, the transfer is a standard-rates transaction. No tax is payable as the amount of the chargeable consideration (£50,000) is not more than the nil rate band for residential standard-rates transactions (£125,000). Nevertheless, the transfer is notifiable, as the amount of the chargeable consideration is more than £40,000. B must make a nil SDLT return within 14 days of the transfer.

8.3 TRANSFERS SUBJECT TO EXISTING DEBT

(Note: This is not exclusive to transfers of property between spouses and civil partners.) In the absence of a relief for transfers of property between spouses and civil partners, the most common reason why tax is payable on such transactions is because the property transferred is mortgaged. The spouse or civil partner that takes on responsibility for repaying a proportion of the outstanding debt suffers tax on the amount of the debt assumed. A special rule treats the proportion of the existing debt assumed by the purchaser to correspond to their undivided share of the property

---

[2] Finance Act (FA) 2003, Sched.4ZA, para.9A; Income Tax Act 2007, s.1011; *HMRC internal manual – Stamp Duty Land Tax Manual* ('SDLT Manual') (HMRC, 19 March 2016, updated 16 January 2020, available at: **www.gov.uk/hmrc-internal-manuals/stamp-duty-land-tax-manual**): SDLTM09820.

acquired. If the co-owners are joint tenants rather than tenants in common, they are treated as owning a 50 per cent undivided share each. See **1.5**.[3]

Example 8.2

A is in a civil partnership with B and they live together. A bought a flat in his sole name before entering into the civil partnership. He now wishes to give half of the flat to B. The flat is worth £750,000. The outstanding mortgage is £300,000. Neither A nor B own another property. B must pay tax on 50% of £300,000 at the residential standard rates. No tax is payable on B's acquisition of 50% of the equity in the property (£225,000) as he does not give A anything for it – A's disposal is out of natural love and affection.

Of course, the same treatment works in reverse. Where a property owned jointly by spouses or civil partners is transferred to one spouse or civil partner, SDLT is payable on the amount of the chargeable consideration given (if any) for the transaction. The exception is if the transfer is made in pursuance of a court order (etc.) (see **8.4**). Such transactions, however, are not higher-rates transactions due to the higher rates exemption, subject to meeting the conditions for the exemption, including the requirement that the couple 'live together' (see **8.2**).

The chargeable consideration would typically consist of cash paid for the share of the equity in the property acquired and the assumption of a share of the outstanding debt corresponding to the share in the property acquired.

Example 8.3

A is in a civil partnership with B. A and B separate but do not begin proceedings to dissolve the civil partnership. They own their home as tenants in common 60:40 in favour of A. B agrees to transfer his 40% undivided share in the property to A. The property is worth £1 million. The outstanding mortgage is £600,000. A pays B £160,000 (40% of the £400,000 equity in the property). Neither A nor B own another property. A must pay SDLT in accordance with the residential standard rates on the total of the £160,000 of cash paid and the £240,000 of debt assumed (40% of £600,000).

Transfers of equity can be taxed in an arbitrary way, especially if the person that gives away the equity owns another dwelling. This is because the property might be treated as if it were acquired by both persons on trust for themselves.

Example 8.4

A and B are not married or in a civil partnership. They live together in A's house. A also owns an interest in a second home overseas. A wishes to give half of his house to B. The house is

---

[3] FA 2003, Sched.4, para.8; SDLT Manual: SDLTM04040.

TRANSFERS BETWEEN SPOUSES AND CIVIL PARTNERS

worth £1.2 million. The outstanding mortgage is £750,000. The house is transferred from A to A and B. As A and B purchase the house jointly, A owns another property, and A and B are not married or in a civil partnership, the transaction is a higher-rates transaction, and A and B would be jointly and severally liable for the SDLT. The chargeable consideration is £375,000 (50% of £750,000). SDLT of £20,000 is payable (an effective rate of 5.3%): (£125,000 @ 3%) + (£125,000 @ 5%) + (£125,000 @ 8%).

It is arguable that in the above example, viewed realistically, A is *not* a purchaser – logically, A person cannot acquire something he held before the transaction. Nevertheless, it would be prudent to transfer the equitable interest in the property *before* transferring the property legally to avoid any risk.

Example 8.5

As above, but A executes a deed of trust of half the house in favour of B. The only purchaser is B; hence, the transaction is a standard-rates transaction (as B does not own, and is not deemed to own, another property). The chargeable consideration is £375,000 (50% of £750,000), as before. SDLT of £8,750 is payable (an effective rate of 2.3%): (£125,000 @ 0%) + (£125,000 @ 2%) + (£125,000 @ 5%). Then, A transfers the bare legal title in the house to A and B to hold for themselves as beneficial tenants in common. No SDLT is payable on the transfer, as no consideration is given.

This is exacerbated where the transfer of equity occurs as part of a remortgage. To prevent a risk of SDLT being incurred on the new debt, it would be prudent to transfer the equity before the legal title, as above.

Example 8.6

As above, but A wishes to remortgage and increase his mortgage by £150,000. Part of the new debt (£900,000) is used to discharge the existing debt (£750,000). The rule that deems the proportion of debt assumed to correspond to the percentage undivided share in the property acquired only applies to the assumption of *existing* debt. In this case, therefore, there is a risk that the acquisition of the property by A and B on its disposal by A is for £750,000. To avoid this risk, as before, A could execute a deed of trust of half the house in favour of B before remortgaging. The only purchaser would be B; hence, the transaction would be a standard-rates transaction (as B does not own, and is not deemed to own, another property). The chargeable consideration would be £375,000 (50% of £750,000), as before. Then, A could transfer the bare legal title in the house to A and B to hold for themselves as beneficial tenants in common, and finally A and B could remortgage. No SDLT would be payable on the transfer or the remortgage, as no consideration would be given for either transaction.

Where the couple own or are to own the transferred property jointly in a partnership (e.g., a general partnership established under the Partnership Act 1890), special rules apply (see **8.6**).

8.4 DIVORCE, DISSOLUTION OF CIVIL PARTNERSHIP, ETC.

A transaction between spouses or civil partners is exempt from charge if it is in pursuance of:

- certain types of court order; or
- an agreement between the spouses or civil partners made in connection with the dissolution or annulment of the marriage or civil partnership, their judicial separation or a separation order. Do not forget that an agreement relating to land cannot exist unless it is in writing and complies with Law of Property (Miscellaneous Provisions) Act 1989, s.2.

Such a transaction is automatically exempt (no claim for relief needs to be made) and not notifiable (no SDLT return needs to be made) regardless of the amount (if any) of the consideration given for the transaction and may be made before or at any time after the relevant court order. Furthermore, it is not restricted to the couple's home, or even to residential property. If the couple carry on business together and own premises, it could extend to those. See **2.5**.

Example 8.7

A and B are married and own their home equally. A applies for judicial separation. In connection with the decree pronouncing the judicial separation, A agrees to buy out B's share of the property. The value of the property is £1.2 million. The outstanding mortgage is £700,000. A pays B £250,000 (half of the equity in the property) and assumes £350,000 of debt (half of the outstanding mortgage). The chargeable consideration for the transaction is £600,000 (£250,000 plus £350,000). No SDLT is payable by A and no SDLT return needs to be made. The transaction is exempt (and not notifiable), as it is in pursuance of an agreement made in connection with their judicial separation.

Where joint owners of a property are unmarried and not in a civil partnership, a transfer of one person's share in the property to the other would be chargeable if consideration is given: e.g., cash is paid and/or debt is assumed. The circumstances for the transaction (e.g., breaking up) are irrelevant. See **8.3**.

Where a spouse or civil partner is required by a court order to retain an interest in the former home, that interest does not count against them when determining whether the higher rates apply to their purchase of a new home or other dwelling (see **3.3.11**).[4]

---

[4] FA 2003, Sched.3, paras.3, 3A, Sched.4ZA, para.9B; SDLT Manual: SDLTM00550.

8.5 ASSIGNMENTS AND SUB-SALES

A special rule applies where a spouse or civil partner (A) exchanges contracts to buy a property in their sole name and before completion of the contract assigns that contract or agrees to on-sell the property to their spouse or civil partner (B). Relief may apply to A's acquisition (see **7.5**) but the chargeable consideration for B's acquisition is deemed to be not less than the price under the A-to-B contract or the sum of the net amounts of the consideration given by B and C. The net amount of consideration given by a party is the amount of the consideration given by that person less the amount of the consideration given to that person. This prevents spouses and civil partners entering into a sub-sale, assignment or other 'pre-completion transaction' for an amount less than provided for under the original contract. It also applies where B and C are not married or in a civil partnership but are otherwise connected or are not acting at arm's length.[5]

Example 8.8

B exchanges contracts to buy a house from a third party, A, for £1 million. Between exchange of contracts and completion, house prices fall by 10%. B agrees to on-sell the property to his spouse, C, for £900,000. The two contracts are completed at the same time. B's acquisition should be exempt if he claims relief. Due to her marriage to B, C's acquisition would be chargeable on not less than £1 million, the price under the original sale and the sum of the net amounts given by B and C. The net amount given by B is £100,000 (i.e., £1 million less £900,000) and the net amount given by C is £900,000. The amount of the chargeable consideration would have been £900,000 but for B's marriage to C (and the fact that it is not an arm's length transaction).

8.6 TRANSFERS TO/FROM PARTNERSHIPS

A property may be transferred from a spouse or civil partner to himself and his spouse and civil partner jointly (and vice versa). Where the spouses or civil partners jointly acquire, hold and dispose of the property in their capacity as partners, special rules apply. A partnership is defined in the Partnership Act 1890 as a relationship that subsists between persons carrying on a business in common with a view to profit. Other works (and case law) should be consulted to determine in what circumstances jointly held property constitutes a legal partnership. It is clear, though, that merely holding a property jointly for investment purposes is not enough and a degree of business activity or organisation is required. The special rules override the usual charging rule. Rather than the chargeable consideration being taken to equal the amount or value of the consideration given, instead it is taken to equal a proportion of the market value of the property transferred. A

---

[5] FA 2003, Sched.2A, para.12; SDLT Manual: SDLTM21560.

formula is used to arrive at the chargeable proportion and a prescriptive set of rules must be used to apply that formula. The rules are discussed in more detail at **Chapter 16**.[6]

Example 8.9

A is in a civil partnership with B. He owns a number of buy-to-let properties. Debt is owed by A and secured on the properties. He transfers an equal share in them to B subject to the debt. They agree to share the income and capital profits derived from holding and selling the properties equally. Assume there is a general partnership and the properties transferred are held by A and B for the purposes of that partnership. A and B would be jointly liable to SDLT arising on the transfer, not merely B. However, the amount of SDLT chargeable would be nil because the chargeable proportion of the market value would be nil applying the special charging rules for transfers of property from a partner (A) to a partnership (A and B). The amount of the consideration given (if any) by B does not affect this conclusion; hence, it does not matter that B assumes 50% of the outstanding debt.

WARNING

- It may not be obvious that the joint holding of property constitutes a general partnership.
- Conversely, it may not be obvious that an arrangement described by the parties as a partnership in fact merely constitutes the joint holding of property.
- The application of the special charging rules for transfers to/from partners can have a significant effect, positive or negative depending on the facts. Identifying in what circumstances there is a partnership and when the special charging rules apply is important.
- The special charging rules are some of the most complex rules in the SDLT legislation. Numerous concepts, conditions, exceptions and anti-avoidance rules apply. Consequently, obtaining specialist advice is recommended.

---

[6] FA 2003, Sched.15, Part 3; SDLT Manual: SDLTM33300; Property Income Manual (HMRC internal manual, 10 April 2016, updated 6 December 2019, available at: **www.gov.uk/hmrc-internal-manuals/property-income-manual**): PIM1030; *Elisabeth Moyne Ramsay v. Revenue and Customs Comrs* [2013] UKUT 226 (TCC).

CHAPTER 9

Gifts, assents, appropriations and appointments

9.1 BACKGROUND

This chapter covers the stamp duty land tax (SDLT) treatment of transfers of dwellings for no consideration. Such transfers include:

- gifts in consideration of natural love and affection;
- appointments of trust property by trustees to beneficiaries;
- withdrawals of capital by partners from partnerships;
- distributions of property by a company to its member(s) in satisfaction of a dividend, return of capital or on a winding up of the company;
- transfers of property to companies or partnerships by way of capital contribution;
- transfers of property by settlors to trustees; and
- assents and appropriations by personal representatives.

The general principle is that transfers for no chargeable consideration are automatically exempt from charge. See **2.5**. This means that no tax needs to be paid and no SDLT return needs to be made. The difficulty arises where the 'real world' and 'SDLT world' diverge. In some circumstances, chargeable consideration is *deemed* to be given for the transaction. This might be by virtue of an anti-avoidance rule designed to stop a particular type of mischief or a special charging rule. There is no distinction drawn between actual consideration and deemed consideration in the SDLT code. The tax is chargeable in the same way on both. It is therefore necessary to understand in what circumstances transfers for no actual consideration (or transfers for no obvious actual consideration) are chargeable. Those circumstances might depend on the relationship between the parties to the transaction, the type of transfer made, the making of a prior claim to SDLT group relief or the application of the SDLT general anti-avoidance rule, Finance Act (FA) 2003, s.75A.

In this chapter, the terms 'purchaser' and 'vendor' are used to refer to the person making the acquisition and disposal, respectively. This is despite the fact that no consideration is given for the transaction. This follows the scheme of the tax.[1]

9.2 DEBT

Transfers of dwellings in return for the assumption or discharge of existing debt are chargeable to SDLT on the amount of the debt assumed or discharged. Consequently, transferring a dwelling for nothing other than the assumption of existing debt owed by the vendor or the discharge of existing debt owed to the purchaser is not exempt from SDLT. This should not be controversial. The assumption or discharge of debt is clearly actual consideration given for the transaction. See **1.5**.

Two exceptions apply where the amount of debt assumed by the purchaser does not attract SDLT. The first relates to transfers in connection with divorce or the dissolution of a civil partnership (see **2.5**). The other relates to assents and appropriations by personal representatives (see **9.3**).[2]

Example 9.1

A and B (a married couple living together) own a dwelling worth £1 million equally as tenants in common. Debt in the amount of £300,000 is secured on the property. A and B are jointly and severally liable for the debt. A agrees to give his 50% undivided share in the property to B subject to the debt. The chargeable consideration for the transaction is taken to be 50% of the debt (£150,000). As an exemption from the residential higher rates applies (see **8.2**), the amount of tax payable is calculated in accordance with the residential standard rates; hence, £500 of SDLT is payable (an effective rate of 0.3%): (£125,000 @ 0%) + (£25,000 @ 2%).

9.3 ASSENTS AND APPROPRIATIONS BY PERSONAL REPRESENTATIVES

The transfer of property by personal representatives to a person (or persons) in satisfaction of their entitlement under the will of a deceased person or on the law on intestacy is an SDLT transaction. However, it is an exempt transaction unless the purchaser(s) (the beneficiary/beneficiaries) gives consideration for the transaction other than assuming debt secured on the property at the date of death (not debt taken

---

[1] For more information see *Sergeant and Sims on Stamp Taxes* (LexisNexis UK), AA4: SDLT–chargeable consideration; FA 2003, s.43(4), Sched.3, para.1.
[2] FA 2003, Sched.3, paras.3, 3A, Sched.4, para.8; *HMRC internal manual – Stamp Duty Land Tax Manual* ('SDLT Manual') (HM Revenue and Customs (HMRC), 19 March 2016, updated 16 January 2020, available at: **www.gov.uk/hmrc-internal-manuals/stamp-duty-land-tax-manual**): SDLTM04040, SDLTM04040A.

on by the personal representatives to discharge the deceased's debt). Where consideration is given for the transaction other than assuming debt secured on the property, the assumption of the secure debt is disregarded as chargeable consideration. See **2.5**.[3]

Example 9.2

A, B and C are the beneficiaries of their late father's estate. At the date of their father's death, his estate was valued at £1 million. The estate consists entirely of the freehold estate of his former main residence worth £1.5 million with an outstanding mortgage of £500,000. Over the course of the estate administration the personal representatives of the estate accept an offer on the property of £1.7 million. A, B and C decide that they would like the property to be appropriated to them before it is sold. A deed of appropriation is drafted and signed by all three of them ahead of exchange of contracts on the property sale. The acquisition of the property by A, B and C is exempt from SDLT and not notifiable. No tax is payable and no return needs to be made by them.

9.4 VARIATION OF TESTAMENTARY DISPOSITIONS

An SDLT transaction following a person's death that varies a testamentary disposition (whether effected by will or otherwise) is exempt provided that it is carried out within two years of the person's death and no consideration other than the making of a variation of another testamentary disposition is given for it. Where consideration is given for the transaction other than the making of a variation of another testamentary disposition, the making of a variation of another testamentary disposition is disregarded as chargeable consideration.[4]

9.5 TRANSFERS BETWEEN RELATIVES

There is no market value rule where the purchaser is an individual related to the vendor. Where the purchaser does not give anything in money or money's worth as consideration for the transaction, the transaction is exempt from charge even if he is related to the vendor. There are, however, rules that modify the SDLT treatment of transfers of property between relatives in certain cases:

- *Sub-sales, assignments of contracts, etc.:* Where a person enters into a contract to purchase a property and before completion of the contract a relative of theirs becomes entitled, under a separate transaction, to call for a transfer of the property, the chargeable consideration for the relative's acquisition may be increased under a special rule (see **Chapter 7** and **8.5**).

---

[3] FA 2003, Sched.3, para.3A, Sched.4, para.8A(1); SDLT Manual: SDLTM00570, SDLTM00570.
[4] FA 2003, Sched.3, para.4, Sched.4, para.8A(2).

- *Transfers between spouses or civil partners:* Where chargeable consideration is given for the transfer of a dwelling, the amount of tax chargeable is calculated in accordance with the residential standard rates provided certain conditions are met (see **8.2**). This is the extent to which the tax affords a relief to spouses or civil partners unless the property is before the transaction or will become after the transaction partnership property (see below and **8.6**).
- *Contributions to and withdrawals from partnerships:* Special charging rules determine the amount of the chargeable consideration given for the transaction. Those rules are affected (positively) where the partners are individuals and related to each other (see **8.6**).

Example 9.3

A and B are brothers. A owns a dwelling. He transfers a dwelling to himself and his brother equally to hold as tenants in common in consideration of natural love and affection. No debt is secured on the dwelling and nothing is given by B. B's acquisition of the property is exempt from charge, as no chargeable consideration is given for the transaction.

9.6 TRANSFERS TO A CONNECTED COMPANY

Where the purchaser is a company and either the purchaser is connected for tax purposes with the vendor or some or all of the consideration includes the issue or transfer of shares in a company with which the vendor is connected, then, subject to certain exceptions, the chargeable consideration given for the transaction is taken to be not less than the market value of the subject-matter of the transaction. In other words, it is not possible to give a property to a connected company for no consideration, even by way of capital contribution, or for less than the market value of the property, to save tax. The provision is one of a limited number of market value rules (see **1.5.2**).

There are three exceptions. Two relate to purchases by trustees and apply where the purchaser is a professional trustee or the purchaser is only connected with the vendor via his position as trustee. The other relates to distributions (see **Chapter 15**).[5]

Example 9.4

A owns the freehold estate in a dwelling for investment (buy-to-let). He transfers it to a company of which he is the only member, B Ltd, for a nominal amount. A's motive is to divest himself of the dwelling before he purchases a new dwelling in order to prevent the purchase being taxed in accordance with the higher rates. The transfer is effective in achieving that

---

[5] FA 2003, ss.53, 54.

aim. However, B Ltd suffers SDLT in accordance with the higher rates on the market value of the dwelling (see **3.3.2.4** and **3.3.9.1**). None of the exceptions to the market value rule applies.

9.7 DISTRIBUTIONS *IN SPECIE*

HM Revenue and Customs (HMRC) might argue that where a company distributes property by way of a final dividend and the subject-matter of the dividend is expressed to be an amount of cash satisfied by the transfer of property, SDLT is chargeable on the amount of cash. This is because, HMRC might say, the member of the company is entitled to receive the cash as soon as the dividend is declared; therefore, the company owes that cash to its member and that debt is discharged in return for the property. The author would argue that this is incorrect. Viewing the facts realistically, the member is never entitled to receive the cash. He is only ever entitled to receive the property. The subject-matter of the dividend, although expressed in cash, is stated to be satisfied *in specie*. Curiously, HMRC's position is contained in its guidance on share transfers, but not on property transfers. The logic is the same, so there is no discernible reason for the omission. Nevertheless, this risk is easily avoided by expressing the subject-matter of the dividend to be the property worth £X. In this way, it is certain that the member is only ever entitled to receive the property, not any cash. In the author's experience, the standard precedent for dividends *in specie* always needs to be amended for this point.[6]

Example 9.5

A Ltd owns a dwelling worth £2 million. Its only member is B. B wishes to 'de-envelope' the dwelling. A Ltd's board recommends paying a final dividend of £2 million to be satisfied *in specie* (being a transfer of the dwelling not cash) to its shareholder, B. HMRC may argue that as soon as A Ltd resolves to pay the dividend the company owes £2 million to B and the dwelling is transferred in satisfaction of that debt; hence, it is chargeable to SDLT, at the appropriate rates, on £2 million.

9.8 CONTRIBUTIONS TO PARTNERSHIPS

The transfer of a dwelling by a partner to a partnership, in whole or in part, by way of capital contribution is chargeable to SDLT under special charging rules. The absence (or presence) of any actual consideration is irrelevant. Complicated rules determine the amount of the chargeable consideration deemed to be given for the transaction. In broad terms, that amount is equal to a proportion of the market value

---

[6] FA 2003, ss.53, 54(4); *Stamp Taxes on Shares Manual* (HMRC internal manual, 7 March 2016, updated 25 November 2019, available at: **www.gov.uk/hmrc-internal-manuals/stamp-taxes-shares-manual**): STSM021130.

of the property transferred. A prescribed series of steps must be followed to calculate the chargeable proportion (see **16.4**). The market value is not reduced by any debt secured on the property transferred. Where a new lease is granted to the partnership, the special charging rules determine the proportion of the market value of the lease *and* an equivalent proportion of the net present value (NPV) of the rent payable over the term of the lease that is chargeable. Any liability arising on the transfer is borne by all the partners, jointly and severally, even where the partnership has separate legal personality.

For these purposes, there is a transfer of property (or the grant of a lease) to a partnership in any case where the property becomes partnership property: i.e., where it is held by, or on behalf of, the partnership for the purposes of the partnership business.[7]

Example 9.6

A owns 10 dwellings in England held for investment (buy-to-let). The dwellings are worth in total £10 million. A transfers the properties to a Scottish partnership consisting of himself and a business associate, B. B is unrelated to A. Each partner is entitled to share equally in the income profits of the partnership. The transfer is made by way of capital contribution. No debt is secured on the properties transferred. Nevertheless, both partners are jointly and severally liable to pay £239,500 of SDLT (an effective rate of 2.4%): (£150,000 @ 0%) + (£100,000 @ 2%) + (£4,750,000 @ 5%). (The tax is calculated in accordance with the non-residential rates, as more than five dwellings are transferred: see **3.2.5**. It would not be beneficial to disapply those rates by claiming multiple dwellings relief: see **4.3**.) It is irrelevant that the partnership has separate legal personality. Nor does it matter that no actual consideration is given for the transaction. In this example, the chargeable consideration deemed to be given for the transaction is equal to 50% of the market value of the properties transferred.

WARNING

The special charging rules for transactions involving partnerships and partners (or connected persons) are notoriously complex. In many cases it would be prudent to seek specialist advice to check.

9.9 DISTRIBUTIONS BY, AND WITHDRAWALS FROM, PARTNERSHIPS

The transfer of a dwelling by a partnership to a partner, in whole or in part, by way of a distribution or a withdrawal is chargeable to SDLT under special charging rules. The absence (or presence) of any actual consideration is irrelevant. Complicated rules determine the amount of the chargeable consideration deemed to be given for the transaction. In broad terms, that amount is equal to a proportion of the market

---

[7] FA 2003, Sched.15, paras.10, 11, 12, 35; SDLT Manual: SDLTM33300, SDLTM33500.

value of the property transferred. A prescribed series of steps must be followed to calculate the chargeable proportion (see **16.5**). The market value is not reduced by any debt secured on the property transferred. Where a new lease is granted by the partnership, the special charging rules determine the proportion of the market value of the lease *and* an equivalent proportion of the NPV of the rent payable over the term of the lease that is chargeable. Any liability arising on the transfer is borne by the partner acquiring the property.

For these purposes, there is a transfer of property (or the grant of a lease) from a partnership in any case where the property that was partnership property (i.e., property held by, or on behalf of, the partnership for the purposes of the partnership business) ceases to be partnership property.

Where there is a transfer of property by a partnership to a partner on a withdrawal made by the partner and the same partner had transferred the property to the partnership within the last three years, there is a risk that the transfer of the property by the partnership might be charged separately under a specific provision.[8]

Example 9.7

A limited liability partnership (LLP) holds a number of dwellings as a source of rents in the course of a property-rental business. It distributes some of the dwellings (all of which are located in England) to one of its members, B. B is entitled to a 50% share of the income profits of the partnership. The total market value of the dwellings to be transferred is £5 million. Debt in the amount of £3 million is secured on the dwellings to be transferred. An LLP had acquired the dwellings on the open market and paid stamp duty/SDLT in full on its acquisition. B has been a member since the incorporation of the partnership and there have been no changes to the income-profit sharing ratio of the members. B is not related to the other members of the partnership. The chargeable consideration for B's acquisition of the dwellings is deemed to be £2.5 million (50% of £5 million), not £3 million. B might consider paying tax in accordance with the non-residential (or mixed) rates if more than five dwellings are transferred or claim multiple dwellings relief (see **3.2.5** and **4.3**, respectively).

WARNING

The special charging rules for transactions involving partnerships and partners (or connected persons) are notoriously complex.

9.10 THE SDLT GENERAL ANTI-AVOIDANCE RULE

The scope and application of the general anti-avoidance rule, Finance Act 2003, s.75A, could be the subject of an entire chapter and possibly an entire book. They are the subject of case law. However, that case law does not illuminate the scope and

---

[8] FA 2003, Sched.15, paras.17A, 18, 19, 20, 21, 37; SDLT Manual: SDLTM33300, SDLTM33700.

application of the rule to simple or benign fact patterns particularly well. HMRC had confirmed in guidance for the first 13 years of section 75A's life (2006–19) that it would not apply the provision where transactions had been taxed 'appropriately'. This prevented the provision from having any negative impact except on tax avoidance schemes. In 2019, however, HMRC argued, and it was found in one case, that the guidance was incorrect. As a result, it is not safe to rely on the guidance until HMRC confirms its position. The relevance of the foregoing stems from a First-tier Tribunal decision in 2019 that held (so far as material to the discussion):

- section 75A is part of the scheme of the tax;
- there is no precondition to its application that the purchaser intended to avoid SDLT;
- section 75A contains objective yardsticks for determining whether there is a tax saving; it self-defines 'avoidance' for the purposes of the provision;
- establishing whether or not there is a tax saving is judged by reference to 'scheme transactions'; scheme transactions (which do not need to be land transactions) merely need to be commercially interdependent on the SDLT transaction.

This means that where there is an SDLT transaction (or more than one), there are other arrangements closely connected to the SDLT transaction (the scheme transactions) and less SDLT is payable on the SDLT transaction than would be payable on a notional transaction, section 75A might apply. Its effect is to charge tax on the notional transaction less any SDLT paid on the SDLT transaction(s). In determining the amount of SDLT chargeable on the notional transaction, and therefore whether section 75A is engaged, the chargeable consideration is taken to be the largest amount (or aggregate amount) given by any one person, or received by the vendor, by way of consideration for the scheme transactions.[9]

> **WARNING**
>
> It is quite a challenge persuading parties that structuring or restructuring that may not be driven by SDLT (or any tax for that matter) could be vulnerable to an SDLT anti-avoidance rule, and SDLT may be chargeable on an amount given by someone other than the purchaser and/or for something other than the subject-matter of the SDLT transaction. Nevertheless, that is the concern. Consequently, wherever residential property is transferred as part of a series of steps (however benign), Finance Act 2003, s.75A should be considered and, if necessary, advice should be taken or confirmation of HMRC's interpretation of the legislation should be requested.

---

[9] *Project Blue Ltd* v. *Revenue and Customs Comrs* [2018] UKSC 30; *Hannover Leasing Wachstumswerte Europa Beteiligungsgesellschaft mbh and another* v. *Revenue and Customs Comrs* [2019] UKFTT 262 (TC); FA 2003, ss.75A, 75B, 75C; SDLT Manual: SDLTM09050, SDLTM09150, SDLTM09175, SDLTM09200, SDLTM09210, SDLTM09225, SDLTM09250, SDLTM09275.

Example 9.8

A Ltd owns the freehold estate in a house occupied by the only shareholder of the company, B. B had made a loan to the company to fund its purchase of the property. B wishes to take the property out of the company. If the company distributed the property in satisfaction of the loan, SDLT would be chargeable on the amount of the debt discharged. Consequently, B discharges the loan owed to him by the company in return for the company issuing further shares to him (debt for equity). This is done prior to the company making a distribution of the property. Neither the conversion of the shareholder debt into equity nor the subsequent distribution of the property are chargeable to SDLT. B must take a view on whether the issue of shares by A Ltd is a 'scheme transaction' within the meaning given by Finance Act 2003, s.75A. If it is, the value of the shares would be taken to be the chargeable consideration on a notional transfer of the property, the amount of SDLT paid on the SDLT transaction (nil) would be less than the amount of SDLT that would be payable on a notional transaction; hence, section 75A would be engaged and B would suffer SDLT based on the value of the shares issued.

CHAPTER 10

Right to buy transactions, shared ownership leases, etc.

10.1 BACKGROUND

This chapter covers the stamp duty land tax (SDLT) treatment of:

- transactions made under the right to buy scheme;
- rent to mortgage transactions;
- shared ownership leases; and
- shared ownership trusts.[1]

These transactions are generally entered into by housing associations and local authorities as vendors and housing association tenants or key public sector workers as purchasers. The rent to mortgage scheme has been withdrawn. However, existing rent to mortgage properties exist.

Shared ownership leases are excluded from the enfranchisement legislation.

Note: The legislation and HM Revenue and Customs (HMRC) guidance in this area are unclear.

10.2 SHARED OWNERSHIP LEASES

Shared ownership leases refer to arrangements under which eligible persons (historically, an existing housing association tenant, or a person on a housing association or local authority housing list, or a key public sector worker) are granted a lease of a dwelling at a discounted rent and the option to purchase a share of the dwelling for an initial payment and the option to purchase additional shares of the dwelling for further payments based on the market value of the dwelling at the relevant time. The discount in rent, at any point during the term of the lease, corresponds to the percentage share of the dwelling beneficially owned by the

---

[1] For more information see *Sergeant and Sims on Stamp Taxes* (LexisNexis UK), AA9.8: Right to buy transactions, shared ownership leases and shared ownership trusts; Finance Act (FA) 2003, s.70, Sched.9; *HMRC internal manual – Stamp Duty Land Tax Manual* ('SDLT Manual') (HMRC, 19 March 2016, updated 16 January 2020, available at: **www.gov.uk/hmrc-internal-manuals/stamp-duty-land-tax-manual**): SDLTM27000.

tenant. This typically equals three per cent of the percentage share of the dwelling owned by the landlord, index-linked for future years.

Where a person acquires a new lease of a dwelling through an approved shared ownership scheme, he must choose how to pay SDLT. There are two possibilities:

1. pay SDLT in one instalment upfront; or
2. pay SDLT in stages.

The first choice involves making an election. SDLT is payable within 14 days of the grant of the lease based on the market value of the dwelling stated in the lease. No further payment of SDLT or SDLT return are due if the purchaser increases his share in the dwelling ('staircasing') or acquires the reversionary interest in the dwelling. The staircasing transactions and the acquisition of the reversionary interest are exempt from charge.

The market value of the dwelling is either the market value of the freehold estate where the lease gives the tenant a right to acquire the reversionary interest or the 'open market premium' where it does not.

The 'open market premium' is the premium that would be payable to acquire the largest share of the dwelling permitted under the lease. Various conditions must be met before an election may be made: see below.

A market value election also relieves the SDLT (if any) that would be payable on the net present value (NPV) of the rent payable over the term of the lease. The NPV of the rent would need to exceed £125,000 before any SDLT would be due on the rent (see **5.2.3**). The minimum rent stated in the lease must be used in the NPV calculation. The minimum rent means the lowest rent which could become payable under the lease if the purchaser chose to staircase regardless of whether or not he in fact does. If the NPV of the minimum rent were to exceed £125,000 causing SDLT to be payable on the rent, the tax paid would not be refunded by HMRC, in whole or in part, if the tenant subsequently staircases such that the rent reduces or the lease ends.

The second choice involves the tenant paying SDLT initially based on the premium paid for the lease, as well as on the NPV of the minimum rent. No tax would be payable if the amount of the premium and NPV of the minimum rent, viewed separately, do not exceed the nil rate band. No payment of SDLT (or no payment of additional SDLT) would be due unless and until the purchaser staircases to more than 80 per cent. It does not matter whether or not any SDLT is paid on the grant of the lease.

At the point that the purchaser staircases to more than 80 per cent, in calculating the charge to SDLT it is important to distinguish shared ownership leases granted before 12 March 2008 and those granted on or after that date. Where the lease was granted before 12 March 2008, the amount of SDLT payable on the premium and the staircasing transactions is based on the total sum paid for the grant of the lease and all the staircasing transactions. This means that staircasing to more than 80 per cent could cause additional SDLT (and a further SDLT return) to become due on the premium paid for the lease. Where the lease was granted on or after 12 March 2008, the amount of SDLT payable on the staircasing transactions only is based on the total sum paid for all the staircasing transactions and the premium paid for the grant of the lease. The premium paid for the grant is *not* aggregated with the payments made under the staircasing transactions to calculate the tax due on the premium; hence, staircasing would not cause additional SDLT to become due on the premium paid for the lease. This is explained below. The exemption for staircasing up to (and including) 80 per cent was introduced for transactions with an effective date after 17 March 2004.[2]

Consequential modifications are made to the usual treatment of contingent consideration. Rather than tax being calculated as if the contingency will occur, instead the contingent consideration (staircasing payments) is disregarded as chargeable consideration.

WARNING

1. In the examples that follow, it is assumed that neither the tenant nor his spouse or civil partner (or their children unless aged 18 or over) own the freehold or leasehold estate (or foreign equivalent) in another dwelling worth £40,000 or more (unless it is subject to a long lease) – see **3.3**. If the tenant (etc.) does own such a dwelling, then the tax due on the staircasing transactions would be calculated in accordance with the residential higher rates unless the tenant has lived in the dwelling throughout the previous three years, the lease has an unexpired term of more than 21 years and the tenant is beneficially entitled as tenant in common to more than 25 per cent of the lease or there are no more than four joint tenants (see **3.3.10.2**). The tax due on the staircasing transactions in the examples has been calculated in accordance with the standard rates based on this assumption.
2. The tenant's choice regarding whether to pay SDLT in one instalment upfront or in stages and the effective relief on staircasing up to (and including) 80 per cent do *not* apply to shared ownership leases granted by private bodies. In the examples that follow, it is assumed that the shared ownership lease is granted by a qualifying body, not a private body.
3. The treatment of shared ownership leases has been the subject of frequent legislative amendment. The commentary and examples that follow apply to leases granted on or after 29 October 2018. Specialist advice should be sought in relation to staircasing transactions in pursuance of a lease granted before that date.

Example 10.1

A acquires a shared ownership lease of a house for a term of 125 years in January 2012. He is unmarried and is not a first-time buyer. The market value of the property is £300,000. He pays £150,000 for a 50% share. The monthly rent is £375: (£150,000 @ 3%) / 12. A chooses to pay SDLT in stages. The amount of SDLT payable on the premium is £9,000 (a flat 3% rate applied for purchases between £125,000 and £250,000 at that time). The NPV of the minimum rent does not exceed £125,000; hence, no tax is due on the rent. A later

---

[2] FA 2003, Sched.9, paras.2, 3, 4A, 4B, 5, 15, 15A, 16; SDLT Manual: SDLTM27020, SDLTM27030, SDLTM27040, SDLTM27050, SDLTM27060, SDLTM27065, SDLTM27080.

staircases. In the first staircasing transaction, in January 2015, he pays £100,000 to increase his share to 75%. In the second and final staircasing transaction, in November 2018, he pays £125,000 to increase his share to 100% and acquire the freehold estate of the property. The total sum paid for the grant of the lease and the two staircasing transactions is £375,000 (£150,000 + £100,000 + £125,000). No SDLT is due on the first staircasing transaction, as the transaction does not result in A's share exceeding 80%. However, SDLT is due on the second staircasing transaction. The tax is calculated on the total amount paid for the two staircasing transactions and the premium paid on the grant of the lease (as the lease was granted after 11 March 2008), before it is apportioned to the transactions. A must make an initial SDLT return and pay tax within 14 days of the second staircasing transaction. The amount of SDLT payable on £375,000 in accordance with the rates in force at the date of the second staircasing transaction is £8,750: (£125,000 @ 0%) + (£125,000 @ 2%) + (£125,000 @ 5%). The proportion of the £8,750 attributable to the second staircasing transaction is £2,917: (£125,000/£375,000) x £8,750. This means that £2,917 of SDLT is payable on the second staircasing transaction within 14 days of the transaction. No additional tax is due in respect of the grant of the lease and no tax is due on the first staircasing transaction.

A market value election must be made in the SDLT return or an amendment to the SDLT return. This means that a market value election cannot be made more than one year after the filing date for the transaction (14 days after completion). Once made, a market value election cannot be withdrawn. There is nothing in the SDLT return that enables the purchaser to bring the making of a market value election to HMRC's attention. HMRC advises that the return should be completed by inputting the market value stated in the lease at question 22 (total premium payable) of the SDLT return. While this should be effective, to prevent potential confusion the author would recommend that the purchaser also voluntarily sends HMRC a letter that cross-refers to the return to state explicitly that he has made a market value election. Other advice on how to complete an SDLT return for shared ownership leases is available in HMRC's SDLT Manual.

The conditions that must be met before a market value election is valid are as follows:

- the lease must be granted by a 'qualifying body'; or
- the lease must be granted 'in pursuance of the preserved right to buy';

and:
- the lease is of a dwelling;
- the lease gives the tenant(s) exclusive use of the dwelling;

and:
- the lease provides for the tenant(s) to acquire the reversion; or
- the lease provides for the tenant(s) to make a payment to reduce the rent payable under the lease;

and:
- the lease is granted partly for rent and partly for a premium calculated by reference to the market value of the dwelling (where the lease gives the tenant a

right to acquire the reversionary interest) or the 'open market premium' (where the lease does not give the tenant such a right); and
- the lease states the market value of the dwelling (where the lease gives the tenant a right to acquire the reversionary interest) or the minimum rent and the open market premium (where the lease does not give the tenant such a right).

A 'qualifying body' is:

- a local housing authority within the meaning of the Housing Act 1985;
- a housing association within the meaning of the Housing Associations Act 1985 or Housing (Northern Ireland) Order 1992, Part 2;
- a housing action trust established under Housing Act 1988, Part 3;
- the Northern Ireland Housing Executive;
- Homes England;
- the Greater London Authority;
- a development corporation made under the New Towns Act 1981; or
- a private registered provider of social housing if the purchase or construction or adaptation of the property has been funded with the assistance of a grant or other financial assistance made under Housing and Regeneration Act 2008, s.19 or by the Greater London Authority.

A lease is granted 'in pursuance of the preserved right to buy' if:

- the landlord is a person against whom the right to buy under Housing Act 1985, Part 5 is exercisable by virtue of section 171 of that Act;
- the tenant(s) are the qualifying person for the purposes of the right to buy; and
- the lease is of a dwelling that is the qualifying dwelling-house in relation to the purchaser.

Example 10.2

A acquires a shared ownership lease of a house for a term of 125 years in July 2019. He is unmarried and is not a first-time buyer. The market value of the property is £350,000. The monthly rent is £438: (£175,000 @ 3%) / 12. He pays £175,000 for a 50% share. A makes a market value election. The amount of SDLT payable is £7,500 (an effective rate of 2.1%): (£125,000 @ 0%) + (£125,000 @ 2%) + (£100,000 @ 5%). No SDLT is due on the rent by virtue of A making the market value election irrespective of the NPV of the rent. A later staircases. In the first staircasing transaction he increases his share to 75%, paying £95,000. In the second and final staircasing transaction he increases his share to 100% and acquires the freehold estate of the property, paying £105,000. The total sum paid on the staircasing transactions is £200,000. No SDLT is due on the staircasing transactions by virtue of A having made the market value election.

Example 10.3

As before, but A does *not* make a market value election. The amount of SDLT payable initially is £1,000. This is the tax due on the £175,000 premium: (£125,000 @ 0%) + (£50,000 @ 2%). The NPV of the minimum rent does not exceed £125,000; hence, no tax is due on the rent. The tax on the premium will not be increased by a later staircasing transaction (as the grant was after 11 March 2008). No SDLT is due on the first staircasing transaction, as the transaction does not result in A's share exceeding 80%. However, SDLT is due in respect of the second staircasing transaction within 14 days of the second staircasing transaction. The amount of SDLT payable is based on the total amount paid for the grant of the lease and the two staircasing transactions, £375,000 (£175,000 + £95,000 + £105,000), before being pro-rated. The tax due on £375,000 (assuming there are no changes in tax rates or tax bands) is £8,750: (£125,000 @ 0%) + (£125,000 @ 2%) + (£125,000 @ 5%). The proportion of the £8,750 attributable to the second staircasing transaction is £2,450: (£105,000 / £375,000) x £8,750. This means that £8,750 of SDLT is payable on the second staircasing transaction within 14 days of the transaction. No additional tax is due in respect of the grant of the lease and no tax is due on the first staircasing transaction.

For shared ownership leases granted on or after 12 March 2008 where no market value election is made, the method for calculating the tax on the first staircasing transaction that takes the purchaser's share over 80 per cent and on each subsequent staircasing transaction is as follows:

1. Calculate the amount of SDLT due on the total sum paid under the staircasing transaction, all previous staircasing transactions and the grant of the lease using the rates in force at the date of the staircasing transaction.
2. Divide the amount paid under the staircasing transaction by the total sum paid under all the staircasing transactions and the premium paid on the grant of the lease to produce a fraction.
3. Multiply the amount of SDLT payable found at the first step by the fraction found at the second step to give the proportion of the SDLT due on the staircasing transaction.
4. Repeat this exercise for all previous staircasing transactions.
5. For each previous staircasing transaction, where there has been a change of rates since that transaction took place:
    (a) calculate the amount of SDLT due on the total sum paid under all the staircasing transactions and the premium paid on the grant of the lease using the rates in force at the date of the staircasing transaction; and
    (b) multiply the relevant amount of SDLT payable by the fraction given by dividing the sum paid for the staircasing transaction by the total sum paid under all the staircasing transactions and the premium paid on the grant of the lease.
6. Compare the amount of SDLT paid on all previous staircasing transactions

with the amount of SDLT now payable for the previous staircasing transactions as a consequence of the latest staircasing transaction.

The possibility of making numerous returns and retrospective adjustments to the tax paid on earlier staircasing transactions is strong where the purchaser staircases more than once after increasing his share to over 80 per cent. In the following example, five staircasing transactions generate the obligation to make six SDLT returns in total!

Example 10.4

In 2010, A acquires a shared ownership lease of a house in London for a term of 125 years. He is unmarried but is not a first-time buyer. The market value of the property is £800,000. He pays £200,000 for a 25% share. The monthly rent is £1,500: (£600,000 @ 3%) / 12. A does not make a market value election. The amount of SDLT payable initially is £5,323. This is the tax due on the £200,000 premium ((£125,000 @ 0%) + (£75,000 @ 2%)). The NPV of the minimum rent does not exceed £125,000; hence, no tax is due on the rent.

A later staircases. In the first staircasing transaction a year later (2011), he increases his share to 50%, paying £210,000. In the second a year later (2012), he increases his share to 75%, paying £225,000. In the third a year later (2013), he increases his share to 85%, paying £90,000. In the fourth a year later (2014), he increases his share to 95%, paying £95,000. In the final staircasing transaction a year later (2015), he increases his share to 100% and acquires the freehold estate of the property, paying £50,000.

No SDLT payment and no SDLT return are due on the second staircasing transaction, as the transaction does not result in A's share exceeding 80%. A must make an initial SDLT return and pay SDLT in respect of the third staircasing transaction within 14 days of the third staircasing transaction. The amount of SDLT payable is based on the total amount paid for the three staircasing transactions and the premium, £725,000 (£200,000 + £210,000 + £225,000 + £90,000), before being pro-rated. The tax due on £725,000 (using the rates in force at 2013) is £29,000: (£725,000 @ 4%). The proportion of the £29,000 attributable to the third staircasing transaction is £3,600: (£90,000 / £725,000) x £29,000. A might need to make a further SDLT return and pay additional tax in respect of the third staircasing transaction within 30 days of the fourth staircasing transaction and would need to make an initial SDLT return and pay tax in respect of the fourth staircasing transaction within 14 days of the fourth staircasing transaction. The amount of SDLT payable is based on the total amount paid for the four staircasing transactions and the premium, £820,000 (£200,000 + £210,000 + £225,000 + £90,000 + £95,000), before being pro-rated. The tax due on £820,000 (using the rates in force at 2014) is £31,000: (£125,000 @ 0%) + (£125,000 @ 2%) + (£570,000 @ 5%). The proportion of the £31,000 attributable to the fourth staircasing transaction is £3,591: (£95,000 / £820,000) x £31,000. This is the tax due in respect of the fourth staircasing transaction. We now need to calculate the tax due in respect of the third staircasing transaction. The tax due on £820,000 (using the rates in force at 2013) is £32,800: (£820,000 @ 4%). The proportion of the £32,800 attributable to the third staircasing transaction is £3,600: (£90,000 / £820,000) x £32,800. The same amount of tax was paid at the time of the third staircasing transaction (£3,600), so there is no additional tax (and no further return) due in respect of the third staircasing transaction. A might need to make two further SDLT returns and pay additional tax in respect of the third and fourth staircasing transactions within 30 days of the final staircasing transaction and would need to make an initial SDLT return and pay tax in respect of the final staircasing transaction within 14 days of the final staircasing transaction. The amount of SDLT payable is based on the total amount paid for all five staircasing transactions and the premium, £870,000 (£200,000 + £210,000 + £225,000 + £90,000 + £95,000 + £50,000), before being pro-rated. The tax due on £870,000 (using the rates in force at 2015) is £33,500: (£125,000 @ 0%) + (£125,000 @ 2%) + (£620,000 @ 5%). The proportion of the £33,500 attributable to the final staircasing transaction is £1,925: (£50,000 / £870,000) x £33,500. This is the tax due in respect of the final staircasing transaction. We now need to calculate the tax due in respect of the third and fourth staircasing transactions. Starting with the third staircasing transaction, the tax due on £870,000 (using the rates in force at 2013) is £34,800: (£870,000 @ 4%). The proportion of the £34,800 attributable to the third staircasing transaction is £3,600: (£90,000 / £870,000) x £34,800. The same amount of tax was paid at the time of the third staircasing transaction (£3,600), so there is no additional tax and (and no further return) due in respect of the third staircasing transaction. Moving to the fourth staircasing transaction, the tax due on £870,000 (using the rates in force at 2014) is £33,500: (£125,000 @ 0%) + (£125,000 @ 2%) + (£620,000 @ 5%). The proportion of the £33,500 attributable to the fourth staircasing transaction is £3,658: (£95,000 / £870,000) x £33,500. Less tax was paid at the time of the fourth staircasing transaction (£3,218), so £440 of additional tax and a further return are due in respect of the fourth staircasing transaction within 30 days of the final staircasing transaction.

First-time buyers may claim relief on the purchase of a shared ownership lease regardless of whether or not they make a market value election. That was not always the case, though. The relief was initially only available to first-time buyers of shared ownership leases that chose to make a market value election. In 2019, the law was changed to enable all first-time buyers of shared ownership leases to benefit from the relief. First-time buyers that completed their purchase on or after 22 November 2017 (the date on which first-time buyer relief was introduced with permanent effect) and chose to pay SDLT in stages were invited to apply for a repayment of the SDLT paid due to not having been able to claim first-time buyer relief. Applications needed to have been made by 29 October 2019. Where the relief is claimed, no tax is chargeable on the NPV of the rent.

Where a market value election is made, the relief may be claimed if the market value of the dwelling does not exceed £500,000. Where a market value election is not made, the relief may be claimed if the premium paid for the grant of the lease does not exceed £500,000. The relief does not apply to any staircasing transactions. The relief, if claimed on the grant of the lease, is not withdrawn if one or more staircasing transactions entered into after the grant mean that the total amount paid for the grant and the staircasing transaction(s) is more than £500,000.

For first-time buyer relief on purchases of shared ownership leases, see **4.2.3**.

Example 10.5

A acquires a shared ownership lease of a house for a term of 125 years. He is unmarried and is a first-time buyer. The market value of the property is £400,000. He pays £100,000 for a 25% share. A makes a market value election and claims first-time buyer relief. The amount of SDLT payable is £5,000 (an effective rate of 5%): (£300,000 @ 0%) + (£100,000 @

5%). A later staircases. In the first staircasing transaction he increases his share to 75%, paying £220,000. In the second staircasing transaction he increases his share to 100% and acquires the freehold estate of the property, paying £115,000. The total sum paid on the staircasing transactions is £335,000. No further SDLT is due by virtue of A having made the market value election.

Example 10.6

A acquires a shared ownership lease of a house for a term of 125 years. He is unmarried and is a first-time buyer. The market value of the property is £620,000. He pays £310,000 for a 50% share. The monthly rent is £775: (£310,000 @ 3%) / 12. A does *not* make a market value election and claims first-time buyer relief. The amount of SDLT payable initially is £500 (an effective rate of 0.2%): (£300,000 @ 0%) + (£10,000 @ 5%). (No SDLT is due on the rent irrespective of the NPV of the rent by virtue of A claiming the relief.) A later staircases. In the first staircasing transaction he increases his share to 75%, paying £220,000. In the second staircasing transaction he increases his share to 100% and acquires the freehold estate of the property, paying £115,000. The total sum paid on the staircasing transactions and for the grant of the lease is £645,000 (£310,000 + £220,000 + £115,000). No SDLT is due on the first staircasing transaction, as it does not take A's share to over 80%. However, SDLT and an initial SDLT return are due within 14 days of the second staircasing transaction. The amount of SDLT due on £645,000 (assuming there are no changes in tax rates or tax bands, see above) is £22,250 (an effective rate of 3.5%): (£125,000 @ 0%) + (£125,000 @ 2%) + (£395,000 @ 5%). The proportion of the £22,250 attributable to the second staircasing transaction is £3,967: (£115,000 / £645,000) x £22,250. This means that £3,967 of SDLT is payable on the second staircasing transaction within 14 days of the transaction. No additional tax is due on the initial capital payment and no tax is due on the first staircasing transaction.

Where the lease is assigned, the purchaser (assignee) assumes the obligation to make further SDLT returns in respect of previous staircasing transactions. To give effect to this rule, anything previously done by the vendor (assignor) in relation to notifying HMRC and paying SDLT is treated as if it had been done by the purchaser (see **5.4.3**).[3]

TIP

When acting for a purchaser of a shared ownership lease, it is necessary to inform them of their right to make a market value election (assuming the conditions for doing so are met), the time period for doing so, the effect of doing so (and of not doing so, including the obligation to make numerous SDLT returns on staircasing transactions) and the fact that, once made, the election cannot be withdrawn.

---

[3] FA 2003, Sched.17A, para.12.

RIGHT TO BUY TRANSACTIONS, SHARED OWNERSHIP LEASES, ETC.

> **TIP**
>
> When acting for an assignee of a shared ownership lease, it is necessary to pull copies of the SDLT returns made by the assignor (or the original tenant if the assignor is not the original tenant) or details of the historic staircasing transactions to ensure that the correct amount of tax is calculated on further staircasing transactions.

10.3 SHARED OWNERSHIP TRUSTS AND RENT TO SHARED OWNERSHIP LEASE SCHEMES

10.3.1 Rent to shared ownership lease schemes

'Rent to shared ownership lease' refers to a scheme under which a person in occupation of a dwelling under an assured shorthold tenancy granted by a 'qualifying body' has the right to be granted, or the right to apply to be granted subject to an assessment of their financial position, a shared ownership lease by the same body. For such transactions, the grant of the assured shorthold tenancy and the shared ownership lease are taken not to be 'linked' transactions for the purposes of SDLT (see **5.2.7**). Consequently, the amount of the SDLT payable on the shared ownership lease cannot exceed the premium paid for the shared ownership lease and the NPV of the rent payable under the lease. In addition, the tenant is not treated as substantially performing the agreement for the shared ownership lease by virtue of being in occupation of the dwelling (though the author would argue that this treatment is for the avoidance of doubt only if the tenant does not take possession of the dwelling under the agreement).

10.3.2 Shared ownership trusts

The SDLT rules for shared ownership trusts are substantially similar to the rules for shared ownership leases – see **10.2**.[4] Shared ownership trusts enable shared ownership purchases of flats held in commonhold under the Commonhold and Leasehold Reform Act 2002. Due to the limited number of commonholds in existence, the number of shared ownership trusts is even more limited.

A 'shared ownership trust' is a trust of a dwelling (or a building that is in the process of being constructed or adapted for use as a dwelling) under which:

- a beneficiary (the 'social landlord') is a qualifying body;
- another beneficiary (the 'purchaser') is an individual;
- the purchaser is given exclusive use of the dwelling;

---

[4] FA 2003, Sched.9, paras.7, 8, 9, 10, 11, 12, 13, 14, 15B, 16; SDLT Manual: SDLTM27071, SDLTM27072, SDLTM27073, SDLTM27074, SDLTM27075, SDLTM27076, SDLTM27077, SDLTM27080.

- the purchaser makes an initial payment (the 'initial capital') to the social landlord;
- the purchaser makes additional payments ('rent-equivalent payments') to the social landlord by way of compensation;
- the purchaser is permitted to make other additional payments ('equity-acquisition payments') to the social landlord; or
- the purchaser's beneficial share of the dwelling at any time is determined by reference to the total amount paid by the individual by way of initial capital and equity-acquisition payments.

The purchaser (note that the social landlord is disregarded as a purchaser for the purposes of SDLT) may choose to pay SDLT:

- in one instalment upfront; or
- in stages.

The first choice involves making an election. SDLT is payable within 14 days of the declaration of the trust based on the market value of the dwelling stated in the trust deed. No further payment of SDLT or SDLT return are due if the purchaser increases his share of the beneficial ownership of the dwelling by making equity-acquisition payments. These equity-acquisition payments and the transfer to the purchaser of an interest in the dwelling on the termination of the trust are exempt from charge provided that the tax chargeable on the declaration of the trust has been paid by the purchaser. The market value of the dwelling – which is determined on a vacant possession basis – should be stated in the trust deed. An election also relieves the SDLT (if any) that would be payable on the NPV of the rent-equivalent payments made over the term of the trust. The rent-equivalent payments are treated as payments of rent. The NPV of the rent-equivalent payments would need to exceed £125,000 before any SDLT would be due on the payments (see **5.2.3**). If the NPV of the rent-equivalent payments were to exceed £125,000 causing SDLT to be payable on the rent-equivalent payments, the tax paid would not be refunded by HMRC, in whole or in part, if the tenant subsequently makes equity-acquisition payments such that the rent-equivalent payments reduce or the trust ends. Note that the NPV calculation uses the rent-equivalent payments – it does not use the minimum rent-equivalent payment (if any) stated in the trust deed (cf shared ownership leases).

There is nothing in the SDLT return that enables the purchaser to bring the making of a market value election to HMRC's attention. HMRC advises that the return should be completed by inputting the market value stated in the trust deed at question 22 (total premium payable) of the SDLT return. While this should be effective, to prevent potential confusion the author would recommend that the purchaser also voluntarily sends HMRC a letter that cross-refers to the return to state explicitly that he has made a market value election. Other advice on how to complete an SDLT return for shared ownership leases is available in HMRC's SDLT Manual. The advice should translate to shared ownership trusts.

The second choice involves paying SDLT initially based on the initial capital (i.e., the payment is treated as a premium), as well as on the NPV of the rent-equivalent payments. No tax would be payable if the amount of the initial capital and NPV of the rent-equivalent payments, viewed separately, do not exceed the nil rate band. No payment of SDLT (or no payment of an additional amount of SDLT) would be due unless and until the purchaser makes equity-acquisition payments to increase his share of the beneficial ownership of the dwelling to more than 80 per cent. It does not matter whether or not any SDLT was chargeable on the declaration of the trust. At the point that the purchaser's share of the beneficial ownership of the dwelling increases to more than 80 per cent, the amount of SDLT payable on the equity-acquisition payments only is based on the total sum of the initial capital payment and the equity-acquisition payments. The equity-acquisition payments are not aggregated with the payment of the initial capital for the purpose of determining the tax due on the initial capital payment.

A 'qualifying body' is:

- a local housing authority within the meaning of the Housing Act 1985;
- a housing association within the meaning of the Housing Associations Act 1985 or Housing (Northern Ireland) Order 1992, Part 2;
- a housing action trust established under Housing Act 1988, Part 3;
- the Northern Ireland Housing Executive;
- Homes England;
- the Greater London Authority;
- a development corporation made under the New Towns Act 1981; or
- a private registered provider of social housing if the purchase or construction or adaptation of the property has been funded with the assistance of a grant or other financial assistance made under Housing and Regeneration Act 2008, s.19 or by the Greater London Authority.

WARNING

In the examples that follow it is assumed that neither the purchaser nor his spouse or civil partner (or their children unless aged 18 or over) own the freehold or leasehold estate (or foreign equivalent) in another dwelling worth £40,000 or more (unless it is subject to a long lease) (see **3.3**). If the purchaser (etc.) does own such a dwelling, then the tax due on the equity-acquisition payments would be calculated in accordance with the residential higher rates unless the purchaser has lived in the dwelling throughout the previous three years, and the purchaser is beneficially entitled as tenant in common to more than 25 per cent of the lease or there are no more than four joint tenants (see **3.3.10.2**). The tax due on the equity-acquisition payments in the examples has been calculated in accordance with the standard rates based on this assumption.

Example 10.7

A acquires a share of the beneficial ownership of a flat under a shared ownership trust in July 2019. He is unmarried and is not a first-time buyer. The market value of the property is £350,000. The monthly rent-equivalent payment is £438: (£175,000 @ 3%) / 12. He pays £175,000 of initial capital for a 50% share. A makes a market value election. The amount of SDLT payable is £7,500 (an effective rate of 2.1%): (£125,000 @ 0%) + (£125,000 @ 2%) + (£100,000 @ 5%). No SDLT is due on the rent-equivalent payments by virtue of A making the market value election. A later makes equity-acquisition payments. By making the first equity-acquisition payment, he increases his share of the beneficial ownership of the property to 75%, paying £95,000. By making the second and final equity-acquisition payment, he increases his share of the beneficial ownership of the property to 100%, acquires the freehold estate of the flat, becomes a member of the commonhold association and the trust terminates, paying £105,000. The total sum of the equity-acquisition payments is £200,000. No SDLT is due on the equity-acquisition payments by virtue of A having made the market value election.

Example 10.8

As before, but A does *not* make a market value election. The amount of SDLT payable initially is £1,229. This is the total of the tax due on the £175,000 initial capital payment ((£125,000 @ 0%) + (£50,000 @ 2%)) and on the £147,965 NPV of the rent-equivalent payments ((£125,000 @ 0%) + (£22,965 @ 1%)). The tax on the initial capital payment will not be increased by A later making equity-acquisition payments. No SDLT is due on the first equity-acquisition payment, as the transaction does not result in A's share of the beneficial ownership of the dwelling exceeding 80%. But SDLT is due on the second equity-acquisition payment within 14 days of making the second equity-acquisition payment. The amount of SDLT payable is based on the total of the initial capital payment and the two equity-acquisition payments, £375,000 (£175,000 + £95,000 + £105,000), before being pro-rated. The tax due on £375,000 (assuming there are no changes in tax rates or tax bands) is £8,750: (£125,000 @ 0%) + (£125,000 @ 2%) + (£125,000 @ 5%). The proportion of the £8,750 attributable to the second equity-acquisition payment is £2,450: (£105,000 / £375,000) x £8,750. This means that £2,450 of SDLT is payable on the second equity-acquisition payment within 14 days of the transaction. No additional tax is due on the initial capital payment and no tax is due on the first equity-acquisition payment.

Where multiple equity-acquisition payments are chargeable, the method for calculating the tax on each is as follows:

1. Calculate the amount of SDLT due on the total sum of the equity-acquisition payment, all previous equity-acquisition payments and the initial capital payment using the rates in force at the date of the equity-acquisition payment.
2. Divide the equity-acquisition payment by the total sum of the equity-acquisition payments and the initial capital payment to produce a fraction.
3. Multiply the amount of SDLT payable found at the first step by the fraction

found at the second step to give the proportion of the SDLT due on the equity-acquisition payment.
4. Repeat this exercise for all previous equity-acquisition payments.
5. For each previous equity-acquisition payment, where there has been a change of rates since that transaction took place, calculate the amount of SDLT due on the equity-acquisition payments and the initial capital payment using the rates in force at the date of the equity-acquisition payment. And multiply the relevant amount of SDLT payable by the fraction given by dividing the sum paid for the equity-acquisition payment by the total sum paid under all the equity-acquisition payments and the initial capital payment.
6. Compare the amount of SDLT paid on all previous equity-acquisition payments with the amount of SDLT now payable for the previous equity-acquisition payments as a consequence of the latest equity-acquisition payment.

The possibility of making numerous returns and retrospective adjustments to the tax paid on earlier equity-acquisition payments is strong where the purchaser makes more than one equity-acquisition payment after increasing his share to over 80 per cent. In the following example, five equity-acquisition payments generate the obligation to make six SDLT returns in total!

Example 10.9

In 2010, A acquires a share of the beneficial ownership of a flat under a shared ownership trust. He is unmarried and is not a first-time buyer. The market value of the property is £800,000. He pays £200,000 of initial capital for a 25% share. The monthly rent-equivalent payment is £1,500: (£600,000 @ 3%) / 12. A does not make a market value election. The amount of SDLT payable initially is £5,323. This is the total of the tax due on the £200,000 initial capital payment ((£125,000 @ 0%) + (£75,000 @ 2%)) and on the £507,308 NPV of the rent-equivalent payments ((£125,000 @ 0%) + (£382,308 @ 1%)).

A later makes equity-acquisition payments. By making the first equity-acquisition payment a year later (2011), he increases his share of the beneficial ownership of the dwelling to 50%, paying £210,000. By making the second equity-acquisition payment a year later (2012), he increases his share to 75%, paying £225,000. By making the third equity-acquisition payment a year later (2013), he increases his share to 85%, paying £90,000. By making the fourth equity-acquisition payment a year later (2014), he increases his share to 95%, paying £95,000. By making the final equity-acquisition payment a year later (2015), he increases his share to 100%, acquires the freehold estate of the flat, becomes a member of the commonhold association and the trust terminates, paying £50,000.

No SDLT payment and no SDLT return are due on the second equity-acquisition payment, as the transaction does not result in A's share exceeding 80%. A must make an initial SDLT return and pay SDLT in respect of the third equity-acquisition payment within 14 days of the third equity-acquisition payment. The amount of SDLT payable is based on the total amount paid for the three equity-acquisition payments and the initial capital payment, £725,000 (£200,000 + £210,000 + £225,000 + £90,000), before being pro-rated. The tax due on £725,000 (using the rates in force at 2013) is £29,000: (£725,000 @ 4%). The proportion of the £29,000 attributable to the third equity-acquisition payment is £3,600: (£90,000 /

£725,000) x £29,000. A might need to make a further SDLT return and pay additional tax in respect of the third equity-acquisition payment within 30 days of the fourth equity-acquisition payment and would need to make an initial SDLT return and pay tax in respect of the fourth equity-acquisition payment within 14 days of the fourth equity-acquisition payment. The amount of SDLT payable is based on the total amount paid for the four equity-acquisition payments and the initial capital payment, £820,000 (£200,000 + £210,000 + £225,000 + £90,000 + £95,000), before being pro-rated. The tax due on £820,000 (using the rates in force at 2014) is £31,000: (£125,000 @ 0%) + (£125,000 @ 2%) + (£570,000 @ 5%). The proportion of the £31,000 attributable to the fourth equity-acquisition payment is £3,591: (£95,000 / £820,000) x £31,000. This is the tax due in respect of the fourth equity-acquisition payment. We now need to calculate the tax due in respect of the third equity-acquisition payment. The tax due on £820,000 (using the rates in force at 2013) is £32,800: (£820,000 @ 4%). The proportion of the £32,800 attributable to the third equity-acquisition payment is £3,600: (£90,000 / £820,000) x £32,800. The same amount of tax was paid at the time of the third equity-acquisition payment (£3,600), so there is no additional tax (and no further return) due in respect of the third equity-acquisition payment. A might need to make two further SDLT returns and pay additional tax in respect of the third and fourth equity-acquisition payments within 30 days of the final equity-acquisition payment and would need to make an initial SDLT return and pay tax in respect of the final equity-acquisition payment within 14 days of the final equity-acquisition payment. The amount of SDLT payable is based on the total amount paid for all five equity-acquisition payments and the initial capital payment, £870,000 (£200,000 + £210,000 + £225,000 + £90,000 + £50,000), before being pro-rated. The tax due on £870,000 (using the rates in force at 2015) is £33,500: (£125,000 @ 0%) + (£125,000 @ 2%) + (£620,000 @ 5%). The proportion of the £33,500 attributable to the final equity-acquisition payment is £1,925: (£50,000 / £870,000) x £33,500. This is the tax due in respect of the final equity-acquisition payment. We now need to calculate the tax due in respect of the third and fourth equity-acquisition payments. Starting with the third equity-acquisition payment, the tax due on £870,000 (using the rates in force at 2013) is £34,800: (£870,000 @ 4%). The proportion of the £34,800 attributable to the third equity-acquisition payment is £3,600: (£90,000 / £870,000) x £34,800. The same amount of tax was paid at the time of the third equity-acquisition payment (£3,600), so there is no additional tax (and no further return) due in respect of the third equity-acquisition payment. Moving to the fourth equity-acquisition payment, the tax due on £870,000 (using the rates in force at 2014) is £33,500: (£125,000 @ 0%) + (£125,000 @ 2%) + (£620,000 @ 5%). The proportion of the £33,500 attributable to the fourth equity-acquisition payment is £3,658: (£95,000 / £870,000) x £33,500. Less tax was paid at the time of the fourth equity-acquisition payment (£3,218), so £440 of additional tax and a further return are due in respect of the fourth equity-acquisition payment within 30 days of the final equity-acquisition payment.

First-time buyers may claim relief on the purchase of a property under a shared ownership trust regardless of whether or not they make a market value election. That was not always the case, though. The relief was initially only available to first-time buyers of properties under a shared ownership trust that chose to make a market value election. In 2019, the law was changed to enable all first-time buyers of properties under a shared ownership trust to benefit from the relief. First-time buyers that completed their purchase on or after 22 November 2017 (the date on which first-time buyer relief was introduced with permanent effect) and chose to pay SDLT in stages were invited to apply for a repayment of the SDLT paid due to not having been able to claim first-time buyer relief. Applications needed to have been made by 29 October 2019. Where the relief is claimed, no tax is chargeable on the NPV of the rent-equivalent payments.

Where a market value election is made, the relief may be claimed if the market value of the dwelling does not exceed £500,000. Where a market value election is not made, the relief may be claimed if the amount of the initial capital does not exceed £500,000. The relief does not apply to any equity-acquisition payments. The relief, if claimed on the declaration of the trust, is not withdrawn if one or more equity-acquisition payments made after the declaration mean that the total amount paid for the initial capital and equity-acquisition payments is more than £500,000.

For first-time buyer relief on purchases of shared ownership leases, see **4.2.3**.

Example 10.10

A acquires a share of the beneficial ownership of a flat under a shared ownership trust. He is unmarried and is a first-time buyer. The market value of the property is £400,000. He pays £100,000 of initial capital for a 25% share. A makes a market value election and claims first-time buyer relief. The amount of SDLT payable is £5,000 (an effective rate of 5%): (£300,000 @ 0%) + (£100,000 @ 5%). No SDLT is payable on the rent-equivalent payments due to the claim for relief. A later makes equity-acquisition payments. As a result of making the first equity-acquisition payment, he increases his share of the beneficial ownership of the dwelling to 75%. As a result of making the second and final equity-acquisition payment he increases his share to 100%. The total sum paid on the equity-acquisition payments is £300,000. No further SDLT is due by virtue of A having made the market value election.

Example 10.11

A acquires a share of the beneficial ownership of a flat under a shared ownership trust. He is unmarried and is a first-time buyer. The market value of the property is £620,000. He pays £310,000 for a 50% share of the beneficial ownership of the dwelling. A does *not* make a market value election and claims first-time buyer relief. The amount of SDLT payable initially is £500 (an effective rate of 0.2%): (£300,000 @ 0%) + (£10,000 @ 5%). No SDLT is payable on the rent-equivalent payments due to the claim for relief. A later makes equity-acquisition payments. By making the first equity-acquisition payment, he increases his share of the beneficial ownership of the dwelling to 75%, paying £220,000. By making the second and final equity-acquisition payment he increases his share to 100%, paying £115,000. The total sum of the equity-acquisition payments and initial capital payment made is £645,000 (£310,000 + £220,000 + £115,000). No SDLT is due on the first equity-acquisition payment, as it does not take A's share to over 80%. However, SDLT and an initial SDLT return are due within 14 days of making the second equity-acquisition payment. The amount of SDLT due on £645,000 (assuming there are no changes in tax rates or tax bands, see above) is £22,250 (an effective rate of 3.5%): (£125,000 @ 0%) + (£125,000 @ 2%) + (£395,000 @ 5%). The proportion of the £22,250 attributable to the second equity-acquisition payment is £3,967: (£115,000 / £645,000) x £22,250. This means that £3,967 of SDLT is payable on the second equity-acquisition payment within 14 days of the transaction. No additional tax is due on the initial capital payment and no tax is due on the first equity-acquisition payment.

> **TIP**
>
> When acting for a purchaser of a shared ownership property under a shared ownership trust, it is necessary to inform them of their right to make a market value election (assuming the conditions for doing so are met), the time period for doing so, the effect of doing so (and of not doing so, including the obligation to make numerous SDLT returns on making equity-acquisition payments) and the fact that, once made, the election cannot be withdrawn.

10.4 RIGHT TO BUY TRANSACTIONS

The 'right to buy' scheme was introduced in 1980. In essence, it helps eligible council and housing association tenants to buy their home by giving a discount of up to £82,800 or £110,500 for properties in London, respectively (correct at the time of writing), index-linked for future years. Eligible tenants are those persons that have been a public sector tenant for at least three years (reduced from five years in 2015) before applying to buy their home.

The SDLT rules are modified in the case of right to buy transactions. Such transactions take one of two forms:

1. the sale of a dwelling at a discount, or the grant of a lease of a dwelling at a discount, by a 'relevant public sector body' (essentially this applies to council tenants); or
2. the sale of a dwelling at a discount, or the grant of a lease of a dwelling at a discount, 'in pursuance of the preserved right to buy' (essentially this applies where the purchaser was a council tenant when the council transferred it to another landlord, such as a housing association).

'Relevant public sector bodies' include:

- government ministers;
- a local housing authority within the meaning of the Housing Act 1985;
- a county council in England;
- a non-profit registered provider of social housing;
- a registered social landlord (RSL);
- Homes England; and
- the Greater London Authority.

'In pursuance of the preserved right to buy' means a transaction under which:

- the vendor is a person against whom the right to buy under Housing Act 1985, Part 5 is exercisable by virtue of section 171A of that Act;

- the purchaser is the qualifying person for the purposes of the preserved right to buy; and
- the dwelling is the qualifying dwelling-house in relation to the purchaser.

For such transactions, the amount of SDLT payable by the purchaser is based on what is given initially for exercising their right to buy (i.e., reflecting the discount given and ignoring the possibility of a repayment of the discount). Any subsequent payment triggered by the purchaser reselling the dwelling-house within five years (discount repayment) is also disregarded. The normal rules that ignore contingencies and tax contingent consideration (subject to the ability to defer tax on contingent and uncertain consideration) are disapplied.

Where the vendor is a relevant provider of social housing, any discounts given by it on disposals of dwellings to tenants do not count as part of the chargeable consideration for a right to buy transaction. The author presumes that this is for the avoidance of doubt only.

HMRC advises that relief should be claimed in an SDLT return by entering code 22 at question 9 ('are you claiming relief?') of the SDLT return, though this is not required by law.[5]

10.5 RENT TO MORTGAGE TRANSACTIONS

The 'rent to mortgage' scheme was part of the government's mortgage rescue scheme.[6] A rent to mortgage transaction is no longer available. It referred to:

- the transfer of a dwelling to a person; or
- the grant of a lease of a dwelling to a person,

where that person is exercising a right to acquire on rent to mortgage terms under Housing Act 1985, Part 5.

The chargeable consideration for the transaction for the purposes of SDLT is the price that would be payable for the transaction calculated in accordance with Housing Act 1985, s.126, as it applies to rent to mortgage transactions.[7]

---

[5] FA 2003, Sched.9, para.1; SDLT Manual: SDLTM27010, SDLTM27015.
[6] The mortgage rescue scheme was a government initiative to help vulnerable households who were at risk of having their homes repossessed.
[7] FA 2003, Sched.9, para.6; SDLT Manual: SDLTM27070.

CHAPTER 11

Alternative property finance

11.1 BACKGROUND

This chapter covers the stamp duty land tax (SDLT) treatment of certain alternative property finance arrangements, including the availability of specific reliefs. The reliefs are meant to prevent multiple SDLT charges arising on the arrangements and therefore give parity with conventional property finance.[1]

There are two types of alternative property finance arrangements relevant to SDLT. Both relate to the main types of Islamic sharia-compliant financing: Ijara mortgages and Murabaha mortgages. They are collectively referred to as 'home purchase plans' and their provision is regulated under the Financial Services and Markets Act 2000.

The first, which applies to Ijara mortgages, involves a financial institution and a person (usually an individual) entering into arrangements under which the financial institution buys the freehold or leasehold estate of a property and, out of that estate, grants to the person a long lease and a call option to buy the freehold or leasehold estate in one transaction or a series of transactions. The amount of rent payable under the lease is equivalent to that which would be payable under a conventional mortgage. The term of the lease is equivalent to the finance term under a conventional mortgage (e.g., 25 years). At the end of the term of the lease, the finance ends and the person is entitled to require the financial institution to sell to him the freehold or leasehold estate for a nominal payment.

The second, which applies to Murabaha mortgages, involves a financial institution and a person (again, usually an individual) entering into arrangements under which the financial institution buys the freehold or leasehold estate of a property and sells it for staged payments to the person, who grants the financial institution a legal mortgage.

In both cases, the interest held by the financial institution – which is, or is equivalent to, a security interest – is an exempt interest for the purposes of SDLT

---

[1] For more information see *Sergeant and Sims on Stamp Taxes* (LexisNexis UK), AA6.4 [AA125] Alternative property finance structures (Islamic mortgages); Finance Act (FA) 2003, ss.71A, 73; *HMRC internal manual – Stamp Duty Land Tax Manual* ('SDLT Manual') (HMRC, 19 March 2016, updated 16 January 2020, available at: **www.gov.uk/hmrc-internal-manuals/stamp-duty-land-tax-manual**): SDLTM28000.

subject to various carve-outs. Consequently, where the carve-outs do not apply, dealings in the interest are not chargeable to SDLT. The carve-outs apply where:

- SDLT group relief was claimed by the financial institution on its acquisition of the freehold or leasehold estate;
- the lease ends; or
- the agreement under which the person can require the financial institution to transfer to the person the freehold or leasehold estate ends or becomes subject to a restriction.

'Financial institution' is defined to include banks; building societies; wholly owned subsidiaries of banks and building societies; and regulated providers of home purchase plans.

11.2 LAND SOLD TO FINANCIAL INSTITUTION AND LEASED TO INDIVIDUAL

Relief is available where a financial institution and a person enter into arrangements under which:

- the financial institution buys the freehold or leasehold estate of a property, either in its sole name or jointly with the person;
- the financial institution grants a lease or an underlease to the person; or
- the person has the right to require the financial institution or its successors in title to transfer to the person the reversionary interest in one transaction or a series of transactions.

The relief provides a full exemption for the person's acquisition of the lease and the reversionary interest and, if applicable, any shares in the beneficial interest in the freehold or leasehold estate over the course of the finance period, subject to meeting certain conditions. This leaves only the financial institution's acquisition of the freehold or leasehold estate in charge, which means the total amount of tax payable under the arrangements is the same as the total amount of tax that would be payable had the person used a conventional mortgage to finance its acquisition. (Under the alternative property finance arrangements, the financial institution rather than the person would bear the tax. However, the author assumes, this cost is passed on to the person.) If the financial institution acquires the freehold or leasehold estate on its disposal by the person or another financial institution, its acquisition is also exempt from charge. This is meant to give parity with a conventional remortgage.

The person's acquisition of the lease is exempt provided that the following conditions are met:

- SDLT is duly paid by the financial institution on its acquisition of the freehold or leasehold estate (unless it purchased the freehold or leasehold estate from the person or another financial institution, see above); and
- the freehold or leasehold estate continues to be owned by a financial institution.

The person's acquisition of the reversionary interest (usually at the end of the mortgage) is exempt provided that the following conditions are met:

- the freehold or leasehold estate continues to be held by a financial institution; and
- the lease continues to be held by the person.

Where the conditions are met, the person's acquisition of the lease and reversionary interest are automatically exempt: relief does not need to be claimed. Nevertheless, this does not mean that each transaction is not notifiable – it is. HM Revenue and Customs (HMRC) provides a relief code (code 24) and the author would encourage its use in the SDLT return to avoid confusion.

The agreement under which the person can require the financial institution to transfer to the person the freehold or leasehold estate is not treated as substantially performed unless and until the person exercises his right to call for the reversionary interest.

The transfer of the freehold or leasehold estate to the person by the financial institution is notifiable.

For the purposes of first-time buyer relief and the residential higher rates, the person, rather than the financial institution, is treated as making the purchase (see **4.2** and **3.3**, respectively). This is to prevent the relief ceasing to be available and the transaction automatically being a higher-rates transaction due to the fact that the financial institution rather than the person makes the purchase in the 'real world'. The financial institution's acquisition is exempt from the residential super rate provided that the person is not a company or, if it is a company, relief from the super rate applies to the person's acquisition of the lease (see **3.4**). The relief from the super rate may be withdrawn if the qualifying conditions cease to be met within a three-year period (see **3.4.4**).

Note that the relief cannot be coupled with sub-sale relief (see **7.5**). Where the financial institution's acquisition is exempt by virtue of the SDLT relief, then the intermediate purchaser (the purchaser under the original contract) is barred from claiming sub-sale relief. This is designed to prevent an SDLT avoidance scheme.[2]

Example 11.1

A takes out a home purchase plan to purchase the freehold estate in a house for £400,000. It is his first purchase. He contributes £40,000 of the price. The rest is financed under the home purchase plan (90% loan to value). The monthly rent is fixed for five years at £1,347 (4.49% of £360,000 / 12). After five years the rental rate increases to the Bank of England base rate plus 3.99%. The term of the lease (and therefore of the finance) is 25 years. No additional acquisition payments are permitted during the fixed rental period; thereafter additional acquisition payments may be made every quarter. After 25 years, the individual

---

[2] FA 2003, s.71A, Sched.4ZA, para.15, Sched.4A, paras.6A, 6B, 6C, 6D, 6E, 6F, 6G, 6H, Sched.6ZA, para.3; SDLT Manual: SDLTM28100, SDLTM28110, SDLTM28120, SDLTM28130, SDLTM28100.

can require the home purchase plan provider to transfer to him the freehold estate in the house for a nominal amount. The home purchase plan provider claims first-time buyer relief. It must pay SDLT of £2,000 (an effective rate of 0.5%): (£300,000 @ 0%) + (£100,000 @ 2%). No SDLT is payable by the individual on acquiring the 25-year lease; nevertheless, the individual voluntarily makes an SDLT return and claims relief. At the end of the 25-year term (or sooner if the individual makes additional acquisition payments), the individual exercises his right to require the home purchase plan provider to transfer to him the reversionary interest in the house and the lease expires. No SDLT is payable by the individual on acquiring the freehold estate, though the individual must make an SDLT return. The individual chooses to claim relief in the return.

11.3   LAND SOLD TO FINANCIAL INSTITUTION AND RESOLD TO INDIVIDUAL

Relief is available where a financial institution and a person enter into arrangements where:

- the financial institution buys the freehold or leasehold estate of a property;
- the financial institution sells the freehold or leasehold estate to the person; and
- the person grants the financial institution a legal mortgage over the freehold or leasehold estate.

The relief provides a full exemption for the person's acquisition of the freehold or leasehold estate. This leaves only the financial institution's acquisition of the freehold or leasehold estate in charge, which means the total amount of tax payable under the arrangements is the same as the total amount of tax that would be payable had the person used a conventional mortgage to finance its acquisition. (Under the alternative property finance arrangements, the financial institution rather than the person would bear the tax. However, the author assumes, this cost is passed on to the person.) If the financial institution acquires the freehold or leasehold estate on its disposal by the person or another financial institution, its acquisition is also exempt from charge. This is meant to give parity to a conventional remortgage.

Where the conditions are met, the person's acquisition of the freehold or leasehold estate is automatically exempt: relief does not need to be claimed. However, HMRC encourages relief to be claimed by entering code 24 at question 9 ('are you claiming relief?') of the SDLT return.

There are two conditions to meet in order to benefit from the exemption:

- SDLT must be paid by the financial institution on at least the market value of the freehold or leasehold estate purchased; and
- the financial institution's acquisition cannot be eligible for SDLT group relief, reconstruction relief or acquisition relief.

For the purposes of first-time buyer relief and the residential higher rates, the person, rather than the financial institution, is treated as making the purchase (see **4.2** and **3.3**, respectively). This is to prevent the relief ceasing to be available and the transaction automatically being a higher-rates transaction due to the fact that the financial institution rather than the person makes the purchase in the 'real world'. The financial institution's acquisition is exempt from the residential super rate provided that the person is not a company or, if it is a company, relief from the super rate applies to the person's acquisition of the lease (see **3.4**). The relief from the super rate may be withdrawn if the qualifying conditions cease to be met within a three-year period (see **3.4.4**).

Note that the relief cannot be coupled with sub-sale relief (see **7.5**). Where the financial institution's acquisition is exempt by virtue of the SDLT relief, then the intermediate purchaser (the purchaser under the original contract) is barred from claiming sub-sale relief. This is designed to prevent an SDLT avoidance scheme.[3]

Example 11.2

A takes out a home purchase plan to purchase the freehold estate in a house for £500,000. It is his first purchase. He contributes £125,000 of the price. The rest is financed under the home purchase plan (75% loan to value). The finance provider buys the property and immediately resells it to A for a fixed price (£800,000). A pays £125,000 towards the £800,000, leaving £675,000 to be paid. A pays the £675,000 in equal instalments over a 25-year term; hence, the monthly repayment is £2,250 or £675,000 / (25 x 12). The home purchase plan provider claims first-time buyer relief. It must pay SDLT of £4,000 (an effective rate of 0.8%): (£300,000 @ 0%) + (£200,000 @ 2%). No SDLT is payable by the individual on acquiring the property; nevertheless, the individual voluntarily makes an SDLT return and claims relief.

11.4 ALTERNATIVE FINANCE INVESTMENT BONDS

An SDLT relief is provided for transactions involved in connection with the issuance of alternative finance investment bonds.[4] The relief is subject to meeting a number of conditions. The conditions include:

- A person transfers to a bond issuer a freehold or leasehold estate to act as the bond asset and held only by the bond issuer for the duration of the bond (not greater than 10 years), at which point it is to be transferred back.
- Out of the freehold or leasehold estate, the bond issuer grants to the person a leaseback for the purpose of generating income or gains for the bond.
- The bond issuer enters a charge on the property in respect of the amount of SDLT that would be chargeable but for the relief.
- Over the term of the bond, the bond issuer issues bonds to the value of at least 60 per cent of the market value of the property transferred.

---

[3] FA 2003, s.73, Sched.4ZA, para.15, Sched.4A, paras.6A, 6B, 6C, 6D, 6E, 6F, 6G, 6H; SDLT Manual: SDLTM28400, SDLTM28410, SDLTM28400, SDLTM28400.
[4] FA 2009 ss.73C, 123, Sched.61.

Relief, which is capable of being withdrawn, applies to the transfer and re-transfer of the property. Leaseback relief is available to exempt the leaseback. Additionally, the issue, transfer and redemption of rights under the bond are exempt from SDLT.

It would be unusual for residential property to be the subject of such a bond.

CHAPTER 12

Transactions involving public bodies

12.1 BACKGROUND

This chapter covers the stamp duty land tax (SDLT) treatment of various types of transaction involving public bodies.[1] That treatment consists mainly of affording reliefs or modifying the general charging rules for such transactions. The transactions in question consist of:

- acquisitions by local authorities following the making of a compulsory purchase order (see **12.2**);
- acquisitions in compliance with planning obligations (see **12.3**);
- acquisitions by public bodies (see **12.4**);
- arrangements involving public or educational bodies (see **12.5**);
- acquisitions made by government departments or parliamentary bodies (see **12.6**);
- acquisitions of diplomatic and consular premises (see **12.6**);
- acquisitions by international organisations (see **12.6**); and
- acquisitions by bodies established for national purposes (see **12.6**).

The author recognises that for some of these types of transaction, it would be unusual for the subject-matter of the transaction to involve residential property.

12.2 COMPULSORY PURCHASE

Where a local authority makes a compulsory purchase order to compel the owner of a property to sell it to the local authority, the local authority's purchase is exempt from SDLT provided that another person (a developer) will develop the land and the local authority claims relief. HM Revenue and Customs (HMRC) appears to accept that it is not necessary that the purchase is made in pursuance of the order. It is enough, it says, that a compulsory purchase order has been made. So sales by agreement are within the relief provided that the purchased property is, in fact, developed by another person.

---

[1] For more information see *Sergeant and Sims on Stamp Taxes* (LexisNexis UK), AA8: SDLT–relief for public and national purposes.

The relief must be claimed in an SDLT return, or in an amendment to an SDLT return, by entering code 10 at question 9 ('are you claiming relief?') of the SDLT return. The relief, once granted, cannot be withdrawn.

No relief applies to the purchase of the property by the developer on its disposal by the local authority.

The purchase must be made to facilitate development of the land by someone other than the local authority. The term 'development' takes its meaning from Town and Country Planning Act 1990, s.55 (meaning of 'development' and 'new development'). Under section 55, 'development' means 'the carrying out of building, engineering, mining or other operations in, on, over, or under land, or the making of any material change in the use of any buildings or other land'.[2]

Example 12.1

Land owned by a farmer is the subject of a compulsory purchase order. The land is acquired by the local authority for road widening as part of a development being carried out by a private developer. He receives £350,000, including an amount for 'disturbance' (e.g., professional costs and SDLT payable on purchasing replacement land). The local authority's acquisition of the land is exempt from SDLT by virtue of compulsory purchase relief. The local authority sells the land to the developer for the same amount. The developer is liable to SDLT.

12.3 COMPLIANCE WITH PLANNING OBLIGATIONS

A full relief is given to specified public authorities that purchase land from developers to comply with an obligation imposed (under Town and Country Planning Act 1990, s.106 or Planning (Northern Ireland) Order 1991, art.40) on the developer by the planning authority when giving planning permission. The only condition is that the land is purchased within five years of planning permission being granted or modified. The purpose of the relief is to prevent developers bearing the SDLT that would, but for the relief, be payable by the public authority on buying back the land duly developed by the developer in satisfaction of the developer's planning obligation.

Qualifying public authorities include:

- ministers of the Crown;
- a county or district council;
- the council of a London borough;
- the Greater London Authority;
- primary care trusts (PCTs); and
- National Health Service (NHS) trusts.

---

[2] Finance Act (FA) 2003, s.60; Town and Country Planning Act 1990, s.55; *HMRC internal manual – Stamp Duty Land Tax Manual* ('SDLT Manual') (HMRC, 19 March 2016, updated 16 January 2020, available at: **www.gov.uk/hmrc-internal-manuals/stamp-duty-land-tax-manual**): SDLTM22000, SDLTM22005, SDLTM22010, SDLTM22020.

The relief must be claimed in an SDLT return, or an amendment to an SDLT return, by entering code 11 at question 9 ('are you claiming relief?') of the SDLT return.[3]

12.4 PUBLIC BODIES RELIEF

A full relief is given to public bodies where an SDLT transaction is entered into in connection with a 'reorganisation' effected between public bodies (or their wholly owned subsidiaries) under a statutory provision. 'Reorganisation' for this purpose includes the establishment, reform or abolition of a public body and the alteration or transfer of functions to be performed by a public body.

Qualifying public bodies include:

- ministers of the Crown;
- a county or district council;
- the council of a London borough;
- the Greater London Authority;
- PCTs; and
- NHS trusts.

The relief must be claimed in an SDLT return, or an amendment to an SDLT return, by entering code 18 at question 9 ('are you claiming relief?') of the SDLT return.[4]

12.5 ARRANGEMENTS INVOLVING PUBLIC OR EDUCATIONAL BODIES

Modifications are made to the SDLT rules on exchanges for certain arrangements involving public or educational bodies – better known as public–private partnership (PPP) or private finance initiative (PFI) arrangements. They take effect as a partial relief. However, no claim needs to be made in an SDLT return to secure this treatment. Nevertheless, this does not mean that such transactions are not notifiable – they are. HMRC provides relief code 28 ('other relief') and the author would encourage its use in the SDLT return to avoid confusion.

Qualifying arrangements are those where:

- there is a transfer, or the grant or assignment of a lease, of land (the 'main transfer'), by a 'qualifying body' (A) to a non-qualifying body (B);
- the consideration given for the main transfer includes the grant of a lease or an underlease by B to A of the whole, or substantially the whole, of that land (the 'leaseback');
- B undertakes to carry out works or provide services to A;
- the consideration given by A to B for the carrying out of those works or the provision of those services includes cash.

---

[3] FA 2003, s.61; SDLT Manual: SDLTM22500, SDLTM22505, SDLTM22510, SDLTM22520, SDLTM22530, SDLTM22500.
[4] FA 2003, s.66; SDLT Manual: SDLTM25000, SDLTM25005, SDLTM25010, SDLTM25030.

Whether or not there is a transfer, or the grant or assignment of a lease, of any other land ('surplus land') by A to B is irrelevant.

Where there are qualifying arrangements, the amount of SDLT chargeable on the main transfer or on the transfer of any surplus land (a liability for B) is calculated without reference to:

- the leaseback granted by B to A; or
- the carrying out of the works or the provision of the services by B.

Additionally, the amount of SDLT chargeable on the leaseback (a liability for A) is calculated without reference to:

- the main transfer;
- the transfer of any surplus land; or
- any consideration given by A to B for the works or services.

This means that SDLT will only be chargeable on any cash given for the main transfer and leaseback. The market value rules that would usually apply to an exchange of chargeable interests are modified (see **1.5.3**).

'Qualifying bodies' are 'public bodies' (see **12.4**) and certain institutions within the further education sector.[5]

12.6 OTHER RELIEFS INVOLVING PUBLIC BODIES

12.6.1 Crown exemption

Acquisitions made by government departments or parliamentary bodies are exempt. The exemption is automatic. No relief needs to be claimed. Nevertheless, this does not mean that such transactions are not notifiable – they are. HMRC provides relief code 28 ('other relief') and the author would encourage its use in the SDLT return to avoid confusion.

12.6.2 Diplomatic premises

Full relief is available for acquisitions of diplomatic and consular premises under specified provisions. The relief does not apply to the purchase or lease of the private residence of a diplomat or consular official. The relief must be claimed in an SDLT return, or an amendment to an SDLT return, by entering code 27 at question 9 ('are you claiming relief?') of the SDLT return.

12.6.3 Foreign sovereign immunity

Full relief is available on the purchase or lease of premises of an international organisation where a statutory instrument confers exemption from UK taxation.

---

[5] FA 2003, Sched.4, para.17; SDLT Manual: SDLTM29500.

The relief must be claimed in an SDLT return, or an amendment to an SDLT return, by entering code 27 at question 9 ('are you claiming relief?') of the SDLT return.

12.6.4 Acquisitions by bodies established for national purposes

Acquisitions made by specified bodies established for national purposes (e.g., the Historic Buildings and Monuments Commission for England) are exempt from SDLT.[6]

---

[6] FA 2003, ss.69, 107; SDLT Manual: SDLTM20500, SDLTM20600, SDLTM26500, SDLTM32000.

CHAPTER 13
Options and rights of pre-emption

13.1 BACKGROUND

This chapter covers the stamp duty land tax (SDLT) treatment of options (both call options and put options) and rights of pre-emption (also known as rights of first refusal).[1]

Both types of interest are described in the SDLT legislation as not being 'major interests'. They are described in this work as 'minor interests', though that term is not used in the legislation. 'Major interests' are limited to freehold and leasehold estates, legal or equitable. All other types of 'chargeable interest' (see **1.2.3**) are 'minor interests'. The relevance of the distinction mainly relates to the treatment of exchanges and notification. The exchange of minor interests is not chargeable unless cash is paid (or there is consideration other than the minor interest given). This is an exception to the market value rule that normally applies to exchanges (see **1.5.3**). The acquisition of a minor interest is not notifiable unless tax is payable or would be payable but for claiming a relief (see **1.9**).

To a lesser extent, the distinction is also relevant to the residential super rate and the higher residential rates, where only major interests count (but where an undivided share of a major interest is treated as a major interest); and also to first-time buyer relief (although almost certainly HM Revenue and Customs (HMRC) would also regard an undivided share as a major interest). The grant of an option to buy a dwelling would not be subject to the super rate, the higher rates or qualify for first-time buyer relief.

A specific legislative provision applies to:

> ... [t]he acquisition of –
> (a) an option binding the grantor to enter into a land transaction, or
> (b) a right of pre-emption preventing the grantor from entering into, or restricting the right of the grantor to enter into, a land transaction ...[2]

---

[1] For more information see *Sergeant and Sims on Stamp Taxes* (LexisNexis UK), AA2.7: Options and rights of pre-emption; FA 2003 ss.46, 117; *HMRC internal manual – Stamp Duty Land Tax Manual* ('SDLT Manual') (HMRC, 19 March 2016, updated 16 January 2020, available at: **www.gov.uk/hmrc-internal-manuals/stamp-duty-land-tax-manual**): SDLTM01300, SDLTM01300A.

[2] Finance Act (FA) 2003, s.46(1).

It goes on to say that it does not apply to an option or a right of pre-emption that is a chargeable interest. As call options are property rights, not personal rights, the provision appears merely to extend the scope of the tax to put options and rights of pre-emption, both of which are personal rights.

An option might be inherent in another chargeable interest, the main subject-matter of the land transaction. For example, a lease may be granted on terms that include an option to purchase the reversion. Such an option is *not* the acquisition of a separate chargeable interest; hence, there is no need to apportion part of the consideration given for the lease to it. Rather, it is wrapped up in the main subject-matter of the land transaction – the lease.

13.2 OPTIONS

An option is a contractual right to require another person to acquire or dispose of something, in this context a dwelling. There are two types of option: a call option and a put option – both are granted for a period (the option period) after which the option expires:

- a call option is granted by the owner of a dwelling (A) to another person (B) giving B the right (but not the obligation) to require A to sell the dwelling to B; and
- a put option is granted by a person (A) to the owner of a dwelling (B) giving B the right (but not the obligation) to require A to buy the dwelling.

13.2.1 Grant of option

The grant of an option is an SDLT transaction distinct from the transaction that results from the exercise of the option. It is an acquisition by the person to whom the option is granted (the option holder). The tax is charged on the amount or value of the consideration given (or deemed to be given: see **1.4.2**) for the transaction. The effective date of the transaction is the date that the option is granted.

An option is a 'minor interest'. This means that transaction is not notifiable initially (i.e., a return does not need to be made) unless tax is payable or would be payable but for claiming a relief because the amount or value of the chargeable consideration is more than £125,000.

The grant of the option cannot be 'linked' to the transaction that would result from the exercise of the option unless and until the option is exercised (see **1.5.4**). This means that the price payable to exercise the option (also known as the 'strike price') is disregarded when determining the amount of tax chargeable on the grant of the option. However, where the option is exercised it is unclear in what circumstances the transaction that results from the exercise of the option is 'linked' to the grant of the option. The implication of the grant of the option being linked to the transaction that results from the exercise of the option is discussed at **13.2.2**.

No distinction is drawn between options that are capable of being settled in cash and those that are not.

The grant or assignment of an option does not count as a 'pre-completion transaction' (see **Chapter 7**).

13.2.2 Exercise of option

The exercise of an option results in an SDLT transaction distinct from the grant of the option. The degree of proximity (if any) between the grant and exercise of the option is irrelevant. It is an acquisition by the person acquiring the dwelling. The tax is charged on the amount or value of the consideration given (or deemed to be given) for the transaction. Where there is an increase in tax rates between the grant of the option and exercise of the option, the tax due at exercise of the option is usually calculated in accordance with the rates applicable at the date of exercise, not the date of grant. This is consistent with the usual form of transitional provision given for rate increases.

Where a call option is exercised, the person making the acquisition is the option-holder: i.e., the same person that acquired the option (whether initially on the grant of the option or subsequently on the assignment of the option). Where a put option is exercised, the person making the acquisition would not be the person that granted the option. In other words, the purchaser of a put option is the vendor of the land. It would be rare indeed if A paid any consideration to B for the grant of a put option, and since on the exercise of the option B would be the purchaser, there could be no linkage between the grant of a put option and its exercise.

In the case of call options only, where the transaction that results from the exercise of the option is 'linked' to the grant of the option, the consideration given to exercise the option is aggregated to the consideration given to acquire the option. The tax is then calculated on a single transaction for the aggregate consideration before it is apportioned to the two transactions by multiplying the tax by the fraction produced by dividing the total consideration by the consideration given for each transaction. Note that the legislation does not say that the exercise of an option is always 'linked' to the grant of the option. It merely says that they *may* be 'linked' transactions.

This might make the grant of the option notifiable if it was not initially or it might mean that the grant of the option is re-notifiable and additional tax is payable on the grant of the option. That means that an SDLT return would need to be made for both the grant of the option *and* the subsequent transaction.

Example 13.1

A owns the freehold estate of a house. He grants a call option to B under which B can require A to sell the dwelling to B for £1.5 million. B pays £50,000 to A for the option. The grant of the option is not chargeable initially as the amount of the consideration given for the option is less than £125,000. (The £40,000 threshold for the residential higher rates does not apply, as the option is not a major interest in a dwelling.) Subsequently, B exercises the option and pays A the £1.5 million to acquire the dwelling. The transaction resulting from the exercise of the option is, HMRC would say, 'linked' to the grant of the option. SDLT would be payable on £1.55 million. Assuming the residential standard rates of tax apply (see **1.4.1**), £99,750 of tax would be payable (an effective rate of 6.4%): (£125,000 @ 0%) + (£125,000 @ 2%) + (£675,000 @ 5%) + (£575,000 @ 10%) + (£50,000 @ 12%). The £99,750 must be apportioned to the two transactions in the ratio 50,000:1,500,000. So £3,217 would be apportioned to the grant of the option (£99,750 x £50,000 / £1,550,000) and £96,533 would be apportioned to the transaction resulting from the exercise of the option (£99,750 x £1,500,000 / £1,550,000). A would need to pay the tax and make an SDLT return for each transaction within 14 days of the exercise of the option.

Example 13.2

A owns the freehold estate of a house. He grants a call option to B under which B can require A to sell the dwelling to B for £1.5 million. B pays £250,000 to A for the option, and if the option is exercised, the option fee is deductible from the price. The grant of the option *is* chargeable initially as the amount of the consideration given for the option is more than £125,000. The residential standard rates of tax apply, as the grant of the option is not a major interest. £2,500 of tax would be payable (an effective rate of 1%): (£125,000 @ 0%) + (£125,000 @ 2%). Subsequently, B exercises the option and pays A the £1.25 million to acquire the dwelling. The transaction resulting from the exercise of the option is, HMRC would say, 'linked' to the grant of the option. Assuming the standard rates of tax continue to apply, £93,750 of tax would be payable (an effective rate of 6.3%): (£125,000 @ 0%) + (£125,000 @ 2%) + (£675,000 @ 5%) + (£575,000 @ 10%). The £93,750 must be apportioned to the two transactions in the ratio 250,000:1,250,000. So £18,750 would be apportioned to the grant of the option (£93,750 x £250,000 / £1,500,000) and £78,125 would be apportioned to the transaction resulting from the exercise of the option (£93,750 x £1,250,000 / £1,500,000). A would need to pay £16,250 (£18,750 – £2,500) of tax and make a further SDLT return for the grant of the option within 30 days of the exercise of the option and pay £78,125 of tax and make an SDLT return for the transaction resulting from the exercise of the option within 14 days of the exercise of the option.

If the higher rates were to apply to the balance of the purchase price, it is arguable that 125/150 of the tax at the higher rates on £1.5 million would apply to the purchase and 25/150 of the tax at the standard rates on £1.5 million would apply to the option. The exercise of the option does not turn the grant of the option into a major interest.

The uncertainty over whether the two transactions are 'linked' concerns how the 'linked' transaction rule should be interpreted. If the purpose of the rule is to prevent the avoidance of tax that, but for the rule, would be achieved by dividing a single transaction into tranches to take advantage of the nil rate band and lower tax rates, then it is arguable that the exercise of the option would not be 'linked' to the grant of the option absent that mischief. However, the reader should note that HMRC would likely disagree. This has particular relevance to lease renewals. If the renewal of a lease resulting from the exercise of an option is 'linked' to the grant of the lease (and prior renewals, if any) the lease is taken to 'grow' on each renewal and the net present value (NPV) of the 'grown' lease should be calculated to determine whether it exceeds the nil rate band or attracts more tax. Many tenants living in rental accommodation in prime central London may (reasonably) be unaware that their decision to renew a lease has caused SDLT to become due. See **5.7.2**.

Example 13.3

On 1 January 2020, A is granted a one-year lease over an apartment for an annual rent of £60,000. It contains an option to renew. The grant of the lease is a chargeable but not a notifiable SDLT transaction. The NPV of the rent payable over the term of the lease (£60,000) is below the nil rate threshold (£125,000). A renews the lease twice. He fails to realise that the renewals require him to recalculate the NPV of the rent. Fortunately, there were no consequences of the first renewal. The NPV of the rent payable over the term of the lease (now for a term of two years) was still under the nil rate threshold (£113,981). However, the second renewal did have an SDLT consequence. The NPV of the rent payable over the term of the lease (now for a term of three years) was more than the nil rate threshold (£168,098); hence, an SDLT return was due and payment of £430 was required: (£125,000 @ 0%) + (£43,000 @ 1%). Interest and penalties are imposed for late payment and late filing respectively.

Where the option-holder is not the original option-holder because he acquired the option by assignment rather than grant, then his acquisition of the option would not be 'linked' to the transaction resulting from the exercise of the option if the parties are unconnected. This is because it is not enough for transactions to be 'linked' that they form part of a single transaction, series of transactions or arrangement. The transactions must also be between the same parties or connected persons.

There is one exception to this rule. As between landlord and tenant, a change of tenant does not break 'linkage', as the incoming tenant steps into the outgoing tenant's shoes for linkage purposes. Most flats are leasehold, but it would be rare for the tenant to be granted an option unless it were contained in the lease – so would not count as a separate chargeable interest.

Example 13.4

A owns the freehold estate of a house. He grants a call option to B under which B can require A to sell the dwelling to B for £1.5 million. B pays £50,000 to A for the option. B assigns the option to C for £10,000. Although this is an assignment of a chargeable interest, it is still a minor interest, so no SDLT is payable and a return is not required. C exercises the option. The parties to the grant of the option (A and B) and the assignment of the option (B and C) are not the same as the parties to the transaction resulting from the exercise of the option (A and C). Consequently, unless A and B were connected, the transactions would not be 'linked'.

'Linked' transactions should be notified by entering 'Yes' at question 13 ('is this transaction linked to any other(s)?') of the SDLT return and inputting the total consideration for the linked transactions.

HMRC states that the further return due on the grant of the option should be made by letter. This is by concession.[3]

13.2.3 Assignment, variation and release of option

Once an option is granted, it is a chargeable interest; hence, an assignment, variation or release of the option would be SDLT transactions. In each case, it is an acquisition by the person to whom the option is assigned or the relevant person whose interest or right is benefited by the variation or release of the option. The tax is charged on the amount or value of the consideration given (or deemed to be given) for the transaction. The transaction is not notifiable initially (i.e., a return does not need to be made) unless tax is payable or would be payable but for claiming a relief because the amount or value of the chargeable consideration is more than £125,000. Any transaction relating to the option that might happen subsequently even if it is envisaged at the time of the grant of the option is a separate SDLT transaction.

Where the purchaser wishes to draw down tranches of land, say, for residential development, rather than entering into a single contract, he might consider acquiring a call option over each tranche. That way, there would be no risk that drawing down a tranche substantially performs the whole contract so as to trigger tax on tranches that have yet to be drawn down (see **1.8**). This benefit has to be factored against the negative cashflow that would arise on drawing down tranches individually: the exercise of an option would always trigger a tax point, whereas paying part of the part due under a single contract may not.

13.3 RIGHTS OF PRE-EMPTION

The right of pre-emption is frequently known as a right of first refusal. In return for making a payment, the right is granted by the owner of a dwelling (A) to another person (B) to prevent A from selling the dwelling without first offering it to B to purchase for the same amount offered by a particular person. The grant of the right is an SDLT transaction distinct from the transaction that results from the exercise of the right. It is an acquisition by the person to whom the right is granted (the holder). The tax is charged on the amount or value of the consideration given (or deemed to be given) for the transaction. The effective date of the transaction is the date that the right is granted.

A right of pre-emption is a 'minor interest'. This means that the transaction is not notifiable initially (i.e., a return does not need to be made) unless tax is payable or would be payable but for claiming a relief because the amount or value of the chargeable consideration is more than £125,000. It would, however, be rare for a

---

[3] FA 2003, s.81A.

right of pre-emption to be given except as part of another land transaction, in which case it would not be considered an independent land transaction.[4]

Example 13.5

A owns the freehold estate of a house. He grants a right of pre-emption to B in return for £10,000. A markets the house for sale and accepts an offer from a person (C) to purchase the house for £1 million. A offers the house to B to purchase for £1 million. B accepts the offer. Both B's acquisition of the right of pre-emption and the transaction that results from B exercising his right are distinct SDLT transactions – but probably 'linked'.

---

[4] FA 2003, ss.46, 117; SDLT Manual: SDLTM01300, SDLTM01300A.

CHAPTER 14
Release of negative obligations

14.1 BACKGROUND

This chapter covers the stamp duty land tax (SDLT) treatment of the release of negative obligations contained in restrictive covenants and rights to light.

A restrictive covenant is an agreement between owners of adjoining land under which one landowner imposes a restriction on the use of his land for the benefit of the other land owner. Examples include:

- restrictions on access over land;
- restrictions on any new building or residential developments on the land; and
- a prohibition on using land for any trade or business activities.

An easement gives the owner of land the right to make use of other land (usually adjoining land) for the benefit of his own land. A right to light is a type of easement. It gives the owner of a building the right to receive, usually through a window, enough natural light passing over adjoining land to enable him to use the building. Unlike most easements, like rights of way and rights of drainage, which allow one landowner to do something on another landowner's land, a right to light is negative: it prevents the owner of adjoining land from doing something on his own land. Put another way, the owner of the land burdened by the right to light is prevented from obstructing the light passing over his land so as to interfere with the ability of the owner of the land benefited by the right to light.

Both types of property right are appurtenant to a freehold or leasehold estate. They are also registrable and 'run with the land', binding future owners of the land. They can be valuable. They allow the holder of the rights to exercise a significant degree of control over that which can be done on adjoining land.

Both are, therefore, 'chargeable interests' for the purposes of SDLT: an interest or right in land or the benefit of an obligation or restriction or condition affecting the value of an estate or interest in or over land.

Restrictive covenants and rights to light may be created by agreement. Rights to light may also be created by implication and by prescription.

Consequently, the release of a restrictive covenant or a right to light is an SDLT transaction. The purchaser is the person whose land is benefited by the release; the vendor is the person ceasing to be entitled to the restrictive covenant or right to light.[1] The release of such interests is common where restricted land is to be developed. The holder of the restrictive covenant or right to light agrees with the developer to release their right in return for a payment. The release benefits the land owned by the developer.

14.2 CHARGEABLE CONSIDERATION

Having established that the release of a restrictive covenant or right to light is an SDLT transaction it is necessary to examine what is the chargeable consideration given for the transaction.

The chargeable consideration is the value added tax (VAT) inclusive amount or value of the consideration given in money or money's worth for the transaction unless a market rule applies.

The subject-matter of the transaction is not a 'major interest' for the purposes of SDLT, as a 'major interest' is defined to include only freehold or leasehold estates. This has two consequences:

- the transaction is not notifiable unless SDLT is payable or would be payable but for a claim for relief; and
- the exchange of restrictive covenants or rights to light is not chargeable unless consideration is given other than the reciprocal release or the exchange also involves a freehold or leasehold estate.

Where the consideration given for the release of a restrictive covenant or right to light includes a freehold or leasehold estate, the chargeable consideration is taken to be the higher of the value of the release and the amount or value of the consideration given.[2]

Example 14.1

A and B are owners of adjoining land. A agrees to release the right to light that benefits A's land in return for B agreeing to release the right to light that benefits B's land. No consideration is given by the parties other than the reciprocal release. The transaction is exempt due to no chargeable consideration and not notifiable.

Example 14.2

As above, except that A agrees to grant a lease of a small strip of land to B as part of the consideration for B agreeing to release the right to light that benefits B's land. The consideration given for A's acquisition is the higher of the value of B's release on the one hand and the aggregate value of A's release and the lease on the other. The consideration given for B's acquisition is the higher of the aggregate value of A's release and the lease on the one

---

[1] Finance Act (FA) 2003, ss.43, 48.
[2] FA 2003, ss.47, 117, Sched.4, paras.1, 5.

hand and the value of B's release on the other. What is the market value of an easement, when it exists only to benefit one piece of land? There is no market for easements or restrictive covenants, so arguably the right is worth nothing. Under the rule in *Stokes* v. *Cambridge* (1961) 13 P&CR 77 where an easement or restriction is the only impediment to development, the owner of the impediment can reasonably ask for a share of development profit. There is no evidence that this rule applies to the valuation of interests for the purposes of SDLT.

14.3 RATES OF TAX

Having established the chargeable consideration given (or deemed to be given) for the transaction, it is necessary to determine which set of tax rates and tax bands applies. This is harder than one might think. Where the restrictive covenant or right to light benefits a dwelling, it is not clear whether the subject-matter of the transaction is residential property or non-residential property. The uncertainty is caused by the drafting in the legislative provision that defines residential property. On a plain reading of the provision (Finance Act 2003, s.116(1)), the conjunction 'and' used in subsection (1) implies that an interest in or right over land that subsists for the benefit of a dwelling is residential property only if it is sold with that dwelling. Subsection (1) reads as follows (emphasis added):

(1) In this Part 'residential property' means –

 (a) a building that is used or suitable for use as a dwelling, or is in the process of being constructed or adapted for such use, *and*
 (b) land that is or forms part of the garden or grounds of a building within paragraph (a) (including any building or structure on such land), or
 (c) an interest in or right over land that subsists for the benefit of a building within paragraph (a) or of land within paragraph (b);

and 'non-residential property' means any property that is not residential property.

If that is correct – and note that reasonable views differ on whether or not it is correct – the subject-matter of the release of a restrictive covenant or right to light benefiting a dwelling is *not* residential property. The impact of the decision lies in the variance between the tax rates for residential property transactions and non-residential (or mixed) transactions. See **1.4.1** for tax rates and tax bands.[3]

Example 14.3

A owns the freehold estate of a house. He agrees to release his right to light in return for B paying £200,000. If the non-residential rates of tax apply, the amount of tax chargeable would be £1,000 (an effective rate of 0.5%): (£150,000 @ 0%) + (£50,000 @ 2%). If the residential rates of tax apply (only the standard rates would be applicable, as the main

---

[3] FA 2003, ss.55, 116.

subject-matter of the transaction does not consist of a major interest in a dwelling), the amount of tax chargeable would be £1,500 (an effective rate of 0.8%): (£125,000 @ 0%) + (£75,000 @ 2%).

CHAPTER 15

Transfers to connected companies

15.1 BACKGROUND

Where a company (regardless of where it is incorporated or tax resident) acquires a property and the company is connected for tax purposes with the vendor (regardless of the type of person making the disposal – e.g., individual or company), the company's acquisition is chargeable to stamp duty land tax (SDLT) on not less than the market value of the property transferred on the effective date of the transfer.[1] Where the amount or value of the chargeable consideration given for the transaction is less than the market value of the property, the chargeable consideration is taken to be equal to the market value of the property.

The rule also applies where a company acquires a property and some or all of the consideration given consists of the issue or transfer of shares in a company that is connected with the vendor.

It is one of a number of market value rules (see **1.5.2**). Other than a different set of rules that applies to transfers between partnerships and partners or connected persons, and a specific anti-avoidance rule for 'pre-completion transactions' there are no other market value rules that apply to transfers between connected persons: see **Chapter 16** and **Chapter 7**, respectively. The transfer of a property between spouses, therefore, is exempt provided that no consideration is given: see **Chapter 8**.

The purpose of the rule is to prevent 'enveloping' – the strategy of putting a property into a corporate wrapper enabling a person in the future to purchase the property without paying SDLT by purchasing the shares in the company that owns the property. There is no indirect charge to SDLT on sales of shares in 'land-rich' companies; hence, this rule is necessary.

The rule means that it is not possible to gift a property to a connected company or to transfer the property to such a company without the company suffering SDLT on the full market value of the property. The exemption for transfers for no consideration is disapplied (see **2.5**).

---

[1] For more information see *Sergeant and Sims on Stamp Taxes* (LexisNexis UK), AA4.8 [AA58]; Finance Act (FA) 2003, s.53; *HMRC internal manual – Stamp Duty Land Tax Manual* ('SDLT Manual') (HMRC, 19 March 2016, updated 16 January 2020, available at: **www.gov.uk/hmrc-internal-manuals/stamp-duty-land-tax-manual**): SDLTM30220.

Certain types of other corporate vehicles are treated as if they were companies for this purpose: namely, unit trust schemes and co-ownership authorised contractual schemes. Partnerships are, though, disregarded as companies even if they are 'bodies corporate' (e.g., limited liability partnerships (LLPs)).

Example 15.1

A, an individual, owns all the issued share capital of a company, B Ltd. B Ltd carries on a property-letting business. A transfers a residential property worth £1 million to B Ltd. Immediately before the transfer, debt in the amount of £700,000 is owed by A and secured on the property. The transfer of the property is subject to B Ltd assuming the obligation to repay that debt. Nothing else is given or done by B Ltd in return for the transfer of the property. B Ltd must pay SDLT based on £1 million, not £700,000. This is because B Ltd is connected with A.

15.2 CONNECTION

The most frequent instances where two persons (A and B) are connected are:

- where A is B's spouse, civil partner, brother, sister, ancestor or lineal descendant;
- where A is the spouse or civil partner of B's brother, sister, ancestor or lineal descendant;
- where A is the brother, sister, ancestor or lineal descendant of B's spouse or civil partner;
- where A is the spouse or civil partner of a brother, sister, ancestor or lineal descendant of B's spouse or civil partner;
- where A is the trustee of a settlement and B is the settlor;
- where A and B are members of the same partnership except in relation to acquisitions or disposals of assets of the partnership pursuant to genuine commercial arrangements;
- where A and B are companies under common 'control';
- where B is a company and A has 'control' of B (or A and persons connected with A have control of B).

The term 'company' includes any body corporate or unincorporated association but does not include a partnership (or LLP, which is a partnership for SDLT purposes).

A unit trust scheme is treated as if it were a company and the rights of the unitholders are treated as if they were shares in the company.

The term 'control' means a person exercising, or having the ability to exercise, or the entitlement to acquire, direct or indirect control over a company's affairs by, in particular, possessing (or being entitled to acquire) the majority of the shares of the company or of the voting power in the company, or a shareholding that entitles him to the majority of the distributable assets or profits of the company. In certain circumstances, the rights and powers of a nominee, company or associate may be attributed to a person.[2]

15.3 EXCEPTIONS

There are three exceptions to the market value rule. It does not apply where:

- immediately after the transfer the company holds the property as a professional trustee (i.e., in the course of the business of trust management);
- immediately after the transfer the company holds the property as trustee and it is connected with the vendor merely by reason of him being the trust's settlor; or
- the vendor is a company and the transfer is, or forms part of, a distribution of its assets whether or not in connection with its winding up. For this exception to apply, the property, or the interest from which the property derives (for instance, out of which a lease has been granted) must have been acquired by the vendor company more than three years ago or, if the purchase is more recent, it must not have claimed group relief.

Where the transaction is the grant of a lease to a connected company, the terms of the lease (including the amount of rent payable) are respected and tax is chargeable on the net present value (NPV) of the rent payable over the term of the lease if it exceeds the nil rate band of £125,000, but the premium would be taken to be not less than the amount that a lease on the same terms would fetch on the open market. In other words, the market value rule does not deem the rent to be at a market rate.

Example 15.2

A grants a 10-year lease of a house to his company A Ltd for £10,000 a year, when the market rent would be £100,000 a year. The terms of that lease are respected. SDLT would be payable on the NPV of £10,000 for 10 years – which is below the £125,000 threshold. However, if that lease were to be sold on the open market, it would have a capital value in excess of £500,000. That invokes the super rate and the need, if applicable, to claim exemption. It would, of course, be possible to insert provisions in the lease that prevent it from having a market value. One might prohibit all assignment, underletting and other dealings with the lease. One might provide that the house can only be used as residential accommodation for A and A's family and invited guests. In such an event, there would not be any SDLT payable on the lease.

As to distributions made '*in specie*', the type of distribution is irrelevant (e.g., dividend or a reduction of share capital) provided that the transfer is treated legally as a distribution.[3]

---

[2] Corporation Tax Act 2010, ss.450, 451, 1122, 1123.
[3] FA 2003, s.54; SDLT Manual: SDLTM30220.

> **WARNING**
>
> HMRC might argue that a distribution made in pursuance of a final dividend expressed in cash to be satisfied '*in specie*' is taxable. Where a company makes a final dividend '*in specie*', specialist advice should be sought. The existence of a charge may not matter if the conditions for SDLT group relief are met. However, the availability of the relief may be in doubt if it is not claimed within one year of the filing date.

Example 15.3

A Ltd owns the full interest (legal and beneficial) in a residential property. It bought the property on the open market from a third party. The entire issued share capital of the company is owned by B Ltd. A Ltd distributes the property *in specie* to B Ltd in pursuance of a dividend in accordance with B Ltd's rights as a shareholder of the company. No debt is owed by A Ltd. The transfer is exempt from charge, as B Ltd does not give any consideration for the transaction and the market value rule does not apply.

CHAPTER 16

Partnerships

16.1 BACKGROUND

This chapter covers transactions between partners (or connected persons) and partnerships, and transfers of interests in partnerships.[1] The rules are some of the most complex in the stamp duty land tax (SDLT) code. One reason is the inconsistency of treatment: in some cases partnerships are treated as transparent; in others they are treated as opaque. Another reason is the prescriptive set of rules and use of formulae. The residential property lawyer should exercise a high degree of caution when advising on the SDLT treatment of transactions involving partnerships and partners (or connected persons). The comments in this chapter are necessarily high level. In this context, more than in any other context within the SDLT code, the residential property lawyer should verify assumptions made on the SDLT treatment by going to the legislation or seeking advice. HM Revenue and Customs' (HMRC's) guidance manual is 'light' and fails to cover all the charging provisions – e.g., the charge on capital withdrawals and loan repayments (see **16.6**).

The part of the SDLT code that deals with partnerships is Finance Act 2003, Sched.15. It is largely self-contained and is split into three parts. The first two are of general application and, in particular, confirm the manner in which partnerships are treated when transacting with third parties ('ordinary partnership transactions'). The third sets out special rules for transactions involving partnerships and partners (or connected persons) and transfers of interests in partnerships ('special partnership transactions').

16.2 GENERAL RULES

'Partnerships' are defined to include all three types of partnership recognised in the UK – (a) general partnerships within the Partnership Act 1890; (b) limited partnerships registered under the Limited Partnerships Act 1907; and (c) limited liability partnerships incorporated under the Limited Liability Partnerships Act 2000 or the

---

[1] For more information see *Sergeant and Sims on Stamp Taxes* (LexisNexis UK), AA3: SDLT–partnerships; FA 2003, Sched.15; *HMRC internal manual – Stamp Duty Land Tax Manual* ('SDLT Manual') (HMRC, 19 March 2016, updated 16 January 2020, available at: **www.gov.uk/hmrc-internal-manuals/stamp-duty-land-tax-manual**): SDLTM33000.

Limited Liability Partnerships Act (Northern Ireland) 2002 – and overseas entities 'of a similar character'.

Other works should be consulted to determine in what circumstances the joint ownership of property constitutes a partnership under the Partnership Act 1890. Notwithstanding that qualification, the following remarks are made:

- The 1890 Act defines a partnership as 'the relation which subsists between persons carrying on a business in common with a view of profit'.
- It continues by warning that joint ownership does not, of itself, create a partnership whether or not the owners share profits from the jointly held property.
- Hallmarks of a partnership include authority to bind, joint and several liability (unless contracted out), sharing profits and losses in common, the pooling of resources, mutual benefit and risk, and being actively involved in the business, whether in the management of the property or the making of decisions setting the strategy of the business.
- An agreement is not a prerequisite for a partnership.

For the purposes of SDLT, except as otherwise provided, partnerships are 'looked through' even where the partnership has separate legal personality. This means that the property held by a partnership is treated as held by the partners and where a partnership buys or sells a dwelling, the partners are treated as the vendor or purchaser.

For ordinary partnership transactions:

- responsibility for making an SDLT return and payment of SDLT falls on the partners at completion and those who become a partner after completion; but
- the tax cannot be recovered from those who become a partner after completion; and
- the responsibility is joint and several but the obligation to make an SDLT return or SDLT payment can be discharged by a partner nominated by the majority of the partners; the nomination must be notified to HMRC to be effective.[2]

Example 16.1

A, B and C are the partners in a Scottish partnership. The partnership has separate legal personality. It purchases a dwelling as an investment (buy-to-let) from a third party. The obligation to make an SDLT return and SDLT payment is on all three partners. A, B and C notify HMRC that B is their representative, and B discharges the obligations of the partners. Subsequently, A leaves the partnership and D joins. For whatever reason, HMRC makes an assessment to recover a loss of tax in respect of the earlier transaction. A, B and C are liable to pay the underpaid tax – D is not.

---

[2] FA 2003, Sched.15, Parts 1, 2; SDLT Manual: SDLTM33210.

16.3 INTRODUCTION TO SPECIAL RULES

The special charging rules determine the amount of the chargeable consideration given for the transaction. The amount or value of the chargeable consideration given in the 'real world' (if any) is disregarded except for the purposes of the SDLT general anti-avoidance rule (see **1.11**).

The chargeable consideration is calculated by reference to the market value of the property transferred or the property held by the partnership.

The market value of the property is the price which that property might reasonably fetch on a sale in the open market. The market value is *not* reduced by any debt secured on the property.

Any value added tax (VAT) chargeable on the transaction is not treated as part of the chargeable consideration.

Although it is not explicit in the legislation, HMRC accepts that the special charging rules take precedence over other market value rules (e.g., transfers to connected companies).

Where the special charging rules are engaged (except the charge on capital withdrawals and loan repayments: see **16.6**), the exemption for transfers for no consideration does not apply. Nevertheless, if the amount of the chargeable consideration is nil by virtue of the special charging rules, the loss of the exemption has no practical effect.

The concept of 'partnership share' is used in the calculation of the chargeable consideration under the special charging rules. 'Partnership share' means, for this purpose, the proportion in which a partner is entitled at that time to share in the income profits of the partnership. The proportion in which a partner is entitled to share in the capital profits of the partnership is irrelevant for these purposes.

16.4 TRANSFER BY PARTNER (OR CONNECTED PERSON) TO PARTNERSHIP

Special charging rules apply where a partner or a connected person transfers property (or grants a lease) to the partnership.[3] The rules prescribe a five-step method to calculate the amount of the chargeable consideration deemed to be given for the transaction. The amount or value of the consideration that is given for the transaction in the 'real world' (if any) is disregarded unless the SDLT general anti-avoidance rule applies (see **1.11**). The chargeable consideration deemed to be given is based on the market value of the property transferred/lease granted and, in the case of the grant (or deemed grant) of a lease, the net present value (NPV) of the rent. The five-step method determines what proportion of the market value of the interest acquired and, if applicable, the NPV of the rent is used. The steps are complicated. The summary that follows should not be relied on as comprehensive. (For simplicity, the references below to 'transfer' include grant.)

The five steps involve:

---

[3] FA 2003, Sched.15, paras.10, 11, 12, 12A, 27A; SDLT Manual: SDLTM33500.

1. identifying the partner(s) or connected person(s) that dispose of the property (each called a 'relevant owner');
2. identifying the partners that are either a relevant owner or an individual (note: not a corporate partner) connected with the relevant owner (called 'corresponding partners');
3. for each relevant owner, identifying the proportion of the property transferred to which he was entitled before the transfer and allocating that proportion between that person's corresponding partners (in whichever way produces the least tax);
4. for each corresponding partner, finding the lower of the proportion of the property transferred allocated to him and their partnership share (called the 'lower proportion');
5. aggregating the lower proportions (called the 'sum of the lower proportions').

The result, the sum of the lower proportions, is deducted from 100 per cent to produce the proportion of the market value of the property transferred (and, if applicable, the NPV of the rent) that is chargeable.

A company that is connected with the relevant owner only by reason of being a trustee is treated as an individual and, therefore, a corresponding partner.

A company that is not a relevant owner and is a member of the same group as the relevant owner is effectively treated as a corresponding partner despite not being an individual subject to meeting the conditions for SDLT group relief (see **18.2**).

The rules that define 'connection' are complex and are borrowed from corporation tax legislation (see **15.2**).[4]

Example 16.2

A owns the freehold estate of a building consisting of five flats let to tenants worth £2 million. He transfers it to a partnership in which he is a partner. There are two other partners, B and C, both of whom are individuals unrelated to A. A is entitled to 40% of the income profits of the partnership. B and C are each entitled to 30% of the income profits of the partnership. The sum of the lower proportions is 40; hence, the proportion of the market value of the property treated as the chargeable consideration is £1.2 million: £2 million x (100 − 40)%. The amount of SDLT payable by A, B and C is £99,750 (an effective rate of 8.3%): (£125,000 @ 3%) + (£125,000 @ 5%) + (£675,000 @ 8%) + (£275,000 @ 13%). (Note multiple dwellings relief would be available but would, if claimed, produce a higher tax cost: see **4.3**.)

Example 16.3

As above, except that B is married to A. The sum of the lower proportions is 70 (40 + 30); hence, the proportion of the market value of the property treated as the chargeable consideration is £600,000: £2 million x (100 − 70)%. The amount of SDLT payable by A, B and C would be £38,000 (an effective rate of 6.3%) if multiple dwellings relief was not

---

[4] Corporation Tax Act 2010, ss.450, 451, 1122.

claimed: (£125,000 @ 3%) + (£125,000 @ 5%) + (£350,000 @ 8%). And the amount of SDLT payable by A, B and C would be £18,000 (an effective rate of 3%) if multiple dwellings relief *was* claimed: £600,000 / 5 = £120,000; (£120,000 @ 3% = £3,600); £3,600 x 5 = £18,000 (see **4.3**).

All the partners at completion of the transfer and those who join the partnership after completion are jointly and severally liable for the SDLT due on the transfer. (However, HMRC cannot recover the tax from a person who did not become a partner until after completion of the transfer.)

The partners may make an election to disapply the special charging rules and instead pay SDLT based on 100 per cent of the market value of the property transferred. The attraction of making such an election is to safe-harbour the property transferred from SDLT on subsequent transfers of interests in the partnership made for no consideration (see **16.7**). The election, once made, is irrevocable and must be made in an SDLT return or an amendment to an SDLT return.

16.5 TRANSFER BY PARTNERSHIP TO PARTNER (OR CONNECTED PERSON)

Special charging rules apply where a partnership transfers property (or grants a lease) to a partner or a connected person.[5] The rules prescribe a five-step method to calculate the amount of the chargeable consideration deemed to be given for the transaction. The amount or value of the consideration that is given for the transaction in the 'real world' (if any) is disregarded unless the SDLT general anti-avoidance rule applies (see **1.11**). The chargeable consideration deemed to be given is based on the market value of the property transferred/lease granted and, in the case of the grant of a lease, the NPV of the rent. The five-step method determines what proportion of the market value and, if applicable, the NPV of the rent is used. The steps are complicated. The summary that follows should not be relied on as comprehensive. (For simplicity, the references below to 'transfer' include grant.)

The five steps involve:

1. identifying the partner(s) or connected person(s) that acquire the property (each called a 'relevant owner');
2. identifying the partners that are either a relevant owner or an individual (note: not a corporate partner) connected with the relevant owner (called 'corresponding partners');
3. for each relevant owner, identifying the proportion of the property transferred to which he is entitled after the transfer and allocating that proportion between that person's corresponding partners (in whichever way produces the least tax);
4. for each corresponding partner, finding the lower of the proportion of the

---

[5] FA 2003, Sched.15, paras.18, 19, 20, 21, 22, 24; SDLT Manual: SDLTM33700.

property transferred allocated to him and their partnership share (called the 'lower proportion'); and
5. aggregating the lower proportions (called the 'sum of the lower proportions').

The result, the sum of the lower proportions, is deducted from 100 per cent to produce the proportion of the market value of the property transferred (and, if applicable, the NPV of the rent) that is chargeable.

A company that is connected with the relevant owner only by reason of being a trustee is treated as an individual and, therefore, a corresponding partner.

The rules that define 'connection' are complex and are borrowed from corporation tax legislation (see **15.2**).[6]

WARNING

1 A company that is not a relevant owner and is a member of the same group as the relevant owner is not treated as if it were a corresponding partner. Consequently, SDLT group relief is only available if all the partners are companies and members of the same SDLT group (see **18.2**). In other words, the availability of the relief is hard-edged: there is no concept of partial group relief for transfers of property from partnerships to partners or connected persons.
2 Where all the partners are companies and the sum of the lower proportions is 75 or more, the chargeable consideration is taken to be 100 per cent of the market value of the property transferred. This is so that group relief is claimed. However, in certain circumstances the override applies without recourse to group relief.
3 Where the property was transferred to the partnership on or after 20 October 2003, then the partnership share of the corresponding partner used in the sum of the lower proportions calculation is taken to be zero, unless the partnership paid *ad valorem* stamp duty or SDLT on its acquisition of the property.
4 Any increases in the partnership share of the corresponding partner between the date they joined the partnership and the transfer of the property by the partnership are only taken into account in determining the partnership share of the corresponding partner in the sum of the lower proportions calculation if *ad valorem* stamp duty or SDLT was paid on the increases.
5 Where the assets of a partnership are sold to a company held by the partners on an incorporation of the business of the partnership, the partnership had acquired some or all of the assets on their disposal by a partner or a connected person and the sale occurs within the period of three years beginning with the transfer of the property to the partnership by the partner or connected person, there may be a risk that the sale triggers a charge on a capital withdrawal (see **16.6**). Reasonable views differ on the interaction between the special rules for transfers by partnerships to partners or connected persons and those for capital withdrawals.
6 Where the assets of a partnership are sold to a company held by the partners on an incorporation of the business of the partnership, the partnership had acquired some or all of the assets on their disposal by a partner or a connected person and the sale is 'involved in connection with' the earlier transfer of the assets to the partnership, the sale may be taxed under the SDLT general anti-avoidance rule (see **1.11**). It is not possible, therefore, to 'route' property into and out of a partnership to avoid the SDLT that would otherwise be payable on a transfer of the property from the

---

[6] Corporation Tax Act 2010, ss.450, 451, 1122.

> original owner(s) to a connected company. The desire to incorporate the business may be driven by inheritance tax or the restrictions on mortgage interest relief.

Example 16.4

A, B and C are partners in a partnership. They are all individuals unrelated to each other. A is entitled to 40% of the income profits of the partnership. B and C are each entitled to 30% of the income profits of the partnership. The partnership distributes a property to A. The sum of the lower proportions is 40; hence, the proportion of the market value of the property treated as the chargeable consideration is £1.2 million: £2 million x (100 – 40)%. The amount of SDLT payable by A, B and C is £99,750 (an effective rate of 8.3%): (£125,000 @ 3%) + (£125,000 @ 5%) + (£675,000 @ 8%) + (£275,000 @ 13%). (Note: multiple dwellings relief would be available but would, if claimed, produce a higher tax cost – see **4.3**.)

Example 16.5

As above, except that B is married to A. The sum of the lower proportions is 70 (40 + 30); hence, the proportion of the market value of the property treated as the chargeable consideration is £600,000: £2 million x (100 – 70)%. The amount of SDLT payable by A, B and C would be £38,000 (an effective rate of 6.3%) if multiple dwellings relief was not claimed: (£125,000 @ 3%) + (£125,000 @ 5%) + (£350,000 @ 8%). And the amount of SDLT payable by A, B and C would be £18,000 (an effective rate of 3%) if multiple dwellings relief *was* claimed: £600,000 / 5 = £120,000; (£120,000 @ 3% = £3,600); £3,600 x 5 = £18,000 (see **4.3**).

Example 16.6

As above, except that the assets of the partnership are sold to a company held by A, B and C on an incorporation of the business. The consideration for the transfer in the 'real world' is the issue of shares by the company. A, B and C act together to secure and exercise the control of the company, having entered into a shareholders agreement to regulate the relationship of the shareholders, the management of the company and ownership of the shares. The sum of the lower proportions is 100 (40 + 30 + 30); hence, the proportion of the market value of the property treated as the chargeable consideration is £0: £2 million x (100 – 100)%. No SDLT is chargeable.

16.6 CAPITAL WITHDRAWALS AND LOAN REPAYMENTS

A withdrawal of money or money's worth and the repayment (to any extent) of a loan made to the partnership are not generally SDLT transactions. An exception applies where:

- some or all of the partnership property was transferred to the partnership by a partner or a connected person;

- the withdrawal or loan repayment occurs within three years of that property transfer;
- in the case of withdrawals, the money or money's worth withdrawn does not relate to income profit;
- in the case of withdrawals, the person making the withdrawal is the person that transferred the property to the partnership, the partner with whom he was connected or another connected person;
- in the case of withdrawals, the withdrawal is made on withdrawing capital or coupled with the person reducing his interest or retiring from the partnership;
- in the case of loan repayments, the loan that is repaid by the partnership was made to the partnership by the person that transferred the property to the partnership, the partner with whom he was connected or another connected person; and
- a specific election was not made to disapply the special charging rules on the transfer of the property to the partnership (see **16.4**).[7]

Where the withdrawal or loan repayment is chargeable, the amount of the chargeable consideration is based on the amount of the money or value of the money's worth withdrawn or the amount of the loan repaid (capped at the market value of the property on the date it was transferred to the partnership) less any amount previously charged to tax. All the partners are jointly and severally liable for the tax.

It is not clear what mischief this provision is designed to prevent. Those alert to the issue can prevent a charge by waiting for the three-year window to expire before arranging for the relevant event to take place. Alternative ways may exist to give effect economically to the relevant event that does not involve a withdrawal or loan repayment. In the author's opinion, no SDLT charge would arise if the partnership repays an amount owed by the partnership to the relevant person other than in the course of lending money: e.g., cash left outstanding following a sale of an asset to the partnership. Likewise, no SDLT charge would arise if the partnership merely pays the relevant person interest not the principal element of a loan.

Example 16.7

A, B and C are the limited partners in an English limited partnership. They each own a 33% partnership share. A transfers a number of dwellings to the partnership by way of capital contribution. The amount of the chargeable consideration given for the transaction is calculated in accordance with the special rules (see **16.4**). Two years later, A retires from the partnership and withdraws cash from the partnership. The cash is not income profits. A, B and C are liable to pay SDLT based on the amount of cash withdrawn by A less the amount previously charged to tax.

---

[7] FA 2003, Sched.15, para.17A.

> **WARNING**
>
> Whenever a property is transferred by a partner or connected person to a partnership, you should warn of the possibility that a withdrawal of money or money's worth or a repayment of a loan made to the partnership within three years of the transfer could trigger an SDLT charge for all the partners.

16.7 TRANSFER OF INTEREST IN PARTNERSHIP

Subject to two exceptions (explained below), the transfer of an interest in a partnership that is not a 'property-investment partnership' is not chargeable to SDLT.[8] 'Property-investment partnership' means 'a partnership whose sole or main activity is investing or dealing in chargeable interests (whether or not that activity involves the carrying out of construction operations on the land in question)'. So farming partnerships, house-builder partnerships, professional services partnerships and other types of trading partnerships are not 'property-investment partnerships' for this purpose. Even if the partnership interest transferred relates to a 'property-investment partnership', a charge only arises if, and to the extent that, the partnership owns property that is 'relevant partnership property'. Whether or not property held by a partnership is 'relevant partnership property' for this purpose depends on factors including:

- when the property was acquired by the partnership;
- whether stamp duty or SDLT was duly paid on the acquisition of the property by the partnership; and
- whether consideration is given for the partnership interest.

Where there is 'relevant partnership property', the chargeable consideration (i.e., the amount of tax payable) is based on a proportion of the market value of the relevant partnership property. The chargeable proportion corresponds to the percentage partnership share transferred. 'Partnership share' means a person's entitlement to share in the income profits of the partnership at that time.

In broad terms only, and note that the rules are more complex than this generalisation, where an existing partnership interest is *sold*, all partnership property is 'relevant partnership property' subject to limited exceptions. (The legislation describes such sales as 'Type A' transfers.)

There is a 'sale' of a partnership interest for this purpose where:

- consideration in money or money's worth is given by the person acquiring or increasing their income-profit share in the partnership; or
- a person becomes a partner, the interest of an existing partner is reduced or an existing partner retires from the partnership and there is a withdrawal of money

---

[8] FA 2003, Sched.15, paras.14, 17, 29, 30, 31, 32, 36; SDLT Manual: SDLTM33330, SDLTM34000, SDLTM34600, SDLTM34610, SDLTM34650.

or money's worth from the partnership by the retiring partner funded by the capital contribution made by the new partner.

In contrast, where a new partnership interest is acquired or an existing partnership interest is increased and no consideration is given, then partnership property is not 'relevant partnership property' if the property was acquired by the partnership on its disposal by a third party (i.e., a person other than a partner or a connected person) and full stamp duty or SDLT was paid by the partnership. (The legislation describes such transfers as 'Type B' transfers.)

Examples of transfers for no consideration that fall into this category include:

- gifts of partnership interests;
- transfers of partnership interests by way of capital contribution to another partnership or to a company;
- distributions *in specie* of partnership interests;
- activation of carried interests in partnerships;
- acquisitions of partnership interests resulting from making capital contributions to partnerships; and
- increases of partnership interests resulting from the death or retirement of an existing partner.

The two exceptions referred to above (where transfers of interests in *any* type of partnership are chargeable) are where:

- there is a transfer of property by a partner or connected person to the partnership followed by a transfer of an interest in the partnership, and the two transfers form part of the same arrangements. In this case, the transfer of the interest in the partnership is chargeable based on the market value of the property transferred to the partnership regardless of the type of partnership;
- a partnership interest is a chargeable interest for the purposes of the SDLT general anti-avoidance rule, Finance Act 2003, s.75A; hence, where the conditions of section 75A are met, the transfer of the partnership interest is chargeable based on the highest amount or aggregate amount given as consideration by any one person or received by the vendor for 'transactions' that are 'involved in connection with' the transfer (see **1.11**).

Example 16.8

A, B and C are equal partners in a general partnership (i.e., one within the Partnership Act 1890) that carries on a property-letting business. All the partnership property – which was acquired on the open market – is situated in England. The total value of the partnership property is £6 million. The partnership owes bank debt in the amount of £1.8 million (30% debt for equity), secured on the partnership property. B sells his share in the partnership to D for £1.4 million (one-third of the net asset value of the partnership: 1/3 of (£6 million – £1.8 million) = £1.4 million). The transfer of the partnership interest is an SDLT transaction. The amount of the chargeable consideration is £2 million: 1/3 of £6 million. It is unclear whether the £2 million of chargeable consideration would be taxed in accordance with the non-residential rates or residential higher rates irrespective of the number of dwellings held by the partnership, and whether the partnership property consisted exclusively of dwellings. Specialist advice should be sought. Note that a claim for multiple dwellings relief cannot be made on this type of transaction (see **4.3**). D must make an SDLT return and pay the tax within 14 days of the transfer.

Example 16.9

As before, except that D acquires his partnership by subscription, B merely retires and B merely withdraws from the partnership the capital he had originally contributed to the partnership. The transfer of the partnership interest is an SDLT transaction. However, the amount of the chargeable consideration is nil. D is not regarded as having given consideration for the transfer of the partnership interest and as all the partnership property was acquired from third parties, none of the partnership property is 'relevant partnership property'; hence, the chargeable consideration is taken to be 1/3 of nil. D must make an SDLT return and pay the tax within 14 days of the transfer.

Example 16.10

As before, except that the partnership had acquired the property on its disposal by A. B and C acquired their interests in the partnership by making matching cash contributions. The transfer of the partnership interest is an SDLT transaction. However, as with the first example (a sale of an existing partnership interest by B to D), all the partnership property that was acquired by the partnership on its disposal by A counts as 'relevant partnership property'; hence, the amount of the chargeable consideration is £2 million: 1/3 of £6 million. D must make an SDLT return and pay the tax within 14 days of the transfer.

Example 16.11

As before, except that the partnership had acquired *some* of the property on its disposal by A. B and C acquired their interests in the partnership by making matching cash contributions. The partnership used the cash contributed by B and C to acquire the property on the open market. The proportion of the £6 million total value of the partnership property attributable to the property acquired from A is £2.1 million. The transfer of the partnership interest is an SDLT transaction. Only the partnership property that was acquired by the partnership on its disposal by A counts as 'relevant partnership property'; hence, the amount of the chargeable consideration is £700,000: 1/3 of £2.1 million. D must make an SDLT return and pay the tax within 14 days of the transfer.

Example 16.12

As before, except that the partnership carries on the trade of farming. The transfer of the interest in the partnership – regardless of how it is effected and whether or not consideration is given – is not chargeable to SDLT on the basis that the partnership property was not acquired by the partnership on its disposal by a partner or a connected person, or, if it was so acquired, the transfer of the partnership interest is not pursuant to arrangements in existence at the time of the property transfer.

An SDLT return only needs to be made on a transfer of a partnership interest where tax is payable or would be payable but for a claim for relief.

Where a partnership interest is sold and the partnership property consists of, or includes, shares in a company, the deed of assignment may attract stamp duty capped at the amount of stamp duty that would be chargeable if the deed of assignment had transferred the shares and the consideration were a proportion of the market value of the shares (less any debt secured solely on them) corresponding to the partnership share transferred.

16.8 OTHER SPECIAL RULES

Other rules modify the SDLT treatment on:

- transfers of property between partnerships where there is (to any extent) commonality of membership;
- transfers of property from a partnership in connection with the incorporation of a limited liability partnership (LLP);
- transfers of partnership interests in exchange for property;
- transfers involving partnerships where all the partners are members of the same SDLT group; and
- acquisitions of partnership interests by charities.[9]

16.9 OTHER AREAS OF DIFFICULTY

Other areas of difficulty generally include:

- *The interaction of the special rules in Finance Act 2003, Sched.15, Part 3 with other market value rules (e.g., transfers to a connected company):* HMRC appears to accept that the special rules take precedence, at least over the market value rule for transfers to connected companies; but this is not explicit in the SDLT code.
- *The interaction of a transfer of a property from a partnership to a partner or connected person (e.g., on the incorporation of a partnership) within three years of the transfer of property (not necessarily the same property) to the partnership:* It is not clear how the special charging rules for transfers made by partnerships (see **16.4**) interact with the special charging rules for withdrawals by partners (see **16.6**).

---

[9] FA 2003, s.65, Sched.15, paras.16, 23, 24, 28; SDLT Manual: SDLTM34080.

- *Transfers from partnerships where some but not all of the partners are charities or members of the same group:* There is no concept of partial relief. It is arguable that partial relief nevertheless applies as a matter of statutory interpretation; but HMRC's position is uncertain and this has yet to be tested before the courts. Partial group relief is expressly given for transfers *to* partnerships (see **16.4**), so the absence of an equivalent provision for transfers from partnerships is curious. See **18.2**.
- *Transfers of property from a partnership to a company held by the partnership (and vice versa):* One would reasonably expect the tax treatment of such a transfer to be benign, especially where the parent partnership is a body corporate (e.g., a limited liability partnership) and can head an SDLT group. However, the transfer would be treated as if it had been made by the partners, not the partnership; hence, unless all the partners are members of the same SDLT group, SDLT group relief would be denied (see **18.2**).
- *Transfers of tiers of partnership interests (e.g., the interest in a partnership owning a partnership interest is transferred):* It is not clear whether HMRC is correct in being able to 'look through' the bottom partnership (and any intermediate partnerships) to determine whether the top partnership the interest in which is transferred is a property-investment partnership and owns property – the conditions for a charge on the transfer of the interest (see **16.7**).
- *The operation of the SDLT general anti-avoidance rule in connection with transactions involving partnerships* (see **1.11**).[10]

WARNING

Each of the aforementioned areas of difficulty deserves specialist advice or making a request for HMRC clearance. The application of the legislation is uncertain, HMRC's guidance is inadequate and there is a range of reasonable views.

---

[10] FA 2003, ss.75A, 75C(8)(a), (8A), Sched.15, paras.2, 14; SDLT Manual: SDLTM33330, SDLTM34000, SDLTM34160, SDLTM34200.

CHAPTER 17

Promote arrangements and development licences

17.1 BACKGROUND

This chapter covers a particular provision: Finance Act 2003, s.44A. It applies to transactions with an effective date on or after 17 March 2004.[1] It is a rare example of a rare provision in the stamp duty land tax (SDLT) code that deems a person to acquire a chargeable interest in the 'SDLT world' when in the 'real world' he does not. It is aimed at development licence arrangements, which were frequently used by house-builders under stamp duty, before SDLT was introduced. Those arrangements involved a landowner and a house-builder entering into an agreement under which the house-builder would be given access to the land to carry out a residential development and market the dwellings for sale. The house-builder would also be given some kind of power to compel the landowner to transfer ownership of the completed dwellings to the buyers. The house-builder would usually give the landowner cash to acquire this right and a proportion of the sale proceeds realised on selling the dwellings. But for section 44A, no SDLT would be chargeable because the house-builder would not acquire any interest in, or any rights over, the land. Parliament considered that this was wrong and legislated for an SDLT charge to arise in these circumstances.

Two comments can be made: first, section 44A has been drafted widely and sometimes it is necessary to interpret the provision purposively to prevent ordinary sale arrangements being charged under it; second, it is possible to structure arrangements of this kind in a way that is not chargeable. As a result, the provision arguably ought to be repealed or amended.

References in this chapter to 'house-builder' are to any person providing services in connection with a residential development.

---

[1] For more information see *Sergeant and Sims on Stamp Taxes* (LexisNexis UK), AA2.6 [AA35A]; FA 2003, s.44A.

17.2 THE SCOPE OF FINANCE ACT 2003, S.44A

An SDLT charge arises where a contract is entered into under which a chargeable interest is to be conveyed by one party to the contract (A) at the direction or request of the other (B) to a person who is not a party to the contract (C) or to C or B.

B is not regarded as entering into an SDLT transaction by reason of entering into the contract, but if B 'substantially performs' the contract, he is treated as acquiring a chargeable interest. The effective date of the transaction is the date of substantial performance.

B would substantially perform the contract by:

- taking possession of all or substantially all of the subject-matter of the contract; or
- paying the whole or substantially the whole of the price payable under the contract.

This is the standard meaning of 'substantial performance' (see **1.8**).

If the contract is (to any extent) rescinded, annulled or not carried into effect, the tax paid by B shall be repaid by HM Revenue and Customs (HMRC). A claim for repayment must be made by amending the SDLT return made by B.

Where B assigns the benefit of the contract to another person (D), the assignment of rights is not chargeable to SDLT. Instead, D is treated as having entered into the original contract in place of B and the total consideration given by D (whether to B and/or A) is the chargeable consideration for the transaction and taxed.

Therefore, the provision mimics the general rule for sale contracts and an accompanying provision mimics the principle that assignments of rights are not chargeable of themselves.

However, the drafting of section 44A causes confusion regarding its scope. After all, ordinary sale contracts frequently permit the purchaser to direct the vendor to transfer the property either to the purchaser or another person nominated by the purchaser. There is no relevant HMRC guidance or case law. It is, therefore, necessary to look at extraneous material to determine its intended scope – e.g., Explanatory Notes and Hansard. That material confirms that section 44A is intended to apply merely to development licence arrangements. The following text from Hansard is illuminating:

> ... new section 44A is there to ensure that stamp duty land tax is not avoided, especially in commercial transactions, by disguising what is in substance the purchase of land for development as a non-land transaction, often described as a 'building licence'.
>
> The Government believe that the tax treatment should reflect the substance. That is our policy on a variety of issues that are to be debated today.
>
> The effect of the amendment [to remove the word 'request'] would be to tempt taxpayers and their advisers to draft building licences that are still in substance the

purchase of land but which provide that the developer will 'request' rather than 'direct' the landowner to convey to a third party. That would no doubt be the sort of request that it is hard to say no to.[2]

The overlap of section 44A and the equivalent provision that applies to ordinary sale contracts (Finance Act 2003, s.44) does not harm ordinary sale contracts that are substantially performed or completed. The substantial performance or completion would be taxed in the usual way. Its impact is felt on assignments of rights and other 'pre-completion transactions' (see **Chapter 7**). This is because the standard regime for pre-completion transactions is prescriptive and provides instructions on how to apply the SDLT code to the transaction effected on completion – e.g., who is the vendor, what is the chargeable consideration, whether or not relief must be claimed, etc. The specific regime for assignment of rights of contracts under section 44A is much more forgiving. It merely substitutes D for B.

At first blush, section 44A is effective in charging 'development licence' contracts. Even though the house-builder may not acquire an interest in the land (under the standard form of development licence contract it merely acquires a licence to occupy, which is an exempt interest for SDLT purposes), its right to direct the landowner to convey the land to its customers engages section 44A to tax the consideration given by the house-builder at the point of it taking possession of the land.

However, what if the house-builder does not make a cash payment to the landowner for acquiring rights under the development licence contract and instead is entitled to *receive* consideration for the construction works carried out by it derived from the sale proceeds from the development? The answer probably depends on whether the consideration received by the house-builder is a fee or commission calculated by reference to the sale proceeds or the right to a share of the sale proceeds themselves. Whereas the former is not a 'chargeable interest' for the purposes of SDLT, the latter probably is under general principles.

If the house-builder acquires a chargeable interest under general principles or is deemed to acquire a chargeable interest under section 44A, then it is not clear what the chargeable consideration given by the house-builder is. Clearly, if the house-builder gives consideration in the form of cash for the rights it acquires under the development licence, then that is part of the chargeable consideration given for the transaction. However, what about the value of the construction works carried out on the land or the services performed by the house-builder? A provision in the SDLT legislation (Finance Act 2003, Sched.4, para.10) disregards 'works of construction, improvement or repair of a building or other works to enhance the value of land' if they are provided on a major interest in land acquired or to be acquired under the transaction. At first sight, this gives optimism. On closer inspection, there are problems relying on this provision. First, the meaning of the term 'major interest' is limited to a freehold or leasehold estate. The developer has not acquired such an

---

[2] Financial Secretary to the Treasury (Ruth Kelly), Hansard, HC Deb 28 April 2004 vol.420 col.915.

interest – in fact it has not acquired any interest in the 'real world'. It is deemed to acquire a chargeable interest, but the type of chargeable interest it is deemed to acquire is not specified. Accordingly, the 'works exemption' does not appear to provide a safe harbour. Second, a recent trend is for house-builders to provide professional services (sometimes referred to as 'promotion services') to secure planning consent. The author doubts that such services fall within the description 'other works' in paragraph 10 as a matter of statutory interpretation, as the term 'other works' is preceded by examples of physical works.

Example 17.1

An owner of bare land (A) enters into a contract with a house-builder (B). Under the contract, B is given a licence to occupy the land, the right to develop the land into residential property and market the dwellings built or to be built for sale. B may request A to grant leases of the dwellings to B's customers, the purchasers of the dwellings. In the event of default by A, B has the power to direct A to grant leases of the dwellings or to transfer the freehold estate to it. The sale proceeds realised by B are shared between A and B according to a specific ratio. B pays £500,000 on entering into the contract. The value of the construction works provided by B is £10 million. The contract is chargeable to SDLT as soon as B takes possession of the land under licence. The chargeable consideration given for the transaction includes the £500,000. It is unclear whether the £10 million of works is also part of the chargeable consideration given for the transaction. It is also unclear whether B acquires a chargeable interest under general principles by acquiring a right to share in the sale proceeds.

Example 17.2

As above except that B agrees to provide professional services to secure planning consent for the residential development; B does not make a cash payment; and B is paid an amount of cash by A calculated by reference to the sale proceeds realised by A. It is unclear whether the contract is chargeable under section 44A. Arguably, it is not. The contract may not be one 'under which a chargeable interest *is to be conveyed*'; and it is not 'disguising what is in substance the purchase of land for development as a non-land transaction'. B might request HMRC to confirm its interpretation of section 44A under the 'Non-Statutory Business Clearance' procedure.

Transactions chargeable under section 44A are only notifiable if tax is payable – i.e., if the amount or value of the chargeable consideration given for the transaction is more than £125,000.

CHAPTER 18

Corporate reliefs

18.1 BACKGROUND

This chapter covers three stamp duty land tax (SDLT) reliefs common to corporate transactions:

- group relief;
- reconstruction relief; and
- acquisition relief.[1]

The first two provide a complete exemption from charge. The last substitutes the relevant tax rates with a special flat rate of 0.5 per cent. All three reliefs must be claimed in an SDLT return or an amendment to an SDLT return and are subject to withdrawal.

The availability of the reliefs is not sensitive to the subject-matter of the transaction – the reliefs apply equally to the acquisition of residential property and non-residential property. However, reconstruction relief and acquisition relief require the land transaction to be entered into for the purposes of, or in connection with, the transfer of the *undertaking* of another company; and, in the case of acquisition relief only, the undertaking must have as its main activity the carrying on of a trade that does *not* consist wholly or mainly of dealing in land. This restricts the availability of acquisition relief where the subject-matter of the land transaction is residential property.

Having an awareness of the conditions that need to be met to claim the reliefs and the circumstances in which the reliefs are withdrawn is important to the residential property lawyer. Determining the availability of the reliefs and whether a withdrawal is triggered can be hard. Those issues require good knowledge of tax technical concepts, including the meanings of:

- 'equity holder';
- 'ordinary share capital';
- 'arrangements';

---

[1] Finance Act (FA) 2003, Sched.7, Parts 1, 2; *HMRC internal manual – Stamp Duty Land Tax Manual* ('SDLT Manual') (HMRC, 19 March 2016, updated 16 January 2020, available at: **www.gov.uk/hmrc-internal-manuals/stamp-duty-land-tax-manual**): SDLTM23000.

- 'tax avoidance';
- 'control' and 'change of control';
- 'undertaking'; and
- 'reconstruction'.

The comments that follow are only a guide to these concepts.

18.2 GROUP RELIEF

18.2.1 Overview

Group relief gives a complete exemption from charge to SDLT transactions between members of the same corporate group.[2] The relief is given where:

- the vendor and purchaser are both 'companies';
- one of the parties is the '75 per cent subsidiary' of the other, or both are the '75 per cent subsidiaries' of another company;
- at completion (or, if earlier 'substantial performance': see **1.8**) there are no 'arrangements' for a person or persons together to obtain control of the purchaser but not of the vendor; and
- the transaction is not in pursuance of, or involved in connection with, certain other disqualifying arrangements.

One can immediately see that the hurdle to pass to benefit from the relief is high and the conditions are prescriptive.

Once claimed, the relief may be withdrawn if a specified event happens within a control period of three years beginning with completion (or substantial performance).

The aim is to relieve fully from charge the transfer of property within a corporate group provided it is to remain in the group.

The relief must be claimed in an SDLT return, or an amendment to an SDLT return, by entering code 12 at question 9 ('are you claiming relief?') of the SDLT return.

18.2.2 Conditions

As stated above, the following four conditions must be met:

- The vendor and purchaser are both 'companies'.
- One of the parties is the '75 per cent subsidiary' of the other, or both are the '75 per cent subsidiaries' of another company.

---

[2] For more information see *Sergeant and Sims on Stamp Taxes* (LexisNexis UK), AA7: SDLT–relief for corporations; FA 2003, Sched.7, Part 1; SDLT Manual: SDLTM23010.

- At completion (or, if earlier 'substantial performance') there are no 'arrangements' for a person or persons together to obtain control of the purchaser but not of the vendor.
- The transaction is not in pursuance of, or involved in connection with, certain other disqualifying arrangements.

They are taken in the same sequence below.

18.2.2.1 Companies

'Company' means a body corporate; hence, it includes a limited liability partnership (LLP). Although a unit trust scheme is generally treated for SDLT purposes as if the trustees were a company and the units were shares in the company, that treatment is disapplied for group relief. In practice, the inclusion of an LLP in the meaning of company only matters where the parties to the transaction are subsidiaries of the partnership: i.e., where the partnership heads a group. A transfer to or from a partnership in this context, regardless of whether the partnership is a body corporate, would fall within special charging rules (see **Chapter 16**). Moreover, as discussed at **18.2.2.2**, it is not possible to 'look through' an LLP, a Scottish partnership or any other type of partnership that has separate legal personality to trace a group relationship between two companies. This is due to the absence of issued share capital.

> **WARNING**
>
> Always check in the case of foreign entities that they answer the description of a company and, where they are intermediate entities within a group, that they have issued share capital (or something equivalent to issued share capital). Complicated questions arise on foreign entity characterisation.

18.2.2.2 '75 per cent subsidiaries'

The condition that the parties to the transaction are 75 per cent subsidiaries can be met in one of two ways: one of the parties may be the 75 per cent subsidiary of the other; or both may be 75 per cent subsidiaries of another company.

A company (the subsidiary) is a 75 per cent subsidiary of another company (the parent) if the parent is the beneficial owner (directly or indirectly through one or more other companies) of at least 75 per cent of the 'ordinary share capital' of the subsidiary and is beneficially entitled to at least 75 per cent of any profits available for distribution to the subsidiary's 'equity holders' and would be beneficially entitled to at least 75 per cent of any assets available for distribution to the subsidiary's 'equity holders'.

'Equity holder' means a shareholder or a loan creditor in respect of a loan that is not a normal commercial loan.

'Ordinary share capital' means all types of issued share capital other than capital that only entitles the holder to receive a dividend at a fixed rate.

Example 18.1

A Ltd owns the entire issued share capital of B Ltd and C Ltd. B Ltd and C Ltd each own 50% of D Ltd. A Ltd is grouped with B Ltd, C Ltd *and* D Ltd. It meets the 75% tests in relation to B Ltd and C Ltd directly and in relation to D Ltd indirectly through B Ltd and C Ltd.

Meeting the 75 per cent tests indirectly through one or more companies requires those intermediate companies to have issued share capital. This means that if an entity in the chain of ownership has separate legal personality and does not have issued share capital or is not a company, then that entity blocks a group relationship from being in existence: it is not possible to 'look through' it to meet the 75 per cent tests. Examples of such blocking entities include companies limited by guarantee, Scottish partnerships and LLPs.

Example 18.2

A Ltd owns the entire issued share capital of B Ltd. It is also the owner of a company limited by guarantee that owns C Ltd. The transfer of property between B Ltd and C Ltd would not qualify for group relief. A Ltd meets the 75% tests in relation to B Ltd but does not meet them in relation to C Ltd: the guarantee company prevents A Ltd from meeting those tests indirectly.

WARNING

Although an LLP may head a group so that SDLT transactions between direct or indirect subsidiaries of the partnership are eligible for group relief, an SDLT transaction between a member of the partnership and a subsidiary of the partnership would not be so eligible. This is because the partnership lacks share capital. More worryingly, an SDLT transaction between an LLP and its subsidiary would also not be eligible for group relief. This is because the members of the partnership would be regarded as making the disposal or acquisition and they would not be treated as grouped with the subsidiary of the partnership by reason of the partnership blocking the group. Note, finally, that an SDLT transaction between a member of the partnership and the partnership would fall within special charging rules (see **Chapter 16**).

18.2.2.3 Arrangements for person to obtain control of the purchaser

Group relief is not available if at completion (or, substantial performance, if earlier) there are 'arrangements' in place for one or more persons together to have or obtain control of the purchaser but not of the vendor.[3]

'Arrangements' is not defined exhaustively. It includes 'any scheme, agreement or understanding, whether or not legally enforceable'. HMRC appears to accept that there cannot be an 'arrangement' without the involvement of a third party. That is to say, an 'arrangement' for a disqualifying event cannot be unilateral. However, identifying the point that negotiations turn into 'arrangements' – arguably an agreement in principle whether or not legally enforceable – may be tricky and difficult to prove.

'Control' means the power of a person to secure that the affairs of the company are conducted in accordance with his wishes through holding shares or voting power or other powers conferred by the company's articles of association.

The relief is similarly restricted where the transaction is in pursuance of, or in connection with, arrangements for the purchaser to exit the same group as the vendor by reason of ceasing to be a 75 per cent subsidiary of the vendor or another company. The 'control' restriction is a wider test.

Exceptions apply where the shares in the purchaser are to be acquired by a company in connection with:

- the reconstruction of the purchaser's parent company provided that the acquisition of the shares will qualify for stamp duty reconstruction relief;
- joint ventures carrying on a commercial undertaking; or
- the exercise of security by a mortgagee.

> **WARNING**
>
> It is unclear whether the condition is met due to the appointment of an insolvency practitioner. This may turn on the type of insolvency practitioner and their powers. See *Farnborough Airport Properties Co.* v. *Revenue and Customs Comrs* [2019] EWCA Civ 118.

18.2.2.4 Other disqualifying arrangements

Group relief is not available if the land transaction is in pursuance of, or in connection with, 'arrangements' under which:

- some or all of the consideration for the transaction is to be given or received (directly or indirectly) by a third party;

---

[3] FA 2003, Sched.7, paras.1, 2, 2A, 2B; Corporation Tax Act 2010, s.1124; SDLT Manual: SDLTM23010, SDLTM23020, SDLTM23030A, SDLTM23010, SDLTM23010.

- the purchaser is to exit the same group as the vendor by reason of ceasing to be a 75 per cent subsidiary of the vendor or another company.

So far as the first limb is concerned, consideration is regarded as given or received by a third party if a person is to be *enabled* to provide it in consequence of a transaction involving a payment by a third party.

So far as the second limb is concerned, there is no express exception for reconstructions, but HMRC accepts that this is implicit.

Finally, group relief is not available if the transaction:

- is not carried out for genuine business reasons; or
- forms part of arrangements that have as a main purpose the avoidance of SDLT, stamp duty, income tax, corporation tax or capital gains tax.

These are two separate limbs, though in practice the two overlap. 'Tax avoidance' has its usual case law meaning: i.e., obtaining a tax advantage that was not contemplated by parliament or 'abusing' tax legislation in some way. Tax advantages based on making reasonable choices or 'responsible' tax planning do *not* infect the purpose of the transaction. A 'white list' of acceptable tax planning can be found in HMRC's guidance manual[4] and is set out below. From a practical perspective, if the intra-group transaction is driven by tax and the description of the tax planning is not contained in HMRC's white list, the purchaser is likely to be on the back foot in persuading HMRC and ultimately a court or tribunal that the nature of the tax planning is reasonable. Determining whether or not the tax planning is reasonable may require a detailed understanding of the purpose and scheme of the relevant tax legislation.

The examples of acceptable tax planning contained in HMRC's manual – the 'white list' – include:

- the transfer of a property to a group company having in mind the possibility that shares in that company might be sold more than three years after the date of transfer;
- the transfer of a property to a group company having in mind the possibility that shares in that company might be sold within three years of the date of transfer, with a consequent clawback of group relief, in order that any increase in value of the property after the intra-group transfer might be sheltered from SDLT;
- the transfer of property to a group company having in mind the possibility that either of the above might occur;
- the transfer of a property to a group company prior to the sale of shares in the transferor company, in order that the property should not pass to the purchaser of the shares;
- the transfer of property to a group company in order that commercially generated rental income may be matched with commercially generated losses from a property income business;

---

[4] SDLT Manual: SDLTM23010.

- the transfer of property to a group company in order that commercially generated chargeable gains may be matched with commercially generated allowable losses; and
- the transfer of property to a group company in order that interest payable on borrowings from a commercial lender on ordinary commercial terms may be set against commercially generated rental income.

Example 18.3

A Ltd owns the entire issued share capital of B Ltd. A Ltd owns a number of residential properties. It sells the properties to B Ltd for the issue of shares. The sale is in pursuance of an arrangement to sell the entire issued share capital of B Ltd (then owning the properties) to a particular person. The arrangement for a person to obtain control of B Ltd (the purchaser) but not of A Ltd (the vendor) and for B Ltd to cease to be a 75% subsidiary of A Ltd restricts the availability of group relief. B Ltd must pay SDLT based on the higher of the value of the consideration shares and the value of the properties transferred.

Example 18.4

A Ltd owns the entire issued share capital of B Ltd. B Ltd owns a number of residential properties. It sells some of the properties to A Ltd for cash. The sale is in pursuance of an arrangement to sell the entire issued share capital of B Ltd (then only owning the properties to be sold) to a particular person. The arrangement for a person to obtain control of B Ltd (the vendor) but not of A Ltd (the purchaser) and for B Ltd to cease to be a 75% subsidiary of A Ltd does *not* restrict the availability of group relief. B Ltd may claim group relief to obtain a complete exemption from charge.

18.2.3 Withdrawal of group relief

Group relief may be withdrawn if a specified event happens within three years beginning with completion (or substantial performance) or in pursuance of arrangements made within three years.[5] It is not possible, therefore, to make arrangements within three years of the intra-group transaction for a specified event to occur after the three-year period expires. In those circumstances, the event, whenever it occurs, would give rise to a withdrawal.

There are two alternative withdrawal triggers:

- an exit by the purchaser from the same group as the vendor; or
- a change of control of the purchaser.

---

[5] FA 2003, Sched.7, paras.3, 4ZA, 4A, 4, 5, 6; SDLT Manual: SDLTM23010, SDLTM23010, SDLTM23080, SDLTM23010, SDLTM23010.

The second trigger only applies where the intra-group transaction was preceded by an earlier transaction for which group relief, reconstruction relief or acquisition relief was claimed, or where the vendor has exited the group (see below).

For both withdrawal triggers, the purchaser (or a subsidiary of the purchaser) must hold the property that was transferred intra-group (or a derived interest) at the time of the triggering event.

Where there is a withdrawal, the purchaser must make a further SDLT return and pay tax within 30 days of the relevant trigger event. The amount of tax payable is based on the market value of the property transferred (and, in the case of the grant of a lease, the rent) at completion of the transaction (or a proportion of the market value of the property transferred corresponding to what proportion of the property is held by the purchaser or a subsidiary of the purchaser).

Exceptions apply where the purchaser exits the vendor's group due to:

- the vendor (or a company above the vendor) being wound up;
- the shares in the purchaser are acquired by a company in connection with the reconstruction of the purchaser's parent company and provided that the acquisition of the shares in the purchaser by the acquiring company qualifies for stamp duty reconstruction relief;
- the transfer of the vendor's business to another company in connection with the demutualisation of an insurance company; or
- the vendor exiting the purchaser's group by reason of a transaction relating to shares in the vendor or a company above the vendor.

However, in the case of the last exception only, where there is a 'change of control' of the purchaser after the vendor has exited the purchaser's group, the purchaser is treated as exiting the vendor's group, meaning that the relief is withdrawn.

There is a 'change of control' of the purchaser where a person who controls the company (alone or with others) ceases to do so, a person obtains control of the purchaser (alone or with other), or the purchaser is wound up.

Where group relief is withdrawn and the purchaser fails to pay the tax within six months, HMRC may recover it from the vendor, any company that was above the purchaser and in the same group as the purchaser, or any person that was a controlling director of the purchaser or a company that controlled the purchaser. Other than an equivalent provision that applies to the withdrawal of reconstruction and acquisition reliefs, this is the only example of a secondary liability in the SDLT code. In all other cases, the only liable person is the purchaser.

Example 18.5

A Ltd and B Ltd are sister subsidiaries. The entire issued share capital of both companies is held by C Ltd. A Ltd holds a number of residential properties worth in total £5 million. It sells them to B Ltd for an inter-company receivable. There are no arrangements in existence for B Ltd to exit A Ltd's group or for the consideration to be indirectly or provided/received by a third party. B Ltd claims group relief in an SDLT return. Two years later, C Ltd receives an

CORPORATE RELIEFS

unsolicited offer from a third party to purchase the properties held by B Ltd for £6 million. C Ltd accepts the offer on condition that the third party purchases the shares in B Ltd. The third party completes its purchase of the shares in B Ltd. B Ltd must make a further SDLT return within 30 days. It must pay tax based on £5 million at the rates in force at the date of the original transaction.

Example 18.6

A Ltd and B Ltd are sister subsidiaries. The entire issued share capital of both companies is held by C Ltd. A Ltd holds a number of residential properties worth in total £5 million. C Ltd wishes to sell some of the properties held by A Ltd. It finds a third party buyer for the properties to be sold and arranges for the properties to be sold in a manner that does not attract SDLT for the buyer in return for receiving a higher purchase price. C Ltd procures that A Ltd sells to B Ltd the properties to be retained (which are worth in total £3 million), leaving only the properties to be sold in A Ltd. B Ltd claims group relief in an SDLT return. C Ltd and the third party buyer complete their sale and purchase of the shares in A Ltd. The group relief claimed by B Ltd is not withdrawn, as the vendor in the intra-group transaction exits the purchaser's group, not the other way round. Two years later, C Ltd receives an unsolicited offer from another third party to purchase the properties held by B Ltd for £3.5 million. C Ltd accepts the offer on condition that the third party purchases the shares in B Ltd. The third party completes its purchase of the shares in B Ltd. B Ltd must make a further SDLT return within 30 days. It must pay tax based on £3 million at the rates in force at the date of the original transaction.

The 'change of control' withdrawal trigger is complex and operates indiscriminately. HMRC had published a detailed guidance note specifically on the trigger where the vendor exits the group, listing a number of cases where it would and would not say there was a change of control for these purposes. That note, therefore, is an important source of reference. It is unfortunate, then, that the status of that guidance is unclear. The note was archived and has not been incorporated into the SDLT Manual, perhaps for fear of criticism that HMRC is seeking to narrow by guidance legislation that it considers to operate too broadly.

There is no concept to elect for the tax due on a withdrawal to be paid by another group company, as there is with capital gains tax.

18.3 RECONSTRUCTION RELIEF

18.3.1 Overview

Relief is available where an SDLT transaction is in connection with the acquisition of the whole or part of the undertaking of a company (the target company) by another company (the acquiring company) in pursuance of a scheme for the reconstruction of the target company.[6] The relief provides a complete exemption from charge, must be claimed in an SDLT return or an amendment to an SDLT return and is subject to withdrawal. The residential property lawyer is unlikely to need to use the relief other than possibly as part of a larger corporate transaction.

The relief is given where:

- the consideration consists of or includes the issue of non-redeemable shares in the acquiring company to all the shareholders of the target company;
- any consideration given for the transaction that is not met by issuing shares must be met by the acquiring company assuming liabilities of the target company;
- each shareholder of the target company is a shareholder of the acquiring company;
- the proportion of shares held by a shareholder in the target company is the same (or as near to as may be the same) the proportion of shares held by them in the acquiring company; and
- the transaction is carried out for genuine business reasons and does not form part of arrangements that have as a main purpose the avoidance of SDLT, stamp duty, income tax, corporation tax or capital gains tax.

One can immediately see that the hurdle to pass to benefit from the relief is high and the conditions are prescriptive.

Once claimed, the relief may be withdrawn if a specified event happens within a control period of three years beginning with completion (or substantial performance).

The aim is to relieve from charge the transfer of property forming part of a reconstruction of a company.

The relief must be claimed in an SDLT return, or an amendment to an SDLT return, by entering code 13 at question 9 ('are you claiming relief?').

18.3.2 Conditions

As stated above, the following five conditions must be met:

- the consideration consists of or includes the issue of non-redeemable shares in the acquiring company to all the shareholders of the target company;
- any consideration given for the transaction that is not met by issuing shares must be met by the acquiring company assuming liabilities of the target company;
- each shareholder of the target company is a shareholder of the acquiring company;
- the proportion of shares held by a shareholder in the target company is the same (or as near to as may be the same) as the proportion of shares held by them in the acquiring company; and

---

[6] FA 2003, Sched.7, Part 2; SDLT Manual: SDLTM23200.

- the transaction is carried out for genuine business reasons and does not form part of arrangements that have as a main purpose the avoidance of SDLT, stamp duty, income tax, corporation tax or capital gains tax.[7]

They are taken in the same sequence below.

18.3.2.1 'Reconstruction'

A reconstruction is a term of art. It refers to the transfer of part of a company's business to another company where the economic ownership of the business transferred is the same. HMRC says that it only considers that part of a company's business is transferred if what is transferred is capable of existing on its own as a viable business. The mere partition of assets or investments is, HMRC says, unlikely to be sufficient.

18.3.2.2 Consideration shares

At least some of the consideration given for the transaction must be met by the acquiring company issuing non-redeemable shares in its capital. Not only that, but the shares must be issued to *all* the shareholders of the target company. If some but not all of the shareholders of the target company receive the consideration shares, the relief is lost entirely, it is not apportioned to the extent that shareholders of the target company receive shares.

'Non-redeemable shares' has its ordinary meaning. Shares of any class may be issued provided that they are not capable of being redeemed.

18.3.2.3 Assumption of liabilities

Where not all of the consideration given for the transaction is met by the issue of shares, the availability of the relief requires that the only other form of consideration given by the acquiring company is the assumption of the target company's liabilities.

18.3.2.4 Matching membership

Immediately after the transaction, the membership of the acquiring company and of the target company must match.

18.3.2.5 Matching shareholdings

Immediately after the transaction, the proportion of shares held by a shareholder in the target company must match (or as near to as may match) the proportion of shares held by them in the acquiring company. There is no requirement to mirror classes of

---

[7] FA 2003, Sched.7, para.7; SDLT Manual: SDLTM23201, SDLTM23210.

shares, merely a requirement to mirror the proportionate shareholdings of the companies overall. The relaxation 'as near to as may be the same' is likely to refer to differences that are unavoidable and insubstantial in value.

18.3.2.6 No tax avoidance

'Tax avoidance' has its usual case law meaning – i.e., obtaining a tax advantage that was not contemplated by parliament or 'abusing' tax legislation in some way. Tax advantages based on making reasonable choices or 'responsible' tax planning do *not* infect the purpose of the transaction. If the SDLT transaction is driven by tax, the purchaser is likely to be on the back foot in persuading HMRC and ultimately a court or tribunal that the nature of the tax planning is reasonable. Determining whether or not the tax planning is reasonable may require a detailed understanding of the purpose and scheme of the relevant tax legislation.

Example 18.7

A Ltd is held by three shareholders, A, B and C, equally. A Ltd runs a number of businesses including a go-karting business. A Ltd recategorises its shares into two classes 'A' and 'B' shares. A Ltd reduces and cancels its 'B' shares in full, transfers all the assets of its go-karting business, including the freehold estate of the land from which the business is carried on, to B Ltd (set up by A) and B Ltd issues new non-redeemable shares to A, B and C. After the transfer A, B and C own B Ltd equally. No other consideration is given by B Ltd. B Ltd claims reconstruction relief in an SDLT return.

18.3.3 Withdrawal of reconstruction relief

Reconstruction relief may be withdrawn if a specified event happens within three years beginning with completion (or substantial performance) or in pursuance of arrangements made within three years.[8] It is not possible, therefore, to make arrangements within three years of the SDLT transaction for a specified event to occur after the three-year period expires. In those circumstances, the event, whenever it occurs, would give rise to a withdrawal.

There is one withdrawal trigger: a change of control of the acquiring company. The acquiring company (or a subsidiary of the acquiring company) must hold the property that was transferred (or a derived interest) at the time of the change of control.

Where there is a withdrawal, the acquiring company (i.e., the purchaser) must make a further SDLT return and pay tax within 30 days of the relevant trigger event. The amount of tax payable is based on the market value of the property transferred (and, in the case of the grant of a lease, the rent) at completion of the transaction (or a

---

[8] FA 2003, Sched.7, paras.9, 10, 11, 12; SDLT Manual: SDLTM23230, SDLTM23240, SDLTM23250, SDLTM23260, SDLTM23270, SDLTM23280.

proportion of the market value of the property transferred corresponding to what proportion of the property is held by the purchaser or a subsidiary of the purchaser).

Exceptions apply where the change of control of the acquiring company due to:

- a share transaction in connection with divorce or the dissolution of a civil partnership;
- a share transaction in connection with the variation of a testamentary disposition;
- a share transaction that is exempt from stamp duty by virtue of stamp duty group relief;
- a share transaction that is exempt from stamp duty by virtue of stamp duty share-for-share relief; or
- a loan creditor ceasing to control the company.

However, in the case of the two exceptions relating to share transactions that are exempt from stamp duty by virtue of a stamp duty relief only, a subsequent exit of the acquiring company's parent from the target company's group or a change of control of the acquiring company's parent would trigger a withdrawal of the relief.

There is a 'change of control' of the acquiring company where the company becomes controlled by a different person, by a different number of persons or by two or more persons at least one of whom is not the person or one of the persons by whom the company was previously controlled.

Where the relief is withdrawn and the acquiring company fails to pay the tax within six months, HMRC may recover it from any company that was above the acquiring company and in the same group as the acquiring company or any person that was a controlling director of the acquiring company or a company that controlled the acquiring company. Other than an equivalent provision that applies to the withdrawal of group relief and acquisition relief, this is the only example of a secondary liability in the SDLT code. In all other cases, the only liable person is the purchaser.

Example 18.8

A Ltd is held by three shareholders, A, B and C, equally. A Ltd runs a number of businesses including a go-karting business. A Ltd recategorises its shares into two classes 'A' and 'B' shares. A Ltd reduces and cancels its 'B' shares in full, transfers all of the assets of its go-karting business, including the freehold estate of the land from which the business is carried on, to B Ltd (set up by A) and B Ltd issues new non-redeemable shares to A, B and C. After the transfer A, B and C own B Ltd equally. No other consideration is given by B Ltd. B Ltd claims reconstruction relief in an SDLT return. Two years later, A, B and C sell their shares in B Ltd to a third party. B Ltd must make a further SDLT return within 30 days. It must pay tax based on the market value of the freehold estate transferred at the rates in force at that time.

18.4 ACQUISITION RELIEF

18.4.1 Overview

Relief is available where an SDLT transaction is in connection with the acquisition of the whole or part of the undertaking of a company (the target company) by another company (the acquisition company) in return for the issue of shares to the target company or some or all of the target company's shareholders (i.e., a partition demerger). The relief provides a *partial* exemption from charge, must be claimed in an SDLT return or an amendment to an SDLT return and is subject to withdrawal. The effect of claiming the relief is to substitute a flat 0.5 per cent rate for the relevant marginal rate that, but for the claim, would have applied. It means that the amount of tax payable on the asset sale is equivalent to the amount that would be payable if shares had been sold. The residential property lawyer is unlikely to need to use the relief other than possibly as part of a larger corporate transaction.[9]

The relief is given where:

- the consideration consists of or includes the issue of non-redeemable shares in the acquiring company to the target company or any or all the shareholders of the target company;
- any consideration given for the transaction that is not met by issuing shares must be met by the acquiring company assuming liabilities of the target company and/or paying cash up to 10 per cent of the nominal value of the consideration shares issued;
- the consideration shares are issued to the target company, and the acquiring company is not associated with another company that is party to arrangements to buy back the consideration shares;
- the undertaking acquired by the acquired company has as its main activity the carrying on of a trade that does not consist wholly or mainly of dealing in chargeable interests (i.e., interests in land situated in England or Northern Ireland);
- the transaction is carried out for genuine business reasons and does not form part of arrangements that have as a main purpose the avoidance of SDLT, stamp duty, income tax, corporation tax or capital gains tax.[10]

One can immediately see that the hurdle to pass to benefit from the relief is high and the conditions are prescriptive.

Once claimed, the relief may be withdrawn if a specified event happens within a control period of three years beginning with completion (or substantial performance).

The aim is to relieve from charge the transfer of property forming part of a partition demerger of a company.

---
[9] FA 2003, Sched.7, paras.9, 10, 11, 12; SDLT Manual: SDLTM23230, SDLTM23240, SDLTM23250, SDLTM23260, SDLTM23270, SDLTM23280.
[10] FA 2003, Sched.7, Part 2; SDLT Manual: SDLTM23200.

CORPORATE RELIEFS

The relief must be claimed in an SDLT return, or an amendment to an SDLT return, by entering code 14 at question 9 ('are you claiming relief?').

18.4.2 Conditions

As stated above, the following five conditions must be met:

- the consideration consists of or includes the issue of non-redeemable shares in the acquiring company to the target company or any or all the shareholders of the target company;
- any consideration given for the transaction that is not met by issuing shares must be met by the acquiring company assuming liabilities of the target company and/or paying cash up to 10 per cent of the nominal value of the consideration shares issued;
- where the consideration shares are issued to the target company, the acquiring company is not associated with another company that is party to arrangements to buy back the consideration shares;
- the undertaking acquired by the acquired company has as its main activity the carrying on of a trade that does not consist wholly or mainly of dealing in chargeable interests (i.e., interests in land situated in England or Northern Ireland);
- the transaction is carried out for genuine business reasons and does not form part of arrangements that have as a main purpose the avoidance of SDLT, stamp duty, income tax, corporation tax or capital gains tax.[11]

They are taken in the same sequence below.

18.4.2.1 Consideration shares

At least some of the consideration given for the transaction must be met by the acquiring company issuing non-redeemable shares in its capital. In contrast to reconstruction relief and the stamp duty reliefs for reconstructions and share-for-share exchanges, the shares do not need to be issued to all the target company's shareholders. Instead, the condition is met if the shares are issued to the target company or some or all of the target company's shareholders.

'Non-redeemable shares' has its ordinary meaning. Shares of any class may be issued provided that they are not capable of being redeemed.

18.4.2.2 Assumption of liabilities

Where not all of the consideration given for the transaction is met by the issue of shares, the availability of the relief requires that the only other form of consideration given by the acquiring company is the assumption of the target company's liabilities

---

[11] FA 2003, Sched.7, para.8; SDLT Manual: SDLTM23201, SDLTM23220.

STAMP DUTY LAND TAX HANDBOOK

and/or the payment of cash, provided that, in the case of cash, the amount of the cash paid does not exceed 10 per cent of the nominal value of the shares issued as consideration.

18.4.2.3 Buyback arrangements

The acquiring company must not be 'associated' with another company that is a party to arrangements with the target company relating to the shares of the acquiring company issued in consideration for the transfer of the undertaking. This condition is not met, therefore, if the acquiring company is party to arrangements with the target company's shareholders relating to the consideration shares issued to the target company's shareholders or if the acquiring company is party to arrangements with an individual relating to the consideration shares issued to either the target company or the target company's shareholders. The purpose of the condition is clearly to prevent arrangements for the consideration shares to be bought back in close proximity to the sale. It is not understood, though, why the condition is so narrow.

18.4.2.4 Qualifying trade

The undertaking transferred must have as its main activity the carrying on of a trade that does not consist wholly or mainly of dealing in chargeable interests (i.e., interests in land situated in England or Northern Ireland). This can be split into two conditions: (a) the undertaking transferred must be a trade, not property investment; and (b) the trade must not consist of property trading. This means that the relief is limited to transfers of trade-related properties: hotels, cinema, pubs, restaurants, etc.

18.4.2.5 No tax avoidance

'Tax avoidance' has its usual case law meaning – i.e., obtaining a tax advantage that was not contemplated by parliament or 'abusing' tax legislation in some way. Tax advantages based on making reasonable choices or 'responsible' tax planning do *not* infect the purpose of the transaction. If the SDLT transaction is driven by tax, the purchaser is likely to be on the back foot in persuading HMRC and ultimately a court or tribunal that the nature of the tax planning is reasonable. Determining whether or not the tax planning is reasonable may require a detailed understanding of the purpose and scheme of the relevant tax legislation.

18.4.2.6 Withdrawal of acquisition relief

Acquisition relief may be withdrawn if a specified event happens within three years beginning with completion (or substantial performance) or in pursuance of arrangements made within three years. It is not possible, therefore, to make arrangements within three years of the SDLT transaction for a specified event to occur after the three-year period expires. In those circumstances, the event, whenever it occurs, would give rise to a withdrawal.

There is one withdrawal trigger: a change of control of the acquiring company. The acquiring company (or a subsidiary of the acquiring company) must hold the property that was transferred (or a derived interest) at the time of the change of control.

Where there is a withdrawal, the acquiring company (i.e., the purchaser) must make a further return and pay tax within 30 days of the relevant trigger event. The amount of tax payable is based on the market value of the property transferred (and, in the case of the grant of a lease, the rent) at completion of the transaction (or a proportion of the market value of the property transferred corresponding to what proportion of the property is held by the purchaser or a subsidiary of the purchaser).

Exceptions apply where the change of control of the acquiring company due to:

- a share transaction in connection with divorce or the dissolution of a civil partnership;
- a share transaction in connection with the variation of a testamentary disposition;
- a share transaction that is exempt from stamp duty by virtue of stamp duty group relief;
- a share transaction that is exempt from stamp duty by virtue of stamp duty share-for-share relief; or
- a loan creditor ceasing to control the company.

However, in the case of the two exceptions relating to share transactions that are exempt from stamp duty by virtue of a stamp duty relief only, a subsequent exit of the acquiring company's parent from the target company's group or a change of control of the acquiring company's parent would trigger a withdrawal of the relief.

There is a 'change of control' of the acquiring company where the company becomes controlled by a different person, by a different number of persons or by two or more persons at least one of whom is not the person or one of the persons by whom the company was previously controlled.

Where the relief is withdrawn and the acquiring company fails to pay the tax within six months, HMRC may recover it from any company that was above the acquiring company and in the same group as the acquiring company or any person that was a controlling director of the acquiring company or a company that controlled the acquiring company.[12] Other than an equivalent provision that applies to the withdrawal of group relief and reconstruction relief, this is the only example of a secondary liability in the SDLT code. In all other cases, the only liable person is the purchaser.

---

[12] FA 2003, Sched.7, para.12.

CHAPTER 19

Compliance and disputes

19.1 BACKGROUND

Stamp duty land tax (SDLT) is a self-assessed tax. Purchasers must form an opinion (a 'self-assessment') on whether an SDLT return must be made and whether tax is payable. Where an SDLT return is made, HM Revenue and Customs (HMRC) may then check the self-assessment by opening an enquiry into the return within a nine-month period beginning with the 'filing date' (the date falling 14 days after completion or earlier substantial performance) before giving its conclusion on whether or not it is correct. Where an SDLT return is not made, HMRC may make an assessment within a 20-year period. Where the purchaser and HMRC do not agree on the correct amount of tax due, the purchaser has a choice of options to try to resolve the dispute. The ultimate decision on the sufficiency of the tax self-assessed by the purchaser rests with the courts. Enforcement of the obligation to make a return in respect of 'notifiable transactions' is linked to registration. Where the purchase of a chargeable interest by the purchaser is notifiable, the purchaser will not be registered as the legal owner of the purchased interest unless he provides a type of receipt (called a 'revenue certificate' or form SDLT5) proving that an SDLT return has been made. That receipt is not evidence that HMRC accepts the self-assessment contained in the return or that tax has been paid. In certain circumstances, one or more 'further returns' may need to be made by the purchaser.

This chapter continues by discussing the obligations on purchasers to make an SDLT return and payment of the tax; the powers of HMRC to monitor and enforce compliance; and the remedies available to the purchaser to resolve tax disputes.[1]

19.2 WHAT TRANSACTIONS REQUIRE AN SDLT RETURN?

The following SDLT transactions require an SDLT return to be made by the purchaser:

- The transfer of a freehold estate for chargeable consideration of £40,000 or more.

---

[1] For more information see *Sergeant and Sims on Stamp Taxes* (LexisNexis UK), AA10: SDLT–administration, compliance and enforcement.

- The transfer of a freehold estate for chargeable consideration of less than £40,000 where the transaction is linked to one or more other transactions and the total chargeable consideration given for the linked transactions is £40,000 or more.
- The grant of a lease for a term of seven years or more for a premium of £40,000 or more, or for an annual rent of £1,000 or more.
- The grant of a lease for a term of less than seven years where tax is payable on the premium and/or the rent.
- The assignment or surrender of a lease that was originally granted for a term of seven years or more for a premium of £40,000 or more.
- The assignment or surrender of a lease that was originally granted for a term of less than seven years where tax is chargeable.
- The acquisition of all other chargeable interests where tax is chargeable.
- A transaction that takes place in the 'SDLT world' due to substantial performance (see **1.8**), or the application of the SDLT general anti-avoidance rule (Finance Act 2003, s.75A – see **1.11**) or the 'pre-completion transactions' regime (see **Chapter 7**).

Tax is chargeable where the amount or value of the chargeable consideration given for the transaction (or the total amount or value of the chargeable consideration given for the transaction and any 'linked' transactions) exceeds the nil rate threshold and therefore is chargeable or would be chargeable but for the purchaser making a claim for a relief (e.g., first-time buyer relief).

Except for certain transactions that are deemed to take place in the 'SDLT world' (e.g., at substantial performance), notifiable transactions cannot be recorded in a land register unless an SDLT return has been made. The restriction on registration applies only to making a return, not to making a correct return or to making payment of the tax.[2]

19.3 HOW TO MAKE AN SDLT RETURN

Returns may be made online via a dedicated portal at HMRC's website or using 'paper returns' by correspondence. The online process is highly recommended over the alternative. This is for two reasons. First, it is impossible to submit online a return that is incomplete. Failure to complete the mandatory fields prevents submission. A high proportion of 'paper returns' submitted by correspondence are rejected, leading to delays in registration due to the failure to complete the mandatory fields. Second, for returns made online a revenue certificate (SDLT5) is usually generated instantly. Inevitably, where paper returns are used, a revenue certificate is produced much later depending on the speed of human intervention and the postal service.

---

[2] Finance Act (FA) 2003, ss.77, 77A, 79; *HMRC internal manual – Stamp Duty Land Tax Manual* ('SDLT Manual') (HMRC, 19 March 2016, updated 16 January 2020, available at: www.gov.uk/hmrc-internal-manuals/stamp-duty-land-tax-manual): SDLTM00310, SDLTM50100.

Guidance on how to complete and submit an SDLT return is available online.[3] It is regularly updated. The guidance gives tips on completing a paper return to stop it being rejected by an electronic scanner. It also gives the main reasons for paper returns being rejected. Those problems do not apply to returns made online.

The comments made in the rest of this section are by exception only. They draw attention to particular parts of the SDLT return that are not obvious.

Question 1 – type of property

One of four codes must be input depending on the class of transaction the property relates to. The codes enable HMRC to identify whether the correct tax rates and tax bands have been applied. The codes are:

- residential standard-rates transactions (code 01);
- mixed-use transactions (code 02);
- non-residential transactions (code 03); and
- residential higher-rates transactions (code 04).

A supplemental form (SDLT4) needs to be completed where code 02 (mixed-use property) or code 03 (non-residential property) is input. Those additional questions appear automatically where relevant when an online return is completed.

Question 4 – effective date of transaction

This is usually the date of completion. But where possession is taken of all or substantially all of the purchased property before completion, the date that possession is taken *could* be the effective date of the transaction. Alternatively, the payment of rent or substantially all the consideration before completion could trigger substantial performance. For further information, see **1.7**.

Question 9 – are you claiming relief?

There are two parts to this question. 'Yes' or 'No' must be entered in the first part and, if 'Yes' is entered, the relevant code for the relief should be input. The most common reliefs in this context are:

- part-exchange relief for house-builders (code 08);
- relocation relief for employers (code 09);
- compulsory purchase relief (code 10);
- compliance with planning obligations (code 11);
- right to buy relief (code 22);
- collective enfranchisement relief (code 25);

---

[3] Available at: **www.gov.uk/government/publications/sdlt-guide-for-completing-paper-sdlt1-return**.

COMPLIANCE AND DISPUTES

- first-time buyer relief (code 32); and
- multiple dwellings relief (code 33).

A code is made available for 'relief' from the 15 per cent flat rate of SDLT (code 35) and it is recommended to use it to prevent an enquiry being opened into the return. But the provisions that afford the 'relief' from the rate operate as automatic exemptions; hence, there is no obligation to use code 35 to benefit from the exemption. Put another way, failure to claim 'relief' from the 15 per cent rate does not make the transaction chargeable to the 15 per cent flat rate. There is room for only one relief code. Occasionally two codes are needed, for example codes 33 (multiple dwellings relief) and exemption from the super rate (code 35). In such cases use code 29: 'combination of reliefs'. It is not necessary to tell HMRC which reliefs are being combined, though this could be done using a covering letter.

Question 10 – what is the total consideration in money or money's worth, including any VAT actually payable for the transaction notified?

Do not enter a figure for premium or rent if the transaction is the grant of a lease. Instead, that information should be entered at questions 20 ('annual starting rent inclusive of VAT actually payable') and 22 ('total premium payable').

If a market value rule applies to deem the chargeable consideration for the transaction to be equal to the market value (or a proportion of the market value) of the purchased property, enter the market value (or relevant proportion of the market value) here.

Question 12 – what form does the consideration take?

If a market value rule applies, enter code 34: 'other (for example market value)'. The market value rules are listed at **1.5.2**.

Question 13 – is this transaction linked to any other(s)?

There are two parts to this question. 'Yes' or 'No' must be entered in the first part and, if 'Yes' is entered, the total consideration for the linked transactions must be input. Linked transactions may be concurrent or consecutive. For more information on linked transactions, see **1.5.4.2**.

Questions 16–25 (leases)

Questions 16–21 should be completed for the grant of a lease, assignment of a lease or transfer of a freehold subject to one or more underleases.

In the case of the grant or assignment of a lease, details of the lease should be entered at questions 16–21. If the grant or assignment is subject to one or more underleases, details of the underlease(s) should be given on a separate schedule. In the case of the transfer of a freehold subject to one or more underleases, details of the underlease(s) should be entered at questions 16–21.

Questions 49–71 (the purchaser)

HMRC requires the purchaser to be identified (in order of priority) by one of the following:

- the purchaser's National Insurance (NI) number if the purchaser is an individual and he has a permanent NI number (question 49);
- the purchaser's VAT registration number (question 50);
- if the purchaser is a UK company or partnership and unregistered for VAT: the purchaser's 10-digit Unique Taxpayer Reference (UTR) (first part of question 51);
- for an individual who does not have a permanent NI number, one of the following: the purchaser's non-UK tax reference number, passport number, driving licence number or identity card number; or for a non-individual: a company registration number (issued by Companies House) or a non-UK tax reference (second part of question 51);
- the country where the reference number was issued where the second part of question 51 is completed (third part of question 51).

Question 60 – to which address shall we send the certificate?

If a return is made online, 'property address' is automatically chosen. This is merely a function of the online system. The certificate will not be sent to the property address. Rather, a link to an electronic version of the certificate will be made available as soon as the return has been submitted.

Question 72 – how many supplementary returns have you enclosed with this return?

This question is only relevant to paper returns. The supplementary returns will automatically form part of the online return where relevant. The supplementary returns are needed where there are more than two buyers or sellers (form SDLT2), the transaction involves more than one property (form SDLT3) and for complicated leases and some residential transactions (form SDLT4).

Each paper return has its own 11-character Unique Transaction Reference Number (UTRN), so photocopies of blank returns cannot be used for different transactions.

Where an online return is made, the UTRN will only be generated once the return is submitted. The number is shown on the bottom-right corner of the return and is also visible on the revenue certificate.[4]

19.4 LIABILITY

The obligation to make an SDLT return and pay the tax only falls on the purchaser except in very limited circumstances (recovery of tax on a withdrawal of certain reliefs). A person is not a purchaser for these purposes unless he has given consideration for the transaction or is a party to the transaction.

The general rule is modified for specific types of purchaser:

- *Joint purchasers:* The obligation to make a return and pay the tax falls on the purchasers jointly but may be discharged by any of them.
- *Partnerships:* Irrespective of the type of partnership and whether it has separate legal personality, the obligation to make a return and pay the tax falls on all the partners but may be discharged by a representative partner if notice is given to HMRC.
- *Trusts:* The obligation to make a return and pay the tax falls on the beneficiaries unless the trust is a 'settlement' (i.e., any type of trust that is not a bare trust) or the transaction is the grant of a lease in which case it falls on the trustee(s).

For paper returns, only the purchaser may sign the declaration that the return is complete and correct unless a power of attorney has been granted by the purchaser. Online returns may be made by the purchaser's agent. Submission of an online return requires the agent to confirm that he is authorised to submit the return and, if appropriate, enter the effective date of the transaction.

19.5 HOW TO MAKE PAYMENT

19.5.1 Domestic payments

Payments of SDLT can be made by Faster Payments, CHAPS or Bacs to HMRC's account using the following details:

Sort code	Account number	Account name
08-32-10	12001020	HMRC Shipley

---

[4] *Guidance – How to complete your Stamp Duty Land Tax SDLT1 paper return* (HMRC, 4 April 2014, last updated 28 September 2018, available at: **www.gov.uk/government/publications/sdlt-guide-for-completing-paper-sdlt1-return**); *Guidance – Stamp Duty Land Tax online and paper returns* (HMRC, 28 November 2018, last updated 1 March 2019, available at: **www.gov.uk/guidance/stamp-duty-land-tax-online-and-paper-returns**).

The 11-character UTRN must be used as the payment reference. That number can be found on the bottom-right corner of the SDLT return after the return has been submitted online and on the revenue certificate (SDLT5).

It is recommended that you make separate payments for each UTRN.

Payments made by Faster Payments usually reach HMRC on the same or next day. Payments made by CHAPS usually reach HMRC the same or next day subject to what time during the day the payment is made. Payments made by Bacs usually reach HMRC in three working days.

19.5.2 International payments

Account number (IBAN)	Bank identifier code (BIC)	Account name
GB03 BARC 2011 4783 9776 92	BARCGB22	HMRC Shipley

19.5.3 Alternative payment methods

Payment may also be made:

- online (note: there is a non-refundable fee if you pay by corporate credit card and you cannot pay by personal credit card);
- at a bank or building society;
- by cheque made payable to 'HM Revenue and Customs only' followed by the UTRN and, for paper returns only, enclosing the payslip from the back of the return.[5]

19.6 WHEN TO MAKE PAYMENT

Payment must be made within 14 days or 30 days depending on whether the SDLT return to which the payment relates is an initial return or further return – see **19.9**.[6]

19.7 HOW TO MAKE A DEFERRAL APPLICATION

For contingent or uncertain consideration (other than rent) potentially payable more than six months after completion, it is possible to apply to defer payment of the tax due on the contingent or uncertain consideration. Failure to do so requires the purchaser to pay tax at the outset based on an estimate of the contingent or uncertain consideration and subsequently to make an adjustment when the contingency ceases or the uncertain consideration is ascertained.

---

[5] 'Guidance – Pay Stamp Duty Land Tax' (HMRC, 30 October 2014, last updated 30 September 2019, available at: **www.gov.uk/guidance/pay-stamp-duty-land-tax**).
[6] FA 2003, s.86; SDLT Manual: SDLT00070.

The practical advantage of a deferral application then is cashflow (depending on the estimate of the contingent or uncertain consideration) and interest. If no deferral application is made and the contingent or uncertain consideration becomes payable, interest would be payable on the unpaid tax from the filing date (usually 14 days after completion) until the date of payment. The rate of interest is the Bank of England base rate plus 2.5 per cent. Whereas if a deferral application is made and the contingent or uncertain consideration becomes payable, interest would only start to accrue 14 days after the filing date if the transaction was not originally notifiable or 30 days after the event causing the consideration to become payable/ascertainable.

Deferral applications must be made, in writing, within 14 days of the effective date of the transaction (usually completion). HMRC will refuse late applications. The application must give:

- the identity of the purchaser;
- the location of the purchased property;
- the nature of the contingency or uncertain payment;
- the amount of the contingent or uncertain consideration;
- full details of the times of the expected payments with reasoning;
- a proposal for a schedule of payments where the uncertain or contingent consideration relates to works;
- a calculation of the total amount of tax payable, including the tax for which deferral is sought; and
- a calculation of the tax for which deferral is sought.

If an application is refused, HMRC should explain why. If the deferred tax is not paid by the payment date (usually 14 days from completion), interest on the late-paid tax would be backdated to the payment date, not the date on which HMRC notified the purchaser of its decision to refuse the application.

An appeal may be notified to the First-tier Tribunal against HMRC's decision to refuse a deferral application provided the notice of appeal is made within 30 days of issue of the notice of refusal.

Confirmation that a deferral application has been made must be included in the SDLT return: see question 4 ('is any part of the consideration contingent or dependent on uncertain future events?') and question 5 ('are you applying for deferment?') of the form SDLT4.[7]

---

[7] FA 2003, s.90; Stamp Duty Land Tax (Administration) Regulations 2003, SI 2003/2837, Part 4; SDLT Manual: SDLTM50900, SDLTM50900A, SDLTM50910, SDLTM50920, SDLTM50930, SDLTM50940, SDLTM50950.

19.8 HOW TO AMEND AN SDLT RETURN

HMRC accepts 'minor' amendments can be made by telephoning the Stamp Duty Land Tax Helpline (0300 200 3510 or +44 1726 209 042). It gives the following examples of 'minor' changes:

- the vendor's details (questions 34–38);
- are the purchaser and vendor connected? (question 59);
- the address of the purchaser if there is more than one purchaser (question 70);
- spelling errors in the property address (question 28);
- wrong title number (question 30);
- changes to the purchase price (question 11) or tax (question 14);
- the effective date (question 4) provided that the return was not made before the correct effective date.

'Substantial' amendments must be made by correspondence accompanied by a copy of the agreement to which the transaction relates. HMRC gives the following examples of 'substantial' changes:

- adding a title number;
- adding or removing a purchaser;
- adding a property;
- errors in the property address other than spelling.

HMRC may require a new return to be made depending on its view of the significance of the change.[8]

For details of how to apply for a refund of overpaid tax, see **19.10**.

19.9 WHEN TO MAKE AN SDLT RETURN

SDLT returns must be made within 14 days of the effective date of the transaction where the transaction is notifiable initially (i.e., where an 'initial return' is due) or within 30 days of the relevant event that causes the transaction to be re-notifiable (i.e., where a 'further return' is due).

Further returns are due where:

- certain types of relief including multiple dwellings relief are withdrawn due to a disqualifying event;
- there is a 'linked' transaction that causes tax or additional tax to be chargeable in respect of the earlier transaction;
- part of the consideration is contingent or uncertain, a deferral application is made and the contingency ceases or the uncertain consideration is known causing the deferred tax to become due;
- a lease for a fixed term or an indefinite term is deemed to be extended by continued occupation;

---

[8] FA 2003, Sched.10, para.6.

- the amount of rent payable in the first five years of the term of a lease ceases to be contingent or uncertain; or
- on completion of the transaction where a return is made in respect of substantial performance.[9]

Example 19.1

A is granted an assured shorthold tenancy of a London flat. The term of the lease is one year. The amount of rent payable is £5,000 per calendar month. A renews his lease three times. The rent increased by 2.5% each year. Although the grant of the lease and the first renewal are not notifiable, the second renewal is. The term of the lease is taken to have 'grown' on each renewal. On the second renewal the net present value (NPV) of the rent for the deemed three-year lease (£172,238) exceeds £125,000. A makes an initial return and pays the £472 of tax within 14 days of the end of the renewed period (£125,000 @ 0%) + (£47,238 @ 1%). On the third renewal, the NPV of the rent for the deemed four-year lease is £228,545. A makes a further return and pays £563 of tax within 30 days of the end of the renewed period: (£125,000 @ 0%) + (£103,545 @ 1%) less the £472 of tax paid. And so on.

Example 19.2

A enters into a contract to purchase off-plan two dwellings from the same seller. The price payable for each (£1 million) reflects a bulk purchase discount. There is a gap of six months between practical completion of the dwellings. A makes an initial return and pays £73,750 of tax within 14 days of completion of his purchase of the first dwelling. The tax is calculated in accordance with the residential higher rates due to A's circumstances as follows: (£125,000 @ 3%) + (£125,000 @ 5%) + (£675,000 @ 8%) + (£75,000 @ 13%). Completion of his purchase of the second dwelling triggers an obligation on A to make an initial return and pay £106,875 of tax in respect of the second dwelling and to make a further return and pay £33,125 of additional tax in respect of the second dwelling. This is because the two transactions are linked. The two returns must be made within 14 days and 30 days, respectively, of completion of the second dwelling. The £106,875 of tax payable on the second purchase and the additional £33,125 of tax payable on the first are calculated in accordance with the rules for multiple dwellings relief. The total consideration for the linked transactions (£2 million) is divided by the number of dwellings purchased (2) to give an average price per dwelling of £1 million. The tax that would be payable on a notional purchase of a £1 million dwelling (£106,875) is multiplied by the number of dwellings purchased to give £213,750. This must be pro-rated to the two transactions, so £106,875 of tax is payable on each. The tax paid on the first transaction (£73,750) is deducted from the tax payable on the transaction (£106,875) to produce an additional tax charge on the first transaction (£33,125). The remaining £106,875 of the £213,750 is payable on the second transaction.

---

[9] FA 2003, s.67; SDLT Manual: SDLTM50100.

Example 19.3

A purchases a family home with an annex. The annex is suitable for independent living. It has, for example, its own cooking and washing facilities. Within 14 days of completion of the transaction, A duly makes an initial return and pays tax in accordance with a claim for multiple dwellings relief. Within the period of three years beginning with completion of his purchase, A reconfigures the annex involving the removal of the kitchen and bathroom. The reconfiguration results in the annex ceasing to be suitable for use as a dwelling. Consequently, it triggers a withdrawal of the relief. A becomes liable to make a further return and repay the relieved tax within 30 days of the annex ceasing to be suitable for use as a dwelling.

19.10 HOW TO RECLAIM OVERPAID TAX

There are two mechanisms to reclaim overpaid tax:

1. by amending an SDLT return (see below); or
2. by making an application for 'relief for overpaid tax'.

19.10.1 Amending an SDLT return

With few exceptions, an SDLT return may only be amended, in writing, within one year of the filing date of the transaction. Conversely, if any type of reclaim is made within one year of the filing date of the transaction it must be made by amending the SDLT return.

A consequence of making the amendment is to re-set the nine-month enquiry period.

The notice of amendment must be accompanied by a copy of the sale contract or agreement for lease and the instrument by which the transaction was effected (e.g., lease or land transfer form).

Applications to reclaim the higher rates of SDLT due to the purchaser having sold his previous main residence are still made by amending the SDLT return, but an extended period and a dedicated online form are given. The period allowed for amending the return is the later of one year of the filing date of the purchase and one year of the effective date of the sale. For the conditions that need to be met to reclaim the tax attributable to the higher rates, see **3.3.10.1**.

Example 19.4

A purchases the freehold estate of a house as a replacement of his main residence. It contains a self-contained annex situated on the grounds of the main house. A pays SDLT in accordance with the residential standard rates. Four months later he receives an unsolicited letter from a company promising to reclaim overpaid tax on his behalf. The overpaid tax, it says, is attributable to his failure to claim multiple dwellings relief. Before the one-year anniversary of the filing date (30 days after completion), A sends HMRC a letter making amendments to the SDLT return originally submitted to give effect to his decision to claim the relief to reduce the amount of tax chargeable. He encloses a copy of the sale contract and land transfer form relating to the transaction. HMRC repays the difference between the tax paid and the tax payable by virtue of A claiming the relief with interest.

Example 19.5

A purchases the leasehold estate of a one-bedroom flat as her first home. She funds the purchase with a five-year fixed rate mortgage. Two years later she marries B, who moves in with A. A and B wish to buy a larger home. B purchases a £500,000 house in his sole name. B pays tax in accordance with the higher rates. He is a first-time buyer and would ordinarily be eligible for first-time buyer relief meaning that he would only pay £10,000 of tax: (£300,000 @ 0%) + (£200,000 @ 5%). However, B's purchase is a higher-rates transaction due to A owning the one-bedroom flat. Consequently, B must pay £30,000 of tax. As soon as the redemption penalty on A's mortgage expires, A sells her flat. As the sale completed within three years of B's purchase and A's flat had been B's main residence at some point within the three-year period, B can make a reclaim of the £20,000 of tax attributable to the higher rates. B reclaims the tax by submitting a form online within one year of completion of the sale of A's flat.

19.10.2 Relief for overpaid tax

An alternative procedure exists for reclaims made in the three-year period beginning one year after the effective date of the transaction.[10] In other words, it begins after the one-year period for amending an SDLT return has expired. It applies where tax has been paid but was not due or tax has been assessed that is not due. HMRC may open an enquiry into this type of reclaim as if it were made in an SDLT return.

HMRC may refuse this type of reclaim for reasons including:

- the overpayment is due to claiming a relief or making a statutory election or failing to do either;
- the purchaser could have reclaimed the tax by amending his SDLT return and knew, or ought reasonably to have known, that he could have done so before the one-year deadline expired;
- the reclaim is the subject of an ongoing appeal; or
- the overpayment was due to a mistake in calculating the SDLT liability and the liability was calculated in accordance with the practice generally prevailing at the time (unless the tax was charged contrary to European Union (EU) law).

---

[10] FA 2003, Sched.4ZA, para.8, Sched.10, paras.6, 34; 'Form – Apply for a repayment of the higher rates of Stamp Duty Land Tax' (HMRC, 1 April 2016, last updated 29 October 2018, available at: **www.gov.uk/government/publications/stamp-duty-land-tax-apply-for-a-repayment-of-the-higher-rates-for-additional-properties**); SDLT Manual: SDLTM54000, SDLTM54010, SDLTM54100, SDLTM54110, SDLTM54110.

> **WARNING**
>
> One year after the filing date of the transaction, purchaser A loses his entitlement to reclaim overpaid tax if the overpayment is due to a failure to claim relief – e.g., first-time buyer relief or multiple dwellings relief. HMRC does not have discretion to allow the reclaim, however reasonable A's behaviour might have been.

Example 19.6

A purchases a residential property as a buy-to-let. He is a first-time buyer. He pays SDLT in accordance with the residential higher rates in error. On learning his mistake 18 months later, he applies for relief for overpaid tax. The overpayment is not attributable to failure to claim a relief – first-time buyer relief does not apply as the property is a buy-to-let – and he was not aware that he could have amended his return within one year of the transaction. The overpayment was due to A wrongly assuming that the higher rates applied. His application is granted and the overpaid tax is repaid with interest.

Example 19.7

A purchases a residential property as a replacement of his main residence. It contains an annex on the grounds of the main house that is suitable for use as a separate dwelling. A year and a half after completion of his purchase, A applies to claim multiple dwellings relief and reclaim the tax that would not have been payable if the relief had been claimed. A's application is rejected, as the overpayment relates to his failure to claim a relief. That A did not know the relief was available, either initially or during the one-year period allowed to amend his SDLT return, is irrelevant.

Where a reclaim is successful, interest is payable on the overpaid tax from the date it was paid at HMRC's standard rate: the Bank of England base rate less one per cent (subject to a collar of 0.5 per cent) per annum.

19.11 HMRC INTERVENTION

19.11.1 Enquiries

An enquiry is the statutory process used by HMRC to check that it is satisfied that the self-assessment made in an SDLT return is correct. A notice (an 'enquiry notice') must be made indicating HMRC's intention to open an enquiry into the return. The notice does not need to be headed 'enquiry notice' or similar. It merely needs to indicate HMRC's *intention* to enquire into the matter. The notice must be made within nine months of:

- the filing date where the return is made on time – the filing date is 14 days after the effective date of the transaction or 30 days after an event that triggers an obligation to make a 'further return' in respect of an earlier transaction; for further returns, see **19.9**;
- the date on which an SDLT return was made, if it was made after the filing date; or
- the date on which an SDLT return was amended.

There is no time period within which HMRC must complete the enquiry. However, the purchaser may apply to the First-tier Tribunal for a direction that HMRC must complete the enquiry within a specified period. Unless this right is exercised, enquiries may continue indefinitely. The author has experience of some SDLT enquiries taking more than 13 years to complete.

HMRC must indicate its conclusion on completion of an enquiry by giving a notice (a 'closure notice'). The closure notice will either confirm that HMRC is satisfied that the self-assessment is correct or make amendments to the return giving effect to its conclusion that it is not correct. As with an enquiry notice, the notice does not need to be headed 'closure notice'. It merely needs to indicate that HMRC has completed its enquiries.[11]

19.11.2 Corrections

HMRC may correct an SDLT return in two circumstances. The first is to correct any obvious errors or omissions. The correction must be made by giving notice to the purchaser in writing within the period of nine months beginning with the date on which the return was made. The purchaser may reject the correction by giving notice within three months of the notice of correction or by amending the SDLT return within one year of the filing date. The second is during an enquiry into the SDLT return where HMRC considers that the correction is necessary to prevent a loss of tax.[12]

19.11.3 Determinations

A determination is a type of revenue assessment made by HMRC where no SDLT return has been made. It indicates the amount of tax chargeable in respect of a transaction 'to the best of [HMRC's] knowledge and belief'.[13] A determination cannot be made more than four years after the effective date of the transaction. If an SDLT return is made within one year of a determination or four years from the effective date of the transaction (if later), that return supersedes the determination.[14]

---

[11] FA 2003, Sched.10, Part 3.
[12] FA 2003, Sched.10, para.17.
[13] FA 2003, Sched.10, para.25(1).
[14] FA 2003, Sched.10, Part 4.

Example 19.8

A Ltd owns a residential property. The company is owned by the occupier of the property, B. B made a loan to A Ltd to enable the company to purchase the property. B wishes to restructure the ownership of the property to save further payments of annual tax on enveloped dwellings having to be made by the company. A Ltd transfers the property to B in pursuance of a dividend *in specie*. The loan made by B to A Ltd is released as a result of, or in connection with, the property transfer. B (wrongly) considers that the transaction is exempt from SDLT due to no chargeable consideration and, therefore, that the transaction is not notifiable. Consequently, B proceeds to register his ownership of the property without making an SDLT return. Three years later, HMRC discover that SDLT should have been self-assessed by B and makes a determination to recover the loss of tax.

19.11.4 Revenue assessments

Where an SDLT return is made, a revenue assessment may be made within four years, six years or 20 years of the effective date of the transaction where:

- HMRC discovers a loss of tax (i.e., tax that ought to have been assessed has not been assessed or excessive tax relief has been given); and
- at the time it ceased to be entitled to open an enquiry into the SDLT return or completed an enquiry, HMRC could not reasonably have been expected, on the basis of the information made available to it before that time, to have been aware of the loss of tax (a 'discovery assessment'); or
- the loss of tax is attributable to fraudulent or negligent conduct on the part of the purchaser, his agent or a partner of the purchaser at the relevant time (a 'misconduct assessment').[15]

There is extensive case law that answers questions including:

- When is a loss of tax brought about 'carelessly'?
- What information is necessary to alert HMRC to a potential loss of tax?
- When is a 'discovery' made?
- Within what time period (if any) must HMRC act after making the discovery?

19.11.5 Time periods for revenue assessments

A revenue assessment (regardless of whether it is a discovery or misconduct assessment) may not be made later than four years after the effective date of the transaction except in the following four situations:

- The loss of tax is attributable to careless behaviour, in which case the time period for making an assessment is extended by two years from four years to six years after the effective date of the transaction.

---

[15] FA 2003, Sched.10, Part 5.

- The loss of tax is attributable to deliberate behaviour, in which case the time period for making an assessment is extended by 16 years from four years to 20 years after the effective date of the transaction.
- The loss of tax is attributable to a failure by the purchaser to make an SDLT return, in which case the time period for making an assessment is extended by 16 years from four years to 20 years after the effective date of the transaction.
- The loss of tax is attributable to a failure by the purchaser to disclose the arrangements under the disclosure of tax avoidance schemes (DOTAS) rules, in which case the time period for making an assessment is extended by 16 years from four years to 20 years after the effective date of the transaction (see **19.21**).[16]

One can see the attraction, therefore, of making a nil return without prejudice to the purchaser's position that the transaction is not notifiable. It ought to prevent HMRC from making a revenue assessment within 20 years of the effective date of the transaction.

As the design of the SDLT return is insufficient to give 'full disclosure' except in relation to the simplest of SDLT transactions, the only way to prevent HMRC from making a discovery is to send a detailed covering letter to HMRC within the nine-month enquiry period that cross-refers to the SDLT return. The use of such a letter is entirely optional. Note, though, that a letter only prevents a revenue assessment if an SDLT return is made. Where a transaction is not notifiable, the purchaser may voluntarily make a 'nil return' without prejudice to his position that the transaction is not notifiable and send a detailed covering letter. In principle, this action should give finality of HMRC's position if HMRC does not open an enquiry into the nil return.

Example 19.9

A uses a wholly owned company to purchase a new residence. He funds the company's purchase by making a loan to the company. Several years later, A wishes to restructure the ownership of the property and remove it from the company. The company makes a dividend *in specie* of the property to A, its only shareholder. As a result of the property transfer, the loan owed by the company to A is released. Despite being given a full set of accurate facts, A's lawyer advises him that the transaction is exempt from charge on the basis of no consideration and not notifiable. No SDLT return is made. More than four years later, A receives a revenue assessment from HMRC to recover the loss of tax. HMRC had discovered that the property transfer was chargeable due to the release of the shareholder loan. A had not acted carelessly, as he had received advice from a competent adviser that proved to be wrong. Nevertheless, the revenue assessment is made in time, as no SDLT return was made. HMRC had 20 years from completion of the property transfer to make a revenue assessment.

---

[16] FA 2003, Sched.10, para.31.

Example 19.10

A transfers his main residence to his mother. His mother, who wishes to downsize, transfers her main residence to A. The properties are of equal value and no cash is given by A or his mother to the other party. A wrongly assumes that the two transfers are gifts, as no cash has changed hands, so the two transfers are exempt from SDLT on the basis of no consideration. He fails to take proper advice to verify his assumption. No SDLT returns are made. More than four years later, A and his mother receive revenue assessments. HMRC had discovered that the property transfers were chargeable due to each being the consideration given for the other. The loss of tax was attributable to carelessness on the part of A and his mother.

19.12 PENALTIES AND INTEREST

19.12.1 Penalties

So far as relevant and material to the reader, penalties may be imposed by HMRC for:

- failing to make an SDLT return by the filing date;
- making an incorrect SDLT return;
- failing to notify HMRC of an under-assessment;
- assisting in the preparation or delivery of an incorrect return; and
- failing to comply with an information notice.

Penalties may not be imposed for failure to pay SDLT. A regime for such penalties exists for other taxes but it has not been 'switched on' for SDLT.[17]

---

[17] FA 2003, s.95, Sched.10, paras.3–5; FA 2007, Sched.24; SDLT Manual: SDLTM85905.

Culpable act	Culpable mind	Amount
Failure to make an SDLT return by the filing date	Not applicable	Potentially three cumulative penalties: fixed: £100 if a return is made within three months of the filing date or, if it is not, £200; and tax-geared: up to the unpaid tax, if a return is not made within one year of the filing date; and daily: up to £60 per day if HMRC applies to the tribunal for a daily penalty
Making an incorrect SDLT return	Carelessness or deliberate errors only	Tax-geared depending on whether the error was careless or deliberate, prompted or unprompted, concealed or not
Failure to notify HMRC of an under-assessment	Failure to take reasonable steps to notify HMRC that an assessment made by HMRC is too low	Tax-geared depending on whether the error was prompted
Fraudulent evasion of tax	Knowledge that return is incorrect. (Separate penalties apply for fraudulent or negligence provision of incorrect information and fraudulent evasion of tax)	On summary conviction: six months' imprisonment or a fine not exceeding the statutory maximum or both On conviction on indictment: seven years' imprisonment or a fine or both
Failing to comply with an information notice	Not applicable	Two cumulative penalties: fixed: £300; daily: £60 per day

19.12.2 Interest

Interest is payable on unpaid SDLT from the filing date (usually 14 days from completion). In certain circumstances, acts or events after completion might trigger another filing date: e.g., the withdrawal of multiple dwellings relief, the continuance of a lease and contingent or uncertain consideration becoming ascertainable or payable. For more information on the filing date, see **19.9**. The interest rate is the Bank of England base rate plus 2.5 per cent.

Interest is payable on overpaid tax from the date it is paid at a lower rate: the Bank of England base rate less one per cent (subject to a collar of 0.5 per cent p.a.).[18]

---

[18] FA 2009, ss.101, 102, 103, 104, 105, Scheds.53, 54; SDLT Manual: SDLTM85910.

19.13 FURTHER TIME, REASONABLE EXCUSE AND SPECIAL CIRCUMSTANCES

A defence to the purchaser's failure to comply with any obligation under the SDLT code is reasonable excuse. Alternatively, if HMRC allows further time for the purchaser to do something required of him, his failure to comply is disregarded. A specific defence applies to penalties for errors made in returns. The penalty may be reduced or suspended for up to two years subject to the purchaser meeting conditions if, in HMRC's opinion, there are 'special circumstances'.

There are numerous decisions of the First-tier Tribunal on what does and, more frequently, does not constitute a 'reasonable excuse'. They are, by their nature, specific to the facts of each case. A general, if somewhat circular, statement was given by the tribunal that to be a reasonable excuse, the excuse must be the cause of the default and it must be reasonable – in other words, the purchaser must have acted as a reasonable person in the same position as the purchaser and mindful of his tax obligations would have acted.[19]

19.14 INFORMATION NOTICES AND INSPECTIONS

HMRC may by notice require the purchaser or a third party to provide documents or information and may inspect premises to check the purchaser's tax position. The notice may not be given without the purchaser's consent or the First-tier Tribunal's approval. An application for approval of the tribunal must be notified to the purchaser unless the tribunal is satisfied that to do so would compromise the collection of tax. Certain documents are excluded – e.g., documents subject to legal professional privilege and documents belonging to an auditor or a tax adviser. Penalties may be imposed for failure to comply with an information notice; providing inaccurate information; falsifying or destroying documents; or deliberately obstructing HMRC in the course of an inspection. Alternative information notices may be given to third parties to obtain the identity of the purchaser. Additional powers are given to HMRC to access records from dishonest agents and monitored promoters.

HMRC has a separate power to request, in writing to the purchaser, such documents that are in the purchaser's possession that HMRC reasonably requires for it to complete its enquiry.[20]

---

[19] FA 2003, s.97; *Nadia Ibrahim Marzouk* v. *Revenue and Customs Comrs* [2016] UKFTT 548 (TC).
[20] FA 2008, Sched.36.

19.15 RECORD-KEEPING

Records relating to an SDLT return and to non-notifiable transactions must be kept for six years or until an enquiry is closed. Penalties may be imposed for failure to comply. It is not necessary to keep original records, copies are acceptable.[21]

19.16 ENFORCEMENT

As one would expect, HMRC has various powers to recover unpaid tax that is due. They include bringing proceedings for distraint and recovery of debt due to the Crown. In exceptional circumstances, HMRC can recover tax debts directly from the bank account of the purchaser. However, HMRC is not a preferential creditor and would rank behind secured creditors in the enforcement of a tax debt owed by the purchaser.[22]

19.17 DISPUTES

19.17.1 Appealable decisions

Not every HMRC decision is appealable. An appeal may only be brought against the decision to:

- amend an SDLT return during an enquiry to prevent a loss of tax;
- amend an SDLT return on closure of an enquiry;
- make a revenue assessment; or
- make a determination.

To make an appeal, the purchaser must write to the relevant HMRC officer that issued the decision within 30 days of the date of the decision and must specify the grounds of the appeal.

The only grounds on which an appeal may be brought against the decision to make a determination are:

- the purchase to which the determination relates did not take place;
- the chargeable interest to which the determination relates has not been purchased;
- the contract for the purchase of the interest to which the determination relates has not been substantially performed; or
- the SDLT transaction is not notifiable.

After an appeal is made, the purchaser may:

- request HMRC to review the decision (see **19.17.2**);

---

[21] FA 2003, Sched.10, Part 2.
[22] FA 2003, Sched.12.

- do nothing, in which case HMRC may offer to review the decision; or
- notify the appeal to the First-tier Tribunal.[23]

19.17.2 Requesting a review

Naturally, if the decision is in accordance with HMRC's practice, it is most likely that it will be upheld on conclusion of the review. In contrast, if the decision is subjective (e.g., it is sensitive to valuation), then there is a greater chance that another HMRC officer may arrive at a different conclusion.[24]

19.17.3 Notifying the tribunal of an appeal

Notifying the First-tier Tribunal of the appeal starts a process that will usually end by the tribunal determining the matter. A form is available online that specifies the information that the tribunal requires.

Where the purchaser has requested a review, he must notify the appeal to the tribunal within 30 days of the date of the notice given by HMRC stating its conclusion of the review or, where HMRC has not given a notice stating its conclusion, within 30 days of the notice given by HMRC stating that the review is treated as if the view had been upheld.[25]

19.17.4 Settlement

Either party in a tax dispute may, at any stage during the dispute, make an offer to the other to settle the matter on specific terms. Acceptance of the offer is binding (subject to meeting the conditions for a valid contract) and takes effect as if a closure notice had been made or the tribunal had determined the matter. If an appeal has been notified to the tribunal, the tribunal must be notified of the settlement. However, the tribunal does not have any powers to reject the settlement or override it and proceed to determine the matter.[26]

19.17.5 Alternative dispute resolution (mediation)

From the point that an enquiry is opened into an SDLT return or a determination or revenue assessment is made, the purchaser may apply to HMRC for 'alternative dispute resolution' (ADR). An exception applies where HMRC has served its Statement of Case or is due to within 10 days. The process is not set by statute and HMRC's participation is at its discretion. If the application is accepted, a mediator would be appointed by HMRC to explore ways to resolve the dispute. The mediator would not act as a judge and take responsibility for determining the matter. Neither

---

[23] FA 2003, Sched.10, paras.35, 36.
[24] FA 2003, Sched.10, para.36B.
[25] FA 2003, Sched.10, para.36D.
[26] FA 2003, Sched.10, para.34E.

making an application nor participating in the process affects the purchaser's rights to seek a review or notify the appeal to the tribunal. HMRC makes an online form available to apply for ADR. HMRC should confirm its acceptance of the application (or not) within 30 days and enclose an agreement known as a 'memorandum of understanding' setting out the process and confirming the purchaser's agreement to participate.[27]

19.17.6 Tribunal rules

The First-tier Tribunal is bound by the rules set out in regulations made in 2009.[28] The overriding objective of the rules is to enable the tribunal to deal with cases fairly and justly. The rules cover things including:

- orders for costs (rule 10);
- evidence (rule 15);
- lead cases (rule 18);
- allocation of cases to categories (rule 23 and chapter 2); and
- application for permission to appeal (rule 39).

19.18 ASKING HMRC FOR HELP

19.18.1 Guidance

There is ample guidance available online in the form of the SDLT Manual. Note that the guidance is prepared for HMRC staff and it is published in accordance with the Freedom of Information Act 2000. Although health warnings are given at the beginning, it is tempting to rely on the guidance as if it were the law. It is not. Although the remedy of judicial review is in theory available to prevent HMRC from acting in a manner that contradicts a taxpayer's 'legitimate expectation', this is a difficult and expensive remedy to access. Some areas of the guidance are objectively wrong (e.g., because they refer to legislation that has been repealed); some are subjectively wrong (e.g., because reasonable views differ on the correct interpretation of the legislation); and others may be found by the courts to be wrong (e.g., because HMRC is seeking to narrow by guidance legislation that it considers to operate too broadly). The best advice is to consult the guidance with caution, seek specialist advice and/or make a request for clearance if the circumstances warrant it (see **19.18.3**).

---

[27] *Guidance – Use Alternative Dispute Resolution to settle a tax dispute* (HMRC, 8 December 2014, last updated 8 July 2019, available at: **www.gov.uk/guidance/tax-disputes-alternative-dispute-resolution-adr**).

[28] Tribunal Procedure (First-tier Tribunal) (Tax Chamber) Rules 2009, SI 2009/273.

19.18.2 HMRC's Stamp Duty Land Tax Helpline

Telephone enquiries	Written enquiries
0300 200 3510 (domestic calls)	Stamp Duty Land Tax
+44 1726 209 042 (international calls)	HM Revenue and Customs
Opening times:	BX9 1HD
Monday to Friday: 8:30am to 5pm	United Kingdom

19.18.3 Pre-transaction and post-transaction rulings

Where you are uncertain about how HMRC would interpret the SDLT legislation and apply it to specific facts (e.g., because the SDLT Manual does not deal with the point), requests may be made to HMRC for confirmation of its interpretation of the legislation. Normally, HMRC limits the subject of such requests to legislation passed within the last four years. However, in the author's experience it does not apply this restriction in practice to SDLT.

There is a single process irrespective of the type of taxpayer – individual or business. For individuals, the procedure is called 'Clearances and Approvals 1' (or 'CAP1'). For businesses, it is called 'Non-Statutory Business Clearance'. However, in essence the process is the same for both. It is called the 'Non-Statutory Clearance Service'. Clearance requests must be made by correspondence either in hard copy to the following address:

> The Technical Team
> Birmingham Stamp Office
> 9th Floor
> City Centre House
> 30 Union Street
> Birmingham
> B2 4AR
> United Kingdom

or by emailing: nonstatutoryclearanceteam.hmrc@hmrc.gsi.gov.uk.

HMRC will refuse to give a substantive response where it considers that:

- not all the necessary information is given;
- its online guidance confirms its interpretation of the legislation;
- it is being asked to approve tax planning;
- a main purpose of the transaction is the avoidance of tax;
- an enquiry has been opened into the SDLT return made in respect of the transaction; or
- the request relates to matters of fact (such as whether activities constitute a business).

Making a request does *not* suspend the deadline for making a return or payment.

An appeal cannot be brought against HMRC's decision not to give a substantive response or to the form of the response. Equally, the purchaser does not have to accept HMRC's response. He may self-assess in a manner that contradicts HMRC's interpretation of the legislation. However, the purchaser must draw to HMRC's attention the ruling request and whether or not the self-assessment is consistent with HMRC's interpretation in the SDLT return.

HMRC aims to respond to clearance requests within 28 days; however, in the author's experience, it regularly takes longer to respond. HMRC does not generally confirm receipt of the request. Follow-up enquiries may be made using the contact details for the Stamp Duty Land Tax Helpline (see **19.18.2**) or by emailing: nonstatutoryclearanceteam.hmrc@hmrc.gsi.gov.uk.

HMRC's response generally binds HMRC. This means that it cannot generally resile from its interpretation of the legislation as stated in the ruling response. However:

- Enforcing the ruling response may ultimately involve making an application for judicial review to the High Court, as well as notifying an appeal to the First-tier Tribunal. The remedy of judicial review is not within the gift of the First-tier Tribunal; hence, an additional action must be brought in parallel at the tribunal at the High Court (see **19.18.1**).
- The success of such an application requires establishing that HMRC's guidance created a 'legitimate expectation' in the purchaser regarding HMRC's conduct.
- The concept of legitimate expectation is still developing.
- For an example of HMRC disowning its guidance in an SDLT appeal, see *Hannover Leasing Wachstumswerte Europa Beteiligungsgesellschaft MBH and another v. Revenue and Customs* [2019] UKFTT 262 (TC).
- If the ruling request is made pre-transaction, the transaction must be carried out as described in the request.
- Full disclosure of all relevant facts and circumstances must be given in the ruling request.
- The ruling does not establish a precedent. It is specific to the relevant transaction only. Even if a subsequent transaction is the same or substantially similar, HMRC is not bound by the ruling made in respect of the earlier transaction.[29]

---

[29] *Guidance – Find out about the Non-Statutory Clearance Service* (HMRC, 8 August 2013, last updated 27 June 2018, available at: **www.gov.uk/guidance/non-statutory-clearance-service-guidance**); *HMRC internal manual – Non-statutory Clearance Guidance* (HMRC, 16 April 2016, updated 25 January 2020, available at: **www.gov.uk/hmrc-internal-manuals/other-non-statutory-clearance**); SDLT Manual: SDLTM51000, SDLTM51010; *R. v. IRC, ex p. MFK Underwriting Agencies Ltd* [1990] STC 873.

19.19 ACCELERATED PAYMENT NOTICES

Accelerated payment notices (APNs) are notices given by HMRC to the purchaser stating that HMRC believes that the purchaser has used a tax avoidance scheme and that HMRC requires the tax that should have been paid to be paid within 90 days.[30] The aim is to reverse the cashflow benefit associated with using a tax avoidance scheme – namely, deferring the payment of tax until the tax disputed is determined, possibly many years later.

APNs can be issued in any of the following circumstances:

- The purchaser has used a scheme that has been disclosed (or ought to have been disclosed) under the DOTAS rules (see **19.21**).
- HMRC has applied the general anti-abuse rule (GAAR) to counteract the scheme (see **1.11**).
- The purchaser has been given a follower notice following his use of the scheme (see **19.20**).

The purchaser cannot bring an appeal against the decision to make an APN, but can make representations on the grounds that the conditions for the making of an APN have not been met, or that the amount specified in the APN is incorrect. Such representations must be made, in writing, within 90 days of the date of the APN. HMRC must consider the representations and confirm its decision to withdraw, amend or confirm the APN in response to them. If HMRC confirms the APN, the purchaser has 30 days to pay the amount specified in the APN.

19.20 FOLLOWER NOTICES

Follower notices are notices given by HMRC to the purchaser where HMRC believes a final decision in another case confirms that the tax avoidance scheme used by the purchaser was not effective.[31] The purchaser does not have to pay the tax specified in the notice and can continue to bring an appeal. However, if a follower notice is made and HMRC is ultimately successful, HMRC can issue a penalty of up to 50 per cent of the disputed tax. It can also trigger the making of an APN requiring the disputed tax to be paid pending the determination of the appeal.

19.21 DISCLOSURE OF TAX AVOIDANCE SCHEMES

The following only summarises the main features of the DOTAS regime so far as relevant and material to the context.

DOTAS requires certain persons to provide information to HMRC about avoidance schemes within five days of the schemes being made available or implemented. The obligation usually falls on the scheme 'promoter', but in certain

---
[30] FA 2014, Part 4, Chapter 3.
[31] FA 2014, Part 4, Chapter 2.

circumstances it may fall on the scheme user (e.g., where the promoter is a lawyer and subject to legal professional privilege).

A person is a 'promoter' if he is responsible, to any extent, for the design of the arrangements or makes a proposal available to others. Where a person notifies HMRC of a notifiable proposal or arrangements, HMRC will respond by issuing a scheme reference number. That number must be given to the user within 30 days. The user then must report the scheme reference number to HMRC within 30 days.

One might reasonably assume that benign arrangements or proposals are not notifiable. That is wrong. Arrangements and proposals are notifiable where the main benefit, or one of the main benefits, is expected to be an SDLT advantage – e.g., the benefit of a relief and the avoidance or reduction, repayment or deferral of the tax. Controversially, the filter that exists under the main regime for most other taxes ('hallmarks') does not apply to SDLT. Subject to two limited exceptions, the test is merely a tax advantage test, rather than a tax avoidance test. The two exceptions refer to a grandfathering provision and regulations[32] that exclude building blocks or combinations of building blocks to produce the SDLT advantage. The grandfathering provision is the most beneficial – it exempts from disclosure arrangements that are the same or substantially the same as arrangements made available by any person (not necessarily the promoter) before 1 April 2010.

The function and purpose of DOTAS have changed since its introduction in 2005. DOTAS was originally intended to be an early-warning device for HMRC, alerting it to what tax avoidance schemes were in the market rather than who was using them. It was subsequently extended to enable HMRC to monitor the use of notifiable schemes. It is now, rightly or wrongly, used to distinguish between acceptable and unacceptable tax planning.

Other consequences (and potential consequences) of disclosing notifiable arrangements or a notifiable proposal under DOTAS (or failing to do so) include the following:

- An APN may be made if an enquiry is opened into the SDLT return or an appeal is brought against a determination or revenue assessment (see **19.19**).
- It may exclude the user from bidding as a supplier under government procurement rules.
- Penalties may be imposed for non-compliance.
- Legal professional privilege may be waived.
- Persons who introduce users to the promoter may be required to provide information to identify the user.
- Conditions may be imposed on the promoter to ensure that the promoter complies with its future obligations under DOTAS and does not promote certain types of tax avoidance scheme.
- The promoter may be monitored by HMRC.

---

[32] Stamp Duty Land Tax Avoidance Schemes (Prescribed Descriptions of Arrangements) Regulations 2005, SI 2005/1868 as amended by Stamp Duty Land Tax Avoidance Schemes (Prescribed Descriptions of Arrangements) (Amendment) Regulations 2012, SI 2012/2395.

- The defence of reasonable excuse is restricted for monitored promoters and their clients.[33]

19.22 DISHONEST TAX AGENTS

Many residential property lawyers routinely outsource SDLT advice. Although that, in itself, is not an issue, and it may be a prudent course of action if the lawyer is not confident, lawyers cannot entirely absolve themselves from liability.

The Finance Act 2012 included a long Schedule 38 ('Tax agents: dishonest conduct'). A 'tax agent' is somebody who, in the course of business, assists others ('clients') with their tax affairs. That obviously includes completing an SDLT return, or calculating SDLT. However, if those tasks are outsourced, it does not exempt the lawyer from responsibility, for (Sched.38, para.2):

(4) Assistance with a client's tax affairs also includes assistance with any document that is likely to be relied on by HMRC to determine a client's tax position.
(5) Assistance given for non-tax purposes counts as assistance with a client's tax affairs if it is given in the knowledge that it will be, or is likely to be, used by a client in connection with the client's tax affairs.

SDLT is a tax on land transactions and residential property lawyers are the ones who document the land transaction. They are tax agents who could face a personal penalty (of between £5,000 and £50,000) if, in the course of acting as a tax agent, they do 'something dishonest with a view to bringing about a loss of tax revenue' (Sched.38, para.3) whether or not a loss is brought about and whether or not they are acting on the client's instructions.

'Doing something dishonest' includes:

- dishonestly omitting to do something; and
- advising or assisting the client to do something the agent knows to be dishonest.

The HMRC compliance handbook[34] describes dishonesty as 'not honest, trustworthy or sincere' by reference to the standards of reasonable people. That would mean 'reasonable practitioners' so far as residential property lawyers are concerned. For instance, if an external tax adviser asked a residential property lawyer to restructure a transaction in order to save SDLT and that involved conduct the lawyer would not normally take, there is a risk that would be seen as dishonest conduct. Similarly, if the amount of SDLT payable seems far too low, and the residential property lawyer does not ask why, or is not satisfied with the answer but completes the transaction anyway, that could be dishonest conduct.

---

[33] FA 2004, Part 7; Stamp Duty Land Tax Avoidance Schemes (Prescribed Descriptions of Arrangements) Regulations 2005, SI 2005/1868; Tax Avoidance Schemes (Information) Regulations 2012, SI 2012/1836; Stamp Duty Land Tax Avoidance Schemes (Prescribed Descriptions of Arrangements) (Amendment) Regulations 2010, SI 2010/407.

[34] *HMRC internal manual – Compliance Handbook* (HMRC, 11 March 2016, updated 30 January 2020, available at: **www.gov.uk/hmrc-internal-manuals/compliance-handbook**), at CH181140.

HMRC is likely to penalise tax agents rarely. However, if it does, the sting is not just the financial penalty, but being reported to the Solicitors Regulation Authority and having one's name published as a dishonest agent.[35]

---

[35] On HMRC's website. See: **www.gov.uk/guidance/dishonest-conduct-by-tax-agents**.

APPENDIX A
Fee-earner checklist

This checklist is not exhaustive. It covers the main areas that a residential property lawyer is likely to encounter on a day-to-day basis.

NO.	QUESTIONS	DONE?	DATE
1	**About the property**		
	Have you considered:		
1.1	Whether the purchased interest is a 'major interest'? *This is relevant to the incidence of the higher rates and whether a stamp duty land tax (SDLT) return is due. A major interest is a freehold or leasehold estate only, except when dealing with the higher rates when (a) it includes an undivided share but (b) it excludes leases originally granted for seven years or less.*		
1.2	Whether the purchased interest is subject to a lease? *This is relevant to the incidence of the higher rates and the availability of multiple dwellings relief. The original term and unexpired term of the lease are both relevant.*		
1.3	Whether the purchased interest is in or over a 'dwelling'? *This is relevant to which tax rates and tax bands apply. A 'dwelling' generally means a building used or suitable for use as a dwelling or in the process of construction or adaption for use as a dwelling.*		
1.4	Whether the purchased interest is in or over more than one dwelling? *This is relevant to the incidence of the higher rates and the availability of multiple dwellings relief. An additional dwelling might include a granny flat or an annex. The value of the additional dwelling(s) is relevant.*		

APPENDIX A

1.5	Whether the purchased interest is in or over more than five dwellings?		
	This is relevant to which tax rates and tax bands apply. HM Revenue and Customs (HMRC) accepts that the six or more dwellings might be purchased in more than one transaction if the transactions are part of a single bargain.		
1.6	Whether the purchased dwelling is used only for non-residential purposes?		
	This is relevant to which tax rates and tax bands apply, and the incidence of the higher rates. For example, part of the land purchased with the dwelling might not constitute part of the garden or grounds of the dwelling.		
1.7	Whether an interest in non-residential property is being purchased with a dwelling under the same transaction?		
	This is relevant to which tax rates and tax bands apply, and the incidence of the higher rates.		
2	**About the transaction**		
	Have you considered:		
2.1	Whether the transaction is 'linked' to another?		
	This is relevant to which tax rates and tax bands apply; the incidence of the higher rates; the calculation of the tax; the obligation to make a further SDLT return in respect of an earlier transaction; and the availability of multiple dwellings relief and first-time buyer relief.		
2.2	Whether part of the price is contingent or uncertain?		
	This is relevant to whether a deferral application needs to be made.		
2.3	Whether part of the price is to be met by giving a land interest to the vendor?		
	This is relevant to whether special charging rules for an exchange apply to increase the chargeable consideration.		
2.4	Whether the transaction is in pursuance of the exercise of an option?		
	This is relevant to whether the transaction is 'linked' to another and potentially whether the transaction is grandfathered by any rate increases.		
2.5	Whether the transaction is interdependent on another transaction for value?		
	This is relevant to whether a general anti-avoidance rule might cause the tax or additional tax to be payable.		

2.6	Whether the transaction is a sale and leaseback; surrender and regrant; sub-sale/assignment; part-exchange; between group companies; collective enfranchisement transaction; between a partner (or connected persons) and a partnership; or funded using alternative finance arrangements? *This is relevant to whether a full or partial relief or special charging rules apply.*		
3	**About the purchaser**		
	Have you considered:		
3.1	What type of person (individual or company) is purchasing the property? *This is relevant to the incidence of the super rate and the higher rates.*		
3.2	Whether the person is purchasing in his/its personal capacity or in his/its capacity as a trustee, partner or company director? *This is relevant to the incidence of the super rate and the higher rates.*		
3.3	For human purchasers only, whether he is married or in a civil partnership and 'living together' with his spouse or civil partner? *This is relevant to the incidence of the higher rates and the availability of first-time buyer relief.*		
3.4	For human purchasers only, whether he (or his spouse or civil partner if appropriate) is replacing his residence? *This is relevant to the incidence of the higher rates.*		
3.5	Whether the person is buying jointly with another person? *This is relevant to the incidence of the higher rates and the availability of first-time buyer relief.*		
3.6	For human purchasers only, whether he (or his spouse or civil partner or minor stepchild) owns (or is beneficially entitled to) another property anywhere in the world? *This is relevant to the incidence of the higher rates and the availability of first-time buyer relief.*		
3.7	Whether the purchaser is a house-builder; property trader; employer; charity; public body; or registered provider of social housing? *This is relevant to whether a full or partial relief applies.*		

APPENDIX A

4	**About the use of property**		
	Have you considered:		
4.1	Whether the purchased dwelling will be used as the purchaser's home? *This is relevant to the incidence of the higher rates and the availability of first-time buyer relief.*		

APPENDIX B

Stamp duty land tax client questionnaire (human purchasers only)

This questionnaire is not exhaustive. It covers the main areas that a residential property lawyer is likely to encounter on a day-to-day basis.

> **Important – please read**
> - References to 'you' are to the purchaser, or, in the case of more than one purchaser, each purchaser of the property.
> - The questions should be answered as at the end of the day of completion of your purchase.
> - If you are purchasing more than one property, the questions should be answered in respect of each property purchased.
> - A 'dwelling' means a dwelling worth £40,000 or more located in England or Northern Ireland and includes an interest in a dwelling.

No.	Question	Y/N
1	**About your purchase**	
	These questions relate to the property you are purchasing (the 'purchased property').	
1.1	Is the purchased property a building used as a dwelling? If not, is it a building that is suitable for use as a dwelling? If not, is it in the process of being constructed or adapted for use as a dwelling?	
1.2	Are you purchasing 'off-plan'?	
1.3	Do you already own an interest in the purchased property?	
1.4	Do you intend to use the purchased property as your only or main residence?	
1.5	Is your purchase part of a series of transactions involving the same vendor?	
1.6	Is the purchased property composed of more than one self-contained dwelling? *Note: If so, please provide a rough apportionment of the price between the dwellings.*	
1.7	Is part of the purchased property used or suitable for use for a non-residential purpose?	

APPENDIX B

1.8	Does the purchased property include land that is not part of the garden or grounds of the dwelling?	
1.9	Is the vendor your spouse or civil partner?	
2	**About you**	
	These questions relate to you, your marital status and your property-ownership history.	
2.1	Are you purchasing the property in your personal capacity rather than as a trustee, partner of a partnership or director of a company? *Note: If you are not purchasing the property in your personal capacity, please go straight to section 4 (About the trust) or section 5 (About the partnership), as appropriate.*	
2.2	Other than the purchased property, do you own (or are you beneficially entitled to) a dwelling or a share of a dwelling anywhere in the world (ignore the ownership of shares in a company that owns a dwelling and leases originally granted for seven years or less)?	
2.3	Have you disposed of a dwelling anywhere in the world within the last three years that was your main residence?	
2.4	If you have answered Yes to question 2.4, after the disposal did you purchase another dwelling (other than the purchased property) that is or was your only or main residence?	
2.5	Are you married or in a civil partnership? *Note: If you are married or in a civil partnership and are purchasing in your sole name, please complete section 3 (About your spouse or civil partner).*	
2.6	If you are married or in a civil partnership, are you permanently separated from your spouse or civil partner?	
2.7	Are you a member of a property-investment partnership or beneficiary under a trust regardless of where in the world it was established or is registered?	
2.8	If you answered Yes to question 2.8, does the partnership hold a dwelling anywhere in the world?	
2.9	If you are the beneficiary under a trust, are you entitled to occupy a dwelling or income earned in respect of a dwelling owned by the trust?	
2.10	Do you have any children aged under 18 who are beneficially entitled to a dwelling anywhere in the world?	
3	**About your spouse or civil partner (if applicable)**	
	Complete this section if: *(a) you are married or in a civil partnership;* *(b) your spouse or civil partner is not jointly buying the purchased property; and* *(c) you are not permanently separated from your spouse or civil partner*	
3.1	Does your spouse or civil partner own (or are they beneficially entitled to) a dwelling anywhere in the world?	
3.2	Has your spouse or civil partner disposed of a dwelling within the last three years?	

SDLT CLIENT QUESTIONNAIRE

3.3	If you have answered Yes to question 3.2, was that dwelling your only or main residence at any point within the last three years?	
3.4	Does your spouse or civil partner have any children aged under 18 that are beneficially entitled to a dwelling?	
4	**About the trust (if applicable)**	
	Only complete this section if you are purchasing in your capacity as a trustee.	
4.1	Are you acting as a trustee of a bare trust? *Note: If Yes, complete 4.2–4.8 in respect of the beneficiary (or, if there is more than one beneficiary, each beneficiary).*	
4.2	Other than the purchased property, does the beneficiary own (or are they beneficially entitled to) a dwelling anywhere in the world (ignore the ownership of shares in a company that owns a dwelling and leases originally granted for seven years or less)?	
4.3	Has the beneficiary disposed of a dwelling anywhere in the world within the last three years?	
4.4	If you answered Yes to question 4.3, after the disposal did the beneficiary purchase another dwelling that is or was their only or main residence?	
4.5	Is the beneficiary married or in a civil partnership?	
4.6	If you answered Yes to question 4.5, is the beneficiary permanently separated from their spouse or civil partner?	
4.7	Is the beneficiary a member of a partnership regardless of where in the world it was established or is registered?	
4.8	If you answered Yes to question 4.7, does the partnership hold a dwelling anywhere in the world?	
4.9	If you are acting as a trustee of a settlement, under the terms of the trust will a beneficiary be entitled to live in the purchased dwelling for their lifetime or to receive the income earned from the dwelling? *Note: If Yes, complete 4.2–4.8 in respect of the beneficiary. If not, complete 2.2–2.11 in respect of yourself.*	
5	**About the partnership (if applicable)**	
	Only complete this section if you are a partner of a partnership and are acting for the partnership.	
5.1	Does the partnership hold a dwelling anywhere in the world?	
5.2	Is the partnership composed solely of individuals?	
5.3	Do you intend to use the purchased property exclusively for the purpose of letting, trading or redevelopment?	
5.4	Will a partner be entitled to live in the purchased property?	

APPENDIX C

Potential problem areas

FACTORS AFFECTING THE PURCHASED INTEREST

- The purchase of a family home with a self-contained annex or 'granny flat' (see **3.3.3**).
- The purchase of more than one dwelling (see **3.2.4**, **3.3.2.3** and **3.3.3**).
- The purchase of a dwelling with land that is not required for the reasonable enjoyment of the dwelling (see **3.2.1**).
- The purchase of a mixed-use building (see **3.2.2**).
- The purchase of a dwelling with land that is actively used or has been habitually used for agricultural purposes (see **3.2.1**).
- The purchase of a derelict dwelling (see **3.2.3**).

FACTORS AFFECTING THE PURCHASER

- The purchaser is a trust (see **3.3.7** and **19.4**).
- The purchaser is a company (see **3.3.2.4**).
- The purchaser is a partnership (see **Chapter 16**).
- There is more than one purchaser (see **3.3.2.2**).
- The purchaser is non-UK resident (see **3.5**).
- The purchaser is a company that is controlled by the vendor (see **9.6**).
- The purchaser disposed of an undivided share of a dwelling used as his only or main residence.
- The purchaser has more than one residence, including the purchased dwelling (see **3.3.10.1**).
- The purchaser intends to use the dwelling as his only or main residence, but not initially (see **3.3.10.1**).
- The purchaser intends to on-sell the property to another person at completion (see **Chapter 7**).

FACTORS AFFECTING THE TRANSACTION

- The purchase is in connection with the incorporation of a property-rental business (see **16.9**).
- The purchase is in connection with death or a divorce (see **8.4**, **9.3** and **9.4**).
- The purchase is the renewal of a rental lease (see **5.7**).
- The purchase is a part-exchange (see **1.5.2**).
- The purchase is an exchange and the values of the properties exchanged are unequal (see **1.5.2**).
- The purchase is made off-plan (see **3.4.2** and **5.5**).
- Part of the price is contingent or uncertain (see **19.7**).
- The purchase was made before 28 October 2018 (see **3.3.10.1**).
- The purchase is a sub-sale or an assignment of rights (see **Chapter 7**).

POTENTIAL PROBLEM AREAS

- The purchase is funded by alternative finance arrangements (see **Chapter 11**).
- The purchase is in pursuance of the exercise of an option (see **Chapter 13**).
- The purchase is involved in connection with other transactions for value (see **1.4**).
- Part or all of the price is to be met by transferring land or granting a lease to the vendor (see **1.5.2**).
- The purchaser is to take possession of the property (perhaps temporarily on a restricted basis) before completion (see **1.7**).
- The purchase is made under Landlord and Tenant Act 1987, Part 1 (right of first refusal) or Leasehold Reform, Housing and Urban Development Act 1993, Part 1, Chapter 1 (right to collective enfranchisement) (see **Chapter 6**).
- The purchase is between a partner (or connected person) and partnership (see **Chapter 16**).

APPENDIX D

Glossary

Words in bold type are defined in this glossary.

Accelerated payment notice (APN) A notice given by HM Revenue and Customs (HMRC) stating its belief that the recipient has used a tax avoidance scheme disclosed under the **disclosure of tax avoidance schemes (DOTAS)** rules or counteracted under the **general anti-abuse rule (GAAR)**, and requiring the recipient to pay a specific amount of tax on account within 90 days.

Acquisition The act or deemed act of acquiring a **chargeable interest**.

Appealable decision The decision by HMRC either to amend a stamp duty land tax (SDLT) return during an **enquiry** to prevent a loss of tax, to amend an **SDLT return** on closure of an enquiry, to make a **discovery assessment**, to make an assessment to recover an excessive repayment, or to make a **determination**.

Arrangements A term used, e.g., in the context of group relief. A scheme, agreement or understanding whether or not legally enforceable.

Assignment of rights One of two types of **pre-completion transaction**. A transaction that gives a person other than the **purchaser** under a sale contract the entitlement to call for a conveyance to him of the whole or part of the **subject-matter** of the sale contract where that entitlement is an entitlement to exercise rights under the sale contract.

Bare trust A trust under which property is held by a trustee for a person who is absolutely entitled as against the trustee.

Body corporate A corporate entity that has a legal existence: e.g., a **company** or a limited liability partnership (LLP).

Chargeable consideration Consideration in money or money's worth (unless otherwise specified) given for the **subject-matter** of the transaction, directly or indirectly, by the **purchaser** or a connected person.

Chargeable interest An estate, interest, right or power in or over land in England or Northern Ireland or the benefit of an obligation, restriction or condition affecting the value of any such estate, interest, right or power apart from an **exempt interest**.

Closure notice A notice informing the **purchaser** that HMRC has completed its enquiries into an **SDLT return** stating HMRC's conclusions.

Company Except as otherwise stated in the SDLT code, any **body corporate** or unincorporated association but not a partnership or LLP.

Completion One of two tax points for SDLT. Completion of the **land transaction**, between the same parties, and in substantial conformity with the contract.

Completion notice A notice given by HMRC confirming that an **enquiry** into an **SDLT return** has been completed.

Connected persons A type of relationship between two persons (natural or legal persons) recognised for certain tax purposes.

Contract settlement An agreement entered into between HMRC and the **purchaser** relating to the purchaser's tax liability.

Corresponding partner A term used in the special charging rules for transactions involving partnerships. A partner that is either a **relevant owner** or an individual that is connected with a relevant owner (see **connected persons**).

Determination A type of assessment made by HMRC estimating the amount of SDLT underpaid by the **purchaser**.

Discovery assessment An assessment made by HMRC to recover a loss of tax where it could not have been reasonably expected to be aware of the loss of tax within the **enquiry period**.

Disclosure of tax avoidance schemes (DOTAS) rules A regime requiring persons, primarily promoters of tax avoidance schemes, to make a disclosure to HMRC describing the arrangements that enable, or might be expected to enable, a person to obtain a tax advantage.

Dwelling (**higher rate, higher rates, multiple dwellings relief**) A building or part of a building (hence **mixed-use** premises qualify) used or suitable for use as a single dwelling or in the process of being constructed or adapted for such use, including land that is, or is to be, occupied or enjoyed with a dwelling as a garden or grounds and land that subsists, or is to subsist, for the benefit of a dwelling. Includes dwellings purchased 'off-plan' subject to meeting conditions.

Effective date The tax point. **Completion** of the transaction or, if earlier, the date of **substantial performance**. It is never the date of exchange unless exchange occurs on the same date as completion or substantial performance. The date of exchange, however, is usually relevant to transitional rules affecting rate increases, etc.

Enquiry The process of HMRC checking that an **SDLT return** has been completed correctly.

Enquiry notice A notice made by HMRC confirming that an **enquiry** has been opened into an **SDLT return**.

Enquiry period The period of nine months after the **filing date** if the **SDLT return** was made on or before that date, or the date on which the SDLT return was made if the return was made after the filing date or the date on which an amendment to the SDLT return was made if the return was amended by the **purchaser**.

Exchange An **SDLT transaction** under which the consideration is met fully or partly by the **purchaser** entering into another SDLT transaction as **vendor** (also known as a land swap). Not to be confused with exchange of contracts.

Exempt interest A **security interest**, a licence to use or occupy land, a tenancy at will, an advowson, **franchise** or manor.

Filing date The last day of the period within which an **SDLT return** must be made (usually 14 days after the **effective date** for **initial returns**).

Follower notice A notice given by HMRC to a person that has used a tax avoidance scheme that has been shown in another appeal to be ineffective, imposing a penalty of up to 50 per cent of the disputed tax if the recipient does not concede.

Franchise A grant from the Crown such as the right to hold a market or fair, or the right to take tolls.

Free-standing transfer One of two types of **pre-completion transaction**. A pre-completion transaction that is not an **assignment of rights** (e.g., a sub-sale and a novation).

Further return An **SDLT return** made after an **initial return**.

General anti-abuse rule (GAAR) A rule enabling HMRC to counteract 'abusive' tax arrangements. Such arrangements are abusive if they cannot reasonably be described as a reasonable course of action.

Higher rate A flat 15 per cent rate of SDLT that applies to the purchase of a **major interest** in a single **dwelling** worth more than £500,000 by a non-natural person, including a **company**, subject to exceptions (referred to in this book as the **super rate** to avoid confusion with **higher rates**). Designed to deter 'enveloping' and prevent a loss of tax on sales of property-rich companies.

Higher rates The rates set out in Table A of Finance Act 2003, Sched.4ZA, para.1(2) (currently three per cent on the first £125,000 of the **relevant consideration**; five per cent on the next £125,000; eight per cent on the next £675,000; 13 per cent on the next £575,000; and 15 per cent on the remainder, if any).

APPENDIX D

Higher rate transaction An **SDLT transaction** chargeable in accordance with the **higher rates**.
Higher threshold interest An interest in a single **dwelling** acquired for **chargeable consideration** exceeding £500,000.
House-building company A company that carries on the business of constructing or adapting buildings or parts of buildings for use as **dwellings**.
Initial return The first **SDLT return** made in respect of a notifiable transaction.
Land transaction The **acquisition** of a **chargeable interest** (also known as an **SDLT transaction**).
Land transaction return A return (also known as an **SDLT return**) used to notify HMRC of a notifiable **SDLT transaction**.
Lease An interest or right in or over land for a term of years (whether fixed or periodic) or a tenant at will or other interest or right in or over land terminable by notice at any time.
Linked transactions Transactions that form part of a single scheme, arrangement or series between the same **vendor** and **purchaser** or, in either case, **connected persons**.
Main subject-matter The **chargeable interest** acquired together with any interest or right appurtenant or pertaining to it that is acquired with it.
Major interest A freehold or leasehold estate, legal or beneficial. However, for the purposes of the **super rate** and the **higher rates**, an undivided share of a major interest is also treated as a major interest.
Market value The price which the **chargeable interest** might reasonably be expected to fetch on a sale in the open market.
Minor interest A **chargeable interest** that is not a **major interest** (this term is used in this book, but is not used by HMRC).
Misconduct assessment An assessment made by HMRC to recover a loss of tax where there has been fraudulent or negligent conduct.
Mixed-use A transaction (or linked transaction) the **main subject-matter** of which is, to any extent, **residential property** and **non-residential property**.
Multiple dwellings relief A partial relief for purchases of more than one **dwelling** in a single transaction or linked transactions. Where it is claimed, the tax is calculated by reference to the average dwelling price.
Nil return An **SDLT return** that is made voluntarily containing a self-assessment of no liability to tax.
Non-residential property Property that is not **residential property**.
Non-qualifying individual An individual permitted to occupy a **dwelling** purchased by a non-natural person and, due to their relationship with the **purchaser**, restricts the purchaser from claiming availability of the relief from the **higher rate** or triggers a withdrawal of the relief.
Notifiable transaction An **SDLT transaction** in respect of which an **SDLT return** must be made.
Partnership share The proportion in which a partner is entitled at that time to share in the income profits of the partnership.
Pre-completion transaction A transaction that gives a person other than the **purchaser** under a sale contract the entitlement to call for a conveyance to him of the whole or part of the **subject-matter** of the sale contract.
Premium Consideration given by the tenant as a capital sum rather than as **rent**.
Property-investment partnership A partnership whose sole or main activity is investing or dealing in **chargeable interests** (whether or not that activity involves the carrying out of construction operations on the land in question).
Property-trader A company, LLP or a partnership composed entirely of companies or LLPs that carries on the business of buying and selling **dwellings**.
Purchaser The person making an **acquisition** (or deemed acquisition) of a **chargeable interest**.

Relevant consideration The total amount of the **chargeable consideration** given for the transaction and any **linked transactions**.

Relevant land Any land an interest in which is the **main subject-matter** of the transaction (or of all **linked transactions**).

Relevant owner A term used in the special charging rules for transactions involving partnerships. A partner or connected person that was entitled to the **chargeable interest** before he transferred it to the partnership or, alternatively, the partner or connected person that is entitled to the chargeable interest after the partnership has transferred it to him.

Rent A payment made by a tenant to a landlord regularly for the right to occupy the demised premises.

Representative partner A partner nominated by a majority of the partners in a partnership to act as the representative of the partnership permitting the nominated partner to act on behalf of all the **responsible partners** in discharging their obligations to pay SDLT or make **SDLT returns**.

Residential property A building (or part of a building) used or suitable for use as a **dwelling**, or that is in the process of being constructed or adapted for such use, and land that is the garden and grounds of a dwelling, or a right or interest in land that subsists for a dwelling or the garden or grounds of a dwelling. Certain institutional property is also residential property.

Responsible partners Those partners in a partnership that have the obligation to pay SDLT and make an **SDLT return** in respect of an **SDLT transaction** entered into by the partnership.

Revenue certificate A certificate issued by HMRC to confirm that an **SDLT return** has been made (Note: It does *not* confirm that the return is correct or that tax has been paid). Also known as a form SDLT5.

Reverse premium A sum of money given by the **vendor** to incentivise the **purchaser** to enter into the transaction: e.g., a sum of money given by the landlord to the tenant on the grant of a **lease**.

Review A self-review made by HMRC in relation to an HMRC decision either offered by HMRC or sought by the **purchaser** after an appeal has been made by the purchaser to HMRC in relation to an **appealable decision**.

Scheme transaction A term used in the SDLT general anti-avoidance rule, Finance Act 2003, s.75A. A transaction (not necessarily a **land transaction** and including any type of arrangement whether or not it could be described as a transaction) that is involved in connection with an **SDLT transaction**.

SDLT return A return (also known as a **land transaction return** or form SDLT1 together with the supplementary forms SDLT2–4) used to notify HMRC of a notifiable **SDLT transaction** containing the **purchaser**'s self-assessment of the amount of tax due.

SDLT transaction The **acquisition** of a **chargeable interest** (also known as a **land transaction**).

Security interest An interest or right (other than a rentcharge) held for the purpose of securing the payment of money or the performance of any other obligation. A type of **exempt interest**.

Settlement Any type of trust that is not a **bare trust**: e.g., an interest in possession trust and an accumulation and maintenance trust.

Standard rates The standard residential rates set out in Table A of Finance Act 2003, s.55(1B) (currently zero per cent on the first £125,000 of the **relevant consideration**; two per cent on the next £125,000; five per cent on the next £675,000; 10 per cent on the next £575,000; and 12 per cent on the remainder, if any).

Standard rate transaction An **SDLT transaction** chargeable in accordance with the **standard rates**.

Subject-matter The **main subject-matter** together with any interest or right appurtenant or pertaining to it that is acquired with it.

Substantial performance One of two tax points for SDLT. Payment of 'all or substantially all' the consideration (in practice HMRC interprets 'substantially all' to mean 90 per cent or more, though this threshold is not specified in the legislation) or taking possession of the whole or substantially the whole of the purchased land and buildings.

Successive linked leases **Leases** granted successively of the same premises usually as a result of the tenant exercising an option to renew.

Sum of lower proportions A term used in the special charging rules for transactions involving partnerships. The total of the **partnership shares** or, if lower, the proportion of the **chargeable interest** transferred apportioned to each partner that is a **corresponding partner** in relation to a **relevant owner**.

Super rate See **higher rate** (note: this term is used in this book, but is not used by HMRC).

Tax avoidance A course of action designed to conflict with or defeat the evident intention of parliament.

Unique Taxpayer Reference (UTR) A unique reference number allocated to a person.

Unique Transaction Reference Number (UTRN) A unique reference number allocated to an **SDLT return**. For returns submitted online, the UTRN is allocated after submission. The UTRN can be found on the bottom right corner of the SDLT return and on the revenue certificate.

Vendor The person making a disposal (or deemed disposal) of a **chargeable interest**.

Index

Accelerated payment notice (APN) 1.11, 19.19
Acquisition
    meaning of 1.2.2
Acquisition relief 18.1, 18.4.1
    assumption of liabilities 18.4.2.2
    buy back arrangements 18.4.2.3
    conditions 18.4.2
    consideration shares 18.4.2.1
    no tax avoidance 18.4.2.5
    qualifying trade 18.4.2.4
    withdrawal of 18.4.2.6
Alternative dispute resolution 19.17.5
Alternative property finance 11.1
    alternative finance investment bonds 11.4
    Ijara mortgages 11.1
    land sold to financial institution
        leased to individual 11.2
        re-sold to individual 11.3
    Murabaha mortgages 11.1
    sharia-compliant financing 11.1
Anti-avoidance 1.11
    acquisition relief 18.4.2.5
    general anti-abuse rule (GAAR) 1.11, 9.10, 16.3
    market value rules 1.5.2
    motive rules 1.11
    reconstruction relief 18.3.2.6
    see also Tax avoidance schemes
Appeal
    appealable decisions 19.17.1
    notifying tribunal of 19.17.3
    see also Disputes
Assents and appropriations
    by personal representatives 2.5, 9.3
Assignments
    of agreements for lease 5.5
    of contracts 9.5
    of leases 5.4.1
        assumption of assignor's obligations 5.4.3
        relieved leases 5.4.2
    of options 13.2.3
    of rights 7.4
Banks
    super rate relief 3.4.4.7
    see also Financial institutions
Buy back arrangements
    acquisition relief 18.4.2.3
Calculation of SDLT 1.4
    chargeable considerations 1.4.2
    see also Tax rates and tax bands
Capital withdrawals
    partnerships 16.6
Caretaker's flat
    super rate and 3.4.4.11
Chain-breakers
    property traders acting as 4.7
Chargeable consideration 1.4.2
    contingent 1.5.1
    debt 1.5
    exchanges 1.5.3
    exempt transactions 1.6, 2.5
    market value rules 1.5.2
    transactions for no chargeable consideration 2.5
    uncertain 1.5.1
Chargeable interest
    acquisition of 2.4
    meaning of 1.2.3, 2.2
    neither chargeable nor exempt interest 2.2
    same person 2.4
Charities relief 4.4
    withdrawal of 4.4.1
Children
    higher rates and 3.3.8

INDEX

Civil partners *see* Spouses/civil partners
Client questionnaire App.B
Collective enfranchisement 6.1
    condition 6.1
    corporate purchasers 6.7
    first refusal 6.2
    higher rates 6.10, 6.12
    identifying the purchaser 6.6
    Landlord and Tenant Act 1987 6.2
    Leasehold Reform, Housing and Urban Development Act 1993 6.3
    meaning of 6.1
    mixed-use buildings 6.9
    multiple dwellings relief 6.11, 6.12
    new landlord acquires reversionary interest 6.2
    nominee company 6.3.1
    non-residential rates 6.12
    price payable 6.3.1
    purchase of extended lease 6.3.2
    qualifying tenants 6.2
    relief 6.1, 6.12
      after 2009 6.5
      between 2003 and 2009 6.4
      multiple dwellings relief 6.11, 6.12
      RTE companies 6.4
    residential standard rates 6.12
    shared ownership leases 10.1
    six or more flats 6.8
    super rate 6.1, 6.12
    tax calculation 6.1, 6.5
    white knight investors 6.3.1
Common reliefs *see* Reliefs
Companies
    connected *see* Connected company
    distributions *in specie* 9.7
    group relief *see* Group relief
    purchasing one or more dwellings 3.3.2.4
    residential higher rate 3.3.2.4, 3.3.9.1
Compulsory purchase 12.2
Connected company
    connection 15.2
    enveloping 15.1
    exceptions 15.3
    market value rule 15.1
    transfers to 9.6, 15.1
    trustees 9.6, 15.3
    unit trust schemes 15.2
Connected persons
    linked transactions 1.5.4.3
    transfers by partnership 16.5
    transfers to partnership 16.4
Consideration shares
    acquisition relief 18.4.2.1
    reconstruction relief 18.3.2.2
Contingent consideration 1.5.1
Continuation of leases 5.7
    extension 5.7.1
    holding over 5.7.3
    renewal 5.7.2
    reversionary leases 5.7.4
Contract
    assignment of 9.5
Corporate reliefs *see* Acquisition relief; Group relief; Reconstruction relief
Crown exemption 12.6.1

Debt 1.5
    assumption/discharge of 9.2
    contingent consideration 1.5.1
    exchanges 1.5.3
    existing debt 1.5
    linked transactions *see* Linked transactions
    market value rules 1.5.2
    uncertain consideration 1.5.1
Deferral applications 19.7
Determinations 19.11.3
Development licence arrangements 17.1, 17.2
Diplomatic premises 12.6.2
Disclosure of tax avoidance schemes (DOTAS) 1.11, 19.21
Dishonest tax agents 19.22
Disputes 19.17
    alternative dispute resolution 19.17.5
    appealable decisions 19.17.1
    mediation 19.17.5
    notifying tribunal of appeal 19.17.3
    requesting a review 19.17.2
    settlement 19.17.4
    tribunal rules 19.17.6
Dissolution of civil partnership 2.5, 8.4
Distributions
    in specie 9.7
    by partnerships 9.9
Divorce 2.5, 8.4
Dwelling
    meaning of
      first-time buyer relief 4.2.2
      multiple dwellings relief 4.3.2
      tax rates and tax bands 3.2.3

Easements 14.1
  see also Right to light
Educational bodies
  arrangements involving 12.5
  see also Public bodies
Effective date 1.7.1
  substantial performance and 1.7.1
Employees
  caretaker's flat 3.4.4.11
  purchases for occupation by 3.4.4.10
Employers
  relief for 4.10
Employment
  relocation for 4.9
Enquiries 19.11.1
Exchanges
  debt and 1.5.3
Exempt interests 2.3
  franchise 2.3
  licence to use/occupy land 2.3, 5.2.2
  meaning of 1.2.4
  neither chargeable nor exempt interests 2.2
  security interests 2.3
  tenancies at will 2.3, 5.2.2
Exempt transactions 1.6, 2.5
  types of 2.5
Expiry of lease 5.6.5
Extension of lease 5.7.1, 6.3.2
  higher rates exception 3.3.10.2

Farmhouse
  super rate and 3.4.4.9
Fee-earner checklist App.A
Filing date 19.1
Final tax position 1.10
Financial institutions
  land sold to
    leased to individual 11.2
    re-sold to individual 11.3
  super rate relief 3.4.4.7
First-time buyer relief 4.2
  conditions for 4.2.1
  higher rates and 3.3.5.3
  market value election 4.2.3.1
  meaning of 'dwelling' 4.2.2
  payment in stages 4.2.3.2
  residential standard rates 1.4.1
  shared ownership leases 4.2.3, 10.2
  shared ownership trusts 10.3.2
Follower notices 19.20
Foreign sovereign immunity 12.6.3
Forfeiture of lease 5.6.1

Free-standing transfers
  pre-completion transactions 7.4
Freehold and leasehold transfers 3.1
  dwelling
    meaning of 3.2.3
    purchase of more than five 3.2.5
    purchase of more than one 3.2.4
    single dwelling 3.2.4
  mixed-use transfers 3.2.2
  residential property, meaning of 3.2.1
  surcharges
    overseas purchasers 3.5
    see also Higher rates; Super rate
  tax rates and tax bands 3.2

General anti-abuse rule (GAAR) 1.11, 9.10, 16.3
Gifts 9.1
Granny annexes
  higher rates 3.3.3
Group relief 18.1, 18.2.1
  75 per cent subsidiaries 18.2.2.2
  arrangements to obtain control of purchaser 18.2.2.3
  companies 18.2.2.1
  conditions 18.2.2
  other disqualifying arrangements 18.2.2.4
  withdrawal of 18.2.3

Helpline 19.18.2
Higher rates 1.4.1, 3.3.1
  children 3.3.8
  collective enfranchisement 6.10, 6.12
  conditions 3.3.2
    company purchasing one or more dwellings 3.3.2.4
    individuals jointly purchasing one dwelling 3.3.2.2
    individuals purchasing more than one dwelling 3.3.2.3
    individuals purchasing one dwelling 3.3.2.1
  exceptions 3.3.10
    inherited dwellings 3.3.12
    lease extensions etc. 3.3.10.2
    property-adjustment orders 3.3.11
    replacement of main residence 3.3.10.1
    transfers between spouses/civil partners 3.3.10.3, 8.2

INDEX

Higher rates – *continued*
  first-time buyer relief and 3.3.5.3
  freehold and leasehold transfers 3.3
  granny annexes 3.3.3
  interactions with other SDLT provisions 3.3.5
  linked transactions and 3.3.5.4
  mixed-use transactions and 3.3.5.1
  multiple dwellings relief and 3.3.5.2
  overseas dwellings 3.3.4
  partnerships 3.3.9
    companies 3.3.9.1
  spouses/civil partners
    buying alone 3.3.6
    transfers between 3.3.10.3, 8.2, 9.5
  trusts 3.3.7
Higher rates regime (HRAD) 3.3.1
Historic Buildings and Monuments Commission 12.6.4
HMRC
  anti-avoidance 1.11
  appealable decisions 19.17.1
  asking for help 19.18
  corrections 19.11.2
  determinations 19.11.3
  disputes *see* Disputes
  enforcement powers 19.16
  enquiries 19.11.1
  guidance 19.18.1
  helpline 19.18.2
  information notices 19.14
  inspections 19.14
  intervention 19.11
  post-transaction rulings 19.18.3
  pre-transaction rulings 19.18.3
  revenue assessments 19.11.4
    time periods for 19.11.5
Holding over
  leases 5.7.3
Home purchase plans
  sharia-compliant financing 11.1
Home reversion plans 3.4.4.8

Ijara mortgages 11.1
Information notices 19.14
Inherited dwellings 3.3.12
Inspections 19.14
Interest on unpaid tax 19.12.2

Joint purchasers
  higher rates 3.3.2.2
  liability to make return/payment 19.4

Land and buildings transaction tax (LBTT) 1.1
Land registry *see* Registration
Land transaction tax (LTT) 1.1
Leases 5.1, 5.2
  assignments 5.4.1
    agreements for lease 5.5
    assumption of assignor's obligations 5.4.3
    relieved leases 5.4.2
  bare trustee 5.9
  continuation of 5.7
  effective date 5.2.4
  end date 5.2.6
  expiry of 5.6.5
  extensions 5.7.1, 6.3.2
    higher rates exception 3.3.10.2
  forfeiture of 5.6.1
  grants of new leases 5.2
  holding over 5.7.3
  licences 5.2.2
  linked leases 5.2.7
  merger 5.6.4
  mixed-use rates 5.2.3
  nominee 5.9
  non-residential rates 5.2.3
  notice to quit 5.6.2
  premium, charge on 5.2.8
  purchase of extended lease 5.7.1, 6.3.2
  relieved leases 5.4.2
  renewals 5.7.2
  rent
    amount payable 5.2.5
    charge on 5.2.3
  rent to shared ownership lease schemes 10.3.1
  requiring SDLT return 5.2.9
  lease variations 5.3
  residential rates 5.2.3
  reversionary leases 5.7.4
  sale and leaseback relief 5.10
  shared ownership *see* Shared ownership leases; Shared ownership trusts
  special charging rules and reliefs 5.8
  start date 5.2.6
  substantial performance 5.2.4
  surrender 5.6.3
  tax rates and tax bands 1.4.1, 5.2.1
  tenancies at will 5.2.2
  termination of 5.6

variations 5.3
    requiring SDLT return 5.3.1
Liability to pay SDLT 1.3
    purchaser 1.3.1
    vendor 1.3.1
Licences
    development licences 17.1, 17.2
    exempt interest 2.3, 5.2.2
    to use/occupy land 2.3, 5.2.2
Linked transactions 1.5.4
    arrangement 1.5.4.2
    connected persons 1.5.4.3
    higher rates and 3.3.5.4
    impact of the rule 1.5.4.1
    meaning of 1.5.4.2
    series of transactions 1.5.4.2
    single scheme 1.5.4.2
Loan repayments
    partnerships 16.6

Market value election
    first-time buyer relief 4.2.3.1
    payment in stages 4.2.3.2
    shared ownership leases 10.2
    shared ownership trusts 10.3.2
Market value rules 1.5.2
    connected companies 15.1, 15.3
    exceptions 15.3
Married couples *see*
    Spouses/civil partners
Mediation 19.17.5
Merger
    leases 5.6.4
Mixed use rates *see*
    Non-residential rates
Mixed-use buildings
    collective enfranchisement 6.9
Mixed-use transactions
    higher rates 3.3.5.1
    types of 3.2.2
Motive rules 1.11
    see also Anti-avoidance
Multiple dwellings relief 4.3
    collective enfranchisement 6.11, 6.12
    higher rates and 3.3.5.2
    meaning of 'dwelling' 4.3.2
    tax calculation method 4.3.1
    withdrawal of 4.3.3
Murabaha mortgages 11.1

National purposes
    acquisitions by bodies established
        for 12.6.4

Negative obligations *see*
    Restrictive covenants; Right to
    light
No chargeable consideration
    transactions for 2.5
Non-residential rates 1.4.1
    collective enfranchisement 6.12
    grants of new leases 5.2.3
Notice to quit 5.6.2

Online payments 19.5.3
Online returns 19.3
Options 13.1, 13.2
    assignment of 13.2.3
    call options 13.2
    definition 13.2
    exercise of 13.2.2
    grant of 13.2.1
    put options 13.2
    release of 13.2.3
    variation of 13.2.3
Overpaid tax
    amending SDLT return 19.10.1
    applying for relief 19.10.2
    reclaiming 19.10
Overseas dwellings
    higher rates 3.3.4
    surcharge 3.5

**Part-exchanges made by
  housing-building companies**
    relief for 4.5
Partnership share 16.3
Partnerships 16.1
    areas of difficulty 16.9
    capital withdrawals 16.6
    contributions to 9.8
    distributions by 9.9
    general rules 16.2
    interest in 16.7
    liability to make return/payment 19.4
    loan repayments 16.6
    partnership share 16.3
    residential higher rate 3.3.9
    special rules 16.3, 16.8
    transfers by
        to connected person 16.5
        to partner 16.5
        to spouse/civil partner 8.6
    transfers of interest in 16.7
    transfers to
        by connected person 16.4
        by partner 16.4

INDEX

Partnerships – *continued*
    transfers to – *continued*
      by spouse/civil partner 8.6
    types of 16.2
    withdrawals from 9.9

Payment of tax
    accelerated payment notices 1.11, 19.19
    alternative payment methods 19.5.3
    deferral applications 19.7
    domestic payments 19.5.1
    failure to pay
      enforcement 19.16
      further time 19.13
      interest on unpaid tax 19.12.2
      penalties 19.12.1
      reasonable excuse 19.13
      special circumstances 19.13
    interest on unpaid tax 19.12.2
    international payments 19.5.2
    joint purchasers 19.4
    liability 19.4
    making a payment 1.9.2, 19.5
    online 19.5.3
    overpaid tax 19.10
    partnerships 19.4
    reclaiming overpaid tax 19.10
    returns *see* Returns
    trusts 19.4
    when to make 19.6

Penalties 1.11, 19.12.1, 19.15

Personal representatives
    assents and appropriations by 2.5, 9.3
    property traders acquiring dwelling from 4.8

Planning obligations
    compliance with 12.3

Potential problem areas App.C

Pre-completion transactions 7.1
    assignments of rights 7.4
    effect of 7.3
    free-standing transfers 7.4
    meaning of 7.2
    registration 7.6
    relief 7.5

Pre-emption rights 13.1, 13.3

Premium
    charge on 5.2.8

Private finance initiative (PFI) 12.5

Promoting arrangements 17.1, 17.2

Property traders
    acquisition from customer of house-building company 4.6
    acquisition from personal representatives 4.8
    acting as chain-breakers 4.7
    relocation for employment 4.9
    super rate on purchases 3.4.4.3

Property-adjustment orders 3.3.11

Public bodies 12.6
    arrangements involving 12.5
    compliance with planning obligations 12.3
    compulsory purchase 12.2
    Crown exemption 12.6.1
    diplomatic premises 12.6.2
    established for national purposes 12.6.4
    foreign sovereign immunity 12.6.3
    reliefs 12.4, 12.6
    transactions involving 12.1

Public–private partnership (PPP) 12.5

Purchaser
    meaning of 1.3.1

Reasonable excuse 19.13

Reconstruction relief 18.1, 18.3.1
    assumption of liabilities 18.3.2.3
    conditions 18.3.2
    consideration shares 18.3.2.2
    matching membership 18.3.2.4
    matching shareholdings 18.3.2.5
    meaning of 'reconstruction' 18.3.2.1
    no tax avoidance 18.3.2.6
    withdrawal of 18.3.3

Record-keeping 19.15

Registered social landlords (RSLs)
    grant of certain leases by 2.5
    relief on grant-funded purchases by 4.11

Registration
    notifiable transactions and 1.9.3
    pre-completion transactions 7.6

Relatives
    sub-sales 9.5
    transfers between 9.5
    see also Spouses/civil partners

Release of negative obligations
    see Restrictive covenants; Right to light

Reliefs 4.1

acquisitions by bodies established for national purposes 12.6.4
charities relief 4.4
collective enfranchisement 6.1, 6.12
  after 2009 6.5
  between 2003 and 2009 6.4
  multiple dwellings relief 6.11, 6.12
  RTE companies 6.4
corporate *see* Acquisition relief; Group relief; Reconstruction relief
Crown exemption 12.6.1
diplomatic premises 12.6.2
employers 4.10
first-time buyer relief 3.3.5.3, 4.2
foreign sovereign immunity 12.6.3
grant-funded purchases by registered social housing landlord 4.11
multiple dwellings relief 3.3.5.2, 4.3, 6.11, 6.12
part-exchanges made by housing-building companies 4.5
pre-completion transactions 7.5
property traders
  acquisition from customer of house-building 4.6
  acquisition from personal representatives 4.8
  chain-breakers 4.7
  relocation for employment 4.9
public bodies 12.4, 12.6
sale and leaseback relief 5.10
Relocation for employment 4.9
Renewal of lease 5.7.2
Rent
  amount payable 5.2.5
  charge on 5.2.3
Rent to mortgage transactions 10.5
Rent to shared ownership lease 10.3.1
Residential higher rates *see* Higher rates
Residential lease rates 1.4.1
Residential property
  meaning of 3.2.1
Residential standard rates *see* Standard rates
Residential super rate *see* Super rate
Restrictive covenants
  chargeable consideration 14.2
  definition 14.1
  examples 14.1

rates of tax 14.3
release of interest 14.1
Returns
  amendments 19.8
    reclaiming overpaid tax 19.10.1
  corrections by HMRC 19.11.2
  disputes 19.1
  excepted transactions 1.9.2
  filing date 19.1
  final tax position 1.10
  grants of new leases 5.2.9
  guidance on submission 19.3
  joint purchasers 19.4
  lease variations 5.3.1
  liability to make 19.4
  making a return 1.9.2, 19.3
  online 19.3
  partnerships 19.4
  payment of tax *see* Payment of tax
  penalties 19.12.1, 19.15
  record-keeping 19.15
  revenue certificate 1.9.3, 19.1, 19.3
  self-assessment 19.1
  transactions requiring 19.2
  trusts 19.4
  when to make 19.9
Revenue assessments 19.11.4
  time periods for 19.11.5
  see also HMRC
Revenue certificate 1.9.3, 19.1, 19.3
Reversionary leases 5.7.4
Right to buy transactions 10.4
Right to enfranchise companies (RTE companies) 6.4
Right to light
  chargeable consideration 14.2
  nature of 14.1
  rates of tax 14.3
  release of interest 14.1
Rights of pre-emption 13.1, 13.3

Sale and leaseback relief 5.10
Scheme of SDLT 1.1
  anti-avoidance 1.11
  calculation of tax 1.4
  compliance by liable person 1.9
    link to registration 1.9.3
    making return and payment 1.9.2
    self-assessment 1.9.1
  components of an SDLT transaction 1.2.1
  debt *see* Debt

INDEX

Scheme of SDLT – *continued*
    effective date 1.7.1
    exempt transactions 1.6
    final tax position 1.10
    liability to pay 1.3
    substantial performance 1.8
    tax rates and tax bands 1.4.1
Scotland 1.1
SDLT returns *see* Returns
Security interests 2.3
Self-assessment 1.9.1, 19.1
Settlement of disputes 19.17.4
Shared ownership leases 10.2
    first-time buyer relief 4.2.3, 10.2
    market value election 10.2
    method of payment 10.2
    open market premium 10.2
    rent to shared ownership lease 10.3.1
Shared ownership trusts 10.3.2
    first-time buyer relief 10.3.2
    market value election 10.3.2
Sharia-compliant financing 11.1
Special circumstances 19.13
Spouses/civil partners
    assignments 8.5
    divorce/dissolution of partnership 2.5, 8.4
    existing debt 8.3
    higher rates exemption 3.3.10.3, 8.2
      buying alone 3.3.6
    mortgaged properties 8.3
    partnerships 8.6
    sub-sales 8.5
    transfers between 8.1, 9.5
      higher rates exemption 3.3.10.3, 8.2
Standard rates 1.4.1, 3.4.1
    collective enfranchisement 6.12
    first-time buyers 1.4.1
Sub-sales
    between relatives 9.5
    spouses/civil partners 8.5
Substantial performance
    effective date and 1.7.1
    leases 5.2.4
    meaning of 1.8
Super rate 1.4.1, 3.4
    banks etc., purchases by 3.4.4.7
    collective enfranchisement 6.1, 6.12
    composite transactions 3.4.3
    conditions 3.4.2
    developers, purchases by 3.4.4.2
    dwellings open to the public, purchases for 3.4.4.6
    employees etc., purchases for occupation by 3.4.4.10
    farmhouse, purchases for use as 3.4.4.9
    flat for caretaker purchased by management company 3.4.4.11
    home reversion plans 3.4.4.8
    interaction with other SDLT provisions 3.4.5
    landlords, purchases by 3.4.4.1
    non-qualifying individuals 3.4.4.5
    property traders, purchases by 3.4.4.3
    reliefs 3.4.4
    trades, purchases for use in 3.4.4.4
Surcharge
    overseas purchasers 3.5
    see also Higher rates; Super rate
Surrender of lease 5.6.3

Tax avoidance schemes
    accelerated payment notices 1.11, 19.19
    disclosure of (DOTAS) 1.11, 19.21
    follower notices 19.20
    see also Anti-avoidance
Tax evasion
    penalties 19.12.1
Tax point 1.7.1
Tax rates and tax bands 1.4.1
    dwelling
      meaning of 3.2.3
      purchase of more than five 3.2.5
      purchase of more than one 3.2.4
      single dwelling 3.2.4
    freehold and leasehold transfers 3.2
    leases 1.4.1, 5.2.1
    mixed-use transactions 3.2.2
    rates of tax 14.3
    release of negative obligations 14.3
    residential property, meaning of 3.2.1
    restrictive covenants 14.3
    right to light 14.3
    see also Higher rates; Non-residential rates; Standard rates; Super rate
Tenancy at will
    exempt interests 2.3, 5.2.2
Termination of leases 5.6
    expiry 5.6.5
    forfeiture 5.6.1
    merger 5.6.4
    notice to quit 5.6.2

surrender 5.6.3
Testamentary dispositions
   variation of 2.5, 9.4
Three per cent surcharge *see*
   Higher rates
Transactions
   components of 1.2.1
      acquisition 1.2.2
      chargeable interest 1.2.3
      exempt interests 1.2.4
   exempt 1.6, 2.5
Tribunal
   notifying of appeal 19.17.3
   rules 19.17.6
Trustees
   transfers to connected company 9.6, 15.3
Trusts
   liability to make return/payment 19.4
   residential higher rate 3.3.7
   shared ownership trusts 10.3.2

Uncertain consideration 1.5.1
Unit trust schemes
   connected company 15.2

Vendor
   meaning of 1.3.1

Wales 1.1
White knight investors 6.3.1